Daphne du Maurier's correspondence with Oriel Malet
began in the early 1950s after they met at a cocktail party in
London. Oriel was a gauche young writer while Daphne,
more than twenty years her senior, was the celebrated
author of international bestsellers such as *Rebecca* and
Jamaica Inn. Yet the friendship flourished over a thirty-year
span, fed by the letters that arrived faithfully from
Menabilly, the du Maurier house in Cornwall.

'Daphne was a wonderful letter-writer, frank, open and
refreshingly honest about every aspect of her creative and,
indeed, her sexual life'

Irish Independent

'A chance to understand the real Daphne du Maurier'

Sunday Independent

Oriel Malet was born in London and spent her childhood in Wales. She completed her first novel at the age of sixteen. Her second was awarded the John Llewellyn Rhys Prize. Since then she has written many novels, two biographies and a children's book. She lives in France.

DAPHNE DU MAURIER

LETTERS from MENABILLY

PORTRAIT OF A FRIENDSHIP

edited by Oriel Malet

ORION

An Orion paperback
First published in Great Britain by Weidenfeld & Nicolson in 1993
This paperback edition published in 1994 by Orion Books Ltd,
Orion House, 5 Upper St Martin's Lane, London WC2H 9EA

A CIP catalogue record for this book is available from the
British Library.

ISBN 1 85797 441 7

Printed and bound in Great Britain by
The Guernsey Press Co. Ltd, Guernsey, C.I.

To
All who remember Menabilly
and
In loving memory of Monsieur and Madame
Jean Barreyre (the Bs!)

Contents

❧

Illustrations

�֍

Acknowledgements

✻

No book can ever be an unaided effort, and I would like to thank all the kind people who have helped me with this one: Beverley Gordet, in Paris, who first suggested it; the family of Daphne du Maurier, who gave me permission to publish their mother's letters, with my special thanks to Christian Browning, for letting me use some of his own beautiful photographs; Margaret Forster, who while at work on her own book, was generous with help and advice; Nesta Roberts and Margaret Biggs, for their constant encouragement; Mademoiselle Marcelle Aufaure, in Paris, for bearing with my instant translation, and giving me photographs from her collection; Madame Goimbault, of Tillières-sur-Avre, for spending two Sundays photocopying my manuscript, after it had gone astray by courtesy of the post office; and last, but definitely not least, my heartfelt thanks to Barbara Noble, who gave up so much time, under difficult conditions, to read and edit the manuscript. Also, to my cat Melusine, for consistently acting (unasked) as a paperweight.

Glossary

꘏

The du Maurier codewords used in everyday speech.

beaming down What Christians know as 'the communion of Saints'!
beeding Looking closely at something.
brewing Thinking out a story, or a character.
C. of L. Change of Life.
cliff, to Throw away, chuck out, ignore.
crumby, to crumb High hopes, anything grand or especially good.
Day (someone's) Daily routines, habits, lifestyle.
Doom Any dire happening.
Frisky An eccentric old person.
Gondal, to To make believe, or pretend.
hard chair, on a To be offended, or in a bad mood.
honky The opposite to royal.
in bal Pregnant.
jam-along Easygoing, informal.
Main Of major importance.
menace, menaced by Attractive, attracted by.
mincy Affected, mincing.
nanny Anything frightening, or threatening.
nim or pal, to Normal bodily functions.
passage wandering Aimlessly killing time.
pegs or to peg Someone whom one momentarily invests with romantic glamour, but more particularly as the inspiration for a fictional character.
psychological politics Interesting discussions.
Robert The curse.
routes or non-routes Familiar routines, or habits.
royal Good-mannered, well-bred.
See Me Conceited, High and Mighty.
shilling, a Anything disappointing, worthless.
Silly Values Anything selfish or superficial; materialistic.
subs Subsidiary characters, or plots.
T.C.W. Private or secret.
teedle, to or T.N.N. Skip, or pass over something or someone.
Tell-Him Long, boring story.
Trit A short walk, particularly with a dog.
waine Embarrassing, or to be embarrassed.
wax, to Sexual intercourse.
Witherspoons Dull, conventional types. (With apologies to real Witherspoons, who may be brilliant.)

Nicknames

𝕏

B, Monsieur and Madame My dearfriends, Jean ('Toto') and Marie-Louise ('Tototte') Barreyre.

Bing, Tray, Track Daphne du Maurier.

Bird Daphne's sister Jeanne du Maurier.

Doodie The Comtesse Costa de Beauregard: an old schoolfriend of Daphne's.

Ferdie Mlle Fernande Yvon.

Flave, or Bee Daphne's daughter Flavia.

Gyggy George du Maurier's brother Eugene.

Hacker/Hakka Olive (Kits' wife).

Kicky George du Maurier.

Kits, Rab, Boo Daphne's son Christian.

Marraine (Fr.: 'godmother') Yvonne Arnaud.

Moper Daphne's husband, Tommy Browning.

Peg, Monsieur and Madame Pierre Fresnay and Yvonne Printemps.

Pen Friend, Goat or Singe Ronald Armstrong.

Piff, Piffy Daphne's sister Angela du Maurier.

Poo, Poonie Daphne's grandchild Marie-Thérèse de Zulueta.

Tod Maud Waddell.

Zulus, the The children of Daphne's daughter Tessa and her first husband, Peter de Zulueta.

'Soyons reconnaissants aux personnes qui nous donnent du bonheur; elles sont les charmants jardiniers par qui nos âmes sont fleuries.'

Marcel Proust

Foreword

There are friendships which, with time, become so woven into the texture of our lives that when such friends depart, a hole is torn which can scarcely be mended, only patched. When we first met, Daphne du Maurier was in her early forties, a best-selling author at the height of her powers, and I was a young and inexperienced writer. That we became, and remained, friends was due to Daphne's patient and tolerant nature. I should have been in awe of her, but owing to her inborn shyness and humility, I never felt the slightest need to be; nor would she have encouraged any such attitude.

Later, when I was abroad, Daphne began to write to me regularly. Her letters reveal an extraordinarily wide range of interests, as well as her vivid imagination and the fantastic ideas which occupied her ever-enquiring mind during solitary walks with her dogs. These letters will surely dispel the myth that she was ever a recluse; nor was she any more neurotic than the majority of writers and journalists, who are a notoriously unstable bunch! She loved her family and friends, and was a good neighbour but – like so many other creative people – she was never very strong or robust, and she needed solitude in which to do her work. An essentially private person, she both cherished and guarded that privacy.

Apart from family news, Daphne's letters to me deal mainly with the subjects that interested her most – the difficult craft of writing, and books – her own, and those she enjoyed reading. It is because I believe that they may be of interest to others, to all who love the world of the imagination which Daphne du Maurier created, and would like to know her better, that I have decided to share them; and to pay a debt of gratitude to a very dear friend, that is long overdue.

'*With a friend, a man tosseth his thoughts,*' wrote Sir Francis Bacon, whom Daphne loved. Looking back, I see that he was right; for this, over the years, is what she was doing in her letters.

Prologue
A LOVING SPIRIT

✿

I do not now remember, since I did not then keep a diary, the exact date on which I first met Daphne du Maurier, but it was in the early 1950s, I was young, and it was spring. I recall walking across St James' Park, on my way to a party being given by Ellen Doubleday, wife of the American publisher Nelson Doubleday, and stopping on the bridge to feed the ducks and to wrestle with a sudden urge to dodge the party and go home to read in peace. Fortunately, I quelled this unworthy urge, reached the hotel, and after being swept up in the lift by a grand personage in a cocked hat and velvet breeches, was disconcerted to find myself planted in front of a pair of firmly closed doors; total silence reigned within the Doubleday suite.

This seemed like a good moment to escape, and I was about to steal away when a voice on the stairs above said calmly: 'I'm afraid Ellen must be late. She sometimes is, but I suppose we had better wait for her.'

I looked up, but could not see who had spoken – nor would I have recognized Daphne du Maurier if I had. After a silence, since Ellen still did not appear, we began to talk. My companion seemed to have little taste for cocktail-party chat, and we plunged almost at once into congenial subjects – books, the theatre, Paris, Life – about all of which, at the time, I thought I knew a good deal.

Nothing she said gave me any clue to her identity, nor did I bother to ask. She struck me as one of the easiest people to talk to, and one of the most amusing. All her remarks were made in a faintly mocking tone, which at times could be slightly disconcerting. Could she secretly be laughing at one? I wished, too, that she would become more visible. The hotel, although grand, was dimly lit, and it began to feel like carrying on a conversation with a ghost.

Suddenly, she asked me, as if she really wanted to know the answer: 'Tell me, what is your Day?' – a question I was to hear her put many times, to both friends and strangers alike, but which then I found slightly confusing (*see* Glossary).

At that time, I had written two books, which had brought me the unexpected good fortune of a £50 prize – a fortune in those days – and a visit to New York to stay with Ellen Doubleday. In fact, I had been exceedingly lucky, but did not yet realize it. I had been writing stories ever since I could hold a pencil, and it had seemed only natural to send my first completed novel to a publisher, and equally natural for him to publish it; this, I explained to my listener on the stairs, was the way I thought things happened.

'I see your point,' she said sympathetically. 'But do tell me, how did you choose your publisher?'

I explained that I had made a list, seized a pin, and stuck it into Mr Faber. This was something I would never have dared to do in real life, since he terrified me, and we never achieved any mutual rapport, although I owe him a big debt of gratitude. I had come to feel more at home in the relaxed atmosphere of my American publishers, Doubleday. All this I confided to my new acquaintance, under cover of the gathering dusk, and it was perhaps fortunate for us both that Ellen suddenly made a dramatic appearance, bowed out of the lift by the personage, her arms filled with flowers and parcels.

'You poor things, how long have you been waiting? My, I never realized the time. I was having tea with Willie Maugham, and he has promised to come on later.'

The double doors were flung open, and we were borne along in her wake. Inside were all the preparations for a party; waiters appeared as if by magic, bearing buckets of champagne and silver dishes of sizzling sausages. Everything became orderly once more, as it always did when Ellen was there.

The room was soon quite full, and my new friend had been swept to the far end of it. No longer a disembodied voice, but standing now in the full light of a crystal chandelier, I could see that she matched her voice, and was beautiful. Tall, slim, blonde, with a skin bronzed by sun and sea air, she reminded me of a figurehead at the prow of a ship; alert, poised, looking into the distance yet perhaps laughing inwardly and no more at ease in so worldly a setting than I was myself. She was surrounded by people anxious to talk to her, and when I remembered the way in which she had made me confide, giving away nothing about herself in return, I suddenly longed to be back in the park with the ducks.

However, Ellen cut off my retreat, saying happily, 'I was sure you and Daphne would get on well, if only you were both less difficult about meeting people.' It was a nasty moment. There was, I knew, only one Daphne in Ellen's world, and so far I had successfully avoided meeting her, put off not only by her fame but by the universal praise bestowed upon her by everyone at Doubleday. This really was the right moment to leave the party, particularly as I was afraid that Ellen, flushed with success, might suddenly want me to meet Willie Maugham, a terrifying old man with a face like a scarab, who had just entered the room.

Everyone's attention now turned towards him, and I was able to weave my way unnoticed through the crowd to the door. To my surprise, I found that Daphne seemed to be doing the same thing.

'I don't want Ellen to see me,' she whispered urgently, 'but I must go home and pack. I'm leaving for Cornwall by the night train.'

Like conspirators, we crept down the stairs and into the entrance hall, where another grand attendant hastened to summon a taxi for us.

'Come back with me,' she suggested suddenly. 'I must pack, but we could find something to eat before I catch the train. That is, if you've nothing better to do,' she added with her usual diffidence.

I could think of nothing except the ducks, and it was raining; a light spring shower. We did not talk much in the taxi – both of us, I suppose, feeling drained by the party. Then, impulsively, she said, 'It *is* kind of you to keep me company. I'm feeling rather low tonight. You see, I had to see my son off to school this afternoon, and I rather dreaded the empty flat.' She laughed, and added deprecatingly, 'Ah, one's *son* ... it's my French blood, I expect,' she mocked herself.

This was a fresh bond between us, for I had always had a passion for France, encouraged by my French godmother, the actress Yvonne Arnaud, and her good French cooking.

The du Maurier flat was in one of those red-brick blocks down the King's Road. The entrance hall smelt of rubber, and the lift gates clattered. There was not much to be seen from the windows except grey London chimneys, and the tops of the trees in the gardens of the Chelsea Pensioners. The square rooms were filled with books and pictures, but it still felt more like a pied-à-terre than a real home and this, Daphne explained, was what it really was. Her husband used it most, since he had to be in London all week, but he came down to Cornwall every weekend, and that was where their hearts were, at a house called Menabilly – a mysterious name to me then, and Cornwall a strange land, for I had never been there.

While Daphne packed, I roamed around the flat, looking at the photographs which were everywhere. There were pictures of boats, and of people dressed as pirates boarding boats, in what was evidently a film sequence; pictures of dogs (West Highland terriers), and of children. My eye was caught by a little blond boy with a wicked, mocking face, rowing a child's boat on grass, wearing a sailor's hat. 'One's son ...' I presumed.

Time raced on, and soon we had to rush downstairs with her suitcase and search for a taxi in the King's Road. 'Thank you so much for coming,' she said, when we had found one, and now I felt that she was glad to be rid of me, her thoughts already turned homewards. 'I wish I could ask you to stay some time, but I always promise the children not to have visitors in the holidays, and I try not to work then, either.'

As the taxi turned out of the King's Road, she waved. I did not expect that I would see Daphne du Maurier again, and rather to my surprise, I was sorry.

Next morning, I went round to John Sandoe's famous bookshop just off the King's Road and bought myself a copy of *Rebecca*. With shame I recalled that we had not discussed her books at all the evening before, only my own. This was not entirely due to youthful egoism; I had yet to learn that Daphne rarely spoke about herself unless pressed, nor had I dared to press her, being only too well aware that I was one of the few people who had not read her books!

I opened *Rebecca* on a number 19 bus, and at once those potent words, '*Last night I dreamt I went to Manderley again . . .*' wove their subtle spell, blotting out the greyness of Piccadilly Circus, and carrying me on several stops beyond the Tottenham Court Road . . .

I was bound for the Doubleday office, in the hope that they kept file copies of all Daphne's books and would lend them to me. The head of the office at that time was Winifred Nerney, a character much loved and respected by all who knew her. Everything about her was reassuring – her calm, authoritative manner, and her sure instinct in dealing with books and authors. She had a large, craggy face, perceptive brown eyes behind horn-rimmed spectacles, and a deep, hoarse laugh. To Ellen, she was a trusted friend; Daphne, I later discovered, also respected her judgement, and whenever I thought up some wild scheme, would recommend me to: 'Ask Winifred, and if she tut-tuts, then DON'T!'

Much of Winifred's earlier life had been spent as personal secretary to Arnold Bennett; she always referred to him as 'Mr Bennett', or very occasionally, 'A.B.' Nelson Doubleday first met Winifred at the Bennetts' and decided, then and there, that she was the right person to run his London office. However, he had to wait a long time for this to happen, since the most alluring offers could not move Winifred until after Arnold Bennett's death.

I always enjoyed my visits to the Doubleday office at 91 Great Russell Street, a Georgian house three doors down from the British Museum. By a strange coincidence, number 91 had once been the first London home of Daphne's grandparents, the young George du Mauriers. The ground floor and basement were now the lair of a surgical shoemaker; when the front door opened, the rich smell of leather and polish almost knocked one backwards.

Winifred's office was on the first floor, in two communicating rooms, one of which had been the young du Mauriers' drawing room. There were always plants in the long window boxes, and in winter a bright fire burned in the hearth. When I banged loudly on the shining brass knocker, the door would fly open to reveal the smiling face of Vi Barton, who sat typing in the outer office, which had once been George du Maurier's – 'Kicky's' – studio. Sometimes the knocking produced a flurry of protest from above, and Margery Allingham the crime-writer would descend from the top floor, where she and her husband, Pip Youngman-Carter, rented a small pied-à-terre. Vi would make coffee, while Winifred and Marge capped each other's stories, punctuated by much laughter. Marge was a large person in every sense of the word, and her kindness and generosity soon swept aside all barriers between us. I loved her books, and still do so today.

The first two books of Daphne's that I borrowed from the office were *The Loving Spirit*, because it *was* her first, and *The Parasites*. I returned many times to borrow more, but it never seems to have occurred to me to write and tell her how much I was enjoying them. She had vanished into a Cornish limbo, of which at that time I knew little or nothing. Then, suddenly, misfortune struck – in the shape of a five-barred gate which should have been open but was mysteriously closed, just as I was riding towards it on a motor-cycle, going rather too fast. The results, if not fatal, were certainly unpleasant, and necessitated several weeks of convalescence. Winifred kindly kept me supplied with books, and she must have passed the news on to Daphne, for one morning I received a sympathetic letter, suggesting that Cornwall might be a good place in which to complete my recovery.

This was too tempting an invitation to refuse, but it threw me into a state of panic, or as Daphne herself would have termed it, 'waine' (*see* Glossary). Why should one dread the unknown, while harbouring secret longings to be the kind of person who can jump on the back of a camel and set off for Tibet at a moment's notice? All I had to do (and did) was to jump into a taxi and set off for Paddington Station, already familiar from journeys to and from my childhood home in Wales. I had not been there since, and was suddenly overcome by a wave of longing. Once the flat green counties of England had been left behind, the train was bringing me closer and closer to the West Country. True, the Welsh mountains were missing, but in their place were softly rolling hills, slate-roofed farms nestling in green valleys, and rushing streams, their banks covered with primroses and cowslips, and a palm tree or two flourishing in the gardens of the seaside boarding houses, where sandy towels already flapped in the brisk spring breeze. The train rocked along beside the sea at Dawlish, a sheer wall of red rocks on one side, and on the other a thin line of shore where a few early visitors were walking their dogs, coat collars turned up.

I do not remember much about my arrival on that first evening, but I am sure that Mr Bunny's taxi met me at Par or St Austell, and that I was increasingly nervous as we motored down the long drive to Menabilly. Daphne, too, may have begun to regret that she had ever thought of inviting me ...

What I remember most clearly from my first visit is waking up the next morning in the spare bedroom known as Blue Lady. It was flooded with bright sunshine, and at the foot of the bed stood a strange figure in wellington boots and a tweed skirt, with rosy cheeks and bright blue eyes. 'My dear, don't let me wake you!' she exclaimed, in the cheerful tone of one who has been up and about her business for hours. 'I just came to dodge in a few of these ...' Her arms were clasping branches of wild cherry, and camellias in full bloom.

'How lovely!' I exclaimed, struggling to sit up.

She beamed. 'I see you like flowers. I must show you my garden later.' She began to push the branches into a tall vase which stood on a writing table at one end of the room, and looked as if it could not hold another twig. 'My dear, how remiss, let me introduce myself. I'm Maud Waddell, but everybody calls me Tod.'

'Why Tod?' I asked, bewildered.

'Mr Tod, the Fox. From Beatrix Potter.' She snipped at a camellia with a pair of secateurs that protruded from the capacious pocket of her cardigan. I thought she looked more like Mrs Tiggy-Winkle, but Tod she had been christened, many years ago, by Daphne and her sister, Angela, and Tod she had remained.

'I see you haven't had breakfast yet. Nothing gets done in this house unless I see to it myself.' She hurried away, positively crackling with purpose, and I lay back on my pillows, and let the peace and silence creep back into the room.

Certain places and houses have strong personalities of their own, regardless of their inmates; perhaps they deliberately cast a spell over those whom they know will love and cherish them. Menabilly was one of these houses, in which layers of time seemed to have worn thin in places, so that the past now and then showed through. There were rooms in which a lot seemed to have been going on before you entered them, and would probably do so again once you, the intruder, had left. Blue

Lady owed its name to a local legend, in which a lady in blue had sometimes been seen looking out of the window. Alas, I never saw her, although I slept many times in Blue Lady, and always found it a cheerful and welcoming room, with its white-painted walls, deep crimson carpet, and chintz curtains patterned with famous ships framed by garlands of oak leaves. The walls were hung with the enchanting sketches which Kicky had made of his family for *Punch*. I had read and loved *Peter Ibbetson* and *Trilby*, his two famous novels written in 1891 and 1894 respectively, long before *Rebecca* and so felt instantly at home with him.

All this was friendly enough, but the bathroom which opened out of Blue Lady, and which had once been another bedroom, was a different matter. There, even at midday, one sometimes had the distinct impression of being watched. In winter, I always tried to spend as little time as possible getting ready for bed, although the watchers were in no sense malevolent; they were just *there*.

On that first visit to Mena, Daphne showed me all over the house, including the old, uninhabited wing that was already crumbling away and has now been pulled down. This, I thought, was really exciting – a house in which you could step from the warm and friendly Long Room, with its bright orange carpet, into long, empty, echoing passages filled with rubble and crumbling plaster, and mouldy panelling. This was the home of bats, and owls nested in the ivy outside. The Old Library still had dusty bookcases lining its walls, and was used as a storeroom. She showed me the buttress where the skeleton of a poor young Cavalier had once been found, walled up, but I never felt that he was one of the Silent Watchers; it was all too far away and long ago.

One of the hazards of staying for the first time in an unfamiliar house is apt to be what Daphne herself had dubbed, in her private language, 'passage wandering'. The guest, with no fixed routine of his own or special place in which to be, wanders into strange rooms, opens wrong doors, or loses his way in unfamiliar passages; retreating at last with a nonchalant air to the guestroom, where somebody may be hovering, wanting to dust. I cannot remember ever passage wandering at Mena, even on that first visit, but I did spend much time hovering in the red-carpeted passage outside Blue Lady, studying the photographs and prints of earlier du Mauriers which lined its walls; that past which, for fifty-six years, George du Maurier drew for the pages of *Punch*, recording his era as faithfully as any camera.

Here were the elegant ladies with their wasp-waists, bustles and fringes, chatting in their overstuffed drawing rooms to gentlemen with side whiskers and velvet jackets. The children Kicky drew were his own (as was the dog), sketched from life as they played in their Hampstead garden, or came down in a long line to the drawing room to be shown off to guests. There were five of them: Trixie, Guy, Sylvia, May and the baby Gerald.

None of his children would ever know the poverty endured by Kicky himself, when he first came to London at the age of twenty-nine to study art, with only ten pounds in his pocket and already haunted by the fear of losing his sight. George du Maurier had made good – becoming one of the most celebrated cartoonists of his day and later, when his sight worsened, writing two resounding best-sellers. He never lost his love for the Paris of his childhood, however, and although he tried to exorcize this in *Peter Ibbetson* and *The Martian*, it remained part of him. Beneath the contentment and security of a happy marriage and a successful career, there was a deeper melancholy which Kicky kept to himself, but passed on to at least one of his children – the youngest, Gerald. Daphne believed this inner darkness to be a family trait, running like a black thread behind the mockery and laughter.

My hostess brought the photographs vividly to life with her own stories of the past: of Trixie, whose son Geoffrey had been her first childish love; of beautiful but doomed Aunt Sylvia, who had died tragically of cancer when a young widow, leaving her family of five boys to be adopted by the playwright J. M. Barrie – thus linking the family with *Peter Pan*; and of Uncle Guy, who wrote the successful patriotic play *An Englishman's Home* and was killed in World War One.

Above all there was her late father Gerald, who seemed as much a part of Mena as any of its living inhabitants. He was the baby of the family, the spoilt 'ewe lamb', clinging on unsteadily behind the others in that forever-sunlit garden. Beneath one sketch, in answer to their mother's anxious enquiry as to what they are playing, the caption, spoken by Trixie, runs: '*We're playing at trains, and I'm the engine, and Guy is a first-class carriage, and Sylvia's a second-class carriage, and May's a third-class carriage, and Gerald, he's a third-class carriage too – at least, he's really only a truck, but you mustn't tell him so, as it would offend him!*'

That truck was later to shoot to the head of the line and become Sir Gerald du Maurier, perhaps the most famous actor-manager of his day, and a widely-adored matinée idol. He introduced an easier, more relaxed style of acting to the London theatre; while offstage, he charmed everyone with his gaiety, generosity and unassuming manner, for he did not take his own gifts, or even life, too seriously. All this was legend, and I had heard some of it before from my godmother, but since acting is the most ephemeral of all the arts, Gerald had never seemed as alive to me as Kicky, whose world I could enter at will, simply by opening a book. Now, however, Gerald came to life as Daphne's much-loved father. His full-length portrait hung at Mena, along with innumerable photographs, his bust in bronze, and a touching collection of fetiches from his dressing room at the theatre.

In 1934, Daphne's book *Gerald: A Portrait* had caused a great furore, since it broke with conventional biography with all its polite limitations, and was instead a frank and honest portrait. *Gerald* was written with great love and sympathy; in it Daphne was never cruel or unkind, but she described the shadowed side of her matinée-idol father, haunted as Kicky had been before him by bouts of nerves and depression, unsure of himself or of those he loved best, and afflicted at times by a doubt that anything at all in life was really worthwhile. I read *Gerald* at one sitting, perched in the sun by the side window at Mena, and even now have only to open the book to find myself back at that wooden garden table, seated in a wicker chair that was shaped like an upturned Welsh coracle ...

Daphne's stories of the past went further back still, to those early glass-blowing ancestors of whom she was so proud – good French peasant stock from the Sarthe and Normandy, swept across the Channel in the aftermath of the French Revolution. She talked freely, too, of her love for Cornwall and of the early days, when she and her two sisters Angela and Jeanne had gone trespassing in Menabilly Woods and had come upon the house – so overgrown with ivy in those days that it seemed less a separate building than a part of the surrounding trees. She had been determined then to rescue it, to fill it with light and love, and the sound of children playing. All this she had done, but the trees remained: one felt they might at any moment advance and recapture their lost ground. Mena was encircled by them, and only from the upper windows could you catch a glimpse of the sea – a thin blue line between banks of scarlet rhododendrons.

All this struck me as *highly* romantic. I could easily imagine myself trespassing in the grounds of some crumbling old French château, I confided to Daphne, and she caught up this idea, adding to it then tossing it back to me, until we had built up a story to which we went on adding fresh scenes and characters. This lasted, I remember, all throughout my first visit, and then it blew away and was lost, as stories do if they are not pinned down on paper.

It was exciting to discover that here at Mena, one could safely give rein to one's imagination, and to the maddest ideas that sprang to mind: while staying with my godmother Yvonne Arnaud, any such flight of fancy was apt to be quenched by her Gallic common sense. Daphne seemed to be more interested in what people *thought* than in what they *did*, and she was always ready to excuse even the most extravagant behaviour, saying with her faintly mocking air: 'Well, that's just the way they are, I suppose!' I never saw her really angry; the worst I ever heard her say of anyone was to accuse them of having 'silly values' – a term which covered anything from selfishness to murder! I sometimes wondered whether this tolerance did not spring from a certain basic indifference towards the outside world, but there was comfort in it, too. Somehow, you knew that no matter how 'silly' your own values might be, she would always be on your side.

The woods round Mena seemed to stretch for miles, an uncharted Amazonian forest; but they were not uninhabited, for various odd characters lived solitary lives here and there, and we came upon them in our walks. A crashing in the undergrowth usually turned out to be old Captain Vandeleur, who lived alone in a ramshackle wooden hut – painted green to camouflage it during the war – with a splendid view out to sea. Dressed in dungarees and an old tweed jacket, with a green pork-pie hat on his head, the Captain spent much of his time cutting down bamboos and despatching them to London in order to feed the Panda at the Zoo. I never knew what else his day might hold, or what he did on the long winter evenings, when his lamp burned late into the dusk.

Daphne and he seemed to get on well enough when they met by chance, but Tod always accused him of tippling, and often seemed to be on what Daphne would call 'a hard chair' with him, over some supposed misdeed. 'My dear, that man, at it again ...' she would complain, over lunch.

In another part of the woods lived two old ladies, their witch's cottage half-submerged by undergrowth; they themselves seemed also to have been overtaken by time, and forgotten. I did not come to know them well until the older of the two died, and poor Miss Wilcox was left blind and alone. Daphne and Tod both called upon them at regular intervals and, unlike Captain Vandeleur, they welcomed visitors.

We rambled through the woods when it was too wet or dull for the beach, or for walking over the cliffs to the Gribben, a local beauty spot, but there were days when it was hot and sunny, and then we basked on the rocks down at Pridmouth, the little beach where Rebecca's sinister cottage had stood. This had long ago been rented to a rich industrialist from the north, and had been turned into a holiday home, complete with terrace and patio. He often flew down at weekends in his private plane, and then one had to be discreet, and look the other way when walking past the low stone wall which separated his garden from the beach.

I longed to swim, but this had been discouraged. My legs were still faintly scarred by my accident, and one hot afternoon Daphne suggested that I bathe them in a rockpool known as 'Dr Rashleigh's Bath' since the latter (the owner of Menabilly, who now lived 'up country' in a modern villa), had put it to much the same use during his old age. Warmed by the sun, the sea water was pleasant and I enjoyed my daily dips, despite the limpets which had taken up residence there and refused to be dislodged. While I dipped, I read *The King's General* in order to catch up on the history of Mena, although Daphne had warned me that it was as much fiction as fact. Meanwhile, she wandered along the shore with Mouse, the West Highland of the moment, at her heels; of all her dogs, he had the most loving, and lovable, nature. It was less pleasant to step out of the water into a chill spring breeze, and we would race up to the house through the woods, which smelt hungrily of wild garlic, to find Tod on the doorstep with a disapproving face. 'My dear, how risky, you'll be sure to catch a chill!' she prophesied daily, but I could never even produce a single sneeze with which to pacify her.

On the days when Daphne had retreated to her workplace, the Hut, to write or to 'brew' over her current story while gazing out to sea, Tod would often invite me up to her flat for a cup of tea. This was down another long, red-carpeted passage, and close to the store cupboard, the key to which Tod guarded with her life.

Her flat, like everything at Mena, was shabby but comfortable, with wide, high-ceilinged rooms, and the ever-present trees pressing against the windows. The furniture resembled herself, in that it was solid and four-square. Books crammed the glass-fronted bookcase, and the walls were hung with her own watercolour paintings. Tod was a talented watercolourist – a difficult art, and one which must have been her solace in a life which had not always been easy, nor uneventful. Between the wars she had spent some time in a Turkish harem, teaching English to the wives of an Eastern potentate. 'My dear, it was hopeless. So scatterbrained, I never could persuade them to concentrate.' Later, she had run a hat-shop in London with a friend, until the war came to close it down, and much else with it. I liked listening to these stories of her past, and Tod told them well, with a dry sense of humour.

Running all through the years like a golden thread was her devotion to the du Mauriers, to Daphne in particular, and a certain nostalgia for the old days at Hampstead, where she had first come as daily governess to Daphne and Jeanne, then aged twelve and nine. Angela at fifteen was older and had less to do with the schoolroom, so Tod had fewer stories to tell of her, but I liked the one in which Angela, in the throes of one of her romantic passions, had jumped up on the Embankment wall, declaring that she was about to cast herself into the Thames. 'Not now, dear, it's tea-time,' had been Tod's characteristic reply.

Naturally enough, Tod always declared that she had known from the first that Daphne was an unusual child – unusually beautiful (the photographs all over the house confirmed this), but also extraordinarily intelligent and sensitive. Later, I came to realize that Angela and Jeanne were unusual, in their own different way. Angela's books are quieter than Daphne's, which may be the reason why they have never reached the wider public they deserve. It is not always an advantage to be related to a celebrity, as Angela herself has recorded with ironic humour in her autobiographical books *It's Only the Sister* and *Old Maids Remember*. She describes a woman who, mistaking her temporarily for Daphne, then exclaimed loudly, 'Oh, it's *only* the sister!' and promptly turned her back. Jeanne, as independent and jealous of her privacy as Daphne, quickly went her own way, becoming a fine painter who lives a free, untrammelled life in a cottage on Dartmoor, among beloved animals and growing things. Any one of these three talented sisters would have been enough for an ordinary family but then the du Mauriers were not ordinary people ...

I often wished I could 'dream true', as Kicky did in *Peter Ibbetson*, and project myself into the garden of Cannon Hall, Hampstead, on a long-past Sunday afternoon in summer, when it was crowded with the visitors and friends with whom Gerald loved to surround himself. To catch a glimpse of the Guitrys? Perhaps, but certainly in order to see Angela in her best pink frock, pursuing her passion of the moment, and a scowling Daphne sneaking off into the shrubbery, longing for them all to go home so that she could become her alter ego, Eric Avon, once again. What made her choose to be this swashbuckling all-conquering schoolboy hero? Years later, when she came to write about her childhood (in *Growing Pains*, 1977), she did not seem to know, or perhaps refused to probe.

Lady du Maurier, Tod once told me, had run the household, imposed its rules and made certain that all was done as it should be. There was nothing Bohemian or Trilbyish about Cannon Hall, nor does it seem to have been entirely Liberty Hall, at least where the children were concerned, although they all looked back upon their childhood with deep affection. A special bond linked Daphne to her father, and Tod maintained that Lady du Maurier had been jealous of this, and it had sometimes made her unfair, if not consciously unkind, lessening her ability to understand this daughter and increasing Daphne's natural love of solitude and independence. It often puzzled me that someone upon whom life had bestowed so much – beauty, talent, a happy marriage – should have remained at heart so shy and diffident, so afraid of life and others. Eric Avon, whom Daphne remembered as being 'just good at everything', must have compensated her for innumerable snubs and scoldings from her mother. Although Gerald asserted boldly that 'daughters were the thing', inspiring Barrie to write this line into one of his best plays, *Dear*

Brutus, perhaps the true might-have-been was the absent son, and Eric Avon the ghost of that suppressed desire caught by the mind of a sensitive and loving child. It was no use expecting Daphne to provide a clue. Imaginary scenes and characters, yes, she would willingly evoke, and she was an adept at giving 'to airy nothing a local habitation and a name', but there were doors that would not open at even the lightest touch; and the test of friendship is surely that of knowing when not to knock.

Time stood still at Mena; it was a sleepy place, and the days slid by in a golden dream, filled with reading, writing, basking down at Prid, or tramping over the cliffs or down through the woods to Polkerris – a little harbour where there was an old black-and-white timbered pub leaning sideways, and a tame fox. We could not go too far afield, for Daphne had not yet learned to drive, and even a modest shopping expedition into Fowey meant hiring Mr Bunny's taxi. There was never time to linger and explore that little town, with its harbour crammed with every kind of craft, from the huge white, powdery china-clay ships, to the smallest pleasure dinghies. Daphne, wanting to get the whole business of shopping over as quickly as possible, would stride swiftly down the main street or, stopping suddenly with a whispered warning: 'There comes old So-and-so, she's sure to want to talk, how waine ...' would whisk me out of sight into a doorway or a shop. She avoided the town at holiday times, when it was full of visitors and the line of cars waiting for the ferry to Bodinnick stretched far down the street. Angela, like many other residents, rowed herself across the harbour from Ferryside, the original du Maurier home at Bodinnick-by-Fowey, in her own dinghy, tying up at the Town Quay.

We visited Ferryside, which Gerald had bought as a holiday home, and Daphne showed me her old room above the figurehead of the *Jane Slade*, where she had written her first book, *The Loving Spirit*. The ferry docked almost in the front garden, and the rocky hillside against which it was built came into the long drawing room downstairs (the original boathouse) with its superb view across the harbour and the town. From here, you ascended to ground level, stepping out into the garden from the dining room or kitchen. It was easy to see why Daphne had found this house to be a refuge from her London life, knowing at once that this was where she belonged, and that she would never be tempted to pull up her Cornish roots. She came at the right time. The town of Fowey was still a small, compact community then; there were few hotels, but many pubs, where sailors met and often fought each other on Saturday nights. The shops had not yet been taken over by chain stores, and sold mostly oilskins and fishing tackle. Living on her own and tasting independence, writing her first book and getting to know the families in the cottages around the harbour, Daphne became integrated in a way that was not possible when the du Mauriers descended en masse for their summer holiday.

One family with whom she quickly made friends were the Quiller-Couches; they lived in a house called The Haven, but 'The Crow's Nest' might have suited it better, for it stood on a hill, looking out to sea. 'Q' – Sir Arthur Quiller-Couch – was, I think, what Katherine Mansfield called a Pa-man; kindly, genial, always ready to give advice to young writers. Daphne was adopted by the whole family, and could even be persuaded to abandon her usual corduroys and oilskins when invited to the ritual Sunday night supper at The Haven. In spite of being so famous an author and essayist, and Professor of Literature at Cambridge University, 'Q' seems to have had some odd ideas on the subject of education. He considered it necessary only for his son, while his daughter Foy, who had even greater intellectual gifts, was never sent to school and left virtually uneducated. It was Foy who had accompanied Daphne on that legendary ride over Bodmin Moor, when a thunderstorm blew them off-course and into Jamaica Inn, thus sowing the seed of that most exciting tale of wrecking and witchcraft.

One day in Fowey, we ran into a severe, upright figure, wearing a round straw hat and gloves, and clasping an umbrella, which set her instantly apart from the summer holiday crowds in jeans and sandals. 'There's Foy Quiller-Couch!' Daphne whispered hastily. I could hardly believe it.

We were invited to tea at The Haven; a real Cornish tea, laid in the dining room round a solid, well-polished mahogany table, and one knew at once that the house had never changed to meet the outside world. Daphne warned me in advance that it was necessary to be on one's best behaviour at The Haven, and almost to curtsey before speaking; to me, Foy's craggy, weatherbeaten face bore a distinct resemblance to the Red Queen's! Unpunctuality had never been condoned at The Haven in 'Q''s day, still less in Foy's, who revered her father's memory and kept strictly to all the old ways. Daphne swore that when Foy's nephew came back late for lunch after sailing in the summer holidays, no dish that had been removed from the table was ever allowed to be brought back again.

All went well, however, and I liked Foy. Her dry, abrupt manner hid a kind heart, and I suspect a lonely one, but I could never believe she had ridden across Bodmin Moor in that thunderstorm ...

Each weekend the sleepy calm of Mena was broken by the arrival from London of Daphne's husband 'Tommy' – Lieutenant-General Sir

Frederick Browning GCVO, KBE, CB, DSO, wartime commander of Airborne Forces and Chief of Staff to Earl Mountbatten in SEAC. I would wake in the grey light of dawn to see a thin streak of light shining under the door of the room next to mine, hitherto cold and empty. On one side of the staircase at Mena all the rooms communicated with each other, as at Versailles; the corridor leading to Blue Lady was on the far side of the well. I usually preferred to take the longer way round, rather than intrude upon the private domain of someone I had not yet met, but sometimes I forgot or was late, and then I rushed through it, still dripping from Dr Rashleigh's bath.

It was very much a man's room, and like everything at Mena, worn and comfortable. The bed was occupied by a collection of equally tatty but obviously well-loved teddy bears! These helped to dissipate my fears about a first encounter, and sure enough I always felt at ease with Tommy and found him good to talk to on many subjects. He was extremely good-looking, which added to his charm, and although he knew this he was never for a moment the foppish character depicted in the film *A Bridge Too Far*. Daphne's fury when this film came out was understandable, although she, more than anyone, must have known that film directors usually adopt a certain artistic licence towards the truth.

Like everyone else, I knew of Tommy's courage during the war. In the early 1950s, the war still felt very close, and those who had fought or who had suffered the horrors of concentration camps and prisons, were still struggling with inner tensions and the aftermath of their experiences, however outwardly serene their civilian lives might now seem. At times Tommy suffered from moods of deep depression, exacerbated by a virus he had picked up in the desert, and which affected his liver. These moods earned him the family nickname of 'Moper'; otherwise, he was Tommy to his family, and Boy to his friends.

This multiplicity of names surprised me at first, but I soon realized that all the du Mauriers were inclined to give each other odd names; from Kicky and Gyggy down to Daphne herself. She had suggested that I call her Bing, as almost everyone else did except for Tod, to whom she was always firmly Daphne. Later she became Tray, from 'Good Dog Tray' – a name bestowed upon her by her son Kits and finally Track, which for some odd reason stuck. To her sister Jeanne she was Scroop, from a childhood game in which she had assumed the role of Lord Scroop of Masham, while Jeanne herself was known as Bird, and Angela as Piff or Piffy.

With Tommy's arrival, our days burst suddenly into a multitude of activities. No longer Mr Bunny, but red-faced George from the boatyard came to drive Tommy in and out of Fowey. This was the old Slade

Boatyard, which had gripped Daphne's imagination when she first came to Fowey and wrote *The Loving Spirit* around the Slade family history. It had long since passed into other hands, but after the war she and Tommy were able to buy it and all Tommy's boats had been built there.

His first, most loved of all, was *Yggy 1*, named after Ygdrasil, the Tree of Life in the Norse Sagas. This was the little boat in which he had so boldly courted Daphne, and which had now come to rest at Mena, close to the Hut. Although she was always kept well-painted, she seemed now to be merely a hollow shell, and it was in *Yggy 11* that I remember sailing up the river in the early autumn in search of sloes. These were made into sloe gin from a special recipe handed on to Daphne by 'Q'; it was a delicious heady brew to swig down on a cold day out at sea. We chugged past the little church at Lanteglos where Daphne and Tommy had been married in what always struck me as the ideal way – no photographers, no fuss and almost no guests, only sympathetic neighbours leaning from the flag-bedecked windows to wave them on their way after a simple wedding breakfast of sausages and bacon, cooked on a primus in the galley. At present, Tommy was absorbed in his plans for building his latest boat, the *Jeanne d'Arc*, named after his favourite saint, also the patron saint of France.

Life became more social at weekends, for Daphne could even be persuaded to accompany Tommy to the Yacht Club in Fowey for meetings, or a drink with the Commodore. This was my chance to explore the town and to become familiar with its steep, narrow streets and bustling quays. Up the hill past the church and the library, a small iron gateway marked the private entrance to 'Place' – an old house with towers and the home of Angela's friends, the Treffrys. Then home to supper on trays in front of the Long Room fire; with no television as yet. Tod discreetly spent much time up in her flat during the weekend; a wary kind of truce existed between her and Tommy. While each was ready to acknowledge the other's good points, they rarely seemed to agree for long on any subject and Daphne, as peacemaker, would sigh with relief when, an argument averted, Tod bustled off to fetch the coffee cups. When all failed and an explosion took place, Tod could be on 'a hard chair' long after Tommy had departed for London by the Monday-night train.

Many families, it seems, adopt a private language of their own. The du Mauriers had done this, so Daphne explained, as far back as the distant glass-blowers. They, like all closed communities such as miners, fishermen, or actors, evolved a common language of their own; and in Kicky's day his children had used an Anglo–French argot among themselves. From the first I had been fascinated by the expressions of her own day which Daphne freely used (*see* Glossary), both in speech and in her letters. These, and many other expressions, I had picked up parrot-wise by the end of my first visit, and very useful I found them – and still do, in private.

I had been deeply impressed at Mena by Track's working routine. She stuck to these 'routes' so firmly, that only if the Hut had been blown out to sea by a hurricane would she have been moved to change them. Every morning, looking round the door of Blue Lady, she'd say in her gentle, almost apologetic voice: 'All right? Good. I'm just off,' and later I would see her striding away purposefully in the direction of her Hut. It was, I thought, the perfect life for any writer to lead, and I managed to do quite a bit of work myself each morning. I would have done more but for the kind-hearted interruptions from Tod. 'My dear, all alone in here? You had better come out and help me weed my garden.'

Tod's garden was a patchwork of colour to one side of the house, for she certainly possessed green fingers. Pinks grew there in profusion, stiff, soldierly gladioli, night-scented stock, and massive dahlias – so useful, she explained, for 'dodging in'. There was always a bowl of red and orange nasturtiums on a round table in the Long Room, and in summer, she planted sweet peas among the raspberries. Everyone in turn was asked to admire Tod's garden, and to offer occasional help (picking the raspberries being a more popular chore than weeding), but the person for whom she performed these feats was the one least interested in them. Daphne enjoyed keeping the many vases in the house freshly filled, and might even do some 'dodging in' herself when necessary, but talk about greenfly or slugs – topics of passionate interest to Tod, as to all true gardeners – was merely a Tell-Him to Daphne who would vanish swiftly, like the Cheshire Cat.

In midweek when absorbed in her work, she would forget all about lunch. Tod, fussing, would ring a large bell outside the front door and a distant figure would at last appear, head down, walking slowly towards the house. These were the only times I felt waine, for it seemed to me foolish to worry someone about boiled beef and carrots when they were obviously leading a more exciting life elsewhere.

To dissociate myself from this procedure, I used to retreat to a room beside the front door, which was then still called the nursery. Tod, coming in to flush me out again, regularly exclaimed: 'My dear, something *must* be done about this room!' I thought it was a pleasant friendly room and, unlike the rest of Mena, it belonged wholly to the present. Upstairs in her own bedroom Daphne had insisted upon keeping the old original wallpaper, so faded now that the walls seemed to be hung with the pale ghosts of white roses, but she preferred it that way. The nursery, with its cupboards stuffed with football gear and old tennis balls, held no such ghosts. I wondered about the occupants, whose photographs were all over the house, beside other children of past generations, Kicky's or Gerald's, all looking so much alike that once again past and present seemed to mingle, or to vanish, I never quite knew which.

At this time Daphne's children Flavia and Kits were still at school; Tessa, who was older, was already out in the world. I do not remember when the ban on no visits in the holidays came to be lifted, for now all these early years at Mena seem to flow into one another. There must have been a day when Mr Bunny's taxi deposited Kits and Flavia at the front door and they burst into the panelled hall, which was lined with racks of bows and arrows, and had a family of lead toads beside the open door. Daphne's husband Tommy was an expert at archery and I once saw him shoot an arrow into the air then split it with another, a feat which, prudently, he could not be persuaded to repeat. Archery became a passion one summer and stuffed animals were perched upon trees in the park to be shot at, and usually missed.

Flavia at sixteen was very like a younger Daphne – slim, fair-haired and blue-eyed. Gentle in voice and manner, she was good at concealing her feelings, which at this time veered as swiftly as the angel weathercock on Mena's roof, from being tomboyish in shorts and jeans, to yearning suddenly to be a great hostess in a garden-party hat. She shared the family aptitude for mockery and mimicry, and took part in all the imaginary games invented by Kits or Daphne, and perhaps by Mena itself, where times so easily merged.

Some days before the holidays began, the long grass in front of the house was scythed and mown by Mr Burt, and turned into Kits' cricket pitch. Mr Burt was another of the characters to be seen around Mena, chopping branches or clearing the Palm Walk, in a vain attempt to keep the woods at bay. He was rather like a tree himself – short and sturdy, his roots deeply planted in the Cornish soil. Going about his business with his faithful little terrier Toby at his heels, he bore a distinct resemblance to Mr Punch, with his twinkling eyes and ruddy face. He had been nicknamed 'Dang Me' by Kits, for this was his favourite expression, as 'My dear . . .' was Tod's. These two were often at cross-purposes, for Tod would have liked some help in her garden more often than Mr Burt was prepared to give it, and when he did, it was not always to her liking.

Mr Burt preferred doing things in his own time and way, which suited Daphne exactly, and they respected each other's independence. Now and then the occupant of the Pridmouth cottage took Mr Burt up in his plane for a joyride and they crossed the Channel to France, but Mr Burt did not think much of foreign parts. While he mowed, Toby sat beside him, stumpy tail a-wag, and ears pricked, aware as all dogs are that something was afoot and that the house would soon be as full of life as Track had wished to make it.

No one could be depressed with Kits around. The ghosts vanished in the holidays, exorcized by his exuberance. Now aged fourteen, he had inherited much of Gerald's charm and gregariousness, and had a wicked gift for mimicry (shared, to some extent, by all the family). Daphne had bestowed upon him her own vivid imagination and between these two there was a bond so open and obvious that no one ever thought of disputing it. It was simply accepted, outwardly at least, by all, but I wondered whether Tommy did not sometimes feel excluded. His affection for Kits was real and strong, but like so many men of his generation he spent little time in getting to know him, and could not enter into his imaginary games as Daphne could do.

One day, in the old condemned wing, he showed me some dusty bottles stacked in the Old Library. 'We'll be drinking this in seven years' time,' he announced with pride. 'On Kits' twenty-first birthday.' I nodded, convinced at that time that seven years, like eternity, was too far off to be contemplated.

Kits loved to tease, and no one's mannerisms were sacred for long, but he never did it unkindly. Tod came in for her fair share, but she was never on a hard chair with Kits, even when he raided her kitchen up in the flat. 'My dear, my cake-tin, empty again! That boy, nothing is safe from him,' she complained, but she always kept the tin well-filled during the holidays.

Kits twisted Tod around his finger as easily as he did everyone, but Flavia was his special ally. These two were as close as a brother and sister can be, but at this time Flavia was about to leave school and their interests had begun to differ. Kits' boon companion was a girl called Noddy, who lived with her grandmother in one of the cottages scattered about the grounds. The pair had come there in the war to escape the bombs, and had stayed on ever since. Together Kits and Noddy played mysterious games with footballs; wherever he went, there was Noddy, a stumpy little figure in a tartan skirt. They raced through the woods on bicycles, or down to the beach where Kelly's ice-cream van daily announced its arrival by a bell, a fact much deplored by Tod. 'My dear, you'll spoil your lunch!' was a cry that, as always, went totally unheeded.

Kits' closest links, however, were always with his mother. From early morning when he came into her room, these two shared private games and ploys that one was invited to watch but rarely to join in; games in which Kits assumed various characters, animal or human. All one summer, he became a character named 'Hung, King of all the Animals', and for the time this lasted everyone else had to become animals too – sowing, who knows, the seeds of 'Blue Lenses', one of Daphne's most frightening short stories. A favourite game was known as 'doing someone's Day'; in this, Kits seized upon some innocent character known to everyone in real life, whose idiosyncrasies amused him, and he and Daphne would then invent the most awful adventures and mishaps for their unfortunate victim.

Kits had a special kind of runic chant with which he tried to lure Daphne away from the newspaper, which she read every day after lunch, so that she would come and play with him. These flights of fancy enchanted me, and in my early years at Mena I found it very easy to slide back into childhood, and join in those in which I was allowed to share. There was always time, too, for solitary pursuits such as reading and writing, for games of cricket, in which as much time was spent hunting for the ball among the rhododendrons as in actual play, and always, talk on every subject under the sun. Kits dubbed all such discussions as 'psychological politics', and disappeared with Noddy when they took place.

There were long walks with Daphne up the beautiful valley of Lux-ullyan, where all the pools and streams were milk-white from the china clay, and afternoons down at Prid, swimming and basking. It was possible in those days, even at the height of summer, to find a secluded spot in which to dry oneself in the sun. On one occasion, Flavia and I opened our eyes to find an upright figure beneath a red umbrella, staring down at us with stony disapproval. It was Foy Quiller-Couch, come unexpectedly to call on Daphne. Seated upon a rock, her hat, gloves and parasol firmly anchored, she gazed pointedly out to sea while we scrambled back into decency, but then unbent enough to share our picnic tea, becoming all at once exceedingly good company.

In spite of the holidays and other distractions, Daphne had been steadily at work upon a collection of macabre short stories called *The Apple Tree*, which were published by Gollancz in 1952. Some of these had been written during my first visit, and over others she was still brooding. I remember the afternoon we were walking over a stubble field, while a crowd of seagulls wheeled and cried above us. 'I've often thought how nanny it would be if all the birds in the world were to gang up together and attack us,' she said suddenly. 'They could, you know.'

Flavia and I were more intent on giving as wide a berth as possible to a large bull, which lived in a corner of the field and was declared to be mild and peaceable. I felt at the time that bulls were a far greater danger to the human race than any number of seagulls. When I came to read her finished story, however, I knew better; it was eventually made into that terrifying movie *The Birds* by Alfred Hitchcock in 1963.

When Daphne was invited to go out to New York to launch an American edition of *My Cousin Rachel*, Ellen Doubleday suggested that I should go with her. I hesitated, fearing that I might merely be a passage wanderer in New York, but this was one of the few occasions on which Winifred tut-tutted, pointing out that it would be ungrateful to Ellen if I refused. So the matter was settled. It was almost as difficult to get to America in those days as it had been for Christopher Columbus; there were visas, fingerprints and endless bureaucratic red tape. It was a long overnight flight. After a plastic dinner, bunks were let down from the ceiling and made up into beds for the convenience of first-class passengers, for everyone was forced to turn out in the middle of the night at a frozen, windswept spot called Gander in Newfoundland. Daphne remained firmly in her bunk with the curtains closed, and got away with it.

We arrived next day, wilting and worn, and were whisked off to Ellen's home on Long Island. This was a beautiful house with sweeping views over Oyster Bay, but even in these luxurious surroundings, and cosseted by Ellen, it took days to recover a sense of reality. Daphne had been determined to stick to her routine of a long walk every afternoon, but this proved difficult since every car we passed stopped to offer us a lift, at which point she would promptly disappear, leaving me to explain to a bewildered driver our odd preference for using our own feet. We came by chance upon a reed-fringed lake, where we often sat to watch for unfamiliar American birds, but these peaceful days were only the prelude to life in New York, where we plunged at once into a whirlpool of parties and people.

New York, New York ... the most exciting city in the world – or so it seemed to me then, and I have not been back since. We woke each morning to hear the tugs hooting mournfully on their way out to sea and at evening, when the lighted windows gleamed like flints against the night sky, it was beautiful, a magical city of towers and pinnacles. From within, it was easy to feel lost among those dark canyons, and the hurrying, jostling crowds. Daphne was whisked off to her various appointments by car, and I was free to walk or go by bus – I could rarely face the subway – and often lost myself and was late. At home, all was still post-war austerity and gloom, and it was a joy to wander up and down Fifth Avenue window-shopping, even if one could not afford to buy.

Daphne took little interest in this activity, since she viewed shopping, whether in Fowey or New York, as a chore rather than a pleasure. On her free afternoons we walked briskly round Central Park, or visited the Frick Collection and the Cloisters, which has stayed in my mind as one of the most beautiful of all museums. We also went to the theatre to see Gertrude Lawrence in *The King and I*. Gertrude was a close friend of Daphne, who had written a play called *September Tide* for her; and there were glamorous pictures of Gertrude among all the other photographs at Mena. Although the two women lived so far apart, they had always kept in close touch. *The King and I* was a sumptuous production, and Gertrude gave a truly memorable performance. Her voice was husky and sometimes seemed a little tired, but her stage presence was extraordinary and she held the audience rapt from the moment the curtain rose. In fact, she was already mortally ill, although no one round her yet realized it, and Daphne remained mercifully unaware that they were meeting for the last time.

Looking back, I can see (as I did not then) what a perilous journey this might have been. Daphne and I were in no way equals, and even at the time it struck me as Silly Values to pretend otherwise, but Ellen Doubleday, from the kindness of her heart, treated us alike. In practice this meant that I could always be included in any amusing events, leaving the dull ones to Daphne; not did it occur to me that she could well have envied me this freedom. She always dreaded large, formal parties, although no one could have guessed this from her calm, serene manner, and the way she managed to put everyone round her at ease. Later, at home with Ellen, the gift for mockery and mimicry returned in full. No one could ever have had a more amusing or thoughtful travelling companion. From the first she was an ally, ready to back me up each time I wanted to dodge some formal party and go off to Greenwich Village with friends of my own, or with Pucky Violett.

Puck was Ellen's younger daughter by her first marriage. She had been christened Ellen, but to save confusion was always called Puck or Pucky, and this difficult name suited her well. She looked like Ellen too, with long dark hair, and her mother's brown eyes and warm smile. She was definitely a creature of her day and age, but had not yet found precisely the right outlet for her very real creative talents; this made us equals and we became friends. At this time she had formed a small theatrical company with a group of professional friends, and was preparing to go out on tour with two classic plays, *The Tempest* and Thornton Wilder's *The Skin of our Teeth*, and for light relief, a one-act musical comedy composed by Puck and the company.

The group were about to leave for Florida when Pucky suggested that I should join them. I had been close enough to the theatre to know that my thespian talents would make Mrs Worthington's daughter look like

Sarah Bernhardt, but Puck brushed such minor objections aside, declaring that there were plenty of jobs to be done backstage. It was a tempting offer and Daphne urged me to accept it, even generously offering to lend me the money, but this I refused, uncertain when, or even if, I could pay it back. Doubleday had turned down my latest novel (a children's story); time was running out fast and meanwhile I was racked with indecision. Then, like a bolt from the blue, a letter came from Little, Brown to say they had accepted my book and were prepared to make an advance, but it would be necessary for me to go to Boston to sign a contract and collect the money. No problem, said the resourceful Puck, we could start from Boston as easily as from New York; and we were off.

I have always been glad I joined that tour. In a few short weeks I learned more about the United States, and possibly myself, than I could have during a dozen formal visits to New York – as the perceptive Pucky may well have guessed. It was the first time I had been part of a team; in spite of my desire to be free and independent I had lived in a protected world, and was as childish in my twenties as the average thirteen-year-old today. When measured against Puck's worldly knowledge and experience, I felt humble. The company were young, talented and professional; two of its members had come from the Abbey Theatre in Dublin, and the leading lady, Peg O'Donnell, later played with the Lunts on Broadway.

We had left winter behind us, and the sight of the palm trees and blue skies of Florida as we stepped from the overnight train raised our spirits. It was necessary to make our funds stretch as far as possible since the outgoing expenses always proved heavier, and the receipts lighter, than anticipated. We always managed to find a bed for the night, and one square meal a day, even if this had mainly to contain large helpings of hominy grits, an unappetizing Southern dish which, like chips in England, seemed to be lavishly served with everything: it looked, and tasted, like fried grey tapioca. The balmy air and white sandy beaches of Florida made it positively inviting to sleep out of doors under the palm trees, and to bathe in a warm sea at dusk or dawn. We made a fire of brushwood and dug for clams in the warm, bubbling sand, roasting them afterwards in the ashes.

I was impressed by the way in which the company managed two complicated productions, using a minimum of scenery and props, and with little or no fuss. In *The Skin of our Teeth*, a skeleton of the Antrobus' house was made from ropes, which collapsed upon the stage just as Mrs Antrobus announced that 'the house is falling about our ears'. The musical comedy was the most lavish in costumes and scenery, and every member of the company was needed here to swell the chorus, and this always received much applause from the audience. Between the acts one of the boys came out in front with a guitar and sang folk songs, spirituals, and what later became popular as 'freedom songs'. This was before the era of Joan Baez; I had not heard such songs before and was filled with enthusiasm for them, and for their messages.

I had not so far experienced hatred or violence at first hand, and my faith in human nature received a rude awakening on the day we found our trucks and scenery, which were parked outside a 'Coloured' university, daubed with graffiti in crude red paint. It took hours of hard work for the boys to clean up before the evening performance. That night, the hall was packed, the front rows filled with little girls in starched white dresses and the boys in Sunday suits and neat bow ties; and over all, a steady hum of expectancy, which it is as good to hear before the curtain rises as a hive of bees on a summer afternoon. It was a hot, still night, and after showing people to their seats and distributing programmes, I stood by the open door, hoping for a breath of fresh air.

As the lights dimmed, there was a sudden explosion. Shots were fired, shattering the windows in the roof and showering the audience with glass. For a moment there was panic: children screamed and dived under the seats. An anger beyond all reason made me dash outside, intent on seizing anyone who might be lurking in the bushes. Perhaps fortunately, all I heard were footsteps dying away in the dark and there were crushed branches where the gunman had crouched. Back in the hall the company quickly took charge and the performance went ahead as planned, to the usual enthusiastic reception.

Afterwards we were entertained to coffee by the Faculty, who were all eminently kind, cultured and civilized human beings. They seemed to feel it necessary to apologize to us for the incident, although it was evident that, to them, such events were commonplace. It had happened before and would happen again; this time, mercifully, no one had been hurt. I could not forget that all the Coloured universities we had visited had been poorly furnished and ill-equipped, often lacking modern laboratories, gymnasiums or swimming pools. The white universities had all these good things; their Faculties, too, were kind, cultured and civilized human beings and they had given us an equally warm welcome. This saddened me and I lay awake for a long time that night reflecting upon the impossibility of changing human nature, merely by a song.

The tour came to an abrupt end for me on a day when the Mayor of St Augustine invited the company for a day out at sea in a fleet of fishing boats. We set sail in the cool early morning, singing 'Shrimp boats are a-coming ...' but as the day advanced and the sun blazed fiercely in a cloudless sky, we shed more and more of our clothes. No one had warned us how fierce the Florida sun could be so early in the year and we had set sail as carelessly as the Jumblies in their sieve, and without a crockery jar in which to hide. On our return that evening, many of the company were badly blistered, and had to be rushed to the local hospital for treatment. All of us suffered in some degree, and I thought it wisest to return to New York since the date of our departure was drawing near.

Ellen insisted on calling in the doctor, who prescribed pills and rest. Later, Daphne came to sit with me and hear about our adventures, which I must have poured forth in an increasingly incoherent stream, for she suddenly got up again, looking anxious. 'Listen,' she said, 'you've got a fever and I'm sure you ought to rest. Better not tell Ellen all this – I mean, about people shooting through windows and so on – it will only worry her, because of Puck. Better not tell Winifred either, she'll only tut.' At the door she turned and said suddenly, 'You know, I rather envy you. It must have been exciting!'

At home once more I felt flat; everyone seemed busy about their own affairs. My godmother Yvonne Arnaud was rehearsing for a concert, to be conducted by her beloved John Barbirolli, and the drawing room now held two grand pianos; glorious music rolled around the house from dawn to dusk. Inspired by this, I sat on the terrace outside and sketched out a sequel to the children's book that Little, Brown had bought, a sequel for which they had asked. In spite of misgivings, I sent this to Daphne for advice with, I hope, an apology. She answered quickly and fully and so our long correspondence began.

The first letters were signed 'Daphne', but this was soon changed to Bing, and later to Tray or Track. Since Bing was the name by which she was known to most of the people around her, it is the one I have used here.

※

LETTERS FROM MENABILLY
𝕽

*Editor's note: the first, undated letters in this collection belong to the early
1950s.*

Mena, Wednesday 7 May.

Dearest Oriel,

Many thanks for your letter, and I would have answered to Marraine's,
but I've been and lost her address, and anyway, perhaps better you should
find this on arriving home, because it's nice getting letters then. (Crumb!)

I *am* cross – I got home, and at once started a fearful *cold*, a real
snorter, and it's made me feel like K.M.* with her TB – why must Fate
do this to me, and drag me down again, just when I wanted to be well
for work? I know it was beastly London that started it off, getting one
moment hot, and the next cold. I stayed in bed yesterday, and you are
quite right about M.M.† – I couldn't put him down! But I did read your
synopsis before I left, and I think it is much more lively than the first
of the series, and even more E. Nesbit-ish, but I do implore you to bring
James‡ in sooner. The strategic place would be the back of the car to
Boulogne, or failing that, *in* Boulogne. I think just around here the story
gets a bit involved, and James would help to get it clearer – I was a bit
muddled by the journalist, and don't see the need of *him* – get Emily
and James away to France, and then make James appear again, and do
his business. Other snag, would the French café woman really engage
Emily to wash dishes? Would they hand her over to the police, or the
English consul at once? But maybe I'm being pernickety, and children
wouldn't question that.

Anyway, do start and get it moving swiftly, and don't *linger* over
Emily's move from her home, and don't dawdle over that. You want to

* Katherine Mansfield.
† Middleton Murry, K.M.'s husband.
‡ A character in *Beginner's Luck*, my book for children published by Chatto & Windus in 1952.

get on to the Goat and the Vase as soon as possible. If you are writing an exciting book, it should move swiftly from the word go. You have to write either a 'sensitive' story about a misunderstood child called Emily (on the Marjory Fleming lines) OR your E. Nesbit-ish Emily–Goat–James–mystery kind. If you try to mix the two, you will fall between two kinds of writing. How tiresome I am, an 'old wise' storyteller talking to a 'young, eager' writer! No, but do you see what I mean? Well, that's you and your story. (You would like me to go on for ages!) Lunch-bell just gone, Tod irritating about some man who wants to measure the house for Rates. I'll go on later.

Sunday

The thing is, I have been enthralled by Middleton Murry. It just explains everything. I had always seen him as quite a different sort of person, and now I understand. That withdrawn sensitiveness, it was not cruelty at all, don't you see? *Why* do you dislike him more than ever? Now at last everything falls into line. He is so honest about himself – always that fear of facing up to life and not wanting to be involved; the interlude with Margaret was a preparation for Katherine – I find it quite absorbing. At last the opposite side of the picture, so we now know what he was thinking and writing to her, when she was wrapped in a dressing gown at Bandol, and elsewhere. Yes, call it weakness if you like. But I feel I now understand the whole relationship. I want to go on reading where he left off, and if you make enquiries, I am sure he has written, quite lately, about a year ago, a *second* part of his autobiography. Do please try and get it. That will tell how he developed, and the next wife, etc.

I do think the Lawrences* must have been a pest to be with, and I find Murry's relationship with Lawrence very difficult to follow, and the intellectual 'ecstasy' with that man called Gordon or something. What made me feel a hundred years old is his face, M.M.'s I mean – his photograph when he and K.M. were together. Because when I first started my 'thing' about them both, I was about sixteen, so they both seemed 'grown-ups' to me, much older, which was half their great fascination. Now they are two youngsters, almost Ken and Tessa,† and it's so queer to realize it. It muddles me, in a strange way. Because I can't stop thinking of them as those two grown-up people, older than myself, great writers, going through distress etc, but now, they are *not*. They are two *young* writers, struggling; and in a horrible 'worldly' way, it's as if I had left them behind. Oh, it's no use thinking about it. They must just stay K.M.

---

* D. H. Lawrence and Frieda Weekley.
† Daphne's daughter Tessa Browning and her friend Ken Spence.

and M.M., as they were, with me younger. But this book is *very* revealing, isn't it? Although the deep intellect part is hard to follow. I would very much like to meet him now, but I should be sad, because he would be about sixty, wouldn't he, which is just as bad as being a very young man! Oh, how muddling!

What else to tell? I saw Clara Vyvyan* and Foy, but I was boiling up for my cold, and it was hard to whip up enthusiasm for the Glacier. She counts on me to go, though, and I feel it would be good for me, though I'm not really mad on the idea. But it's a way of looking at mountains, even if I don't climb them, and I'm sure I must get that out of my system, the feeling of being near mountains (rather Murryish? Well, intellectual!). But now I think I shan't get my Monte Verità† story right until I have been out there. There are twenty pages to do, and it seems Fate I should go out, and then write the last twenty pages afterwards. Do you see?

My next story – I hope to get on to it when the dreary cold goes – is one you will hate. Not macabre, really. About a sensual, rather foolish woman who, through idleness, lets a honky man from a shop make love to her, and then when he begins to get serious she gets frightened – she only meant it as a pastime – but I shan't tell you how it ends. It must give the impression of very hot weather, abroad, and the shutters of foreign shops down, because of the noonday siesta, and flies droning, and dogs asleep in dusty roads, and a lot of ferns and bracken on a cliff-top, and this woman yawning, lazily, sensuously, to the sun. You will *hate* it‡. But I see it very clearly.

Now there is nothing more to say. Perhaps we shall both get to work next week, and have that nice 'busy' worthwhile feeling of creation. If you are ever near a shop, could you find me a belt that one puts money in, like the one you have, because if I go to my Glacier, that would be the answer for walking, wouldn't it? I shall have Robert, I know, on the tour! And Lady Vyvyan will despise me, if I don't walk up a mountain with it. What shall I do with the Robert things? I see myself furtively changing behind a Glacier. She is prepared to sleep in a haystack but I don't think I am. You know my awful ritual of creaming my face, and my hair in pins, and breakfast in bed! Obviously I must rid myself of these foibles. How ease of life does creep into one's bones! Of course, nothing matters as long as one feels well. But to be stricken with a pain – on a haystack – or even just a cold, like I have now, how horrid!

---

* A neighbour and travel writer.
† 'Monte Verità' is the first short story in the collection *The Apple Tree*, Gollancz, 1952.
‡ I didn't. It was 'The Little Photographer', one of the best stories in *The Apple Tree*.

But then think of Japanese prison camps, and things, one has not really experienced *anything* in life. So perhaps a haystack with Lady V. is the nearest one will ever get to Reality! And out of it will come – no, not an epic – a dilatory romance about a jazz-band leader in Monte Carlo!

Lots of love, Daphne.

———

One wet and windy afternoon at Mena, when we were seated comfortably round the fire reading, the window of the Long Room rattled with sudden violence. We looked up to see a figure swathed in black, gesticulating wildly behind the glass. For one moment I thought the encroaching woods had sent forth an elemental spirit, but Daphne said calmly, 'There's old Clara Vyvyan!' and got up to open the window. 'You haven't tramped it here all the way from Trelowarren?' she asked anxiously, as the figure struggled out of its dripping oilskins, shaking itself like a dog, and spraying Mouse, who hastily retreated under the sofa.

'No, no, my dear, only from Fowey. I'm spending a few days at The Haven,' she explained, but even this seemed no mean achievement in such weather, and we were not surprised that Foy Quiller-Couch had declined to accompany her.

The visitor had a brown, weatherbeaten face, like a friendly pirate, and piercing eyes twinkling with humour. Over tea, the talk turned at once to distant places, Arabia and Kanchenjunga; atlases were dragged from their shelves and laid open on the floor, and it was as if the world had suddenly opened wide its doors. Later, Daphne explained that Clara Vyvyan had indeed travelled all over the world, mostly alone, with her few worldly possessions in a pack on her back. She had explored the Greek islands, had met with bandits in Montenegro, had crossed Canada to camp out with trappers in Alaska ... but she always came home again to Trelowarren, a beautiful eighteenth-century Gothic-style house close to the River Helford, where her roots lay. These were embedded as deeply in the garden as in the house, for Clara was a passionate gardener, and was often rewarded by the discovery of some particularly rare plant in one of the unlikely places to which her pioneering spirit led her. She wrote excellent books about her travels, which won her a small but faithful public, and which were published by Peter Owen; but, like so many good things, are probably now out of print.

Fairly late in life, Clara had married a man old enough to be her father – Sir Courtenay Vyvyan. His home and family traditions were far removed from her own vagrant life, and of course all who knew them predicted that it could not last, but it did, and they were happy together. During these years, Clara was content to settle down at Trelowarren, and make the garden into a place of rare beauty. Only after her husband's death did the old restlessness come upon her again but never, I think, to quite the same extent. Daphne had been Clara's travelling companion on several of her shorter European journeys, but she liked more comfort and above all better sanitation, than Clara ever bothered about.

Clara's old age was tragic, for she went blind. She had made Trelowarren over to the next heir, a distant relative, and was confined to one wing, and finally to one room, in increasing isolation. But for the loyalty of old friends like Foy Quiller-Couch, who came to share her solitude until she, in turn, grew too old, her last years would have been sad indeed.

One of the pleasures shared at Mena was a perpetual fascination with people removed from us by time, and temperament. We did not always agree about these. I could not share Daphne's passion for Bacon, while she was equally reticent about my love for Dr Johnson and Madame de Sévigné, but we had both fallen, at different times, under the spell of Katherine Mansfield. For Daphne, this began in childhood, when she had noticed that the window of the night nursery in their Hampstead home looked out upon the back of the house opposite; a light was always burning there when she went to bed. She would wave to it every evening before getting into bed and only discovered, many years later, that this house had been 'The Elephant', the London home of the Murrys, and that the light had been shining from K.M.'s own bedroom. She often mused upon what might have happened if she had walked round to Acacia Road one day and simply rung the bell, adding sadly: 'We shall never know now!'

Any scruples I might have felt at bothering Daphne with my own writing seem to have vanished. Her patience was inexhaustible, and she was a helpful and constructive critic. I had written a novel called *Jemima*, which I had set in Paris, of which I still knew very little. As I had been relying mainly upon guidebooks, and the nostalgic memories of my godmother's elder brother – a gentle, courteous Frenchman exiled in Surrey since the war – the atmosphere of the book felt distinctly *fin de siècle*, although the action took place in the twentieth century. I knew this, and felt slightly guilty when it was published. For some time afterwards, the characters refused to die, probably because I had nothing constructive to put in their place. At this point, I sent Daphne a *cri de coeur*, to which, as always, she replied promptly.

⚮

Mena, Saturday night, 25 October.

Dearest Oriel,

Here we go again, it's like Chesterfield or someone, or Madame de Staël! They ought to be read by students years hence! Listen, first of all, don't get all hot and bothered about this thing you insist on calling 'a plot'. You don't have to have a 'plot'; it sounds like Guy Fawkes in his old cloak, creeping with a lantern. You don't even have to have action (think of Proust). But you must have a real *reason* for it all, a reason for the things you want to say. Not just send Jemima off to Paris without knowing what you are going to do with her, but hoping something will happen. That's not professional, it's amateur. Charades, in fact!

You can keep the Jemima girl and Arthur sitting on a chair and their thoughts banging away at each other right through the book if you like, but their thoughts *must* get you somewhere. And I still am for a beginning, a middle, and an end, but it doesn't have to be a 'plot'. (Infuriating, I keep seeing all these conspirators whispering in corners!) The thing is, you know, Jemima won't die, and Niall* won't either, and we shall be doomed in some way to drag them in until we are completely purged. You see, your Arthur book will have to be a bit Jemima-ish, because of you being Jemima-ish, and in love with Arthur; if you make her quite a different sort of girl, it won't come right. On the other hand, it might be a good idea if we got away from ourselves completely with *new* books. I can't drag Niall into *Mary Anne*,† and you couldn't drag Jemima into a *Life of Lord Chesterfield*! We would, though. Niall will *creep* in as a sort of young captain in the artillery, hanging about Mary Anne in her off moments when she's bored with the Duke of York, and Jemima will be a dreamy sensitive young cousin of Lord Chesterfield, *observing* him. (Why Lord Chesterfield? Well, I don't know. I mean, he does as a symbol!)

Oh, to be purged, to be purged. Yes, the I in *Rebecca* was me, well purged. I've never been her since, but I think I shall be on Wednesday when P.P.‡ comes, and I trip up, shaking hands.

Oh, *not* a country vicar's daughter (back to Jemima the second), a young nurse is much better, or a doctor's daughter. Or Arthur could be a young surgeon. I'm menaced by surgeons, I don't know any, but I always think it's a menacing profession.

Tod used to point with a pencil over my shoulder at sums, and it came clear, when I was about eleven – but think of Tod now? Nothing comes

---

* In *The Parasites.*
† This novel was published by Gollancz in 1953.
‡ Prince Philip, the Duke of Edinburgh.

clear, it gets more muddled, the poor old thing. So years hence, you will come to visit me to hear words of wisdom about writing, and I shall be aged, and my mind gone. How sad. I agree, I'm not adult at all, I just have perspicacity. And a sort of thing that makes me see other people's points of view. But I don't think I have views of my own.

Listen, have you heard of Jung? He is an old psycho man, but nicer than Freud or Adler because he's spiritual. He tells one about one's subconscious self, but is not saying that *all* one wants is endless bed, like Freud. Only he does say that the ordinary life of an artist or writer can never be satisfactory, because of this awful creating thing that goes on inside them all the time, making them Gondal* – so I am deeply interested. Try and get some of his books. Also, he harps, like Freud, on dreams. But he says they *always* reveal the subconscious. So we must start to take track of our dreams, and reveal ourselves.

Anyway, I dreamt last night that I was climbing that great mountain called Kitchenjunga, or whatever it is, so it means I'm not purged of climbing, but as I love mountains anyway and know it, I don't see it's anything to do with the subconscious. If I suddenly dreamt that I was made to be a porter or a lift person, then it would be significant, because I *don't* know it. See? So study your dreams and tell me, and I will interpret. *But*, what is interesting is that I never dream of death or awful things happening, which means my subconscious self is quite happy; it's the outer one that is lost. Which is better, I believe, than the other way round. I mean, if one was gaily dashing about all day, and then had fearful anxiety dreams at night, it would mean there was something *very* wrong with one. Interesting? What do you think? Well, I must stop.

Sunday
All second-wife in *Rebecca*-ish. Tommy† is getting P.P. panic and polishing things, and decanting port, and there's an awful thing about people must be at the gates to open it for the Royal Daimler to sweep through, but WHO will do this? I say, we *can't* compete with crumby people who have minions, so why try? P.P. must learn how ordinary people live, and he shouldn't come here unless he is prepared to be ordinary, and we shouldn't ask him. We've only got four knives with handles that aren't bust, and one silver candlestick must be glued! But what of it, I say? No more for now.

Lots of love, Daphne.

🙥

---

* A reference to the Brontë sisters' childhood writings about an imaginary kingdom of that name.
† From 1952 to 1959, Daphne's husband Tommy was Treasurer to the Duke of Edinburgh.

Mena, 1 December.

Dearest Oriel,

Listen, I got in a muddle about ringing you, because it's so difficult getting through from here, and I never know the right time. It was funny when your wire came.* Tommy and I were out, and old Shaw took it down, and obviously thought I had a poor, very ill friend in a mental home with D.T.'s! She wrote a discreet message (so that Gladys shouldn't see it) – but of course the telegram people all think, 'Dear, dear, how shocking!' and you can never come and stay again, because it will be known at the post office!

I am glad the book is going so well. I really have no news, except that Tod rang up in a flap to say she had a bad varicose vein in her foot, and had been to her doctor in London, and he said it must be operated on at once! And the poor old thing is whizzing into hospital Wednesday, tomorrow, and she says that she will be there a week – but what if it is quite bad? It's rather awful. She goes into the Gordon Hospital, quite near the Tate Gallery. Then Maureen† has to have her tonsils out, and that's next week too, so a couple of dreadfully ailing invalids will descend down here in time for the holidays, can't you imagine it? Tod with a bandaged foot, and Maureen with the swathed neck, and both will vie to see who is the illest. I shall probably come up about the 14th, and we will have a date some time that week, perhaps on the Monday for tea at the flat, though really you are due to be taken out to lunch, but it is such a shilling, I much prefer coming to the flat, and talking. I shall probably have 'Mary Anne' talks with Sheila,‡ the first part of the day. I have had endless Robert, and feel rather 'weak' – it's probably C. of L. or cancer of the uterus, though I don't see *why*!

It's drab and dreary down here, and you are missing nothing, not even the Spirit moving on the face of the Waters. I am surrounded by books on Jesus, and books on gods, and books on psychology; I don't know where I am! Send a note back saying your silly plans, and where you will be next week, in case of writing or ringing up. Poor old Pen Friend§ has been two weeks in hospital with a thing called a *double* rupture. What on earth is it? I feel women aren't supposed to ask, a kind of delicate thing.

Love, Bing.

---

* My telegram read *'Sorry, having D.T.'s writing.'* I had used the abbreviation for Deep Thoughts.
† Maureen Baker-Munton, Tommy's secretary at Buckingham Palace.
‡ Sheila Bush, Daphne's editor at Gollancz.
§ Ronald Armstrong, a retired diplomat living in Switzerland.

'The Spirit moving on the Waters' was the name Bing had given to a certain light which, after a stormy day, streamed down in bright ribbons upon the sea. It was supremely beautiful, and I hoped it would appear on my visits, but like all strange and lovely things, it could not be commanded at will.

On receiving this letter I hastened to the Gordon Hospital, feeling anxious for Tod, but even before I reached the ward, down the long, forbidding corridor a familiar clarion voice rang out: 'My dear, the dust in this place! You would never think it was a hospital. I can't think what those girls are doing. Workshy, that's the trouble!' and I knew all was well.

Tod was sitting up in bed, surrounded by flowers, pink-cheeked and triumphant. She beamed when she saw me, eager to hear all the news, her main preoccupation being to know how things were going without her down at Mena. I knew it would please her best to hear that all was going to rack and ruin. In fact, all was running smoothly, for Shawkie, that old and trusted family friend, whose free and easy ways suited Bing perfectly, had once more stepped into the breach. I was careful not to let Tod guess this, however, and as I left she called me back and begged me to tell Bing on *no* account to let Mr Burt loose in her garden.

I never knew when Pen Friend entered Bing's life, nor when he ceased to be merely a correspondent and became a chosen companion on her trips abroad. He was one of Kits' favourite victims for mimicry, and when we eventually met in Paris I could hardly keep a straight face, on finally encountering the well-known voice and mannerisms. He had been in the diplomatic service and was now retired. He was, perhaps not surprisingly, a snob – but then isn't almost everyone, at heart? Pen Friend was kind, cultured and intelligent, and had led a varied and interesting life. He now lived quietly, in a modest way, at Sierre in Switzerland. Pen Friend enjoyed his creature comforts and, unlike Clara Vyvyan, fully appreciated the comfortable hotels to which Bing lured him on their travels.

᷾

Menabilly, Wednesday.

Dearest Oriel,

I really *am* sorry, I have kept meaning to write, but everything is such a bustle in the holidays, and quite truthfully, I don't seem to have had time to sit down to a long chat.

The mornings (Tod away) are filled with rush – to the store cupboard and back to get Tell-Him things, and then fitting in my letters in between. There have been an awful lot of dull things to answer – the kind that secretaries would, if one had one. Then the afternoons with dashing off to the boat, and only getting back to supper. We had our Regatta thing when your first letter came – it took three days – and then Margot Fonteyn over the weekend (Tommy is rather menaced by her, she is the ballet person. Awfully nice and easy, and reminded me of a Red Indian). Then Ken* was down, and there was bathing. Tommy is down for his holiday, the house seems full. Tommy and I went off for a short cruise in the boat to the Helford River, and so on and so on. So do you see? Also again, I didn't know where you were. I thought vaguely, Wales? Well, forgive me. But now I am writing I don't know what to tell you, because nothing has happened but the Tell-Hims above!

Weather, until today, lovely, so there has been lots of bathing. This I always love, it gives me such a healthy feeling, and I am browner than ever I was. Tessa enjoyed Paris, but had a beastly cold all the time, which was a shilling for her. She had that Peter person† staying for the weekend, but Tommy and I were at Helford, so we missed him. I did this on purpose, so as not to be here to make conversation! I can't make out if she is really menaced or not, but she is going through rather an irritating phase of talking about nothing but men and menaces, I can't think why *now*, suddenly. It *is* an irritating phase, but I feel all girls go through it, and it really comes from not having enough to do or think about. Like you and your pleated menace, you were not working at the time! Now I shall start, I suppose, because of not working, except that I really am too old, and bored stiff with menace and sex talk these days, a real sign of C. of L., I feel!

The dread of Balmoral draws nearer. Margot Fonteyn absolutely saw my point in not wanting to go. The horror of one's clothes, and I *won't* buy a lot of new things, such a waste. It's no good saying I shall like it, I know I shan't.

Clara Vyvyan is on the last lap of the Rhône and will have finished by the last week in September, so my going out to join her is 'out'. I have a feeling, from her letter to Foy, that she is getting a bit tired of it all, and that dog-bite must have had a shaking effect, and now Foy is home, she is all alone again.

But now I have a fresh worry. It is that poor Gertrude‡ is dreadfully ill, and is in hospital. (This is not supposed to be known, I don't know why, but that old dragon Fanny Holzman wrote to me in great privacy, as if I were a next-of-kin, rather a crumb in a way; anyway, don't say anything about it.) She has a bad virus of the liver (how awful if it was cancer, and they won't say), and every consultant has been called in, and she is in agony and sort of kept under, and given 'infusions' (what are they?) and I have told Fanny that if Gertrude wants me to go and be with her when she gets better, of course I'll go, but I've not told anyone this, not even Tommy. But it's pretty sure she won't go back to her play, but will need a long convalescence. Anyway, I feel in a kind of state that I must not plan too far ahead, and I keep thinking how awful if I suddenly had a cable to say she was dead. I can so see it in all the papers. Oh dear, how morbid of me. Think if it happened, and then I had to be all cheerful at Balmoral. Oh well, it's no use looking ahead in that way. Now no more. Write, not on a hard chair.

Tons of love, Bing.

Gertrude Lawrence died three days later. I was in the kitchen of my godmother's farm, shelling peas to the distant sound of the Grieg Piano Concerto, I remember, when the news came over the radio. I rushed to the telephone. Bing had received a cable only a few hours before, and she was shattered. I do not think she had really believed in Fanny Holzman's letter, and all had been mercifully quick at the end.

For some time, Bing had been brooding on the idea of a play, to be based on the life of her notorious eighteenth-century ancestress, Mary Anne Clarke, believing that so flamboyant a personality would be a perfect part for Gertrude. They had discussed it together in New York, and Gertrude was enthusiastic. Now, with her death, the inspiration for this died, too, and it was never written. However, any creative idea that has really taken root in the mind ends, sooner or later, by putting forth fresh shoots – and so it was with Bing's novel *Mary Anne*. Apart from the scandal that rocked London society and brought disgrace to the Duke of York, little seemed known about this lady. At Mena, there was a set of highly coloured contemporary cartoons, showing a fat and blowsy lady being pursued by a mitred Bishop and other dignitaries, with balloons coming out of their mouths ... but the rest was silence.

Bing could never be lured to London for any length of time; she sent for reference books from the London Library, and engaged researchers to delve into the past. I must have been passage wandering at the time, for she suddenly suggested that I might like to do some mild detective work for her, as the following letter reveals.

Incidentally, with regard to Bing's horror of formal social occasions, her visit to Balmoral proved less harrowing in reality than in imagination, and she enjoyed it as a unique experience. Fortunately, there was no time for royal passage wandering; each morning the guests were presented with a programme of the day's events. These were mostly sporting, but they were offered a wide choice of alternatives. Bing did not shoot, fish, ride, or play cards, but she loved being out on the moors, in such beautiful country, with or without a gun. Indoors, she later confessed that her most relaxed moments had been spent in the soothing company of the Queen Mother.

⚜

Mena, Friday night.

Dearest Oriel,

Here are the notes that Derek* made on the Court Martial in September. You will see his handwriting on one page, and I have added my queries above, in my writing. If you read these carefully before going to the Records Office (and of course take them with you) you will not need to copy down anything that he has already done. I feel rather awful about you going off to do this, because you probably want to do something else, or perhaps have Deep Thoughts? But it may be rather interesting to get inside the Public Records Office. I believe they have everything under the sun there, things like Shakespeare's Will – almost. But your bit may be dull, just an old filing room.

The reason I am so keen to know about Charles Thompson is that he is Mary Anne's young brother, and from all the information I can get they were devoted, and I have a feeling that it was only after he was cashiered in May 1808 that she turned revengeful, and wrote threatening letters to the Duke. (She hadn't bothered, before.) I see him as a sort of Branwell, always clinging to her skirts. His character, rather unpleasant, will emerge as you read the Court Martial closely. I do hope the writing isn't too difficult. Can't wait to know how you get on with Derek. He's very pleasant really, and as you are *not* a du Maurier he will think nothing of you! But he is terribly interested in the eighteenth century, and in the

---

* Derek Whiteley, who helped Bing with research.

Regency, and really Gondals himself into those days, and is not interested in the present, so I do think that is a bond in common – not that you and I are particularly interested in the eighteenth century, up to date I haven't taken much interest in it.

Thank heaven, at last the sun has shone, and today I sat out all day by my Hut – no work – just basking. I wish I knew what it meant to love the sun so much. Honestly, one's nature completely changes in the sun. I think it's a harking back to some old past, Ancient Greece or something. I am 'off' Adler, and still very much 'on' to Jung, who is much cleverer and more spiritual, and he doesn't think Gondaling is silly, and striving for power, like Adler. In fact, he says that great genius can come from phantasy, so that is us! And we have two unconsciouses. The ordinary, individual unconscious, made up of a sort of second self, and a bit Adlerish; and a 'collective unconscious' which goes streaming back to old Assyrians and cavemen and people, and we can't *help* that. Of course, this collective unconscious *could* be a case for reincarnation, couldn't it? Instead of just old Assyrians inherited in our bones, as he says it is, it could be that once we *were* Assyrians, in another shuffle. I don't know, I shall have to think.

I have been thinking about Marraine, and her throat. And I wonder if her laryngitis is an unconscious *protest*; something nervous. You know, it is her *way of speaking* that is so attractive, and for which she is so famous. Supposing her unconscious self somehow *resents* this, is against acting, and (although she wouldn't know it) now and again the unconscious self becomes conscious with the laryngitis that *stops* her acting. This is very deep Daphstein, and I don't really know what I mean myself; anyway, I would have to know Marraine better, to 'interpret' her. Now I must stop and go to bed.

Lots of love, Daphne.

———

I paid little heed to this at the time, nor to the unconscious mind in general; the conscious world claimed all my attention. Looking back, I think Bing's own subconscious may have been wise about my godmother. Marraine's first love was always her music, but this was constantly being frustrated, as she was not allowed to give a concert during the run of a play. She had come to the theatre almost by chance, and at this time could not afford to retire, although she was all too often forced to carry the play of the moment on her shoulders. More and more frequently, her voice let her down, and she would be 'off' through ill-health. I had not understood this at the time, for she hid her deepest worries, at home and at the theatre.

I accepted Bing's request to find out more about the elusive Mary Anne, but once in the Record Office, or the British Museum, was always getting sidetracked. Derek Whiteley, Bing's official researcher, treated me with kindly condescension, and we got on well together although he plainly wondered why Bing thought it necessary to involve me. The Reading Room at the British Museum proved to be a fascinating world-within-a-world; and delightful characters lurked there, including an ancient Authority on Medieval Beekeeping. He was as happy as a bee himself, poring over his pile of books in a quiet corner.

One day, we met by chance in a dusty little tearoom off the Tottenham Court Road, and talked about Dr Johnson, whom he greatly admired – perhaps on account of the bees in *his* bonnet, too. His satchel bulged like a comfortable pair of old shoes, but when he fumbled in it for his purse, revealed a packet of football pools, and a postcard of Lily Elsie, that star of Edwardian musicals. This made me love him, and I wished with all my heart that he might win a fortune, and be able to set up a worldwide Centre for Medieval Beekeeping. I reported this to Bing with my meagre gleanings on Mary Anne; she instantly saw the point, and begged me to find out about a Medieval Beekeeper's Day, in case we should need one. When *Mary Anne* appeared, I found my name included with Derek's among the list of people thanked, which in my case was quite unjustified since I had gained far more than I had given.

Some time in the autumn of 1954, Bing was asked to write the preface for a new edition of *Wuthering Heights*. This came at a good moment for her. *Mary Anne* had been successfully launched, and there was as yet only the faintest gleam of a story set in France, developing in her mind. At Mena the Brontës were always a favourite subject for psychological politics. I had just come across a copy of *The Brontës' Web of Childhood* by Fanny Ratchford, the American lady who first transcribed those tiny books of Brontë Juvenilia, which were the source of much of their inspiration, and passed this on to Bing, who was as fascinated by it as I had been.

From a childhood gift of a box of wooden soldiers, which Mr Brontë gave the nine-year-old Branwell, sprang those imaginary worlds of Gondal and Angria, the source of the Brontës' imagination, and their doom, for in adult life they were unable to break free from them. Charlotte sought refuge in the Angrian Chronicles whenever life became too much for her, and suffered agonies of guilt in consequence. Emily, untroubled by conscience, immersed herself in Gondal, the country of her mind, until inspiration failed her, and she died. 'Gondal' became our codeword for all make believe and pretence, whether conscious or not.

Daphne had always longed to visit Haworth, and suggested that Flavia and I should go with her. In those days, the Parsonage was still a quiet and fairly secluded spot. Haworth, too, remained much as the Brontës must have known it – a dour, flinty village, but warm and friendly when seen from within. There were no souvenir shops, in fact few shops of any kind. We had hoped to stay at the Black Bull, but this was not possible for some reason, and so we found rooms at the small but hospitable guesthouse nearby. It was bitterly cold; we woke each morning to find the windows decorated with delicate patterns of ice, and it took considerable courage to leap out of bed. After a substantial Yorkshire breakfast, we walked up the narrow lane to the Parsonage, and spent happy hours among the books and papers there. Bing, with her objective firmly in view, got down to work at once.

Each evening after supper we went for a walk, coming home through the churchyard and seeing the lighted windows of the Black Bull shining out into the dark, as Charlotte and Emily must have seen them while waiting up for poor drunken Branwell's return. Bing was becoming increasingly intrigued by Branwell (the son, predictably, interesting her more than the daughters), but for the time being she thrust her gleanings down into the place where all ideas lie fallow; until years later they rise to the surface with a fresh life of their own.

Shortly after our return from Haworth, we heard that Doubleday were giving up the apartment occupied by their Paris representative. The lease still had six months to run, and they offered this to Bing, possibly in the hope that she might be inspired to delve more deeply into her glass-blowing forebears; but even so generous an offer could not lure her away from Mena, nor from Tommy, whose work kept him in London. Instead, she decided that Flavia and I should spend this time in Paris; Flavia would learn French, and I would write. She insisted that every aspiring writer should spend some time in a country other than their own, to gain experience, and she herself had always been happiest in France.

Flavia and I agreed, with little idea of what awaited us there. The humdrum 'office' we had envisaged turned out to be a sumptuous, *très chic* apartment on the edge of the Bois du Boulogne, and nothing could have been further from the shabby, friendly reality of Great Russell Street. We rattled around like two peas in a pod in the high white-panelled rooms, all opening out of one another, their crystal chandeliers tinkling derisively each time we closed the doors. The whole *immeuble* was so exclusive that not a sound penetrated it from the outside world, and we lived there for six months without ever seeing our neighbours, or exchanging a friendly word in the lift which swung precariously between the floors like a gilded birdcage, and which was nearly always out of order.

Flavia and I did not spend too much time within the imposing walls; outside, close at hand, was the Bois, with its lakes, ducks and boats, and the lovely gardens at Bagatelle. Our everyday ploys took us still more often by the stuffy, garlic-smelling *métro* to the Left Bank, where Flavia attended classes in the studio in which her grandfather had once studied drawing, and I wandered, soaking up Paris like a sponge, and dreaming of K.M. in her shabby hotel room behind the Sorbonne. It was all a joyful interlude, as divorced from real time as the visit to America had been, and it was to have certain unforeseen consequences in my life.

Bing came out to visit us, and brought to life an older, no less fascinating Paris – the city of *Trilby* and *Peter Ibbetson*. It was not so easy to discover the past in modern Passy, with its shops and tree-lined boulevards. In Kicky's day, Passy had been a village on the edge of Paris, and the old house in its green garden that he remembered so nostalgically all his life and which he recreated in *Peter Ibbetson* and *The Martian*, was now a block of flats in the busy rue de la Tour. We searched, with more success, for the house in the rue de la Demi-Lune, in a far less salubrious *quartier*, where Mary Anne and her three children had eked out a precarious existence after the Duke of York's death, waiting for the tide to turn (which for her, sooner or later, it always did). Bing returned home more determined than ever to visit the Sarthe *département* of France and discover her French roots, as soon as possible.

ॐ

Mena, Thursday morning, 6 Jan 1955.

Dearest Oriel,

Many thanks for your letter this morning, and also for the one you wrote Flave, because I read that, too. I think she will ask your advice about clothes in London, when she is actually packing her suitcases. I should go round to Whitelands, if you have a moment, and give advice, like you did once to me, before I went to Rome, or somewhere. As it's her first grown-up trip away, she is inclined to want to be in tottery heels and wearing black – although remembering myself, I never had that black thing, but got myself up in scarlet, like a bird in plumage! – but the point is, that day-by-day, going to the Louvre and so on, one *must* wear sensible, *warm* clothes at this time of the year. That 'flu people get in towns, I am sure is due to hanging about on cold pavements in thin shoes, and not heavy enough coats. For yourself, too – better be muffled up and fumphy, than tottery and mincy!

About going about alone – you must use commonsense about this, the pair of you! I mean, *you* are even more likely to be 'picked up or followed' by leering men, because of flashing Welsh eyes, and in spite of non-adult appearance! No, teasing apart, what I don't think either of you should do alone is walk in the Bois: men *do* go to the Bois to beed, and in the lonelier parts it can be nasty, with a beeder suddenly peering from behind a tree. I have had it happen to me in the past, but the Alsatian dog I walked with generally kept prowlers at bay. (Keeper!)* Some people unfortunately do get followed and spoken to, others don't. I remember Doodie always said *she* was followed, when she was young, and I wasn't, but I think she was on the lookout for it!

Flave knows very little French, and until she gets the hang of things, I don't think she would be capable of finding her way, or asking directions, from one part of Paris to another. I can't think of anyone I know who will suddenly ask her out alone, and say 'meet me at the Bourse', or something. That Doodie, who is called the Comtesse Amédée Costa de Beauregard, and lives in the rue Barbet de Jouy, is the only one I can think of, and she will ask you *both* to lunch at her mother-in-law's house, to which you could take a taxi or bus (if you knew how!) or métro. (The métro, until you know it, can be muddling.) As to menaces, Flave has none, and if one of yours turns up, or appears with a friend, I presume they would call for you both at the apartment, and get you back there. I couldn't care less about Flave going out at night with menaces, if she meets proper ones; but not some pick-up nobody knows about! If you suddenly have a cold, or Robert, I hardly think Flave will want to go on some great excursion alone, there would be no point – it really is commonsense, to decide your Days!

If Flave shows signs of wanting to go three days a week to an Art School, which might be nice, Doodie told me there was a very good one, where 'everyone' went to, called Jullien's, in the rue de Berri, the street off the Champs Elysées, where Deirdre Butler has her office. Deirdre could probably find out about it, and what the hours were, and then you could discuss it. She ought to be able to get there and back, easily enough. But no need to press the Art School. It's only if it appealed to her, and it might be good for her to do. Also, this would give you some freedom for writing, if you felt like it. I suggest you both do something of the sort – you tapping away at the desk Frank used, in the library part of

* Emily Brontë's dog.

the salon, and Flave could paint, on her own, at the other end of the salon. It would be rather fun, and give her a sort of Bohemian feeling, two creative people at work! I'm all for encouraging this painting thing of hers, because if she shows any talent, she could carry on with this when she comes back to England, and have some aim, not become just a 'deb' waiting to be asked out.

As to your own Doom – *No*, I don't see a Doom in *Woman* turning down the book. They make it sound so crumby, with its 'psychological atmosphere', and you ought to be See Me. What Silly Values their readers have, if they can't grapple with it! I think the editors are silly, and the readers *would* like it. It's the same silly attitude that film and theatre managers have, that you must 'write down' to the public. For once, I think Winifred is wrong in telling you to get on quickly with another book. You don't want to be the kind of writer who just writes anything to show she is writing. It will give you angst, to do so! All right if you were a journalist, and had to get out an article once a week, that is a matter of training. But for a sensitive (crumb!) writer like yourself to feel bound to turn out something is morally wrong. You have got to feel it well up in you, like K.M. and her stories! Nice that Hodder's want to sign you up for two more books, but don't ever be tied to a date. I *never was*, and therefore wrote with freedom. Thank goodness old V.G. never pressed me, but in my more prolific days I generally had one book follow another within about two years, not closer. I think it's a mistake to rush them together. It's quite silly to follow your *Angel with a Sword* due September, with another at Christmas. They must be *mad* – but perhaps they mean, get the MS then, because their old imprint takes so long. Anyway, *don't* worry. Take your time. I think being in Paris will be much better for writing than in London. You will have time to concentrate, especially if you and Flave settle to a routine.

My coming out in February will depend a lot on Tessa's baby's arrival, and also, indirectly, with your March plans. And of course a lot depends on how you both like Paris. I mean, you both might loathe it, and want to come back at once! I may say, Flave is looking forward to it madly, and I am sure you will both enjoy it. Old Pen Friend is flying over on the 10th, and staying at the Hôtel Loti, and I am sure he will ask you both out. So do go. If Winifred is still there, he might ask Flave alone, so as not to be stuck with three people, mean old thing! If he does, of course she must go. The old thing is very trustworthy, and he would be admirable for showing you galleries and museums. If you want any last-minute things, do me a Reverse Call over the weekend.

My editor of the Macdonald Classics has written so nicely about my Introduction that I sent off to him last week. He said he had read many books about Emily, and lots of essays, but he had never read anything before that gave him such a vivid and convincing impression of her work and personality, which was such a crumb for me, I thought! If you think for a moment, there was me, once, a silly young girl, just gloating on Emily and her book – and now I am an old writer myself, actually doing an Introduction on her great classic work – it is both noble, and humble-making, don't you agree?

Well, now I must write a line to Winifred, hoping her cold is better! Piffy says that the Channel boats are owned by British Railways, and that they will strike if the trains do so. Do you suppose it's true?

Lots of love, Bing.

𝕏

Mena, Thursday 7 April, 1955.

Dearest Flave and Oriel,

Do forgive a joint letter, but I am alone in the house, nursing Kits with measles, and literally have no time except for brief news. I rather suspected the hoarse voice that greeted me at the airport, as a first brewing sign, but he said all was well, and we went off to the match on Saturday, and then got down here on Sunday morning. By afternoon he had a temp, but it's been such a slow brewing, which O'Reilly says is the case this year. Endless temp and cough and cold, and then nearly a week after out comes the beastly livid rash. It is a horrid disease. I let Tod go off for her Easter break ('My dear, I'm worn out, it will be nice to see some folks!'), and she would no doubt have got on Kits' nerves. Moper comes tomorrow. Apparently he has never had measles, so heaven help us if he gets it.

Now, the other thing is that yesterday I had a wire from Le Mesnil St Denis, saying that Ferdie had been removed to a hospital in Rambouillet, *gravely ill*. An op, I imagine. That she had asked I should be told. There is nothing I can do from here, but could you perhaps ring up, either the hospital, or the house in Le Mesnil (Mansard 84-37), to enquire if the old mother is being looked after, and if Ferdie is all right? Who knows, they may want money, rather awful. The grim thing is that I know poor Ferdie looks upon me as her 'heir', and if anything should happen I believe everything is left to me, of her house etc, but of course she always imagined the old mother would go first. It sounds cold-blooded all this, but I can imagine nothing worse than being suddenly summoned to take charge of the old mother and the house – I don't believe they have any relations. So if you can make enquiries, I would be so grateful. God knows who sent the wire, perhaps the doctor? Because the old mother is blind and bedridden.

                                        All love to you both, Bing.

————

'Ferdie', Mademoiselle Fernande Yvon, was a remote figure in a hospital bed, whom Flavia and I visited once or twice, taking her (so memory curiously recalls) avocado pears – of which she was particularly fond. To Bing, she was a beloved figure from the past – Directrice of the school in Paris to which she and her childhood friend Doodie Millar had been sent to 'finish' their education which, at seventeen, had hardly begun. No one could have been less like Tod, with her tweed skirts and no-nonsense outlook. Mademoiselle Yvon had slanting green eyes, a sarcastic wit, and dressed with true French chic in neat black skirts *à la Chanel*. Bing, who had viewed her sister Angela and Jeanne's frequent 'crushes' with detached amusement, fell under the Yvon spell and became a favourite pupil and later, a loyal friend.

With the years, Ferdie too became somewhat remote, and her lengthy tales of the feuds and friendships in the village of Le Mesnil where she was Deputy Mayor, appeared more and more often as Tell-Hims to Bing; but she was careful never to let Ferdie guess this. Tessa had stayed with Ferdie at Le Mesnil to learn French – an arrangement which might have been more practical for Flavia, too.

Mercifully, Ferdie recovered, and once we went down to visit her at the dark, rather cramped little house in Le Mesnil St Denis, now no longer a village, but a dormitory town for commuters. We did not meet her old mother, who died shortly afterwards. Bing came down with measles, which was to be expected, and took far longer to recover than Kits had done. Her birthday, on 13 May, was spent quietly, in a convalescent state, but she managed to write cheerful letters.

🌺

Mena, 13 May 1955.

Dearest Oriel,

Thank you so much for the lovely book of photographs. I beeded at them with joy yesterday. Oh, France and Paris, how can you bear to leave it? Perhaps you would both have liked to have gone on through June –

the terrible thing is that one *never* wants to come back. I used to go almost mad with grief at leaving in the old days, when Ferdie had her lovely house at Neuilly; and the awful dreariness of going back to Hampstead, and the shilling routes of one's home, and the feeling of disapproval.

I feel all I want to do at the moment is to lie on a chaise-longue and listen to the birds! You *are* a mean old furtive thing not to tell me about your menace; I bet things are brewing up, and you won't say? It's a rainy day, a shilling for my birthday as I can't sit out, and to sit *in* is the end. Tell Flave that Moper gave me a dear little peeper glass, which I wanted, and not a photo of the boat, which is my usual routes dread! He seems better, but still has coughing fits, and gets dreadfully mopish and down at the least thing. I *am* glad I am not a person who gets depressed, it must be so awful. Even if one is too weak to read or write, one can always *think*; and there is so much to think about in an abstract way. I mean it doesn't have to be about one's life or anything. Just kind of browsing. It's now on lunchtime, and so forgive this scrappy kind of letter. But I was so pleased about the book you sent me. The writing was a bit waine and precious I thought, but then it often is in those sort of books.

Poor Flave, does she dread coming back to England? It almost seems a pity she can't have some sort of job in Paris, but I don't know quite what! You know your flat – do you mean you would *lend* it to her? But that wouldn't be right. There must be a proper sort of thing about it. (My pride, like your French francs pride!) Tessa and Peter think of taking a flat in London, though Tessa does not want to as she likes being outside – it's nicer for Moppet.* She does all the things well that I did badly, which is rather Jung-ish, that thing of one's children being one's unconscious opposites!

Tons of love, Bing.

ॐ

Mena, 6 June 1955.

Dearest Oriel,

I had a great clear-out of my Hut (preparing the ground for work, like a cat getting ready for kittens, but heaven knows when I shall start), hence am using up old sheets of paper.

Now you mustn't mind my having begged Flave to tell me about your menace. Nobody else will know there is even a person in the air, but I

---

* Tessa's daughter Marie-Thérèse (Poonie).

did so want to know. I have been reading so many psycho books lately on the Anxious Woman, and the Harassed Parent, and so on, that I had better avoid getting on to psycho-politics, or I shall put you off, but I do hope you are also physically menaced, because I do think this is much more important than people give it credit for. 'Oh well, with Jim I was only physically menaced,' someone will say, 'whereas with Harry we like listening to the same music, or read the same books.' This makes me suspicious of a lasting relationship with Harry, and not the other way round, as people would think! Physical 'in-tune' can bring mental 'in-tune', or at any rate adaptability in its wake; but mental in-tune may never bring physical in-tune, and then you are faced with incompatibility in waxing, like my poor friend X (a Catholic, to boot!).

I know that awful fever of 'in love' does tend to go off inevitably with time, but my new great Professor Daphstein of 'in love' is that the whole thing is nearly always a complete illusion! People are apt to be Pegs, on to whom we hang our emotions and we invest these people with the qualities we want them to have, ignoring whether they do actually possess those qualities. Pegs, poor dears, have their emotions also, and if the particular problem that produced the emotion is quite a different type of one from ours, *then* one is likely to have trouble! The great Daphstein speaks!

One must always differentiate between *instinct* and *emotion*. Instinct makes one hungry, thirsty, sleepy, active, hot, cold, want to wax, not want to wax (see also glands); instinct also makes one want to protect one's young, and fight for food or cover. I do not believe there is emotion in this, merely fundamental feeling. Emotion is more cultivated, and is where all problems start! A baby cries because it's hungry. That's natural, and instinctive. A baby cries because its mother is cross with it. That's emotional. And away starts the first problem, on a long long line of problems! Oriel sits in her pram; an old woman beams, Oriel preens herself. Old woman comes again, doesn't beam; Oriel is Doomed. Oriel connects the non-beam with the idea that the old woman doesn't like her, whereas old woman is probably thinking of something else entirely, but emotional problems for the baby Oriel begin!

I would very much like to know what would happen if a child was brought up so that it never had *any emotional* problems whatsoever. Parents were always wisely kind, without spoiling, the instincts were satisfied, hunger, sleep etc – what *would* its mind be like? I never thought of this before. Seriously, it's worth thinking about, but then you have to have two parents without any emotional problems at all too, otherwise they'd project it on to the child. It really would be Paradise at last, wouldn't it? Because everything that goes wrong in the world is through some false *emotion* – Hitler, strikes, anything. Wait a minute, though. I suppose basic hunger must have started up some original wars, but the emotional reaction of 'that lot have got more than we've got' many more, surely? Ah well, I don't see what all this has got to do with you!

It's ceased raining, and I must get out for a breath of fresh air. Old Lady Vyvyan's Greek book is now out, as well as the Rhône one; you must read both. I loved them equally, but then I would, as I get mentioned (Silly Values!). The Greek one is dedicated to me. I had no idea she was going to, so it's a crumb. Now be sure and tell me *all*, when you write. You should get this when you return.

                                                    Heaps of love, Bing.

                                      ✳

Mena, 14 June, 1955.

Dearest Oriel,

Your great long letter came this morning. I agree with all your summing up, and you appear to have the emotions under control.

Yes, that business of wanting to be independent, and to be married too, is, I should say, the great conflict that goes on in so many women's minds nowadays, not only the artistic ones like us (crumb, our being artistic!). There are not such a vast majority everywhere who only ask for green pastures, and I should say that much of the many, many divorces today comes about because the woman no longer demands *only* green pastures, but her independence, and possibly career too. This thing of career and independence has increased so enormously during the last fifty years, that it amounts to a great revolution! It's as though the fundamental outlook of women has been jolted upside down. It's not surprising that individual women are unsettled, and find it increasingly difficult to make up their minds about anything. Talk about wanting their cake and eating it ... it's really that. How to combine making a home for husband and children, and retaining career and independence? That's the crux. It would be tempting to launch forth into a great discussion of patriarchal society and matriarchal society – a subject I find fascinating, and would like to read deeply about, but books are hard to find.

I think society has been patriarchal now for many thousands of years (except with certain native tribes), which means the rule of the Father. It was matriarchal in Greece and Asia about 10,000 BC, I believe, which means the rule of the Mother; and in those days the Mother was the head of the tribe, like a Queen wasp, and everything centred round her.

The males were used in a slavish way to wax with, and to get food, but a husband *as* a husband hardly counted; I don't think there was such a thing, but the *Son* was very important. I'm not yet quite certain *why* – whether he was nourished and trained to be a hearty young fighter and waxer, to minister to the Mother, or whether because the Mother set such store on him, he was set apart as a sort of god; and *so*, the conception of Dionysus came about, the singing god with hordes of trailing, excited women following him. These things are at the basis of religion, but then were covered over when patriarchal society took over, bringing the Father element into play, with the northern Greek Zeus, and the Hebrew Jehovah; and women were then subdued, and relegated to the home, and to minister to the husband.

What interests me, is *whether* Woman, as such, has been quietly seething to get back to a Matriarchal society ever since (though unconsciously), and whether individual women with careers, rather T.N.N.-ing their husband, and spoiling their sons, are all part of a huge, unconscious, rather terrifying Movement! WHERE ARE WE GOING??? Professor Daphstein peers into her crystal, sees the powerful ruling Mothers, sees the pansy young sons leaping like little goats, spoilt and god-like, sees the wretched husbands toiling dingily to bring in food, and of course none of this is really any advance on the rule of the Father, rather angry and disapproving and frowning, subduing everyone; but merely the other side of the picture! The aim of Society should be to achieve complete Balance. Actually, I think women divide into three types – the ruling type, the ministering type, and the prostitute. The prostitute being the rather lazy spoilt sister of the other two, and I'm not sure that for two pins, *you* couldn't be the prostitute!!! (Shrieks from you, of 'You horrid Bing, I shall never speak to you again…!') The prostitute won't quite make the effort to minister, but wants some sort of spoiling, petting power backlash, that can be got by taking a third line, and by employing their female charms!

Needless to say, I have only just thought out these three female types, and am now going to have a lot of fun fitting them to all the women I know! Of course, one can change from one to the other. I realize I started out in married life by trying to be the ministering type, and succeeded – *but* at the cost of great mental disturbance to myself, and a squishing of the ruling type, who simmered. Came the war, and the ministering type began to fade, and the ruling type emerged, bringing a feeling of mental power to myself (and, I suspect, a feeling of squished humility to Moper). So … the balance has swung too much the other way. It is the correct *balance* you must strive for in marriage, and the correct *balance* of your own individual self.

By the way, to switch to what you say of you and Flave longing for approval, and yet so often critical of other people, it puts a lovely wise finger on a personal fault. We always criticize *others* for doing what we do ourselves, and it hits back like a boomerang. Which brings me to a very interesting new Daphstein I have suddenly thought out, which is that in old age, we fail in those faculties that we have inwardly refused to use. For example, those who lose their sight do so because they have refused to see clearly what has happened in their own lives. Those who lose their hearing, lose it because they have never developed understanding, and have refused to listen to what went on around them. Those who become paralysed, become so because they did not take action at some vital moment, or crisis. Those who develop heart disease, develop it because their emotions, whether of anger or affection, became too strong. Those who get TB get it because they allowed the atmosphere they lived in to stifle them, and those who get cancer allowed some single quality of their character to devour all the other qualities, and so destroy them. It's a fascinating 'stein', and I could go on forever! Oh, about being a chameleon, it *can* mean taking colour from others, but it can *also* mean adaptation to others, seeing their point of view, or in the very large sense, speaking in parables that others can understand – tuning in, in fact, otherwise there would be no contact. The great wise Tray-Bing has spoken!

Heaps of love, Bing.

———

That summer of 1955 proved to be a Meeting of the Waters in all our lives. Flavia decided to try her luck on the stage and enrolled in the preliminary branch of RADA; she possessed the fertile imagination of the du Mauriers, but as yet had no clear idea how to use her gifts. Like many children of famous parents, she had an ingrained sense of inferiority about her own abilities. Before she had been many terms at RADA, it was suggested that she might be considered for the part of the young girl in Enid Bagnold's play *The Chalk Garden*, to be produced at the Haymarket, with Edith Evans in the lead. After much heart-searching, Flavia turned this down, feeling herself to be ill-prepared for such a spectacular début. It was no doubt a wise decision, but reason alone would scarcely have prevented an ambitious young actress from seizing this chance with both hands. Flave was not ambitious; as a result of the fuss she lost interest in her course, and began instead to turn her thoughts towards the many young menaces hovering in the wings.

Half Moon Cottage, Manaton, Devon, 1 July, 1955.

Dearest Oriel,

Your letter was waiting for me when I arrived on Tuesday, but I have not answered it before, because it's never so easy when one is staying away. Wednesday was not fine, so we had a typically Kits sort of day, going to the market and then lunching off snacks in a pub, and going to a Western film in the afternoon. And then yesterday was gloriously fine, so I went off by myself all day on the Moors, and it was bliss, for Deep Thoughts and psycho-politics; and thinking that all things are equal in the sight of God, sort of thing! I munched a pasty in an old earth-dwelling on the top of a tor, and mused upon an aeroplane far above me, thousands of feet up, perhaps flying to America, and then a rock-pippet soaring his little nuptial flight and parachuting, as they do, into the heather – definitely 'to the glory of God', if you know what I mean. I began to wonder why Man had evolved at all. The earth was surely more lovely before they did – nothing very glorious about the businessmen with despatch cases flying to America, yet the plane itself was lovely, like a bird and a crucifix in one. Perhaps that's the point. Today it's a thick moor mist, which is a shilling as I feel myself in good walking trim and could have had another full day.

I had a nice letter from Irene Hentschel* saying she was so pleased with Flave, and I *am* glad; it will be encouraging for her, and she need not dread her audition (perhaps she doesn't anyway!). To switch – I am *outraged* that you and Flave should say that I am a chucker of people! I simply don't know what you base this on. I have never chucked anyone in my life! The friends I knew when young are still my friends, as wide apart as poor old Tod, and Shaw, and Doodie – and if I mock them, it does not mean any more than that mockery is my nature, but they are far from chucked. As for menaces, I never chucked a menace, but have always remained friendly, unlike some people who part in rage or sorrow! I even asked Jeanne and she agreed with me, it's the last quality she would associate with me. I think you must be muddling chucking with being able to live without my friends. I am able to do without them very well, and to see them infrequently, which is very different to chucking. So please comment on this when you next write! I will *not* be called a chucker! (Force of circumstances often compels one to see friends not often, like Ellen and Frank† in America, for instance).

Re. chucking friends on marriage, this almost invariably happens at

---

* Theatre director, coaching Flavia for RADA.
† Frank Price, editor and formerly Paris representative of Doubleday.

first when anyone marries. The two people who are married become a unit, and go everywhere together, and it's never the same as seeing one, however nice they may be as individuals. The *footing* is different. This is why men often get sad when their bachelor friends marry. 'Old Tom is lost to us' sort of thing! It can't be avoided. Tom and Mary are not the same as Tom alone. You notice how even me, married for so long, is probably a bit different at Mena when Moper is at home. When he is there, I am conscious, I suppose, of being part of a unit, and so not wholly the self that you know alone. Which is the reason I like seeing my friends when *they* are alone, and I am alone! Individual attention can then be given. This is part of what one has to face when one marries, that merging into *their* life, and not feeling quite the old routy person, when one takes one's husband to see one's old routy friends. Three people are not two, it's logic. This may sound depressing, but it is true. What *is* tricky is to be torn between one's unit, and one's former individual self. I felt this strongly when I married, and I do still, but being older now I manage to keep some sort of level. A complete 'green pastures' unit should have no need of other sources; it should 'cleave only' unto itself, as it says in the Bible! It's a law of nature, like birds leaving the nest.

The sun comes out, and the moors look inviting. Flave's Woodham-Smith must be the son of that very crumby Florence Nightingale writer.* She seems to be having great fun in London. (Flave, I mean, not Mrs Woodham-Smith!)

I shall be here until Thursday morning, then go to Shaw's for Kits' Long Leave, and home by Tuesday 12th.

Lots of love, Bing.

🐝

Mena, 13 August, 1955.
Dearest Oriel,

Many thanks for your letter. I did so laugh at that sentence 'the conventions of life must be observed, otherwise where are we?' Such a Tut-tut Papa remark! It reminds me of Lady Vyvyan's old husband, who once said: 'If the line isn't drawn somewhere, there would be no line at all!'

Yes, we did have a lovely peaceful week, and I loved it. So good for swimming, basking, and D.T.'s, and psycho–politics. I think you are right about your unconscious not wanting to be adult, and now the realization has come to the surface, it won't be so bad. I didn't know about the unconscious in my young married days, and when I felt vaguely dissatisfied and unhappy, I did not understand it, and thought I was being disloyal to Moper, who was being a very loving husband, and I got guilt. It's the things we *don't* know about ourselves that are the nuisance.

---

* Cecil Woodham-Smith, the biographer and historian. 'Crumby' was a compliment.

The Baker-Muntons seemed very happy, and he really is a *lamb*. Like an older Kits, with rather Kits' ways, except one felt he was steadily reliable, too. Maureen inclined to boss a bit, but I think he would show sturdy independence when the need arose. He is quiet, but at the same time joins happily in conversation, and he was one of the most natural people I have ever met. This thing of Maureen begging him to eat was so funny. 'Now, please, have another helping of beef. You know you like beef ... etc, etc.' And him quietly saying, 'No, really, I have had enough.' I remember my Mummy used to do it to Daddy, and it shows anxiety on the part of the wife!

Old Shaw is cooking tasty dishes and – so unlike Tod – prefers to eat her own humble meal in the kitchen, and wash up at the same time, and then goes and reads her paper in the nursery. Imagine how infra-dig Tod would think this!

Weather continues bliss, and I am still bathing twice a day. We are a bit bored with V. She reminds me rather of how Neltje* was when younger – endless smoking, and sophisticated air, and doesn't join in anything. But, unlike Neltje, she is so unattractive. She seems to be menaced by Moper, and smirks whenever he opens his mouth, which perhaps pleases him. (The Older Man!) I do find it awfully difficult to talk to her about anything. She just says, 'Yes, I guess so,' and goes on drinking gin and tonic. We now dread that she crumbs to stay longer than a weekend.

Flave will be coming up for Marraine's First Night, and will tell you any more news. It's been rather a shilling week all round, but for the blissful weather.

Heaps of love, Bing.

———

Maureen Luschwitz had been Moper's staff officer during the war, and later became his secretary at Buckingham Palace. From then on, her life was woven into the family's routes. Bing turned to Maureen in times of crisis, and it was to Maureen that she wrote the highly personal letter which was published as the appendix to Margaret Forster's biography. After their marriage, Bim Baker-Munton, too, was speedily adopted into the family; he helped Bing with her finances, acted as her trustee, and was later appointed her literary executor. Maureen responded generously to the frequent calls for help from Kilmarth, often at great inconvenience to herself and her own family. Without these faithful friends, in the last painful years, Bing would have been lost indeed.

꒾

* Neltje Doubleday, Ellen's youngest daughter.

Mena, 24 August, 1955.

Dearest Oriel,

Many thanks for your letter, and for the book,* which looks jolly nice (the dedication is a crumb), and I think the title, now I see it on the cover, is very good and striking. I am sure you will get good reviews; I shall be very cross if you don't. What if the critics dislike me so much that you get tarred with my brush: 'We are sorry to see a promising young writer like Miss Malet dedicate a book to a hack-writing, best-selling spinner of yarns like Miss du Maurier etc, etc,' and you are spurned by the highbrows for ever more!

It is still that blissful weather, and I continue with routes twice-a-day bathes, and not too crowded. Poor Moper had his liver and then lumbago for the Regatta, and couldn't sail, wasn't that awful? He just had to sit humped, in a Mopish way. Flave's Charles came for the Sunday. I rather liked him, and he was surprisingly good at washing up, but rather awful having to ask him, as I believe they have footmen and silver trays, so he will probably go back to his nanny mother, and say Menabilly is a dump. I was in my shorts, too, which may have shocked him. Alastair comes next week. I don't think Flave is badly menaced, just nicely so. If badly, she would always be huddled in corners, writing letters. Kits still never goes near the sea, and is always on a bus or in the cinema, horrid little boy!

All love, Bing.

P. S. Nothing sinister in this torn page, merely that I can't go on for a full main page! My plans have got all changed, as Moper at the last moment doesn't want to motor me to France, as it would be a rush for him to get back to Prince P. and Denmark. So I am making Jeanne take me in her car instead, Noël† too! I don't know yet whether I shall gang up with the Singe later or not. The old dilettante can't find himself a hotel in the Loire district, with a nim-place next to his bedroom! To show my middle-aged state, I am looking forward to this trip as eagerly as I have ever done any of my trips, because of finding out the soil of my forebears, and to tread their ground; whereas once upon a time, I should have needed a menace to have given the whole holiday a zip! Which goes to show that the heyday of the blood is over, or it has taken another course! No good writing a long letter to me in France, because

* *Angel with a Sword.*
† Noël Welch, a friend of Jeanne du Maurier.

even if I gave you the address, the hotel might turn out to be a shilling, and we move on. I shall be back in England around the 24th, I suppose, and I hope inspired to write, not the story of my life, but what-might-be, if once-upon-a-time-there-had-been, and if black had been white, and male had been female, and the world had been different etc, etc, which is just another story, in fact!

Lots of love to the great doomed romantic Welsh Maid-of-the-Mountains, who can't find a green pasture to suit her Nomadic soul!

                                                                    Tray.

———

Daphne spoke of *Angel with a Sword*: once again I had forgotten, or ignored, her wise words about plotting, for this book had so melodramatic a plot that no one seemed able to swallow it. Yet it was based upon a true story of Moper's, in which an officer who was universally detested had been shot in the back by one of his own men in the heat of battle – which proves that truth is often unacceptable as fiction. I had enjoyed writing it, and living for months with the family who had been caught up in this dilemma. I parted from them, and their black, seal-like labrador, with true regret. At the time, a menace suddenly grew serious; he was the kind of man for whom one should 'Thank Heaven Fasting', but I was no good at fasting, and little better at knowing my own mind. I felt I had rushed into an engagement for which I was not ready, and needed time in which to sort myself out while he, more conscious than I of Time's wingèd chariot rumbling away behind us, wished to be speedily settled. 'Le coeur a ses raisons, que la raison ne connaît point', as Pascal so wisely said ... and now, both my heart and my reason were drawing me more and more towards France.

𝕏

Mena, Wednesday 30 November, 1955.

Dearest Oriel,

So glad to get your letter this morning, and to see that things have really sorted themselves out. Certainly, going away was much the best solution, though the letter I got from Paris sounded as though you might make up your mind in the other direction. I wonder if poor old Princess

M.* went through all these same problems; probably she did. I think she clung to her independence, in the same way that you do, and found after two years of separation that he was not really menacing enough to make such a fearful Thing about, and perhaps make a lot of people unhappy. This was a bit different from you, because in your case you have made your decision *against* family hopes, but for all that I am sure you have made the right one. Your only fault really is that it seems to have taken such a time to know what you felt. No, of course I shan't go telling anyone – if I am asked, I shall say the truth, that you decided you were really not suited, and that was that. Anyway, nobody *has* asked me, everyone is always much too occupied with their own affairs! But I should tell Winifred, because Ellen really *did* say in her letter to me that she was so sorry she could not get over for your wedding! Just think what a relief it is, really, that it is just a case of waffling, and perhaps stupidity on your part, and *not* some fearful thing of being miserable, with some menacing man suddenly saying *he* did not love *you*! So perhaps the months have not been wasted, but both of you have lived through a time of facing up to Life, if you see what I mean?

It is rather interesting what you say on Page 3 of your letter, about finding out about yourself etc, because if you remember, when I wrote my long Tray-Bing screed to you in September, this was the very thing I put to you, about having to decide what kind of person you wanted to be? You wrote back, rather indignantly, saying you knew quite well what kind of person you wanted to be, and that wasn't the point at all; but actually, I think it *was*! The trouble is, of course, that our ideas of what we want to be do vary very much with our age-group, I suppose. Twenty doesn't want to be the thirty person, and the thirty person doesn't want to be the forty one, and so on; and of course it must be terrifying to cling to the age that is passing, because then one becomes a clutching type that feels it has been cheated (if nothing much has happened) or, if a lot has happened, then afraid that it won't go on!

I am becoming more and more interested in the factor of Greed in human nature, which of course is basic Hunger unsatisfied, that wants to be filled, but somehow just misses the point. In fact, my whole new book† is going to be based on this great Main theme, but nobody will know it because it will be (I hope!) an exciting story of relationships in a French family! I am much intrigued by the Greek word for sin (Jewish), which was 'Missed the Mark'. Which apparently Jesus always used, when he told people: 'Go, and don't miss the mark any more,' meaning that

* The Princess Margaret.
† *The Scapegoat.*

they had been aiming in the wrong direction. It seems to me that this has such a wider and deeper meaning for everyone than the Jewish word 'Sin' – which always suggests to me people bowing and beating their breasts, as they call themselves Miserable Sinners, all nanny at a frowning Father!

Did you know Frank was leaving Doubleday's in the New Year, and returning to Paris to become a story-picker, or whatever it is called, for Metro-Goldwyn? A very good job; he wrote me in ecstasy about it, he was so pleased. I am so glad to think of him being in Paris again.

I have not written since I got back from France, and it seems ages ago – well, it's over a month! I simply adored it, and adored all my part of the country, Sarthe and the Loir-et-Cher, and I found all the places of my forebears, birth and death certificates as well, and the proper real Maurier and everything, which was so exciting. Jeanne and Noël were very nice to be with, and I was glad for Jeanne to have the chance.

Then I had a week in Tours with the old Singe, who was in good form and helpful too, in looking up archives, which must have been rather a Tell-Him really. But his old comforts do have to be pandered to so, his food etc, and he complained his room at Chenonceaux was noisy so we had to go back to Tours and things like that, which was a bit of a bore, but then I suppose an Aged Singe can't be expected to hop it like a youngster. His old nose will be out of joint if I go for a trip with Frank some time in the future! I hope Frank has lost his arrogance and See Me ways, but has kept his nice side.

Heaps of love, Bing.

———

I travelled hopefully to Paris with little idea of what I would do when I got there, but with the desire to shake up my life, as one shakes a kaleidoscope, in the belief that it would instantly form a new and exciting pattern. Like others before me, I imagined that to change countries was to slough off one skin, like a snake, and to assume a different personality; unaware that the journey I had so lightly embarked upon was in reality to be a lifelong one – the search for maturity. Hitherto, I had lived other people's lives, conforming to their ideas, and it was high time I struck out for myself, as Bing had long been urging. A stay-at-home herself in later life, she was then all for travel and adventure. Marraine was also encouraging, although she warned me that once one left a time or place, one could rarely return. She herself had been married for over twenty years to an Englishman, but was still regarded as a foreigner, and had never wholly succeeded in pulling up her French roots. I sympathized, but naturally felt that for me, everything would – and *must* – be different. Others, whose judgement I also valued, such as Winifred Nerney, were frankly disapproving; and there were plenty of Job's comforters to warn me of the perils to be found abroad, especially in France, where it was well known that every dog had rabies and the natives, if not positively hostile, were known to be inhospitable. To all of this, I turned a deaf ear.

⚜

Mena, 4 January, 1956.

Dearest Oriel,

I have not written before, because my cold has still been so beastly, and somehow I could not get down to it. When the house is full it does upset the routes, if you know what I mean! Kits has to be back at Eton on the evening of Tuesday 24th, so you might have to come for his last week and I might have to let you take him up to London, rather than go myself!

Once I go up, the hard-chair people like Irene (Haenschel) etc want me to lunch, and then I find myself having to have a few days in London, which cuts so horribly into the week, and I really *must* get down to proper work at the Hut, instead of this messing about. My awful new thing is wanting to *paint* – did Flave tell you? I mean, I know I can't, I'm not trained, and it couldn't be good, but that's not the point. The point is this fearful desire to slap on to canvas what my mind sees, especially the deep ruddy earth! Furtively I bought oil paints and a few boards, and when Tod and people think I am doing notes at the Hut, I am really getting smothered in oil, and covering these boards with great smears! It's rather like Therapy for Schizophrenics! Actually, you can see what the thing is meant to be – the Grib is the Grib, some trees are some trees, but they are very crude and queer, like those modern French people who are not abstract! Also I keep writing poetry! I sent two to Noël, that highbrow friend of Jeanne's who writes poetry, and she said they were very good – I expected her to mock, because she is so modern! What if Tray, in old age, became a strange old being, deep in paint and poetry?

Well, I read the Brontë book *The Passionate Search** with interest, and I think the bare life is adequately done, but I am really annoyed that the

---

* by Margot Peters.

writer has so *completely* ignored modern research, and except for one or two meaningless references to Angria and Gondal, says nothing about them, which is now known to be the clue to everything. What is the point of rehashing Mrs Gaskell yet again?

Are you interested in the opening up of Walsingham's tomb, to look for Shakespeare's MS? I wish they would find something, if only to irritate the Stratford people!

The gong is going for lunch. Tod has a pain in her side. Too much on her feet!

Lots of love, Bing.

————

That first winter of 1955–6 proved to be one of the coldest on record; all over Paris pipes froze, icicles of fantastic length and strange shapes dripped from the eaves, while icebergs drifted down the frozen waters of the Seine. On the earnest recommendation of a friend, I had rented a room in an apartment on the Left Bank – rashly, without first visiting it, but with the written assurance that it would be a suitable place in which to work as my landlady was out at work all day and the concierge took charge of all the household chores. It sounded ideal, but all too soon I discovered that the concierge had not been paid and my landlady worked part-time, so came home each day for lunch. It was her thrifty habit to turn down the heating every morning when she left for work; my fingers consequently froze to the keys of the typewriter as, cocooned in blankets, I crouched over my desk. She left behind her an old but exceedingly odoriferous Aberdeen terrier, with few redeeming qualities. I grew fond of it, however, and took it for daily walks in the Tuileries Gardens, and round the narrow streets of our *quartier*. Soon growing tired of the exercise, it would drag at its lead, or lie down in the middle of the road with a martyred expression, arousing pitying looks from passers-by and indignant murmurs of: 'Ah, le pauvre vieux chien!' (my godmother's repeated conviction that her compatriots were insensitive to animals proving totally untrue). Never had so much attention been paid to its whims, and it blossomed under this treatment, and became quite human.

I could not bring myself to abandon this furry friend, much as I wished to do so, for working conditions were proving less and less satisfactory. My landlady, whose emotional life was highly complicated, added to the general chaos by constant scenes. Under such trying conditions, Bing's letters were a great solace; they made me laugh, and were an encouragement to work. I found myself looking out for the odd characters and incidents that might amuse her in return, and wrote about them in my letters. One day, she posted a packet of these back to me, with a terse note saying: 'Why not a book?' Why not, indeed? My ideas, which had been as frozen into immobility as the Seine, began to flow. I had frequently found myself comparing, with wry amusement, my present spartan existence with last year's opulence in the Doubleday apartment; as I wrote, the past and present became curiously mingled in memory.

༄

Mena, 4 February, 1956.

Dearest Oriel,

What a damping Doom! I *am* so sorry! But I thought you had checked on the *femme de ménage*, and the bath, and all those sort of things? You have been dreadfully misled. Now, Miss Tray-Bing thinks most briskly, tapping with her pencil, that the thing to do is to clear out as soon as possible, making any sort of excuse, that you must go somewhere where you can get meals cooked, and take a room at the old Spontini, or even a small hotel. Your anaemia *will* boil up again if you just stay put, and don't get enough to eat, and feel unhappy. It wouldn't matter so much if you were forced to live in this place in a K.M.-ish way, because you had no home – then it would be brave, like poets in a garret – but to pay through the nose for a shilling, when as you say, you could be at Marraine's, does seem ridiculous. But *don't* panic too soon, and come flying back. I am sure better things will turn up. Check with Deirdre, Frank, everyone, to see if you can find something better. Actually, when you talk about doing a present book rather than a past one, your present arrival makes a first chapter in itself! The coldest night in Paris for seventy years (says our wireless!), and then your shilling room, and no bath, cold water, and ancient crone of a concierge, up five flights of stairs, it all adds up to a famous first chapter, and much more striking than the original *de luxe* arrival with Flave! I still feel you can mix the two things up.

How frightful for you, suddenly to feel that Paris is an alien city! It's like how one feels in London. One always felt that however much one was alone, Paris would not seem alien. But I do remember a time when Tommy and I were in a hotel, and he suddenly got lumbago and had to be in bed, and I went out for walks by myself, and there was rather what Flave would call a 'passage-wandering' feeling. Children in the Tuileries had homes to go to, but I only had an impersonal room on the top floor of a hotel, with Moper moping! (That was better than your present thing, but I had been used to being looked after, in Paris.) Now, just try and see if there *is* a possible room at the Spontini, that would shelter you even for a fortnight, and consult with a few people that you know, and *don't* fuss about the book until you are more settled in your mind unless, of course, the very agony makes you want to write, like Keats with T.B.! I do feel it will all come right before very long. And do write.

Tons of love, Bing.

☩

Mena, 9 March, 1956.

Dearest Oriel,

Many thanks for your long letter, and I am so sorry you have a cold, but sure this is the second in a month, or five weeks, or am I mixing it up with your Robert? Anyway, tut-tut and Winifred will be clucking like a hen. This letter will be a bit scrappy because we have Neltje and John coming down overnight with Moper for the weekend, and so there is the usual ferment, before guests! You know how for some reason we are always taken aback, and Fortnum's had to be rung up to produce *poussins* and cheese, and we have no cocktail-shaker, and Gladys doesn't stay as a rule for Saturday lunch, and the best sheets are torn, etc, etc, and Moper's old razor blades in the bathroom cupboard! I suppose this is where I pay, and am found out in inadequacy in domestic life, and Tess and Flave will score when they have houses, because of their more natural feeling, but it *does* take time to think about it, and at the moment I'm in the vault of a bank in La Ferté Bernard, looking for a Marriage Settlement, and I really can't attend to anything else! Besides, someone has just told me that my little girl, who *isn't* my little girl really, has gone off in a lorry with some workmen, and I'm rather worried ... so you must see my point!

I am thrilled about your publisher friend, who must obviously know every inch of the district, and please go and stay at once, because I may have made some errors of topography (if that's the word). I wonder if he knows the verrerie, and also the château which I am imagining is the one in the book – I dare not tell you the name, in case he turns out to go there every Sunday for lunch, and I should have another case, a libel one, on my hands! You see, I am bringing the verrerie into it, called by a different name, but the real French marquis who owns it, might crumb I mean this rather scurrilous Count and family in my book to be him –

wouldn't it be awful? Like you, and mocking at Yvonne Printemps! What we authors endure! When one is in the midst of work it is a good feeling to be a writer – I am in such firm day-by-day routes it is quite agony to break off for people at weekends. I even speak to myself out for walks, and yesterday I said, 'Oh ...' in that way French people do, generally saying 'Voyons' with it, in a half-protesting way, and poor Iddy* whirled round and stared at me – he thought I was cross about something, and I had to apologize! I wonder if I was actually writing it on the spot, in that bit of country, I should feel it as strongly. Probably not, you know. The distance makes it closer: if I was there, the reality would kill the fancy. Do you know what I mean?

Frank talks *nonsense* about my having skimmed through your proofs! It's his touch of jealousy again. I loved it, as you know, and was gripped by the whole story, so naturally I didn't notice little fine points, like editors do. But I *had* forgotten a great chunk of *his* book, that he was mentioning, and I bet in a queer way he turned this inside out! I am sure there is a feeling of resentment there that women, as we are, can work and produce books which are probably inferior to what he thinks he could do himself. Another thing – your book was dedicated to me, which he was always going to do with his, and so you have got in first, and another thorn, even old Clara has put her oar in too! So I think we must try and understand if he is tricky about these things. Also, he has always *crumbed* and thought of me – not as a Peg – but as a sort of symbol. I think he sees himself as Niall in *The Parasites* – heaven knows how; Niall was much more a facet of myself.

Oh hell, Tod keeps coming in to interrupt about the food for the weekend, and that Gladys is being disobliging, and Mr Burt has had too much tea at eleven – I shall go dotty! I do apologize for this fearful scrap of a letter. There is of course no sort of news about anything, because it's just a case of steady book, book, book.

Positively no more. I *must* get a walk before going back to the Hut.

Tons of love, Bing.

I had met Frank Price upon several occasions, usually with Winifred, when he was doubtless on his best behaviour. I heard no more of him until he returned to Paris, to work for MGM. To my surprise, I found myself treated almost as an enemy, an attitude for which I was unprepared. When Bing attempted to enlighten me about the possible reasons for this dislike, I found them hard to believe. At the time, Frank was swanning

* Bibby, a West Highland terrier.

in a luxury apartment, so very different from my landlady's top-floor room, that I could see nothing in my life for him to envy.

The final *débâcle* took place one evening, when we had both been invited to dine with the Stuart Gilberts, in their pleasant apartment on the Île St Louis. Stuart had been a close friend of James Joyce, and of the circle of writers and artists in prewar Paris, who had gathered around Sylvia Beach's famous bookshop, 'Shakespeare & Company'. He was also famous as a translator, having turned both Malraux and St Exupéry into beautiful English, and was now working for Skira, a Swiss firm publishing superbly illustrated art books. His wife Moune, who did some part-time reading for Doubleday, was one of those brisk and competent French housewives who can produce a six-course meal for twelve or more guests at the drop of a hat, which she did that night. Each course, cooked by herself, was superb, and the wines were to match, selected by Stuart from his own remarkable cellar. It was my first invitation, and only the usual fear of disappointing Winifred had made me accept it. To add to my waine, I found myself seated next to my host, with Frank facing me across the table. Throughout the meal, he never ceased to needle and bully me, contradicting me every time I opened my mouth (which I did as seldom as possible).

The last straw arrived with the dessert (or perhaps with the champagne, which is often served in France at the end of a formal meal). The talk had turned to James Joyce, and I thought it best to admit at once that I had not read *Ulysses*. Frank exploded at this, and loudly proclaimed that such a cultural lacuna was only to be expected of someone so entirely uneducated. Moune hastily turned all our attention to the lovely peaceful Seine outside the windows, where gaily-lit *bâteaux-mouches* kept streaking the ceiling with bright ribbons of light as they passed by. Later, when we had left the table, Stuart took me quietly aside and, thrusting a slim paperback into my hands, whispered: '*Don't* go home and try to read *Ulysses*. If Joyce hadn't been my friend, I doubt if I should have tackled it myself. Skim through this, and it will tell you all you need to know, in a nutshell.' 'This' was a concise and brilliant critique of Joyce and *Ulysses*, written by Stuart himself, and to which he had added a copy of *Dubliners* from his own shelves. It was the beginning of a warm friendship, which might never have come about, but for Frank's boorishness; so I am grateful to him, too.

After this, I often dined with the Gilberts, and always found myself in interesting and stimulating company. Stuart was a small, wiry man, with very bright, sharp eyes like a bird. Moune was also small, but rounder. He had started out in life as a judge in Burma, where he and Moune had met, with the firm intention of retiring early on a good pension and settling down in Paris. Paris had been his secret love, his Gondal, since childhood. (When I explained about Gondals and Pegs, he saw the point at once.) What I remember best are the cosy winter teas, beside a roaring fire, Stuart leaning contentedly back in his green velvet armchair, and Moune hovering with the teapot. A substantial English tea, complete with buttered crumpets and several kinds of cake, was Stuart's delight, and when they were alone, I think it was often their last meal of the day. I used to bring Stuart bags of crumpets from England, and he once ate six at a sitting, much to Moune's dismay; after this, she rationed them. I pointed out that Dr Johnson used to eat fifteen muffins at a time, washed down with as many cups of tea. 'Lucky man!' said Stuart but Moune, with a cry of, 'Mon dieu, quelle horreur!' moved the dish further away still.

One day, I arrived for tea to find Stuart reading one of my books (*Angel with a Sword*) with one hand, and eating a crumpet with the other. 'I say, this *is* funny!' he said, chuckling happily to himself. 'I *am* enjoying this!'

Preening, I glanced at the title, and my See-Me face fell. 'It's not funny at all,' I protested. 'It's a story full of doom and disaster!'

'Oh, I shouldn't bother about that,' Stuart said briskly. 'People have enough Dooms in their lives today. I should try to cheer them up, if I were you.' After giving this some thought, and several crumpets later, I decided that he was probably right.

One of the more sensible things I managed to accomplish was to bring Stuart and Monsieur B. together. They both had the same twinkly, dry sense of humour, and knew many of the same people (Stuart had once written a film script for Sacha Guitry); both were jam-along, and had no false pretensions. Moune and Madame B. got on less well together. At times, Moune was inclined to be over-conscious of her position as Stuart's wife, and a friend of the Joyces. Madame B. found this amusing, but remained totally unimpressed.

ꕔ

Mena, 15 March, 1956.

Dearest Oriel,

I am so delighted that you are getting on so well with the book. And most certainly Mr Gilbert is a very good person to go by. Not only has he lived in France for years, and so knows the feeling, but he is the translator of all those very crumby highbrow books, like Malraux, so you are well away! What I suggest you do is write the Yvonne Printemps chapter, just as you 'see' it, with Priscilla and all, not toning it down, and then once again get Mr Gilbert's advice. I can't see *you* being maliciously mocking, and an amusing mockery done lightly, with an understanding eye, is really much cleverer and nicer, and I think people often like being brought into other people's books! Old Clara quite mocked me in her Rhône and Greece one, and I didn't mind at all. It's when it's done in a nasty, seeing-the-worst Willie-Maughamish way, that it leaves a nasty taste.

You will like John and Neltje. John is so like Mr Dunn of the farm here, and very jolly, and Neltje all human and nice, now she is grown up, and gentle too. They were easy to have to stay, but it was a bit of a cope, as I wanted to make an effort. Except that they were very nice, and even came for walks, and got so tired afterwards that they rested in their room from four till seven, most obliging! Tommy had his liver, and was in bed, rather typically, but better that than if he had been in a bad mood perhaps, downstairs. He has stayed here all this week, and though better now, was very testy – pitching in fury at old Makarios (who I, being Tray, of course was *for*!) and so on! I'm now groaning in anticipation of the Blacks. I'm going to try and keep them at bay, because it really is agony trying to entertain people when one is working. I think the holidays can be the excuse, as Flave and Alastair come for Easter.

Do tell me your Sarthe man's surname, and exactly where he lives; I might know the place. No more for now, but so glad all goes well.

Fondest love, Bing.

ॐ

Mena, 25 March, 1956.

Dearest Oriel,

Many thanks for your long letter. I will start my Easter one today, and keep it back to post later, so you get it more to the time. I shall be working very hard all next week before Easter, and it would be more scrappy if written then.

Yes, you are right, the daffodils are all out, and better than they ever have been, and people haven't picked them as they usually do – perhaps those notices have done some good. But there are no rhodies even budding, and the camellias were nipped by the frost, so that is sad. Gales all the week, and on my routes walks the sea very huge and powerful – great fun to be beside, but appalling to be on. I'm in such a steady day-by-day routes that I truly grudge any interruption, like going to Ferryside, or weekends, and I'm afraid the break at Easter will set me back. You remember that old Miss Compton Collier, the photographer? She crumbs to come again on the 4th, and I know I shall get hysterics. She was to be in the district, and as Flave and Alastair will just have announced their engagement, it will be very suitable for them to be taken together. She used to do him as a child, too. She is such a champion Frisky, I must tell you about it afterwards!

I am reading Maurois' *Victor Hugo*, which is absolutely absorbing; you must get it. I'm afraid I'm reading a translation (very good) because it is the Book Society for March, but you could get it in French. One of the best biographies I've ever read. I'm also reading, in French, *En Route*, by that old 19th-century Huysmans, also intriguing – how he got very Catholic suddenly, and had guilt about his sins. He had fearful 'down, Rufus, down' impulses of the flesh, always in such embarrassing places too, like suddenly at Mass, or somewhere. I should think it was nerves, and then of course his guilt was overwhelming!

Don't forget one day to go to St Roch, or whatever it's called, in the rue St Honoré, and ask if they have the marriage certificate of Robert Mathurin Busson and Marie Bruyère in June 1789. They might let you copy down the entry. Perhaps churches don't have pre-Revolutionary records, though. Perhaps they are kept in some great Main hôtel de ville.

Flave and Alastair come down on Thursday. Yes, she wants a Main wedding, like Tess, and it's to be the end of July (after Lords), at St Peter's, Eaton Square. I dread it already, because of clothes. I have not seen her since Christmas, so I expect to find her changed, and very grown-up! It still seems funny to me, to want to get married! Won't it be awful if he suddenly gets sent to Israel or somewhere – it's all so what Tod calls 'nasty' in the Middle East. (I am madly for Cyprus being Greek, did I tell you? I daren't mention the subject to Moper! I'm so for old Makarios, too. It takes me back to my childhood days, when 'the troubles' were on in Ireland. I was 10, and *madly* for the IRA! It's my natural thing about hating authority!) Kits writes very funny letters from Eton, but he will get into trouble with his imitations. He breaks up *after* Easter, which is rather a shilling for him.

I am so glad you are getting on so well, and have good 'contacts'. I don't think Stuart Gilbert would say your work is good because he likes you. Nor would Winifred. Or me, for that matter. Do you ever regret not being some Lady Witherspoon person? I'm sure you don't. Just think, you might be in this bitter east wind, with some husband rather thin and mean, and you in early bal, not having liked the waxing! How you are spared! Don't go to your fortune person again. She might say all was

Doom. Now I shall leave this, in case I have anything else to add before I post it.

Wednesday

No news, except the Blacks arrive in London at any moment, and I feel I *must* ask them down after Easter, otherwise Winifred will think me neglectful! It is all for her. Why does one dread her Tut-tut so much? Better be liked by Winifred than almost anyone – if *she* thought one bad-mannered, one would fly the country! Weather suddenly exquisite, like spring as a child. I want to dash out with my dress tucked into my knickers, and say 'Can I take my socks off?' And then I'd play! I sometimes feel I could write a whole chapter on play. (Perhaps I've never done anything else – how grim!)

There is something I wish you would do for me, and that is to find me (in some old shop, perhaps on the Quais), an old French missal – you know what I mean, a Catholic prayer book, but it must be in French. Someone has to die soon in my book, and I feel I must have a French missal before she does, so that I can feel myself at the funeral. Don't go to any expense – any shabby little book would do, actually the shabbier the more I shall like it! And now no more!

Heaps of love, Bing.

※

Mena, Sunday 8 April, 1956.

Dearest Oriel,

Many thanks for your interesting letter, and I wish this could be more, but I am in a flap! The Blacks have just driven off (only stayed for one night), but I feel they have been for months, and Tessa has just rung to say she has got to go whisking into St Mary's Hospital, Paddington, on Monday, to have this Rhesus baby 'brought on'. It is rather alarming, because I don't quite see why it has to be done, and I must now cancel the Riviera, and go dashing up to be handy. Of course, Kits is furious, only just back from Eton, and anyway he is in quarantine for German measles, so everything is in a muddle! I do hope Tess will be all right, and the baby too. It's rather awful, because in my book I have just got to the bit where a wife has to die after having a stillborn baby! It's like a judgement on me: I wonder if I ought to alter the book?

I am thrilled about your contacts in France, and I am sure you are on the right road in all that you do. I was sure you hadn't regretted not marrying. I kept the letter you wrote when you were still trying to imagine that you were menaced, and one of these days I will show it to you, to show how you were fooling yourself! What I want to tell you first, is that you *have* advanced as a person, since then. I think you have advanced both spiritually and mentally! You are *not* as Frisky as you were, and the type of Friskiness that remains is not superior and grown-up, but understanding. I am sure the flow of your writing will have its own reward, and if you do get menaced some time out in France, well and good, but no need to hurry it. I do so applaud your decision to live out there, and it's very plucky too. I wish I had time for a longer letter to go into these things, and to tell you about Flave. I *do* find her changed. When I say changed, I mean that she seems for the moment to have no personality: she might be any ex-deb having got herself engaged, I can't quite tell how or why. It's frightening to have all her eggs in that one basket! As my grandpapa said, when his daughter Trix married at 19: '*Il est beau ... elle a 19 ans ... pourvu que ça dure ...*'* I know what he meant! A. is perfectly delightful, but will he mature the same way as Flave? Will she suddenly wake up, and find *they* think differently? If she does, she may be doomed. If she doesn't, she's doomed equally, so I give up!

I do hope you have a lovely time in Elba. Write from there. I hope I shall only be in London a few days, but who can tell?

All love, Bing.

🜛

Menabilly, 26 April, 1956.

Dearest Oriel,

Sorry to leave you with a gap of news, but the week's break in London was so disorganizing, and then, typically, almost as soon as I got back here Robert emerged, giving me that numbed feeling in the head which made working almost impossible! I was down to about one sentence an hour, and sitting in front of the typewriter with the same page, and all at a crucial moment in the story. Hardly had Robert taken its course, before Kits woke up with a rash, and it was German measles, after all.

---

*He is handsome ... she is nineteen ... long may it last!

Not serious, like the measles last year, but woe, woe to Tray and her work, because he always demands to be read to, and that business of trying to do an hour at the Hut, and then back to him is quite fatal! I may have done it in the past, when I was younger, but now it is much too difficult – poor Tray has to have a quiet routine, to accomplish anything.

Did I tell you that Frank rang me at the flat at the worst possible moment? Moper, in rather a bad mood, had gone to bed early, and the bell rang beside him, and I had to answer – myself worried about Tess and Paul – and it was silly Frank being all nostalgic (and, I suspect, tight!) from his new apartment. It couldn't have been worse timed. However, *not* his fault. I don't know if I told you either about the Blacks' visit of 24 hours? It was more like a lifetime, Maud being on a diet and having to have all her food put through a sieve! They are kindness itself, but I just can't cope with that sort of thing nowadays, it bores me terribly. Let's face it, Ellen did talk endlessly until all hours of the morning, and Tell-Hims quite often, but I did not mind it because she is such a dear, and a glorious Peg! But now that my day of Pegs seems to be over, I don't know that I could face it. Which goes to prove that everything is in the imagination, as I always say.

I'm so glad you have had such encouragement from the agent woman. That is really good news. You don't say how the actual work of the moment progresses, and if you are doing last winter's Paris, or this, or a mixture of both? Sometimes I get waves of despair with mine, thinking no one will see the Deep Underlying Point! You will, I am sure, but definitely not critics, who will dismiss it as stupid and sentimental, with melodrama thrown in. I meant to tell you that any old modern missal will do – when I said 'old' I did not mean 'ancient', but second-hand for cheapness! It could be your birthday present, an attempt to bring me to the True Faith! I'm all *for* the True Faith, actually, if people must be up to date, though personally the Cretan Mother Goddess and her Son, and Horus, mean just the same thing – it's only a question of the development of a universal instinct (Tray-Tray in one of her moods!).

Tess and little Paul go on all right. Kits incredibly cheerful, as always. His new 'make-up' is that Pen Friend has been kidnapped, and smuggled aboard the Grace Kelly–Rainier yacht! What should we do without the Goat to entertain us? Forgive no more, I must snatch some work.

All love, Bing.

卐

Mena, Whit Sunday, 1956.

Dearest Oriel,

Do forgive my silence, but I went and caught Kits' silly German measles, and it has held up everything. I am struggling with the last chapters of the book, but my powers of concentration, and in a way interest, have snapped away, and writing now is exactly like prep when one was a child. Only dogged determination keeps me going, and the feeling that I haven't properly 'palled' – you know my comparison that writing is like a purge!

Now, your *heavenly* missal! I gloat and adore it. What a find. I have practically turned Catholic overnight. The only thing is, I am so steeped in my queer London Libe* books about Origin of Consciousness and Great Snake Mothers that I feel Catholicism is too modern for me, like living in a block of flats, instead of in a cave! Still, it all works to the same thing in the end.

I *do* think all you are doing out in France is being valuable, don't you? As if you were a plant coming on in the right soil. I can't make any plans about coming over, or taking any holiday until this book is off my mind, and revised. Have an awful feeling that I shan't get away, with Flave's wedding looming in July. Incidentally, rather odd, not even a wire from Frank for my birthday. Other years he has always remembered, even from New York. Do you think he's away, or steeped in liquor? (Probably both!)

Heaps and heaps of love, Bing.

Among the new friends I made during that first winter living in Paris was Monica Sterling. Her father had once been the actor-manager of the English Theatre Company in Paris, until the outbreak of war, when the family had been forced to return to England. Monica remained loyal to France, and the instant Paris was liberated she came back again, attached to an American newspaper. She was an over-sensitive, generous person, only too willing to take the troubles of the world on her shoulders – and this pain was threaded through her novels like a dark ribbon, but she could also be an amusing, light-hearted companion. She taught me to love Paris, and its past, as Winifred had once tried to teach me to love London, and failed. Paris seemed familiar, as it has done to others before

* The London Library.

me, just as Bing, on first coming to Cornwall, had cried: 'This is where I belong!'

Monica sometimes dropped in around tea-time, her arms full of books, and enveloped in a flowing black woollen cape against the cold. One day, she glanced at the papers on my desk and asked if she might take them home to read. A few days later, to my surprise I found that I had acquired a French literary agent. Monica worked for Odette Arnaud (no relation to my godmother), a terrifyingly efficient and businesslike lady. In no time at all, scattered sheets of my writing were winging their way across the Atlantic to New York, and were later made into a book* which Victor Gollancz published – much to Bing's amusement. I never managed to feel wholly at ease with Madame Arnaud. I resented her autocratic manner and had no wish to be taken over and re-made into someone I was not. She also believed firmly in self-discipline, in which she rightly considered me to be deficient. New faces, new places, and the heady knowledge that I was free to go my own way, were proving too exciting and unsettling.

🎍

Menabilly, 4 July, 1956.

Dearest Oriel,

Many thanks for your lovely long letter, which was here waiting when I got back from Dartmoor. I must quickly tell you that my 'recuperating' visit was the funniest thing that has ever happened. Poor Noël, Jeanne's friend, was bitten on the nose by her horse the day after I arrived. She had to be rushed into hospital in Bristol to have it coped with by a plastic surgeon. Jeanne went with her, and Tray was left alone in the cottage with the sole charge of: two mares (one savage), one foal, thirty hens, two dogs, one cat, one Esse Cooker, all cooking, no help!! I was alone from Saturday until Thursday! Actually, it was such a complete change that it *was* a change, if you know what I mean! But I did get pretty tired. Only it was good for me, like mortification in a sort of way, and I managed very well. The worst chore was cleaning out the nesting boxes of the hens, with all their revolting pal. I pretended I was lay Brother in a monastery, and as there was no one to speak to, it *was* rather like, and actually, I loved every moment. But of course it was not exactly the baskified holiday I had intended. So Tray has now returned more grizzled and Trayish than ever, with the Main wedding to face, and not having

---

* *Jam Today* – the story of my (sometimes extraordinary) adventures in Paris with Flave.

coped with clothes. Tess, Marie-Thérèse* and Flave are all down here at Mena for a few days – rather fun on my own with my daughters of marriage age, like a matriarch in a tribe.

Fancy about your anaemia, the Swiss *are* good. And what a good thing you did not marry. I don't see much hope of meeting in London apart from the wedding, but let me have Marraine's number, just in case. And don't you think she ought to have a wedding invitation? She was very kind to Flave, and you could have gone together. Could you ring Flave about this? She will be back at the flat Friday night. I have got to come up for a fearful See Me ball at St James' Palace on the 11th, and I dread it. Then Boo's Long Leave, and we are supposed to go that weekend to Maureen, which is a bore. I feel a complete rustic. I have no summer clothes, and am such a shaggy Vixen Tray, you can't imagine!

I have finished the book but don't tell anyone, as I have sent it all in furtive secrecy to Victor's secretary to retype in places, and keep till he gets back from Italy. I am pretending it is still being checked over by me, so no one can see it. Oh, I know *you*, if no one else, will like it and understand it. Obviously our 'work' (crumb) takes it out of us, we are such sensitive people!

Fondest love, Bing.

卐

Mena, Friday 24 August, 1956.

Dearest Oriel,

If this letter is disjointed, it is because I am tapping at my routes alcove desk, but also 'minding' Poonie, who is squatting on the floor, emptying and filling my waste-paper basket. She is a dear little soul, and likes her Tray, but it is difficult to concentrate with her around! Paul is heaven, and I am menaced by him, and already planning how he becomes a Cardinal, and I die in his arms! It's rather the end, to make up Gondals about one's grandson. Perhaps it is the final proof of C. of L.!

No, Ellen was ragging about Balmoral, and the Queen. I know just the way she would have said it, squishing out a cigarette as she did so, and floating from the room in a flowing gown. I only hope she is still like that, and not a nearing-sixty type of American matron. I do wish I could have a few days with her in Paris, after Boo returns to Eton, but I can't make definite plans about anything, as Tommy will not 'come clean' as to whether he is going on the Olympic Tour or not. He says he doesn't want to, and is trying to get out of it, but does not say when he will

---

* Tessa's daughter.

know, so I can't make any plans for my own sort of holiday. I am now going to have Gran and Nurse directly the children go, on 8 September, because old Shaw says she will come and cook, and Tod wants to go to town, 'to see some folks', so I can get Gran over then. Kits is still harping on going to Blackpool! Do you think Ellen would like *that*, instead of Paris??!

Why didn't you tell me about that new 45-ish menace? And *why* should he be queer? I am terribly interested. Anyway, it's always nice to have new contacts. I have written a line to Doodie, to ask her to beed through the keyhole at Yvonne and Pierre! I like the title of *The Horses of the Sun* but I can't see it as being about your Contessa person. It makes me think of Helios, who drove the chariot across the sky every day, in Greek mythology. It's a sort of male title!

How are you getting on with *The Outsiders*? I have got Nijinsky's Diary on the strength of it, and he is so pathetic and sweet – not properly mad at all, but so humble. He has such a good line in it: *'I felt very depressed today, as if cats were scratching at my soul.'* Don't you see his point?

Kits is playing cricket with his friend Richard Cutbill (I always think it's Cutfish), who is staying in Fowey. Moper is moping somewhere, but better. He likes Paul, and says he is going to be a 'first-class chap', but is rather bored with Poo. She is now getting grizzly, so I must finish this letter, and actually there is no news, you know. I've had one or two bathes, but the weather is getting very autumnish. My time is pretty full, because of the children, and also cricket, and walks with Moper – everyone to be fitted in. Good job I'm not working!

Heaps of love, Bing.

🕉

Mena, Friday 4 September, 1956.

Dearest Oriel,

I was trying to think *why* I never wrote to you after all, on that day you lunched with Flave, but I think a lot of things cropped up, and other letters had to be done, and there were awful telephone calls. And this went on for the next few days, interspersed with Kits wanting me to hit that frightful football into a net he had rigged up, and another new amusement for him, which is golf. We have set up a nine-hole golf course right across the park, with red woollen socks tied to cricket stumps, for flags! I must say it is rather good, and even more fun than tennis. You must try it when you come. Then there have been endless things with

Spencer and film rights,* and I am supposed to be having lunch with Alec Guinness when I come to London. Crumb! He has been sent the story and would like to do it, but there have been lots of delicate discussions about it first, before anyone commits themselves. Jubilant cables from Ken McCormick, saying that the Guild have chosen it for March. Also a thing called *Reader's Digest* have chosen it. So it is certainly going to be off to a good start in America, but I am sure to have sniffs and jeers in this country, especially if old Victor does those irritating adverts about it selling a lot before it is even published, which I am sure makes critics despise me more than ever. I am sure if he said, 'This book has sold no copies, and nobody who has looked at it can understand a word,' the critics would be nice, for once!

I do hope I get over to Paris to see Ellen, and that Frank is not tiresome, and wanting to run the thing the whole time. It will be fun to go around quietly with Ellen, and I don't think she wants to be smart, or anything. How awful if she has altered, and become full of fearful Tell-Hims – I couldn't bear it. I don't somehow think she *will*, but one never knows! Also I know I can't do that thing of talking until four in the morning; it will kill me. I die if I don't have a good night's sleep.

I heard from Doodie. She was getting all ready to beed at Pierre and Yvonne again through the bathroom window, and had stuck it open with her brush, when an infuriating man with a red beard emerged from *their* bathroom window, and glared at her, and slammed it. It was a newcomer, and the Fresnays had left stealthily in the middle of the night!

I hope your journey to Switzerland has gone all right. I keep having letters from the Goat, wanting me to make some holiday date with him, but I can't do so until I know if Moper wants to do anything or not. The Goat's latest idea is Ostend! Can you imagine anything more of a shilling? He must see himself strolling up and down a promenade, and wandering into a Casino. Nothing would induce me to go there.

I wonder why Peter Owen wanted more descriptions of *places*, rather than of people, in your book?† I always thought publishers grumbled if there were too many descriptions of places, and it was people they wanted. They must rather have missed the point! Perhaps they wanted you to say, 'There was a dear little café called the Boule d'Or where, etc, etc,' or, 'The shimmering green trees, etc,' but it's silly, because you have got so much Paris atmosphere into it all that further description would be unnecessary. I *bet* Frank is tiresome, when he reads it after it's published. Do just let me say I have read bits of it, at least, and that it is *very*

---

* Spencer Curtis Brown, her agent, who was negotiating over *The Scapegoat*.
† *Jam Today*.

amusing and K.M.-ish, and then he can't tell you afterwards that I have skipped through your book, and don't really know about it.

Listen, how interesting about your doctor being with the person who died at dawn. I wish you had asked him more about all that sort of thing. It's the first time I've heard of a doctor saying he felt a thing about the spirit going on. I have so often heard it said of doctors, that they *don't*. And of course old Maugham, in his book *Human Bondage*, about a medical student, says the more you see of death, the more you are sure the body is all, but then of course that's typical of Maugham. I wish you had asked about your group, he must know it. *I* think you are an old Monkey Positive! But I hope the anaemia picks up in Elba.

Actual plans are as follows. Leave for Blackpool crack of dawn on Thursday morning the 20th, and back to London on Sunday evening. Perhaps lunch with Alec on the Monday (crumb, probably won't come off!) and over to Paris, I hope, for a week, on the late-afternoon plane. I don't know which hotel yet, it depends whether Frank puts Ellen off the Bourgogne.* Actually, I can see her being a bit stubborn, and saying she will try it. I know it would always do for me when I go again. No more news really. Write to Whitelands from Elba, so that I get a letter there before I leave on Monday the 24th.

Heaps of love, Bing.

🏵

In a coiffeur, somewhere in the Faubourg Saint Honoré (qui n'est pas fermé le lundi!).

Dearest Oriel,

Just a line to say how sorry I am I have just missed you. It is the film i.e. Alec Guinness, that I must see Wednesday in London, to match up against the MGM people, who are also bidding. Meanwhile, on the quiet, I have told my French agent Hoffman to give it to a French directeur to read! Thus I may do all the rest in! But T.N.N. my film. I cannot say truthfully that this has been altogether a success – I mean Paris this time. I *loved* the little hotel, and will come again to stay on my own, and only let you know that I am here! The point is – Ellen was a dear, and very much the same, not altered at all, but she is much better in her own country, which I have always said. I don't think she really likes Paris, and au fond she would like to do the chic things. (She went to an

---

* A small hotel, close to where I was staying, in the rue de Bourgogne.

Embassy At Home, the first day!) I don't think she liked the hotel much. She was perfect when it was the early part of the day, and we were on our own, but Frank *never* left us, and also got *crying drunk*. (It's his new thing, Ellen was very worried about him.) But the best thing was that he drove us to La Sarthe, where we went to check up on the environs for my book, and both were charming there, and relaxed, and did not get Martini-ish! In Paris, Frank would have about three before dinner, and then brandy afterwards, and Tell-Him after Tell-Him about the office, and the old staff. Honestly, to be with Pen Friend is like being with *Plato*, in comparison. This sounds cruel, and you will say, as you always do, that I go 'off' people! It's not that, but I just can't *take* it, when people I am fond of take too many drinks, and I am dead sober!

You and I would have great fun here, lunching 'round the corner' in your quartier, and enjoying the true French feel of Paris. One lovely thing was, that after Sarthe we *did* visit l'Abbaye de la Grande Trappe (reason for this, you have to see my book!) and I thought you and I must go there some time, and find a little hotel nearby. Ellen was very sorry not to see you. She comes to Mena for a few days, before she leaves on the 15th. I have no autumn plans, it will depend on Tommy.

Oh, Oriel, I do so love France, and the French countryside, and Paris too – but *not* Barbarian Paris and anyone being smart – one might just as well be at the Berkeley – and Tourist Paris is a shilling too, like standing in Piccadilly Circus with a camera! By the way, Hoffman says that the background and characters in my book are absolutely authentic, and I have not made a silly English gaffe. Just one point of law was incorrect, easily altered. So I'm See Me for that. If I *don't* go anywhere with Tommy, I will try and come over before Xmas. I have liked my week, but truthfully, it's more fun with the old Goat.

Lots of love, Bing.

卐

Menabilly, 13 October, 1956.

Dearest Oriel,

Many thanks for your long letter, which I found waiting for me here when I got back on Thursday. Never came down with Ellen after all, because my Horses of the Sun* turned out to be so madly rushing through the skies that I couldn't drop the reins! The thing being, that it was a terrible either-or between accepting a staggering crumby MGM offer,

---

* The epigraph in my *Horses of the Sun* read, 'Who rides the horses of the sun shall lord it but a day.' Bing used it as a code word for high hopes which might be dashed – here, the film of *The Scapegoat*.

with the top chap flying over to Paris to persuade me and then following me to London, or having Guinness as my man (whom MGM didn't want), and doing it with him in a smaller way, not nearly so much money, but having much more say. It really was torture. It was like choosing between *All This and Heaven Too*, and *The Moon and Sixpence*. I chose *The Moon and Sixpence* and I only hope that it really will come off, because I did take so enormously to Alec Guinness. We lunched together, and supped together, and I *knew* he was right for my man in my book, and when he told me he had spent five days in a Trappist monastery before becoming a Catholic six months ago, it absolutely tipped the scales! Because – as you will see when you read the book – it's queerly apt. And silly old MGM with their talk of Cary Grant (whom I admit is menacing, but Alec G. is Fresnay-ish, and a wonderful actor) had just the wrong idea. Anyway, the woman who did the script of *The Prisoner* (did you see it? The wonderful *serious* Guinness film), is mad to do the script of this, and Alec G. would do it in France, and I believe it would all work out right, and just what I meant. So you see, if one casts one's bread upon the waters, it is returned to you after many days! We are now Daphne and Alec to each other in letters (it's all right, he is married to a devoted wife, and has a son of Kits's age, and they are all Catholics!). But I feel like you with the Pegs that here is a stage person with *values* at last, and might be the start of a nice friendship. So that seems to be going all right, so far.

As to Ellen, she was much better in London, and we had a happy day together at Hampton Court, and then two more quiet evenings in her sitting room at the Berkeley, and there were no Tell-Hims or Martinis! The thing is, she is never at her best in Paris, and that business of being à *trois* with Frank was such a mistake. *He* was all right when *she* had gone, and it just bears out my thing that one must never mix one's friends, but only see one at a time. Probably if I saw *you* with anyone else you would either be silly, or bouncing and irritating, and not the nice understanding, discussing-everything person you are at Mena! I agree that he has somehow gone downhill, and frankly I think it is drink. He is all right in the morning, before he has had any! I noticed that his hand trembled all the time, which is surely *very* bad. Ellen was shocked at his downward path, though poor thing, he was polite to her. But Americans' talk *together* is so Tell-Himish, all about Adlai and Eisenhower. The best evening was dinner, crumb, with André Maurois.

How awful about Doodie. I nearly said in my letter, don't say I've been over. The thing was, it was all so rushed, and I never rang her or poor old Ferdie, as I didn't want to get involved with too many people, that thing of mine. I will of course see her on my next visit, which may be before Christmas, I don't know. You see Tommy now doesn't want to go anywhere, but just to come and have routes down here. So, being rather exhausted after Horses of the Sun, I am quite content to potter here through October, and perhaps November. The old Goat feels let-down at not having what he calls 'an encounter'! But I don't know where I would meet him so late in the year as November, unless Paris again. But if I should come I would have to be 'free', and not tied by him, or Frank, or Doodie, or Ferdie, or you, or anyone. I love your *quartier*, and did I tell you I went to Mass, 10 a.m. at Sainte Clothilde? I got giggles at the stamp, stamp, of the old beadle! It's so panic-making as he draws near, and one wonders if one can find change in one's purse – and that other priest-person shoves that bag on a stick at one in such a ruthless way! I took my Missal, and more or less found my place, but they seem to jump about a bit. Also, it was not such a High Mass as I had hoped. I like *three priests*, bowing and standing one behind the other, and great puffs of incense choking one.

I went to see Tess and them for last weekend, and Poonie gave me such a welcome, it really warmed my heart, and I felt I was continuing my race, do you see my point? She called 'Tay-Tay', all excited, and hurled her little frame upon me, and wouldn't let me out of her sight. Paul still rather lollopy, but sweet. I also dined with Flave and them. They were both very nice and seemed to be cosy in their flat, and they have a poodle.

I went to see Kits at Eton, who was bliss, and made me laugh all through lunch, as he had at Blackpool. His new thing is not the Goat, but my poor little typewriter man, Mr Harris, and so we have to talk in *his* talk, all the time. Mr Harris has an office in a basement in Truro, and Kits's line is to say, in Mr Harris's voice, 'Well, of course my little office *is* below street level, but I have thirty years continuous experience, and I *do* keep a supply of desk equipment. No, the wife and I have no children, and we lost our dear old dog Prince last month, it nearly broke my heart.'

Now no more, as I am trying to get through all my accumulated mail, and it takes time. Write again soon, and say what you do, also if you have found out yet where your Frenchman lives in Sarthe. You never told me the train man had illegitimate children! Or am I muddling him with the *real* man? You have so many new men!

Heaps of love, Bing.

When do you come over in November?

✠

Mena, Friday 19 October, 1956.

Dearest Oriel,

I hope your cold is better? So typical to get one just as you come back healthy and brown. It is mortification, and shows one that all is vanity! I also have a streamer – not bad enough for bed, but for going round with a buzzing head and Kleenex, and now poor Tod has succumbed ('My dear, my head, and is that Mr Burt I hear prowling on my stairs?'). Wet autumn weather, dank dripping trees, and the grass all shaggy. If one was a child, one would be getting out one's winter coat. Did you ever have a hoop, or were they before your time? The things one bowls, I mean, not hooped skirts!

Listen, I really am so tremendously pleased you like *The Scapegoat*. I hoped you would see the psychological politics, and the religious significance, but I still think this will be seen only by the few, and that most people will read it as a semi-thriller, a chap involved with a crowd of women sort of thing. Infuriating, but it is my cross! I am pretty sure Frank had all sorts of criticisms, but he didn't tell me them – chiefly because I think he hoped I would sell to MGM, and shrewdly realized if he was too patronizing it would put me off! (Actually, it wouldn't have done. But I just knew Alec Guinness was right. He is very like Pierre Fresnay, did you realize that?) It is rather interesting that you feel in *Scapegoat* I got *into* my characters, because as far as I can realize, though I'm still a bit too close to it to judge, they are completely imaginary, and not one Peg, or even tiny bits of real people. And when you say *Rachel* was not real to you, it was just the opposite. *Rachel* was so Pegged, i.e. so much of what I felt about Ellen at that time, and Nelson, all incredibly mixed-up of course, that if I was writing my autobiography, I would have to say it was the most *emotionally-felt* book I had ever written. After it, I felt *dead*! And part of me did die, with it. I tell you all this, because your foolish old Granny Tray goes through many more inner experiences than you have perhaps credited her with, and when you say, as you have in the past, how beaming my life must be, you have not perhaps realized the rather fantastic inner world I have so often dwelt in. Re *Scapegoat*, I know that has been written from a sort of spiritual awareness, which is not emotional, and that is why the people are *not* Pegged. (I shall probably begin to Peg Guinness, if I am 'in' with him, over the film!) Actually, in *Scapegoat*, I've tried to say too many things at once. How close hunger is to greed, how difficult to tell the difference, how hard not to be confused, how close one's better nature to one's worst, and finally, how the self must be stripped of everything, and give up everything, before it can understand love. But one can't tell that to the ordinary reader. He that has ears to hear, let him hear.

To change the subject, I had a nice letter from Doodie, not on a hard chair, so I wrote and explained why I had not let her know I was in Paris. I think she would have been in the country anyway. I have been reading an interesting book about La Trappe, which I bought there, and in it, describing the Monastery, it says there is an 'Hôtellerie des Dames'. It surely can't be true? I know men go for a Retreat, but surely not women? Could you bear to write and ask? We might have gone together some time! Jeanne wants me to go to Stanbrook with her, having both of us read *In a Great Tradition*, which is Benedictine. And Guinness has just sent me a terribly interesting book called *The Nun's Story*. So all these Catholic people are trying to push me into the Faith. Little do they know my pagan depths!

Here all next week, and then have to go up to London again to see Guinness, also the Goulds of *Home Journal*. A bore, because once here I get set in routes. André Maurois sent me his book signed, wasn't it a crumb? Actually, I was a bit *déçue* in it.

Tons of love, Bing.

笨

Mena, Monday 5 November, 1956.

Dearest Oriel,

I don't suppose this will be much of a letter now, although I have meant to write for some time. Everything is so beastly in the world, that I feel more like going to La Grande Trappe than ever, but what can one do? First, thanks for your last letter, in answer to mine about old *Scapegoat*, and I am glad your cold is better. Mine still goes on, and now has become stiff-necked, like St Paul – at least, I think it was St Paul who had a stiff neck at some moment in his life!

I went up last week to London again, to see my 'Peg' Guinness before he flew to Ceylon, where he is now probably being interned, or something. We had lunch twice. I took him to that rather shilling place in Sloane Square, where we go with Kits, and he produced a great book for me, all wrapped up, called *The Lord*, and then he showed me with pride a rosary he had bought, which he was taking to Rome to have blessed by the Pope! And between serious talks about religion, he will be all jam-along and ordinary about other things – having the wrong clothes in London, hating parties, and being what I call 'one of us' – do you know? Well, anyway, as far as business went we did not get much further, but he swears he *will* do it, and it's just a case of getting the right movie firm to back us; the negotiations are under way (I sound like Sick-Dog!*). The woman who did the script of the *Prisoner* film wants to do this; she is very clever and crumby, and I met her, Miss Bridget Boland, so that is another crumb.

I must tell you, but it will take too long, how I got involved with having to meet a fan from America, who had pestered for ages to meet me. Some author person, and I went along to the Ritz, expecting quite a crumby-looking American, perhaps like Alastair Cooke – and to my snobby horror, a *frightful* old hunched man got up from a chair, with one eye and a mouth all paralysed at the side, and said in a mid-west voice: 'Little Miss Daphne at last!' And his voice boomed out over the whole of the Ritz, which was crowded for tea, and I had to sit and talk for an hour to this really rather ghastly (though harmless) man, and it was True Mortification! I kept wondering if people I knew might come in. Then finally I said, 'I must go' (his face fell, if it *could* fall, it was all sideways anyway) and I went and hid in the cloakroom for ten minutes, to give him time to go, and then had to sweep out to meet another person for drinks there, at 5.30. The Ritz porter stared as he saw me meet another man, and I am sure he thought I was a prostitute meeting different men! My dread was that Flop-face would not have gone, but thank heavens he had. (The new man did not matter, it was that accountant man.) Well, what with Alec, and meeting Boland, and then Flop-face, and then the awful World Situation, I was glad to get back here, but have to go up again this Friday for Kits's Long Leave.

I don't know what you think of the world? This country is split in two. People like Tommy, and lots of others are firmly for the Sick-Dog's tactics, and myself feel it is all wrong, and tho' I am against stupid Nasser and Co., I am sure we should not have invaded them, and where will it all end? And now, poor *Hungary*! (All Tod can think of is 'Will Oil be rationed, because what of her stove?'!) I'm torn between wanting to go and bury myself in La Trappe, and wanting to fly to Hungary, to help poor bleeding people (and preferably with Alec dressed in International Red Cross uniform at my side!).

I do hope all goes well for you? Alastair has had his varicose veins done, so can't go to Suez yet, but his battalion has been ordered off; it's all so horrid. Write, so I get a letter on my return here from Kits's Long Leave.

All love, Bing.

---

* Nickname invented by Kits (at a moment when everyone had to be some kind of animal) for the then Prime Minister, Sir Anthony Eden.

Mena, 6 December, 1956.

Dearest Oriel,

Thank you so much for the letter that was waiting here when I got back at the beginning of this week, from staying with Jeanne on Dartmoor. I had a lovely week up there to make a healing change, if you know what I mean. Going there for me is rather like coming here for you. I get into a sort of holiday routes, and fit into their ways, and go off for long tramps by myself on the goodly high ground, and have wise thoughts! I feel much stronger for it, even if my stay was barely a week, but the air is so good, and I do love that high ground, as opposed to 'sea level'. Now I am back to warm muggy air and drizzle, but it can't be helped. Tod has gone up to London to do my Christmas shopping, as I couldn't face to go up again, and I hope she will get something nice for you.

We are having the whole crew for Christmas, and my one fear is that Zulus and Towers may kind of scratch – how is it with your sisters when they arrive with husbands, or are they very 'in'? The trouble is that Peter may say tactless things, and then Alastair go cold, and then Tessa red, and Flave waine, and Moper start to pitch! I do hope we shall all be happy. I shall hide in my room with Poo and Beatrix Potter, if things get really tricky. Flave is very sweet post-marriage, and easy, but I still feel her personality is damped, for the time being. She wore nylons and heels and great London skirts all the time she was here, and it seemed so non-routes, not to want to get into trousers and jerseys, but I suppose she feels 'new' dressed that way, and grown-up. I dare say she will settle to her new status in time. I have a dim feeling that when I first married Moper I used to put on a skirt to go into Fowey, but that didn't last very long! What I shall always be glad of is that Kits hasn't changed from going to Eton. He might so well have become snobby, or spotty, but he couldn't be more himself, and all in with the Burts still, and Tessa's shilling Nanny. Only poor Noddy is rather neglected, but that is because she and her Gran have moved to Fowey, otherwise she'd be kicking a football as always, I have no doubt.

I have heavenly letters from my blissful Peg Alec. We have interesting religious discussions by post. No, he's not a bit irritating about his Catholic thing, but actually awfully funny, and also humble. Tessa saw an article about him in *Good Housekeeping*, and there was a picture of his wife, and a son. I know Kits and I will ruin everything by turning him into another Mr Harris. And once we get our frightful giggles, it's the end.

Now I must go down and look at TV News. Moper has been here for a few days, and goes back tonight, and Tod is in London, so I shall have about a week of 'Retreat', as he can't get down for the weekend. I have a spate of Deep Thoughts when I'm alone, so it will be a real Retreat. Now no more, and be sure and ring me up with a reverse call when you get back.

All love, Bing.

Monday, 28 January, 1957.

Dearest Oriel,

I *am* so sorry about chucking your birthday. The thing was, yes, we were down at Tessa's, and I did remember it in the evening, but I had not got my book with your telephone number. Next day, going back to London, it went from my mind as I seemed to be in a whirl of Horses of the Sun things; with a visit down to Elstree to meet Michael Balcon, that old MGM British producer person, and then a session with Peter Glenville, the young director person (you remember, he did *The Innocents* we went to?) and Kits's last day before Eton, and so on. I don't forget you when I don't see you, but I *had* just seen you anyway, so there was no great going-into-of-Main-news-or-Main-Deep-Thoughts that could be written, anyway!

I'm sorry we didn't have more time for Main discussions while you were here. But one *does* have to be alone, you must admit! And when Moper sits and glues on the sofa it is so difficult, as I always feel Main talks are Tell-Hims in front of him. And then Kits with his old football holds one up too. I think in my old days I shall have to have a Salon, like crumby people in the eighteenth century, and friends will come in to have Main talks while I get up, and dress (tho' I can't concentrate then, either!). I wish you could pay a visit to the Bib. Nat.* one day for me, and ask to see the List of Émigrés for the Paris quarter, rue St Honoré, in 1789. I have a feeling my Robert Mathurin Busson (du Maurier might be added) would be amongst them, and it might say what property he left behind him. I am getting all the books I can at the London Libe about the life of the French émigrés over here, as I think it would be so interesting to know how they lived. My man would probably be down as 'faencier'

* The *Bibliothèque nationale.*

or 'gentilhomme verrier', and I know he emigrated pretty soon after his marriage in May 1789, probably after the fall of the Bastille. Anyway, it would be an experience for you to go to the Bib. Nat. and they do have full lists there in the archives, I know. Something to write in an article!

　　　　　　　Write your news soon. And heaps of love, Bing.

☆

Mena, 14 February, 1957.

Dearest Oriel,

　I can't think what else I asked in my last letter, except to go to the Bib. Nat. I'm in lovely contact with some Professeur at a *lycée* in Tours who has found out all about my great-great-grandfather's (the émigré I want you to find) *brother*, who apparently was a terrific republican down in Loir-et-Cher, and he calls him a 'patriote enragé'! He rushed about leading his workmen from my verrerie to arrest nobles, and old clergé, and was so 'enragé' that even the Assemblée of the Convention Nationale had to rebuke him for being so violent! The other brother was equally 'enragé' at Le Mans, so perhaps this explains my hatred of smart things, and the reason I loathed Balmoral! On the other hand, I don't see why my great-great-grandfather, the eldest brother, emigrated, if his family were so republican? But I think, having been living in Paris, in the rue St Honoré, he got above himself, and crumbed that he was *in* with smart people, and that it was the thing to do to imitate them, and emigrate.

　I do wonder if you will find anything in the Bib. Nat.? You may be put on the wrong track, by finding a curious little book on abolishing passports, of all things, by the émigré's son, Louis-Mathurin Busson du Maurier, who wrote it about 1835 or later, I believe. Or, you may get an even more muddling line by finding a book written by someone called Louis du Maurier, who was nothing to do with us at all, but lived years before, or an Aubéry du Maurier of that same family; they are *nothing to do* with the Bussons. It was these people that put my poor *Trilby* grandfather on the wrong track, in the last century. He heard about them, and of course thought they were ancestors. I've been into it all, and they are no relations, so don't be sidetracked by these people. The chap you want is Robert Mathurin Busson (may have du Maurier tacked on, or may not), who emigrated in 1789, and was a gentilhomme verrier, and I am practically sure lived at this time in the rue St Honoré. I know he married in l'Église St Roch in May 1789, and is supposed to have emigrated that year.

No, I have had no great Deep Thoughts, just reading a lot, got Hoffman* to send me from Paris the new book by the French professor person about Emily Brontë. You ought to get it as it's worth having, though I still think no one knows as much as you and I do about the Brontës! One day we must do our Branwell and Anne book. I get a bit cross when people harp so much on great cosmic suffering and wild tumult of thought of Emily, when I am sure all four of them just existed for their 'making out', which completely engulfed them. Anyone who remembers anything of imaginative childhood life knows how completely one identified oneself with moody Byronic heroes, and the more one read, the more one identified oneself, and it then came out in the poems and stories one wrote. When Emily wrote: 'No coward soul'† etc I'm sure she was imagining some Great Person saying that, not just herself being brave, making her bed while Tabby swept! A writer is a kind of medium, who can think him or herself into almost any character.

Must stop. A bit of sun, after ghastly endless rain. Isn't my typewriter irritating, the way the 'S' is fading? It sounds like someone lisping.

Lots of love, Bing.

———

Bing questioned me intently about every aspect of life in France. Every street in Paris fascinated her and every *Place*, from the Tuileries to the Concorde (where the guillotine had once stood); the Église St Roch, where her great-great-grandparents had been married, had to be described in detail, and then looked up in old guidebooks. I began to feel that we were living in two centuries at once, like the ladies who had wandered into Marie-Antoinette's time at Versailles. Bing's ideas were becoming more and more Revolutionary, but this was a period in history that I had always deliberately avoided. She was convinced that her ancestor Robert Busson had lived above his boutique, beneath the arcades of the Palais Royale, and that his young wife had died there. (Their shop is still there, and does not look very different today.) As she set me searching for records in the Église St Roch and at the Bibliothèque nationale I, too,

* Michel Hoffman, literary agent.
† From *Last Lines*.

gradually, became infected with this Revolutionary fever. I was particularly gripped by a book called *The Way of the Tumbrils* by John Eliot, which traces, house by house, the route taken by those dreadful carts as they rumbled along their *via crucis*. I often voiced my horror of the Revolution, and the sheer waste of it to Bing, but she, swept by fervour for her 'patriote enragé' ancestors, was becoming more and more enragée herself.

Fortunately, her interest in the Brontës, although momentarily extinguished by Danton and Robespierre, still survived. Here we were on safer, and familiar, ground. We even planned a book, to be presented in the form of letters to Charlotte and Emily, from Anne and Branwell during their fateful time as tutor and governess to the Robinson family at Thorpe Green. This would have made an intriguing game for the long winter evenings at Mena, but life in Paris left me less time for Brontës, and the idea faded. Bing's interest in Branwell, however, simmered quietly underneath, biding its time.

𝔖

Mena, le 10 Ventôse, l'an 155 de la République.

Dearest Oriel,

Many thanks for your letter. You *are* getting into an interesting milieu. And I shall love to read the new story. What fun to get suddenly inspired, so that you couldn't stop, like K.M. I used to feel like that when I was about twenty-two, and wrote one short story after another. But it's very different in my ageing days!

Along with interest in my French forebears, I've been beeding at the Brontë Juvenilia again, and suddenly wrote to the old man who edited *Shakespeare Head* with T. J. Wise. (You know Wise turned out to be an awful forger of signatures?) Well, the old man, Symington, who is still alive, wrote back to me and said he so agreed with me that poor Branwell had been chucked by everyone from Mrs Gaskell to Fanny.* He said he was sure that lots of the Juvenile tales attributed to Charlotte had been written by Branwell, and that someone (he didn't say who) had written *Charlotte* Brontë on the manuscripts before they were sold to America and the Brit. Mus. (A Charlotte signature would fetch more than a Branwell.) He said would I 'treat this confidentially', and of course I can't wait to tell *you*! The point is, of course, that T. J. Wise and Clement

* Fanny Ratchford, author of *The Brontës' Web of Childhood* and the first person to 'unravel' the Brontë Juvenilia.

Shorter got all the Juvenilia from old Nicholls* in Ireland, and sorted it all out between them before my correspondent, Symington, got them to edit, so – I wonder if the wicked pair got to work on the signatures? It doesn't matter, really, as it's only the Juveniles, but it's rather unfair to Branwell, if it's true.

No more now. Lots of love, Bing.

🜨

le 18 Ventôse (it's not Germinal yet. Germinal starts on the 20th of our March. It's very confusing! The New Year starts 1st Vendémiaire, i.e. 20th Sept!)

Dearest Oriel,

I am looking forward to reading your story. I always like anything that is a bit eerie, with dead people doing things. Supposing *we* are really dead, and don't know? I hope *Ladies' Home Journal* take it, because they do pay so well. It's much more fun being a writer like you with All before you, and everyone so keen. When you reach my age and status you become a Tell-Him, and really rely on old faithful fans to go on reading your books. I wrote Victor to beg him not to advertise me as Best-Selling, because nowadays it puts people off, and has almost become something to be ashamed of (though God knows why, inverted snobbery), but I'm sure he won't take any notice. You are very right about the film of mine. I can't help wishing I had got the whole thing done in France, although I am sure Alec will be good as the man. But it's the rest of the cast one wants frightfully to be French, and yet if they say "Ow do you do, pleez,' it's hopeless. You *are* in with interesting people, it's very good for you, and old Rebecca West's person† too! D'you mean you went off *alone* with him to the Trianon suddenly? How madly See Me.

At the moment, I am rather toying with the idea of a brief trip to Italy in early May. Old Pen Friend has harped so long for me to meet him somewhere, and he is good in Italy, showing 'in the steps of' St So and So, and pictures, and I have an urge to see places like Assisi and Perugia. The only thing is, the silly old man doesn't drive, and it always means hiring cars to get to places; so expensive.

My correspondence with the ancient Brontë man goes well, and he may sell me anything I want out of his Brontë library – all his entire

---

* Charlotte Brontë's husband.
† Her husband, Henry Maxwell Andrews.

Shakespeare Head edition, and all the Transactions since the year Dot! The poor old thing says my interest has given him a new lease of life ('I live in retirement, suffering from poor health') and he is going to look up all his notes and things he made about Branwell thirty years ago.

I made an awful gaffe with my old French man of ninety. I had a *Revue historique*, all about my Bussons in it, but he hadn't written inside it, only sent a *carte de deuil* – heavy black – and I thought it meant the poor old brute was dead, and that the *Revue* had been sent by his confrère. So I wrote to the confrère sending him my *condoléances*, and would these be expressed to *Madame sa fille* etc, etc, and yesterday got a horrified letter from the confrère, saying, '*Non, non, madame, La carte de deuil signifie que M. de Linière a eu un deuil récent dans sa famille. Vous pouvez donc encore lui écrire, sans, bien sûr, lui parler de sa "mort"; car il a 90 ans, et est déjà tres souffrant d'une maladie intérieure grave ...*' It's the sort of thing that gives me hysterics when I think of it. I can see the raised shocked hands of the confrère, also probably ninety, when he got my letter of condolence! But all these old people are such bliss.

Meanwhile, did I tell you that the Professeur d'Histoire at Blois never stops looking up things, and he says that that desperate old brute Marat, who was murdered in his bath by Charlotte Corday, '*avait un parent très proche à la verrerie de Montmiraille.*' How ghastly if he turns out to be an uncle!! That really would be the end! I don't mind being 'un patriote enragé', but I won't admit relationship with Marat. Go and look at him in the Musée Grevin. He is in a tub with a nightcap, and blood running down him.

Now no more, I must write to mumpish Kits.

Tons of love, Bing (la citoyenne Traie!).

※

Mena, le 5 Germinal (does that muddle you?) i.e. 25 March, 1957.

Forgive the hotch-potch sort of letter, but I want to get one off to you, though I may miss the post now. I have been in bed with a stinking cold, one of my worst, caught off Poonie at Tessa's I am certain. She had a streamer, but I couldn't be like those Victorian grandmothers and push her away – 'Don't come near me, child' – as I longed to hug her, and she was so blissful, and 'on' to her Tray, her little face all lit up. Anyway, the result was I caught this absolute snorter, and it was such waine, because it began to get bad the next day at the Guinness's. That awful thing of trying to be bright in another person's house (especially a Peg's house) and my mind all whuzzy when we were going through the Bridget Boland script (which turned out to be rather shilling, with all the atmosphere gone, though she stuck closely to the story).

Anyway, we ploughed through it making notes, and I couldn't make too much of a Peg out of Alec, because of feeling deathly with my cold. The wife, Merula, was there – a very shy little thing. She scarcely uttered, but did the cooking and also sat on a stool drawing, while he sat humped in sweaters and shoes like Kits wears for house football, and now and then put on lovely Deep Thought gram records, and we also had Religious discussions. Wainer still, he *called* me in the morning with my brek, which I didn't expect, and was laying [in] having had two pills because of my cold, and very greasy face and hair in pins, and I just had to brazen it out, and he will be so put off! Their house was very new, like in adverts of *Ladies' Home Journal*, very American and labour-saving. I am sure they adore it, and it was very nice, but it made me long for shabby old Mena.

Thanks terribly for your letter, and I must tell you that I read your story going up in the train, and was absorbed by it. I love the way you write, and the things you write about, but my criticism would be that this atmosphere and story are *wasted* on a short story – you should develop it into a novel. As it is, I feel we don't know enough about what the 'I' did or will do with her psychic gift, and that in a way, the length makes it neither one thing nor the other. Other people may think differently and say it is perfect as it stands, but I think you have the potential material here for a lovely long and interesting book. Love to know what you really feel.

The Main thing why I wrote: Victor has sent me a proof of your book* (immediately grabbed by Tod) and says will I write him a few lines about it, I suppose to quote. I won't do so unless you want me to, as I know you feel waine about these things when we know each other so well, almost as if Flave had written a book and I wrote a quote for her! On the other hand you might like me to, but whichever way let me know.

Tons of love, Bing.

————

Before I left for Paris, Pip and Marge Youngman-Carter (Margery Allingham the crime writer) urged me to look up an old friend of theirs, Madame Meg Catusse-Villars, who as 'Priscilla in Paris' had, for some forty-odd years, contributed a weekly *Letter from Paris* to the *Tatler* magazine, of which Pip was then editor. Like most people, I ruffled through its pages at the dentist or the hairdresser, skipping the saccharine columns of the *Social Diary*, and had been captivated by Priscilla's caustic humour and her vivid descriptions of Paris. These were mainly concerned with theatre and the arts, with here and there, intriguing glimpses of her private world – a cottage on the island of Noirmoutiers, off the coast of Vendée, then wild and primitive, a dog (about which she appeared to feel passionately), and a crusty old *bonne* called Josephine.

'Meg's a tough old bird,' Marge had said briskly, 'but very good value. If she likes you, she'll do anything for you. If not, you won't hear from her again. Do go, and try your luck.'

Secretly, I thought it all sounded terrifying and, at the risk of offending Pip and Marge, the letter of introduction remained unposted and was finally mislaid. It came to light one day at the back of a drawer, and I noted with surprise that the address on the envelope was only two streets away. Guiltily, I popped it into the nearest letterbox, and two days later found myself climbing the steep staircase of an old house in the rue Vaneau.

The door was opened by a round lady wrapped in black shawls, with a bun like a brioche on the top of her head and the rosy, wrinkled cheeks of someone whose roots are still firmly embedded in the country. Josephine belonged to a vanished race, who gave their services with a devotion which money can never buy. She and Meg were friends and conspirators, linked by the common experiences of their long lives. She ushered me

* *Jam Today.*

into a large room, with one royally splendid piece of furniture – a red and gold lacquer Chinese secrétaire, which gave dignity to its shabbiness – a dignity shared by the fierce-looking old lady seated in a green armchair. She apologized for not getting up, saying she was old and tired, but I knew this was not the whole truth; her spirit burned brightly, but she resented her body for not keeping pace with it, and had determined to do battle with it to the end.

Meg's devotion to Pip and Marge was obvious, and I quickly realized that I was only there on sufferance. Our conversation began by being politely conventional, but presently it tipped over into the theatre, and from then on all was plain sailing. Meg admitted to a longstanding admiration for my godmother Yvonne Arnaud, not only as an actress but as a musician. Later, I was fortunately able to bring them together, on one of Meg's last visits to London. She kept nostalgic memories of her own career on the music-hall stage in Paris, and I listened entranced to stories of those she had known in the past – of Colette, of Cocteau and the Guitrys. When Josephine came in to clear away, looking distinctly disapproving, I found that I had long exceeded the acceptable time for a first visit but as I was ushered out, Meg called, 'Come back soon!'

As I suspected, Meg's early years had not been easy, nor uneventful. Her family had settled in London after the stirring events of the Commune, and there she had led the life of any well-brought up young girl, except that her parents enjoyed the society of artists and writers, to whom their London house was always open. At the age of eighteen, Meg fell under the spell of her father's old friend, Henri Gautier-Villars, the enigmatic 'Willy' who was thirty-five years older than she, and still married to Colette. At twenty-one, Meg ran off with him to Paris, causing a breach with her outraged family that was never entirely healed.

Willy preferred his wives to work for him, rather than to exert himself, although he was not without talents of his own. Having forced the young Colette to produce the Claudine novels (which he then published under his own name), he could hardly go through the same performance twice. Instead, he put Meg on the music-hall stage; like Colette before her, she took readily to this new free life, and was quickly successful. Yet when she found that she was pregnant she was delighted too, but she always suspected that he deliberately engineered the accident which caused her to miscarry.

Willy seems to have exerted an almost hypnotic effect on women, and Meg admitted that she was afraid of him. Finally, she gathered the courage to put the Atlantic Ocean between them, and in 1913 she sailed for New York. There, in order to survive, she began to send a weekly account of a Frenchwoman's impressions of life in America to various papers, illustrating these with her own pen-and-ink sketches. When she returned to France at the outbreak of war in 1914, she continued to send a weekly letter to the *Tatler*, this time from Paris; an association that was to end only with her death.

After the war, life brought Meg into smoother waters. She met and married Charles Catusse, a kindly man whose family background had destined him for the diplomatic service, but who had a secret passion for the theatre. His family were outraged at this *mésalliance* with a music-hall artiste who had been scandalously divorced, and it was not until seven years later, after the death of Charles' mother, that they were free to marry. Meg did not often talk of these happier years, but when she did so it was always with deep affection for her 'cher Charles'. Nor did she often speak of her service to her country in 1940, when she was no longer young, driving ambulances for the French Red Cross in the front lines, with a courage which earned her the Croix de Guerre.

At the time we met, Meg was still active, rattling around Paris in her small car. She wished me to know and love her beloved city, and we spent many happy evenings together at the theatre, but she was already spending more and more time in her island home. In late spring, when the chestnuts began to droop, she would set out for Noirmoutiers by car, with Josephine and Vicki, her beloved Skye terrier, tightly packed in among piles of books and luggage. This was then a fairly hazardous journey, for at high tide the Atlantic came in so fast over the causeway linking the island to the mainland, that unwary travellers were often forced to abandon their cars and climb to the safety of one of the watch-towers built for that purpose.

The summer after we met, Meg had invited me to visit her island; I was to fly to La Baule, and take a train down the coast, timed to convey me safely across to Noirmoutiers at low tide. All was in order, and my ticket to hand, when a telegram arrived, announcing that she had suffered a heart attack. Only the prompt action of a friend had saved her life; an action for which Meg later reproached her bitterly, for it condemned her to two years of semi-invalidism, complicated by painful bouts of cardiac asthma.

Hearing of this event, Pip rang to ask if I would stand in for Meg and take over the Paris *Letter* for the *Tatler* during her long convalescence. I knew how much the *Letter* meant to Meg; it kept her in touch with a world she had always known, and she jealously guarded her right to a press card. I accepted, although I had little knowledge of professional journalism, and no training. When I had attended two or three Collections in the morning, an exhibition or two in the afternoon, with the *générale* of some new play to round off the day, I often returned home exhausted in the small hours. But it was a challenge: everyone was kind and helpful, and I made many new friends.

Nevertheless, when Meg returned to Paris, I handed over to her with relief, hoping to go back to my own work, but I soon found that Meg still had need of my services. She could no longer go about as she had once done, and her car had to be abandoned in favour of taxis. Kind friends had organized her removal from the rue Vaneau, whose five flights were now as inaccessible as the Himalayas, to a *rez-de-chaussée* in the avenue de la Bourdonnais. However, this dark, tank-like little basement flat never felt like home to her, and soon it became a prison, and one last painful year was spent virtually riveted to her chair.

Like her old friend and rival Colette, Meg never gave up working, but fought her increasing infirmity with courage and without complaint. I would bring her news of the exhibitions she could no longer visit, and the *générales* she could not attend; she would then write an account of them in her own inimitable style. No one could have guessed they were the work of a mortally sick woman.

Meanwhile, life had become increasingly difficult for me owing to the vagaries of my current landlady's fortunes, and of her temper, and I knew the time had come to make a change. I owned little beyond my books and a typewriter, firmly believing that one should travel lightly through life, unhampered by material possessions. One day, I was summoned to lunch with my agent, Odette Arnaud, in the rue de Téhéran; this was another *hôtel particulier* or private house, with a somewhat forbidding exterior. The Agence occupied the top floors, but visitors were received in Madame Arnaud's own apartments. There was only one other guest at lunch that day – Madame Colette de Jouvenel, once the young Bel-Gazou of her mother Colette's books, but now a lively, middle-aged lady who spent most of her time in the south of France.

Over lunch, Madame Arnaud (who rarely took her mind off her work) accused me of becoming too much involved with the Paris *Letter*, with little time left over for other work. This I hotly denied, revealing in self-defence the difficult conditions under which I was living and working. My vehemence may have surprised her, for she said no more but later, when she had gone back upstairs to her office, Madame de Jouvenel quietly said that she knew of a place where it was possible to work in peace. Friends of hers owned an old house on the Left Bank, and willingly let rooms to people (usually writers or painters) who wished to work undisturbed. It was, she insisted, very peaceful and it even had a garden, in which her mother had celebrated her eightieth birthday. She promised to ring them at once, and the next day found me standing in the middle of one of the busiest, noisiest streets in Paris, feeling slightly bewildered.

Number 76 proved to be a shabby, nondescript house, wedged in between a *pharmacie* and a dress shop, with an outer door from which the paint was peeling. But it was too late to turn back, so I pushed open the door and found myself in a cobbled alley, of the kind that in London would be called a mews. A row of small *boutiques* ran down each side, all now shuttered and barred, for the *grandes vacances* had already begun, when Paris traditionally empties, leaving the city to the tourists and the pigeons.

An enamel plate fixed to the concierge's *loge* informed me that the Villa Racine was to be found at the end of the alley, on the left. This seemed to be blocked by an equally tall, down-at-heel house. To one side, however, there was a narrow passage with an iron lamp-post, and behind it, a green wooden gate. Peering above it, I saw a flight of stone steps leading down into a garden, tangled with lilac bushes and the midsummer foliage of tall trees. Between their branches could be seen a low, rambling house with a tiled roof, its walls so covered with roses and creeper that the windows seemed to blink through them. One felt the house had been planted here centuries ago, when this part of Paris was still open country (as indeed it had, for I once found it marked upon a pre-Revolution map) and here it had stayed, dreaming the years away, while Paris grew up round it.

As I rang the bell, I could see straight through the house to another garden beyond, and I knew that I *must* live here – even if all they had to offer was an attic under the eaves. But to my relief, I was shown into a wide, cool room of pleasant proportions on the first floor. All the rooms were furnished with antique furniture, which from time to time mysteriously disappeared, whenever the owners found it necessary to restock their shop on the rue Jacob. They apologized for this, but I found it an entrancing habit; it was part of the easy atmosphere of the Villa Racine.

I made no enquiries about the other, invisible guests, although it was obvious that we must all be living, at times, in close proximity. On their side, the owners of the house accepted me without question, vouchsafing equally little information beyond a casual mention that the room next to mine was occupied by a friend of theirs, a Belgian poet engaged in translating the poems of Gerard Manley Hopkins into French. As I left that day I turned for one more look at the old house, and from somewhere came the thin, haunting sound of an old French air, picked out on a lute – so faint that it might have been a figment of my imagination. I would have liked to turn back, to investigate, but the proprietor was still standing in the doorway to wave me away, and I did not like to linger.

I went down to Mena that summer in jubilant mood, which even Tod's dire forebodings could not shake. 'My dear, a *poet*? A Belgian? It all sounds very risky to me. You had better make sure you lock your door.'

Bing, as usual, was encouraging. In spite of being so attached to her own 'routes', she liked to hear of others striking out on unknown paths. Yet even she voiced certain doubts. 'Isn't it rather waine?' I remember her asking me. 'To move into that strange house without meeting the other people first? Suppose it all turns out a disaster. What on earth will you do?'

I had no idea. As the summer faded and the autumn *rentrée* loomed, I began to feel that she was right. Once again, I had let my heart rule my head – a procedure which in the past had often brought disaster in its wake.

Those readers who knew Paris in the 1950s and 1960s will remember the Abbaye, that small and friendly club tucked away behind the church of St Germain des Prés, where Gordon Heath and Lee Payant sang folksongs in French and English, every night from nine-thirty to midnight. Gordon's rich velvet voice perfectly suited the melancholy or dramatic melodies of *Le Prisonnier de la Tour* or *Le Roi Renault*, while Lee specialized in English and Irish folksongs. His rendering of the *Vicar of Bray*, or the misadventures of the Unfortunate Miss Bailey, who died by her own hand and then came back to haunt her lover, were inimitable. Their voices blended together perfectly as they sang the lovely Auvergnat shepherd's song *Lou Balou* or one of the rousing spirituals which rounded off the first half of the programme. During the *entr'acte*, they came to each table in turn, asking for requests; as each song ended a candle was blown out, until only one was left burning – the signal for Gordon to round off the evening with a plaintive little air, *Time for Man Go Home*.

Afterwards, people lingered, talking and laughing, until shepherded out into the street. This was the faint music I thought I had heard, drifting over the garden, on my first visit to the Villa Racine. Now I heard it almost every day, with increasing delight. Gordon and Lee had lived at the Villa Racine almost since the Abbaye existed, and were its principal inhabitants. Apart from my own, and the Poet's, all the rooms on the first floor were theirs, and they had turned these into a friendly, comfortable apartment. It would have been spacious, too, had it not been crammed from floor to ceiling with books, pictures and wood carvings, recording equipment and musical instruments. I grew to love them both dearly; Gordon and Lee were the older brothers I had never known, and they opened up new worlds to me, in music, theatre and literature.

The whole house hummed with creative activity. The Poet was a shy man, who flitted in and out like a shadow, and ate his meals with the family in their private apartments. When he found that I shared his love for Gerard Manley Hopkins, he let me see his translations, which were beautiful and sensitive; and he gave me fresh insights into the difficult art of translation. We sat at our desks all morning, leaving only in order to let the cleaner and the cats hold sway. At first, it was dazzling to plunge from our peaceful garden into the hubbub of the busy rue de Sèvres. In spite of a substantial evening meal provided by the Villa, I was always hungry then, and often dropped in to a bistro in the nearby rue Vaneau, where a bowl of home-made soup, a glass of wine and *pain à volonté* cost only 50 centimes. The regular clients came from the hospitals and lycées in the area, and kept their own red-and-white checked napkins in a mahogany box fixed to the wall.

The patron, Monsieur Chevallier, was a huge man with bulging muscles like Popeye, and the kindest heart imaginable. He performed his culinary miracles in a kitchen no bigger than a ship's galley, which may have influenced the pictures he painted in his spare time, in which shipwrecks figured prominently, among more pastoral scenes of his native Burgundy. His wife was a gentle, self-effacing woman, who managed the service single-handed, and never seemed rushed or harried. They had worked together in the Resistance during the war, and the bistro was still the annual meeting-place for the group of British airmen they had helped to safety. I liked the Chevalliers, and continued to visit them long after I had left the Villa Racine, until the fatal day when I found that the bistro had vanished overnight. In its place stood a Chinese pagoda, all tinkling bells and joss-sticks, and the new proprietors bowing with oriental politeness upon the threshold.

When, in my mind's eye, I see the Villa Racine, it is always spring or summer. All my memories are of waking early, to the chattering of little birds in the ivy, and flinging open the windows on to the garden, to find the monks in the garden of the Clinique St Jean on the other side of the wall, already hard at work, raking the gravel paths into a neat pattern. At certain times a bell would ring, summoning them to mysterious duties elsewhere. Bing was endlessly fascinated by the monks and their monastic life, and urged me to trespass over the wall one day and find out more about their Day – but this would have been waine, and I refused.

One person who did not share my idyllic view of the Villa Racine was

Pen Friend. He came to take me out to dinner one evening, enveloped in a flowing cape, a rosette in his buttonhole, and looking every inch a retired diplomat from some Ruritanian court, for he was a handsome old man. We dined in a small epicurean restaurant of his choice; he studied the menu carefully through a monocle, and fussed about the exact temperature of the wine. I listened as he described a recent visit to some old Duchess in her crumbling palazzo in Venice. 'The Marchesa di Frascati, a very old family ...' I sipped my wine, which was delicious, and felt relieved that neither Bing nor Kits were present, to disturb my equanimity. When we parted later at the gate of the Villa Racine, he kissed my hand, and murmured: 'A warning from an old man.'

It was so obscure a warning that I could make no sense of it, but light dawned a few days later when Bing rang me, and revealed that Pen Friend had written her in a fever, demanding if she was aware that I was living *alone*, in *Paris*, in a house with *four* men. This, I decided, would confirm Tod's gloomiest predictions, but as so often happens, on my next visit to Mena she did not fail to surprise me. 'My dear, what nonsense!' she declared, adding stoutly: 'Honi soit qui mal y pense, that's always been *my* motto!'

⚶

Mena, Monday 19 August, 1957.

Dearest Oriel,

You really have missed nothing by not being here this August. The weather has been shilling-ish, and I have not felt the deep urge to bathe, because the crowds on Prid are really awful, also it's awfully difficult to fit in with everyone's plans! The whole crew are down here now, and actually a great help – though the children are a bit whiney. I think the thing is that small children really don't like having their routes altered, and at this stage are actually much more settled in their own home doing their own day-by-day things. But they are both very sweet really.

Moper seems a good deal better, and I'm sure will continue so if he can keep off liquor – it's always that which is so bad for him in every way. But there are still a great many difficulties to be overcome. I am awfully sorry I couldn't see you to ask you one or two rather private things, which I think could have had some slight bearing on things which have lately come about, though possibly only slight, and if there is anything you could have told me, referring to the person as the Snow Queen, and Moper as Kay (!), it might help me in piecing a few things together. Sometimes people – like in that fairy tale – somehow get a piece of glass or ice in their eye which makes them *see* things wrong, and do strange things, and eventually they get into a sort of jam, and it's awfully difficult to get the piece of glass or ice out of their eye, and have them themselves again. Do you remember poor Kay, and how altered he became through harmful influence? Though I don't think the Snow Queen I mentioned has been much to blame in this case, only that she may be a link in a strange chain of events.

As to myself, my C. of L. is no worse really than it has ever been. Would be feeling *fine*, if it were not for the past months of anxiety, which were so utterly and completely unexpected. It's so difficult to know what the future will be. And I do feel very much like Gerda in that fairy tale, knowing that the ice is not yet out of Kay's eye, and wondering what is the right thing to do about it. Doctors have given me no lead whatsoever, and I am inclined to think have made matters worse in some respects.

You dear old thing, I am so glad about the book* doing well. Did you know Gollancz had sent about five copies of it here to me, and I always wondered if they were meant for you? No, I have no writing plans at the moment – *can't*, but there is always Branwell waiting, and after what has happened lately, I should say material for a dozen 'tec or crook novels!

Lots of love always, Bing.

————

Shortly after I returned to Paris, Bing became obsessed with some plot which she believed was being hatched against herself, and especially against Moper. She feared his life was in danger from these evil plotters, and for a time she even persuaded herself that they might try to get at her through me, in Paris. She rang me several times, warning me not to go out at night alone, and to avoid all public places, such as the métro. I was unaware then that such obsessions frequently occur at the change of life. I had either to believe that Bing had gone completely off her head, or that some sort of fearful plot was actually afoot, which might lead, in true Guy Fawkes fashion, to bombs at Buckingham Palace. Apart from these dire warnings, Bing sounded perfectly normal, both on the telephone and in her letters. Kits eventually cured her, as only he could do, for he encouraged her to turn her fears and obsessions into a game of Red Indians, calling himself and everyone else by weird tribal names and so,

* *Jam Today.*

by making her laugh at herself, banished her obsession. Later she exorcized the memory, turning it into that brilliant but terrifying story, 'The Blue Lenses', in which a patient recovering from an eye operation in hospital sees everyone around her, including her husband, as sinister animals. They are all wearing animal masks, which reveal their true, hidden characters – and all have become potential enemies. This strange episode was never repeated, and once the cloud was lifted Bing seemed stronger, in mind and body. She was to need all her strength, to see her through the coming months.

ॐ

The Flat, 8 November, 1957.

Dearest Oriel,

I was so glad to get your letter, because I felt we were 'out of touch', as Tod would say. And though I don't want to 'see folks' like she does, I love hearing from you! Well, you are being a clever, crumbing sort of person, and I am so glad. I can't wait to see the *Tatler* at a hairdresser, or make Kits bring his collection back at Christmas. I know it's not what you call *real* work, but it's a job, and I should think very good for you in all sorts of ways.

I heard from old Victor last week, asking if he could count on a book of stories from me next year, to be delivered by June, and I had to tell him I could do nothing at the moment, because my family life was a bit disorganized with being backwards and forwards to London. I didn't go into details, but said Moper had not been well, and I felt myself selfish if I stayed down at Mena and worked, rather than be with him. Moper seems better and more cheerful, but he's still what I call very 'quiet', and one doesn't know if he's just plain tired, or has things on his mind. His memory is poor, and he forgets things, but then lots of people his age do that. *I know* I am doing the right thing, just as you knew you were doing right to go to Paris, but of course it's very different. I mean, I don't get any excitement out of this, or real pleasure, just a sort of quiet feeling that what is happening to me, is *meant*.

Do tell me your *personal* news. You must have some, and I don't tell Flave or anyone. Who are your friends and menaces?

Tons of love, Bing.

———

Although Bing's letters to me were brave and cheerful, and she made light of her problems on the telephone, I was desperately worried about both her and Moper at this time. My instinct has always been to fly to the help of anyone I love who is in trouble, but this was now impossible. I was tied to Paris by my work, and for the first time realized fully the difficulties of leading a divided life. No sooner, it seemed, had I turned my back on England than everything seemed to go wrong. When I met Bing in London, it was for a hurried visit, snatched from an anxious day; there was no real time to talk, and I could feel the tensions under her assumed calm. She did not want to talk about her problems, she said. They were there, and had to be faced, and that was that. She begged me, when I wrote, not to comment on the things she told me, but to write about Paris and all I was doing there. It was, she insisted, the best way I could help her, and would take her mind off the daily boredom of her London life.

An Edith Piaf song, which came trickling out of every window in Paris at this time, stated that *'Sans amour, on n'est rien du tout'*, and it struck me that love inevitably brings suffering. Bing's love for Moper was being put to the test, and she was facing any mistakes she might have made in the past, with courage. His love for her was equally strong, but he was unable to show it, being locked into a dark private world of the ego (from which all breakdowns ultimately spring). Bing had not been far wrong when she likened Moper to Kay in the Hans Andersen story, whose heart had been frozen by a sliver of ice. I desperately longed for some charm to break the spell, but all I could do was to continue to send Bing long, newsy letters from Paris. I knew she loved to hear about the Pegs, and must have built them up and their importance in my life, for in reality I was busily exorcizing them in my new novel *Horses of the Sun*, which Gollancz published. How I came to transpose them from a sophisticated Parisian existence to wild Elba was one of those mysteries which make the writing game so fascinating.

❦

The Flat, Friday 29 November, 1957.

Dearest Oriel,

It was lovely to get your letter here when I arrived up. And to know that all goes so happily for you. If I answer it rather with 'my' things, I know you will understand. Poor Gran died on Wednesday, just about the moment I was arriving here in the Riviera.* The last two weeks she had been what is known as 'sinking', and I can't tell you how heartbreaking it was. I dared not stay down in Fowey, because I can't let Tommy be on his own here, in case a sort of hysterical nerve-fit should start again, and drinking. Knowing I had to come up to London on Wednesday, I went in to look at her on Tuesday, and alone in the room, bent down and touched her cheek. From her *deep coma*, with closed eyes, and the most incredible spiritual look on her features, she moved her head towards me and kissed me twice, and I put my little Grande Trappe Rosary on her cheek, and she turned her head again, and was deep in the coma. From which she never stirred again. Don't you think it is a strange, very *good* sort of thing to have happened?

You are so right, the backwards, forwards life is neither one thing nor the other. I don't know who I am. I can cope when I am here, but then once home it's such torture to come up again, I always seem to be in a train. Moper's physical health is better, but I don't think his mind is all right. All he seems to want to do is to sit glued to his desk at the office doing rather routine things, and when at home, he doesn't know what to do with his time. I think his brain is going on like a kind of machine, but the power has gone, and he's terrified of relaxing, in case it goes a blank. I wish to heaven one knew of other cases where this has happened. I dread him getting into the hands of the psycho boys again.

So you see, dear old thing, this is a bad patch for us, and I can only hope and pray it works out. Rest of family all well, and being helpful. Don't bother to write about Mummy, I know you will understand.

> Take care of yourself, and fondest love, Bing.

For years, Lady du Maurier had been suffering from a depressive form of senility, devotedly cared for by Angela and a nurse. Every year, Lady du Maurier and the nurse were installed at Mena for a time, while Angela had a much-needed break. Bing had never been very close to her mother in adult life, and Tod declared that in her childhood she had even been afraid of her. I always felt this explained much about Bing's fear of emotions, and her secretiveness. It was all the more consoling to know that there was peace between them at the end, and that a loving kiss

---

* The 'Cornish Riviera' train.

could even break through the barrier of a deep coma, to reach out to her. It comforted Bing, at a time when she was desperately in need of comfort, and for a while gave her the feeling that death is not loss, but a beginning.

🜨

Mena, Monday 16 December, 1957.

Dearest Oriel,

It was lovely to get your long letter.

When we see each other next we can talk our various talks, and heavens yes, I know only too well that thing about being submerged, and so on. But then what about that awful severe word of, 'He who must save his life must lose it' – which might mean, for me, that everything I have loved – my life at Mena – must be given up. Has it been very selfish living here over the years? A Marriage Council person might say it has been, and that had I been ministering to Moper he might never have cracked. I ought to count myself lucky that the crack did not come while the children were growing up. As it is, by living more in London, I am only hurting myself (and, I suppose old Tod) – no one else.

By the way, I must have been barking up the wrong tree about the Snow Queen, because I found two very ordinary, jam-along letters written by her just after she was engaged; but of course he might have crumbed a bit last year before she got herself engaged, when in his cups. Yes, I was carried away by guilt in the summer, all my fault etc, etc – which is one of the reasons I must see it's not my fault now. After all, it's my devotion to Moper that keeps me with him now, not just solemn duty. My thing of family, too, which is very French. I do long to see you, dear old thing, and not in a rushed way. Let us look forward to a happy day together.

All love, Bing.

———

Bing's letters from the King's Road flat, where she was trying hard to establish a new London routes, were fairly optimistic at first. Gradually, boredom set in with her aimless city life, especially when she felt that it was not having the desired effect. Although Moper was now well enough to go off to his office each morning, at home he continued to be silent and withdrawn, and Bing complained that she could not get through to him. Perhaps he found it equally hard to adapt, knowing that he was keeping Bing tied to a place she had always disliked, and in which she found it difficult to work. She was feeling guilty at not having shared his life in London sooner, and their mutual guilts clashed.

ॐ

The Rat-trap, 7 February, 1958.

Dearest Oriel,

Do forgive me for not writing, and T.N.N.ing your birthday, and everything. The truth is, I became awfully depressed after you left, and I thought of you whizzing back to Paris, and your lovely free life, and a kind of despairing gloom and doom came over me! I began seriously to wonder why I did not just pack up and run away! Really, it has been suicidal. There seemed no way out. Shaw has found another little house – rather sweet, I wouldn't have minded it a bit – next to an archery ground to which one would have a key, and I thought I could bask there. But then I thought I would only be pretending after all, and when the first playing-at-house (Flave!) was over, it would be just like the flat again, and Mena going to waste. Anyway, Moper did not want to fork out from his Trust to pay. That's the awful bitter thing, I have provided for *all* of them, and have no capital myself. It's such dreadful King Lear! We have just had another bout at home, which was lovely, but for the fact (terrible admission!) that I am *never alone*. I sneaked out to do some painting – which shows I am beginning to brew – and Moper hung about looking hang-dog, and kept asking when I would be in for tea. You see, I'm sure deep down he grudges my work, and wants to see me as a person waiting to cook his steak. Anyway, I have said I will do this until Easter, and then I don't think I *can* go on like this between London and Mena, and he said he would be down at home more, and perhaps Shaw would come and cook his supper when he was up, which showed he does not want to be off with other creatures – it's just that stupid loneliness men get. So I must just hang on, and hope I don't crack before Easter.

As to Puck's visit, I knew Ellen would like me to ask her for a weekend – the only one of the family never to have been, and all on her own in England for the first time, and *not* on Doubleday money making a splash, either! She seemed grateful when I said she had only to ring up before the weekend if she was at a loose end. Moper, because she was someone new, made an effort, but as it was, Puck and I were never alone to talk, so I could not psycho-politics her, but I *do* like her. I don't think she knows what she is looking for, I suppose an abiding security and affection from someone, and I think she has only had bitty friendships, perhaps Pegs, with people, and her writing hasn't really made out yet. As to Frank, I am *horrified*, but not actually surprised. Probably MGM are not as generous over expenses as Doubleday was, and he obviously thought poor Puck had come over primed with Doubleday money! Poor Puck, I quite thought he would take her to the theatre, because I am sure he does get theatre tickets free. How deadly putting off it all is. And I really was genuinely fond of him – he was a 'Peg' for Kits grown-up, but with a kind of menace in it too, because in his day, and when in a good mood, he did have such charm, and was lovable, and – for him! – somehow menaced, which is always menacing to *one*, if you know what I mean! Well, there it is. All power corrupts, or whatever the expression is.

As to your own life, I do hope the gay menace continues to go well, but don't let it go *too* deep! And try to keep off the other more serious person and menace. I realize now more and more the fearful unhappiness that one piles up for oneself when one interferes with married people. I was so ruthless with my war person, and hurt him and his poor wife so much, and I thought it had all come right. But now I think this business over Tommy must have been God's way of showing me, like a boomerang, what drink and the wrong kind of selfish waxing can do.

Carol* has madly rung me this second, from down the King's Road, and said would I go and see him *at once* – he can't wait to talk to me! He does this once every two years. Of course I have to go! No more for now. I go home again (D.V.) on Thursday.

Fond love, Bing.

☬

Menabilly, 27 March, 1958.

Dearest Oriel,

Lovely to get your long letter. It was so funny, because the next day I had a crumby great lunch at Claridge's. There were two other men, and I was the only woman (rather a power thing, that Flave would have liked!). I got silent giggles, thinking how funny it would be if you were suddenly to see old Tray at a Claridge lunch (I wasn't dressed for the part, either).

* Sir Carol Reed, the firm director and producer.

I had a bloody long ten days in London, not knowing what to do. My only pleasure was to paint the horrible view from my bedroom at the flat, and I made it all strident and screaming, because of my hate, with glaring chimneypots, and those awful Power Station Battersea things, belching evil smoke. Tray's paintings are very out of proportion and crude, but in a queer way they have a sort of power, like paintings done by madmen. (Perhaps I am!) I went to Mass one Sunday, and there is a thing in one of the prayers which says: 'And save us from Everlasting Doom.' I think I am having Everlasting Doom at the moment. I'm going to try and stay down here in April, and be here for poor Kits, who I had to chuck so in the summer. He has passed his test and got his car, and everything, and he is so jolly to be with, and just *can't* be depressed. And faithful old Shaw says she will go and cook Moper his sups every night in London, when he is up. So if he starts drinking again, then we shall know he really is as hopeless as a child that can't be left.

I heard from Ellen that she won't be going to Paris after all, which is perhaps a relief to you? One does hate one's routes to be upset, and you must get ahead with the book and everything. You know, I somehow feel now, since your last letter, that what I had vaguely suspected was true, and that your Peg No. 1 is not the person who I first thought it was, but himself? I won't probe if you don't want to mention it to me. But *if* it is, it makes me feel more than ever that it's one of those Dream Pegs, which I beg you not to let become an issue. You have such a unique sort of friendship with both, which is valuable and fun, and I am sure that if you ever actually what is known as 'spoke your feelings' it might be disastrous. I *do* know how artists and writers can have these friendships with people, with women, with girls, and in a way it's a sort of blend of attraction and admiration, and all the things wrapped up, and they like it that way. It's a sort of safety valve – especially needed by him, because of a rather great extraordinary personality on *her* side – but if you threw a spanner into the Peg-dream with your own emotions, I think it would break the whole thing up, and waine would follow, and you would lose the friendship. Which would seem to me pointless, when you have so much value from it. If, on the other hand, he is one of those normal French people just brewing up to have 'an affair' on the side, I suppose it would be different. But surely then, being French, he would have made the obvious move?

I think a lot of people have Pegs. I dare say he does. He may make you a Peg – this young, attractive person who obviously is fond of him, but because of being somehow withdrawn and a bit shy, does not make the obvious sexy invitation. And if you *are* this Peg, he feels it is a safe Peg – he does not have to do the obvious thing and it remains a sort of dream relationship. If I have blundered in writing to you about this, don't be cross. I am all *for* Pegs, having lived on them for most of my life, and got them out of my system with books, but my God, you have to be jolly careful when you bring them into practical living issues. They either explode like bubbles and vanish, or else turn catastrophic.

I do think with Peg No. 2 (the ordinary waxing person), you are not doing anything wrong. If it ends, you know what you were in for. But equally, don't let that make you think that waxing is just as easy as pi, and like kissing a person, because then you get into that thing of becoming promiscuous – which I wildly remember doing for a few months, thinking I had Power when I was about twenty-one – because it's like putting on too much lipstick, one suddenly doesn't know how to stop! And it becomes Silly Values, as silly in its own way as Tut-Tut Witherspoons are in theirs.

When you next write, tell me your dreams, and the wise Tray will expound and say whether there is anything hinting in them that you should do. My own recurrent dreams are so often about an overwhelming high tide. Sometimes I am trying to swim and can only just keep afloat, and I do not know if this is the tide of my emotions, which threatens to drown me from time to time, or just a hint that I get overwhelmed by my own tidal C. of L. which makes me unable to settle to London. It could mean both. I don't have any other C. of L. symptoms, but just no Robert now for a year. Only the high-tide dream is rather strange, don't you think, and must mean that *Something* keeps recurring, and threatens to overwhelm me! Perhaps my own unconsciousness?

No news of old *Scapegoat*. Alec keeps winning great Oscar things, and having his Power, so it must be hard for him to think of anything else. I still feel he may slip out of *Scapegoat* after all, although when I gave him his chance last September, he would not take it. But he hadn't had all these awards, then.

Tons of love, Tray.

———

It would be a mistake to assume that only those with overworked imaginations, such as writers, make use of Pegs. Consciously or not, most people need a Peg upon which to hang their dreams and illusions. They may Peg their partners, or children (which perhaps explains why so many close relationships finally disintegrate); others may peg royalty, their vicar, a guru, or even God. Some writers range further still – into the past, as Bing did with the Brontës and Francis Bacon, while Dr Johnson is as real to me as anyone I have met in the flesh. One should always be grateful to Pegs, for without them the world would be a harsher place. It is only when Pegs are allowed to intrude into real life and become disruptive, that they are dangerous – as Charlotte Brontë discovered when swept off her feet by Monsieur Héger. Significantly, Emily could not stand the man.

The Monsieur and Madame Peg of our correspondence were Yvonne Printemps and Pierre Fresnay, two of the best loved, almost legendary actors in the Paris theatre. When in 1934 they eloped together, their romance was as enthralling to the public as any Gondal, for both were married: Yvonne Printemps to Sacha Guitry, the wittiest of all French playwrights, who with his father Lucien Guitry dominated the 'théâtre du boulevard' in Paris for years. It was for Yvonne Printemps that he wrote his most sparkling comedies, and engaged the foremost musicians of the day, Reynaldo Hahn and Francis Poulenc, to write the scores. She had been blessed at birth with every gift a good fairy could bestow: beauty, wit, talent, and a rare and exquisite singing voice. 'There is a quality in her (Yvonne Printemps') voice, not only when she sings, but when she speaks, too, that tears at one's heart ...' declared Noël Coward, who wrote *Conversation Piece* for her.

Pierre Fresnay came from a more serious Classical world, of universities and professors, but there were no objections when he decided he wished to be an actor. He joined the Comédie française at the age of eighteen but, rigorously honest and uncompromising by nature, he became disillusioned by the abuses of petty power and privilege he found there. His efforts to persuade the august House of Molière to move with the times created something of a scandal, and he left them in one of his rare but furious rages and was condemned to pay a fine, which weighed heavily upon him for many years.

Twenty years separated the Guitrys in age, and when Sacha could no longer play a 'jeune premier' role and engaged Fresnay in his place, the outcome was inevitable. Everyone predicted that without Sacha's guidance, Yvonne Printemps would cease to exist, but they were proved wrong. In 1937, with *Les Trois Valses* – an operetta with music by Oscar Strauss – Yvonne Printemps and Pierre Fresnay took Paris by storm, and they were never again to lose the hearts of their faithful public. In 1947 Fresnay appeared in *Monsieur Vincent*, a film that was to bring him international recognition, and a Hollywood Oscar. In his autobiography, *Blessings in Disguise*, Alec Guinness cites Fresnay as one of his three favourite actors, and the one who most influenced his own career.

By the time I had woven the Fresnays (suitably disguised) into a novel, they had become too real to be Pegs any longer. Bing was triumphant, feeling that this proved her point. She had always made her own Pegs into the focal point of some story, and once purged of the creative impulse, her interest in them waned, although a few, such as Ellen Doubleday or Gertrude Lawrence, remained lifelong friends.

Pierre Fresnay's public image was of someone courteous but *très sérieux*; however, he had a lighter, more imaginative side and even a touch of fantasy – without which it would have been impossible to live with Yvonne Printemps. Most people in the public eye are inclined to take themselves rather too seriously; the French are particularly fond of pomp and circumstance – of medals, and rosettes worn in the buttonhole. Pierre Fresnay constantly refused all such honours, although he was proud enough of his wife's *Légion d'honneur*. He was one of the most genuinely modest people I have met; Yvonne Printemps, too, was humble about her voice, which she recognized as being a gift from God. Of all gifts, this has always seemed to me to be the most mysterious, and I once asked her to explain it. She said it was quite simple: all one had to do was to fold air into one's diaphragm, gently, in layers, much as one folded clothes into a suitcase, and then expire it again, equally gently and slowly. I have never tried it but I have no doubt she was right – she usually was.

When Yvonne Printemps was annoyed, it was best to keep out of her way. She had certain idiosyncratic expressions for quickly disposing of the things or people that displeased her: *'à la poubelle!'* (bin it!) was one which particularly amused Bing, and which she often used as a codeword in her letters.

My friend Monsieur Barreyre had known Yvonne Printemps almost from her childhood, and loved her dearly. He was also her 'cher Toto', and she gave him a simple, undemanding affection that she showed to few others. As a very young theatre critic, he had wandered one night into the Folies-Bergères, and had been astounded by a frail twelve-year-old who, dressed in feathers and balancing upon a rose-bedecked swing, sang like a bird. Later, he used to lunch every week with the Guitrys, and when the bird eventually took flight, he was one of the few who remained faithful to Yvonne; and later to Pierre, whom he also loved, and respected.

The Fresnays lived on the other side of the Bois de Boulogne, which is suddenly no longer Paris, but Neuilly. When Flave and I first visited them there, the streets lying between the Seine and the Bois were still the narrow streets of a country town, with lilac and syringa hanging over the high garden walls. Here, they built a house which suited Yvonne Printemps exactly. Today it has been pulled down and a block of luxury flats erected, with a plaque commemorating the previous owners. Perhaps, on a summer evening, someone may be fortunate enough to catch an echo of that enchanting voice, but I have never been back again to try.

The house was as perfect as the garden, and almost as full of flowers. (I remember a full-grown flowering cherry tree, which stood in a Chinese jar, at the bottom of the staircase.) Downstairs, squares of black and white marble gave an effect of coolness and light, with light also reflected in the eighteenth-century panelling, carved with flowers and lutes hanging by ribbons. There was colour, too, in Vuillard's portrait of Yvonne, which hung in the salon, and in the Renoirs and Boudins on the walls. I always loved going to that beautiful house – on summer evenings when the table was laid out on the terrace, facing the lamplit garden, but especially on Christmas Eve, when a party of close friends would gather round the fire in the salon. At midnight Yvonne would sing the traditional French carol *Il est né, le Divin Enfant*, and invite others to join in, although no one did. After the delicious *réveillon* (traditional midnight supper), Pierre would sometimes be persuaded to read poetry to us, in his own beautiful voice; to my eternal waine, I once fell fast asleep, never having been able to sit up much later than midnight.

The Bs and Pegs all met constantly, either at the theatre, in our overcrowded flat, or possibly at some grand Paris restaurant, to which Yvonne would suddenly ring up and summon us – and no excuse was ever accepted. If separated for too long, or away on tour, she would ring the Bs each evening, and the conversation could go on for hours; like Bing, she had to be told every detail of their Day. Pierre would often call for Monsieur B. alone, in order to consult him about their latest production.

By one of life's curious chances, when Monsieur B. wandered into the Folies-Bergères on that long-ago evening, the leader of the troupe of 'girls' had been none other than Meg Villars. She, too, had remained faithful to Yvonne, and was equally devoted to Pierre. Thus, when I returned to Paris, I discovered that all these people, whom I had known and loved separately, were linked together in a mysterious way. With hindsight, I think that I must have been a perfect nuisance to the Fresnays in those early years, and I can only pay a belated debt of gratitude to their immense courtesy and patience. My pre-Villa Racine landlady liked me to go out in the evenings, but as yet I did not have anywhere in particular to go, so would often drop in casually to the theatre, as I had done with my godmother – but without the same excuse. I cannot imagine now why Yvonne Printemps did not *poubelle* me at once, but neither then, nor later, did I hear a word of reproach. Instead, the Fresnays always insisted on driving me home, although doubtless tired themselves by the evening performance.

Mena, the Hut, Wednesday morning, 6 August, 1958.

Dearest Oriel,

I've been trying to put myself in your position, and then I realize that in a sense I've been in it, though in another way, or many varied ways. It's strange, and agonizing, how when one's shuffle seems so 'set fair' the whole thing falls apart, and for that moment there seems nothing left. As though God, supposedly merciful, was saying: 'Very well, since Oriel seems so pleased with life, let her take this one!' (Which people have been feeling down the ages, whether it was old Jehovah, or Zeus.) And then Christ is meant to make this difference. Not, I suppose, to soften the blow, but to say: 'When these things happen, don't be afraid. In my values, there is no death.'

It took me four years or longer, to get over that thing of Gertrude dying, and she was *not* a person who had filled my whole life, as Marraine has filled yours, but a Peg, and a lovely illusion. The Peg had become so vital, and so mixed up with writing, that I felt for the time being, there was nothing left in life at all. The writing had gone too. Rock bottom. When Tommy had that crisis last year (and I was all happy and at ease in my shuffle, with no problems), it was again like a great knock-away of the ground from one's feet. That someone whom I respected and loved should have no sort of backbone, and be indeed a pitiful, weak, *sick* figure. Nearer to Marraine, though so long expected, was the agony of watching poor Mummy have her two strokes and die. I want you to believe that the loss of consciousness, total and complete, of your Marraine, is merciful. But I will say one thing. I can never really fear the finality again, after that strange and unbelievable kiss Mummy gave me from the deep coma. It can't be explained. It just happened. And it was the absence of all pain and ugliness and misery, and the extraordinary *purity* of the kiss, that was so overwhelming. So, wherever Marraine is at this moment, on the borderline, you may be assured that all is well, and her particular shuffle has come clear. I expect you have been through the inevitable routes regrets. *Had* you come over before ... *had* you arranged the stay earlier in the week ... *had* you explained last time you were over that etc, etc. It makes no difference. Che sera, sera.

It's strange that, in your last MS (which I did *like*, you know, it's just that knowing you so well I am more involved in what you do), I still saw the struggle of the non-adult you, the child who protests, 'Don't let the world and "them" hurt me.' Your island could be Marraine – the place of safety. Perhaps this is part of why it all has to happen. You have to stand alone, and not a bitter, Doomed alone, but independent of the Mother. Because really that is what she has been, and a Peg too, in a great deep sense of the mother that went before, and the eternal one that we carry inside us. For some, this dependence is stronger than others. I've carried it for years, because of missing it, hence my 'women' pegs. I think Mummy dying at the same moment that Robert stopped, practically, it's all over.

It's good to help, and you are helping her poor husband, who will be so moper-ish and lost. Active things will help. And I wish I could have been *alone*, so you could come to Mena, and lie in bed, and cry. You will cry later, back in Paris. But don't let the crying make you feel, 'Anything goes now.' That is the test – God's test: shall we see what Oriel is made of?

So much love, Tray.

In July 1958 my beloved godmother had suffered a severe cerebral haemorrhage, and had been rushed to a London hospital for an immediate operation, which failed. For weeks she lay in a deep coma, unable to speak or move, but now and then she would raise one hand in the air, as if playing an imaginary piano. It was my first experience of the mystery that is death, and I had made up my mind to go with Marraine to the very edge of it. I knew the decision was a wise one when, a few days before her death, she suddenly regained consciousness as I was sitting quietly beside her one afternoon. The doctors had warned us that she could not speak, her vocal chords being completely paralysed; nevertheless, after a brief struggle, she opened her eyes and with a radiant smile, whispered quite distinctly: '*Ce n'est pas drôle, ma chérie, mais c'est la fin!*'

This extraordinary event shook my faith in doctors (never very strong), but it revived my belief in the power of the spirit. All happened so quickly, there was no time to call her husband, and later I did not speak of it in case he should feel cheated, for she never spoke again. It brought me great peace, just as Bing had been comforted by her mother's kiss, but I soon discovered that it was wiser not to speak of this to others who had not had a similar experience. To do so was to be met with incredulity, or a hint that my imagination had been working overtime.

My insistence on being with Marraine when she died also seemed to shock people, and there were embarrassed silences when it was mentioned, death being the only taboo left in modern society. Bing was sceptical about those we love still being interested in the world they have left behind, and declared that she herself would like to go on to other, wider spheres; and so we adopted the expression 'beaming down' (*see* Glossary) as a codeword for all such manifestations.

One of the people who had been most faithful during Marraine's illness was the author Naomi (Micki) Jacob. From her home on Lake Garda, she rang the hospital for news each week, and realizing her anxiety, I sent written bulletins in return. Micki was a Yorkshirewoman with a compassion as wide as the ocean for all God's creatures, animal or human, but particularly animal. She and Marraine were at one in this, and each bore the other unstinted admiration. They had acted together several times, notably in *The Nutmeg Tree* by Margery Sharp, in which Micki played the mother of a troupe of acrobatics, with whom Marraine became involved.

To my shame, I once criticized Micki for her eccentric appearance. At first nights, she would appear dressed in a masculine evening suit, complete with monocle, and carrying a silver-headed cane.

'How dare you make fun of someone you do not know?' Marraine had demanded with unusual asperity. 'Micki is one of the kindest women, and one of the bravest. She worked for the Resistance during the war, and has many decorations for her courage. Besides, she has four pekes and five cats, and does stalwart work for those poor, downtrodden donkeys in Spain.' The donkeys clinched the matter, and I never criticized Micki again, although secretly I continued to think her rather peculiar.

I was to know better when, in a typically generous gesture, she invited me to visit her in Sirmione after Marraine's death. Micki loved her home, and had every right to feel proud of it, for all she possessed had been achieved by sheer hard work, and courage. It was a cool but friendly little house, tucked away in a shady garden where the pekes could chase elusive butterflies and bark at intruders through the wrought-iron gates. In her youth, Micki had contracted TB; unable to afford a sanatorium cure, she arrived in Italy with a suitcase and her typewriter. In those days, Sirmione was merely a cluster of cottages on the shores of Lake Garda. Micki lodged with a fisherman's hospitable family, learned Italian, produced her first novel, and fell in love with Sirmione. The theatre remained her first love, however, and I enjoyed hearing her reminiscences of the old music-hall artistes of her youth. Her favourite had been Marie Lloyd, but she spoke equally warmly of Lily Elsie, Ellaline Terriss or George Robey. I listened, as spellbound as when I had tapped Meg's memories of Colette and Willy.

Micki allowed no one to interrupt her working hours, and guests were comfortably lodged in a small albergo further down the street. It was a friendly place, bursting at the seams with large Italian families on holiday, and my Italian improved rapidly. At Micki's request, I had been given a large, cool room on the first floor; every morning, I flung the shutters open upon a blaze of blue sky and, leaning on the sill, watched the fishing boats out on the lake. Across the street from the albergo stood the imposing entrance gates to the Villa Cortina, an exclusive hotel with its private beach. The proprietors were also friends of Micki's, and I was allowed to enter these august portals every morning, and to wander through the shady garden, in which huge scarlet canna lilies grew beneath the umbrella pines, down to the beach. Every afternoon, Micki's devoted secretary called for me in her car, and took me sightseeing round the Lakes, for Micki's social life only began at tea-time.

As usual, I sent Bing a full account of my activities. Piffy was an old friend of Micki's, sharing her passion for pekes, and she too had often stayed at Sirmione. At Bing's suggestion, I despatched a postcard of the Villa Cortina to Pen Friend, choosing the grandest view I could find, although I would not go so far as to pretend I was staying there. In return, I received a delighted letter from the old man, urging me to visit some equally elderly Marchesa on the other side of the lake. I felt this had gone a long way towards making amends for the dissolute life he presumed me to be leading at the Villa Racine.

⚜

Mena, 6 February, 1959.

Dearest Oriel,

I snatched a few days on my own, because Moper being on an upgrade patch was able to go to London alone this week, and seems to have survived OK.

I can't tell you what bliss it was to be by myself in an empty house. (Tod still away, 'seeing folks'.) One day Piffy drove me to the north coast to lunch with an old aunt on holiday there, and I thought afterwards, 'Lord, it's come to this, that driving to Tell-Him talk with an aunt of eighty-one is a change and a stimulation!' Then we called on a cousin of mine, who lives that way too – one of the 'Peter Pan' boys, now sixty-five – and I became very depressed, at him and his brusque wife, living in a dreary little house with an east wind biting at them. I thought back to being three, when he was a midshipman and very menacing, and brought me back a balloon, and jigged me up and down, and was very gay and entertaining, like Kits today – and now he is that grousing, grey-haired man.

Bing at Mena

ABOVE Bing at Mena with Mouse, 1955

LEFT Kits when young

OPPOSITE Oriel at the Villa Racine

BELOW Tod resting after lunch at Mena: 'My dear, I'm worn out! ...'

The Hut, Menabilly

Bing and Kits at Mena

ing meditating in her Hut

ABOVE Bing with Kits and Flavia at Mena

ABOVE LEFT Bing and Moper on *Jeanne d'Arc*

LEFT Family group at Mena, but lacking Tessa

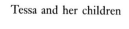
Tessa and her children

Bing and Kits, 1967

I have been thinking about Life, and the shuffle of cards, and you know I have found a better description. At birth, just before conception, God gives us a handful of little coloured strips, and He says to us: 'Look, you can make this into any pattern you like. It is so shaped and coloured that it can become glorious, or depressing, or in-between – whatever you care to trace it for design – and, like a fingerprint, no one else has this particular set of strips. Now, off you go.' And we go whizzing down into our mothers. It is our *choice* that fits them in the shape we make them. And after death, holding our pattern, we go to God and say, 'Look.' And then God says: 'I see. Of course, you could have done this, you know,' and shows us the other combination. And we either say: 'Pheugh! That was a close shave!' or 'Oh *damn*, what a b.f.,' and so on and then, it is quite possible we are given the same pattern again and go whizzing off once more, either here or elsewhere, to see if we can fix a better combination.

I have obviously helped to jiggle Moper into a badly fitting pattern, of this wrong colour, but I still have some pieces in hand before the pattern is complete, which might alter the final design. (Possibly the analogy of a picture in oils might be better than a pattern.)

Marraine *had* to die, but that death can either be put into a great Doom-like cloud showing the picture, or something extraordinarily rare, with the light shining through, and you are now standing in a studio, with the brush in your hand, and undecided about the colour. You hover for a moment or two, over a deep sort of purple – you're not sure – and maybe you decide to lighten it, and when you do, it looks quite different. *It isn't sunset you are painting but sunrise* ... and that makes the rest of the picture out of focus. So you have to alter the design ... Do you see what a fascinating game it can be?

Go out for a walk in two definitely opposite moods. Go determined to see the pain in the faces of people, and the ill-temper, and then after half an hour, say, you must switch, and look for the beauty and the depth. I can't do it here, because I don't see anyone, except Mr Burt sweeping leaves, but I will try when next in London as I hurry along the King's Road! Write a thrashing letter. I'm 'on' to Branwell again and my Brontë collection – for a hobby after tea, not proper work.

Fond love, Bing.

The Flat, Thursday.

Dearest Oriel,

I've just read this,* during the two hours I was waiting for Tommy to come back.

I think it is *very* good indeed, a perfect tribute, and most moving; like Victor, I cried at the end. You have done it quite beautifully, and Marraine would be so proud. It is just the right length, too.

No more for now. Loved seeing you.

All love, Bing.

T. just in. Not too bad. He has been made a GCVO. The Queen very sweet to him.

———

Although outwardly resigned to my godmother's death, inwardly I had not truly accepted it. Well-intentioned people assured me that those we love can never die, while we keep them alive in memory, but I had always considered this a singularly specious argument. Why should existence depend upon anything so fallible as human memory, which diminishes with age? Either there *is* life after death, or we are snuffed out like candles; there is no way round this age-old dilemma, wriggle as we may.

I came home one evening, furiously determined to write down all I could remember about Marraine. I wrote for three successive nights at white-hot speed, filling an exercise book with personal memories, and threw down my pen feeling, for the first time in my life, that for once I had achieved what I set out to do. This *was* Marraine, as I remembered her at home – not merely Yvonne Arnaud, the actress. Bing urged me to publish it, but that did not prove easy. Every editor who read the manuscript wished me to expand it into a full-length biography, and this I did not feel qualified to do. In the end, it was published by Heinemann in time for the opening of the Yvonne Arnaud Theatre at Guildford. What surprised me was the shoal of letters I received subsequently; there were many tributes to Marraine from those who had known and loved her, and these I had expected, but there were also many sincere and moving letters from those who, recently bereaved, had found comfort in its pages; and by these I felt paid in full.

✠

* *Marraine.*

Mena, 19 July, 1959 (Tommy's and my Silver Wedding).

Dearest Oriel,

Bless you for the letter I found on coming back here from London, where I had been to see doctors etc. Tommy is now here, and a good nurse. It is rather like Gran over again in a strange way, and I just know I have to give, and give, and eventually all will come right. I don't mean give in a stupid way, but in a healing and understanding way. I can't go into any details about the breakdown, it is something that has been coming on for months, perhaps years. Only by understanding now can one hope for his health, and mind, for the future. I have been right down into the depths of horror, but I am coming out now. I cannot write a long letter because at this moment part of Tommy's cure is for me to do everything I can for him, all his letters, everything, and be with him. So I must hope my friends – and I know you are very close to me – will understand if I cannot write a long letter. I am so glad your new room at the Villa Racine is such a happy one.

Fondest love, Bing.

———

Later, at Mena, Bing explained to me that Moper had threatened to shoot himself. No one really knew what had sparked off this final gesture; his periodic fits of depression had always been accepted as passing moods, but that this was a cry for help seemed evident. In searching for a reason, Bing cast about in her mind for any, and every solution. Moper was never involved with the person she called the Snow Queen, as she herself later realized. It may have been the culmination of years of tensions, within and without; his courageous war, his work – in which he was perhaps not as settled as he appeared – or his life in London. Bing has often been criticized for not keeping him company there, but this is to ignore the fact that she was the chief breadwinner of a family with expensive tastes, not the least of them being Moper's own desire for bigger and better boats. Her peaceful life at Mena was a necessity for her, if she was to continue to lay the golden eggs with which to satisfy her family's demands, and with her generous nature, she could deny them nothing. Her own tastes were few, and simple; but to maintain a house the size of Menabilly, and later Kilmarth, would have daunted most people in the postwar world.

Someone really qualified might have been able to help Moper come to terms with his highly sensitive and complex personality, but as so often, the only solution seemed to be increasing doses of tranquillizers and pills. Moper's own solution was no less unfortunate; he knew that his capacity for drink was small, the pills reduced it still further, and he suffered acutely from remorse after each lapse. A vicious circle was created from which it was difficult for anyone leading a public life to break free. When the breaking point was reached, Bing bent all her energy on helping Moper survive and win through. With all her love and loyalty, she put her own wishes aside to be with him in London, and to give him her support.

⚜

Mena, 5 December, 1959.

Dearest Oriel,

Many thanks for your letter, which was waiting here when I got back from Yorkshire. Do forgive me for not sending a postcard from Haworth, but I was so madly busy all the time, trying to copy things at the Museum, and escaping Mr Mitchell's Tell-Hims, that I nearly went dotty! Tess was so helpful and efficient in Yorkshire. Not only did she drive the car, but read the maps, which I am hopeless at, and also was interested in tombstones and church records, and we hunted through that Little Ouseburn church – the Thorpe Green place, where Anne and Branwell were – for old marriages and things, and all sorts of things that would have been a fearful Tell-Him to anyone not in the Brontë know, but she did not mind. We went to York, and to Leeds (for Brotherton manuscripts) and to Halifax, to see Sowerby Bridge and Luddenden again, and then to the Black Bull at Haworth, where she left me on my own. The guesthouse had new people, and I was made very comfy at the Black Bull – the pathetic landlord and wife turned out of their room for me! And I did not have to run a gauntlet of the bar; the sitting-room above has a roaring fire, and I had my meals alone in a room at the back, where Branwell used to sit.

Mr Mitchell all over me at the Parsonage, but I nearly died from his Tell-Hims. He had manuscripts ready for me to see in a little student's room apart, in a new building, but instead of letting me dash to look at them, the entire first morning was spent in telling me how difficult the workmen were being, building his new quarters, and how his wife did not want the stove where they put it. I nearly *cried* with frustration, thinking of the manuscripts waiting for me, but dared not move to them, for fear of offending him. He poured out his heart, looking just the same – unhealthy and pale, and making jokes I did not understand. He loathes Miss Gérin (I suppose she would not listen to the Tell-Hims), and said she and her husband were adventurers, just trying to make what they could out of the Brontës. I found myself defending her, because after all, that book on Anne was very good, but *he* said it was just a rehash of everyone else's work. Well, of course, *all* Brontë books are, in a way. The Parsonage was very spruced up with new wallpaper and paint, and will look better when it has worn a bit, but the Tell-Him Bonnell things are all moved, which is good. They had to do up the house to preserve it, and one wishes it could be a bit more shabby.

The other Tell-Him thing about Mr Mitchell, is that when one asks him about the people of *old* days – John Brown, and them – he always *will* start telling one about their descendants, saying: 'Why, old Jimmy Brown, I saw him only last night, John Brown's great-grandson. Now, he went to Australia, and married a girl out there, and they had three children,' etc, etc, but who *cares*? It's the *old* John Brown one wants! If you ask me, nobody there really knows anything any more. And Miss G. can sit in their cottages till she's blue in the face, she will only hear the old Gaskell stories repeated over and over again, and embroidered. Imagine a person a hundred years hence, going down to Polkerris, and asking Gladys' twin's nephew or great-nephews about me – I mean, what *would* they say? 'Well, I know as my Great-Auntie Glads used to tell of her. She was a nice lady but never came down to the village much, but she was always in corduroys, and she had a little Hut, she said, somewhere in the woods, where she would write,' and the old interviewer person would go to the remains of Miss Phillip's cottage in the woods, and get it all wrong. And then a grandchild of that Polkerris person who used to go round saying I was a spiritualist, would remember that, and say, 'My Gran cooked once up at the big house, and she said they were spiritualists up there, and Lady Brown, as she was, used to call up the spirits and get them to write her books. She was always in a trance they used to say . . .'

Really, the only things they *can't* get wrong are probably Wills and Death Certificates, but they would make dull reading! By the way, I got Mrs Robinson's: Lady Scott as she became, Branwell's person, and she had diarrhoea for ten days in London in 1859, and died – poor thing. So that was the end of her!

Tons of love, Bing.

Menabilly, 31 March, 1960.

Dearest Oriel,

I have waited to answer your goodly long letter, because I was on the last lap of Branwell.* I finished this week, and went through him. When I came to the last few pages (which I have put separately, and called 'Post-Mortem') as it is really an extract from Charlotte's letter, about the poor dogs sniffing round and giving her a welcome, when everyone was dead – I cried so much, I couldn't see through my specs!

My own non-Branwell news is that Ellen is flying over in April, and I have promised to unveil a plaque to my grandfather outside the house in Great Russell Street (Doubleday office). Winifred and Barbara, all beaming, want me to do it, with them watching, and Ellen insists on representing the firm! I don't know what I *do*; just pull a string, I suppose. I *shan't* make a speech!

Kits and I have a plan for both of us in June. His TV series will be over, and he wants me to go with him, plus his car, and tour round Italy for three weeks! I must say, I would adore it, and such fun to be with him abroad – Venice, etc. I have not yet broken the idea to Moper, but I do pray he won't be sniffy, and that it will work out. He is so much better now, and over his flu and pleurisy, and that nerve thing also seems so completely gone. So I do hope it will be OK in June. We plan to go after Whitsun.

Flave and Alastair are here for a few days. Flave has done her hair in a bun, and it makes her look ten years older. Piff saw Rupert last week, when she was up that way, and loved him, and said he looked like me! I can't *wait* for a Track-like grandson! Moper is potty on him. It's psychological politics, he would probably have liked a little afterthought son, far better than the children we had!

I'm sure I did not want security when I married. But I was very menaced by Moper, and he was not the sort of man who would *not* have married, he was not the 'affair' type. And after all, my mother was a very basic type of woman, so I must have inherited the normal thing of a woman wanting to be married from her, and from Daddy's mother, also a basic type. It's the Witherspoon and 'chore' thing that I unconsciously hated (just like Flave does now), and in spite of all his tantrums, I really loved Moper. You *must* really love a person to marry them, and be prepared to put up with faults galore. That old 'better-for-worse' thing must be faced!

I don't foresee the Villa Racine for you for ever but I think, with Pegs

* *The Glass-Blowers.*

put aside, it's time for another Main stock-take, as to what you see yourself moving towards. Small flat? Small house? France whate'er betide? Or not?

All love, Track.

————

The Poet, his task accomplished, left the Villa Racine and I inherited his room. It was larger than my own, and had three windows overlooking the garden; I could still watch the monks at work, raking the gravel paths. One end of the room had been arranged as a sitting room, with a sofa and armchairs grouped about the fireplace, and the walls were lined with book shelves. I loved this room for its elegant proportions, but I had not been in possession long when our life at the Villa came to a sudden end. One bright spring day, I came home to find a polite note, informing me with infinite regrets that we must soon begin to look for a new place in which to live. The proprietors, who spent more and more time now in the country, had come to find the house and shop a heavy burden, and had decided to sell, and retire.

For Gordon and Lee, the blow was greater, for they had been there so long, but the choice was simpler for they *had* to stay close to the Abbaye, and before long found a charming duplex further down the street, where our concierge, Madame Pernod, continued to cherish them. I could count on no such certainties, and when Bing asked me what I saw ahead, I had no answer to give her. 'France, whate'er betide?' she asked, and I was not even sure of that. Every morning I searched the property columns in the *Figaro*, but the truth was that the Villa Racine had set too high a standard for my purse, and nothing less would please me.

I had almost given up hope, when one day a few lines of small print at the bottom of the page caught my eye. They read: '*Houseboat for sale, close to the Bois. Tout confort, jardin.*' It was the garden which settled it; within an hour I was on my way to the furthest edge of the Bois de Boulogne, where it joins the leafy suburb of Bagatelle. In those days, the Bois was still a pleasant place where it was possible to feel the country close at hand. There were no traffic lights, and people could picnic or walk their dogs in perfect safety; no taxi would refuse to cross the Bois, even late at night. Later, I sometimes came home at dawn when all was fresh and green and once, at full moon, heard a nightingale singing his head off. The taxi driver stopped his engine and we listened, enthralled.

The houseboat was one of a long line of boats moored between the

Pont de Neuilly and the Pont de Puteaux. Some had once been to sea, but were now firmly attached to the land by all mod. cons. – mains water supply, electricity and telephone. Others were converted barges, like the ones we saw plying their trade up and down the Seine, while one or two were simply wooden chalets on stilts. These were always the most nautical of all, with lifebelts festooned about them and door-knockers in the shape of anchors. The one I had come to visit had once been the ticket office of those pleasure steamers known as the *bâteaux mouches*, further down river. It was comfortable and roomy enough within, with a modern kitchen and bathroom; and on the bank was its garden, containing a stone urn filled with geraniums, and willow trees trailing their branches in the water. It was for sale, fully furnished and equipped. I had only to write out a cheque, walk in and take possession. Thanks to my agent Odette Arnaud, I had money in hand – and I forgot that summer does not last forever.

I still remember the consternation that greeted me that evening, when I burst into the dining room at the Villa, and announced with pride that I had bought a boat. 'Are you sure you haven't burned one?' Gordon and Lee demanded pertinently, but once they saw I was serious, they were kind and helpful. I needed encouragement, for everyone else predicted Doom. The boat would be damp and unhealthy in winter, I would be robbed and murdered by *clochards*, who would be lurking in the garden at nightfall ... If nothing else, the boat would sink and drown me in the Seine. Had I thought to have the structure surveyed? Was the boat insured? I had done none of those sensible things, and the wise held up their hands in horror. To my surprise, Meg Catusse was one of the few people who supported my choice. 'If you want it, then do it,' she advised. 'Never look back. Life is too short for regrets.'

She was right. The five or so years I spent in *La Ronde des Heures* ('the Dance of the Hours') were supremely happy ones – and sound investments do not always buy happiness.

Once settled on board, I could not have taken more pride in my boat if she had been a stately Spanish galleon, and much time was wasted in swabbing decks and polishing brass. Moreover, by the acquisition of *La Ronde des Heures*, my desire to live in a purely French community was granted in a way that would not have been possible elsewhere. One can live for years in a Paris flat without getting to know one's next-door neighbours; especially since the concierges, who once buzzed like flies in their curtained *loges*, have all now been replaced by letterboxes. The houseboats formed a closely-knit community, by necessity if not always by choice. Living on a river has its dangers as well as pleasures, and everybody had to be willing to lend a friendly hand when the dreaded cry went up: *'La Seine monte!'* This happened almost every spring, and sometimes in the autumn, for although the Seine is not a tidal river, at this time there were few barrages to control the floods.

Our boats were moored along a pleasant Boulevard (which has since become a *voie express*) facing the island of Puteaux, which divided the river and protected us from the sand-barges on their way to Paris, which were forced to use the other side. I often used to cross the river and visit the lock at Suresnes on the opposite bank, to watch the barges go through and talk to the people who worked on them. At Christmas, each barge carried a lighted tree on its prow, winking cheerfully through the dusk. The *marché* was cheaper on this side of the river, also bigger and noisier, although the same stallholders could later be found in the small covered *marché* of our exclusive district, Neuilly. Those who were forced to count their *sous* would cross the Pont de Puteaux and take advantage of this. I had not yet realized how exclusive were those who lived on land, for the corner of Neuilly where our boats were moored was full of big houses and gardens with high stone walls over which, in spring, lilac and wisteria blossomed. The narrow streets were still cobbled in places, and lit by old-fashioned gas lamps. But even then, their hour had struck; one by one, the old houses were being pulled down, to be replaced by blocks of expensive modern flats, of the kind advertised in Paris as being of *'grand standing'*.

There was something odd, some touch of fantasy or imagination about my neighbours on the river, however grand their boats might be – and some were grand indeed, with swimming pool or garden on the roof, trellised with climbing plants. Some of the owners had lived on, or near the sea for most of their lives, but there were musicians, painters, actors, and even explorers.

My next-door neighbour was the possessor of the largest, most imposing boat on the river, but it was also one of the shabbiest. Once, long ago, it had plied its way up and down the Rhine, and had two enormous mahogany paddle wheels like the Mississippi steamer in *Show Boat*. She could not afford to keep it running, however, and the wheels had been laid up in dry dock or perhaps even lost overboard, for she was an extremely scatty, temperamental lady, albeit an artist of talent (when she had time to concentrate). Many of her pictures were in private collections, and an enormous mural decorated one of the Paris post offices. She had been married three times, but when I knew her had settled down and was bringing up her third child, a son, in the most conventional manner possible. To achieve this, she was forced to take in paying guests, who frequently went off without paying. Fortunately, during the years I knew her, her own private apartments were let to a businessman who went off to work each morning, complete with briefcase. They rarely met, but he paid the rent with commendable regularity, which was all that was required of him. He had asked my Mississippi neighbour to engage a *femme de ménage* to clean his apartment once a week, and I often wondered whether he suspected that this task was performed by his landlady herself, who gratefully pocketed the extra cash which he left out for her each Saturday. The fiction was maintained to the end, and polite messages left for this invisible charlady whom, wisely, he never asked to meet.

Other smaller cabins were let to students in return for help with painting and maintaining the boat. They were of varied nationalities, but were all uniformly helpful and charming. Apart from painting, my neighbour's other passion was music. She had installed a grand piano in the deckhouse, on which she played *fortissimo* – the sound floated over the water between us, and I loved to listen.

⚓

Mena, 7 July, 1960.

Dearest Oriel,

Your letter of 23 June reached me here at home yesterday, having trekked all the way from Venice, then Rome, then to Whitelands, and so here! I was glad to hear from you, and by now you will have made firm plans about the houseboat.

Yes, I did write to you from Venice, so you should already know something of our trip. It was all great fun, but pretty exhausting, because Rab's car is very cramped for a passenger. Of course, seeing Venice or Rome with someone like Kits is very different to old Pen Friend. There is no doubt that old Pen Friend is jolly good as a travelling companion. His bearded old appearance makes waiters swarm, one gets the best attention, and he is so good for sightseeing, which I love. Kits has no interest in any culture, or old building. All he wanted to do was to watch people, or go shopping – and I hate shopping! On the other hand, he was not like Flave and shy of languages. He made a flourishing effort, with gesture and accent, at both French and Italian, and of course was very amusing company, mocking everyone. I told him those two stories from K.M. about the purple-faced Englishman calling out '*Où est* Cook's *homme?*' from the train, on arrival in France; and the same man saying, '*Niente, niente*, these Italians are famous beggahs!' on arrival in Italy. This so amused him that he was quoting them all the time – in a Pen Friend voice – and I was terrified real Italians would hear him say,

'These Italians are famous beggahs!' as touts approached with postcards!

Like you, he has a fearful thing against English Witherspoons, whom he calls Cutfishes (from some Eton slang), and yet is fascinated when they are at the next table in hotels. He says one knows what they are going to say before they open their mouths. I was terrified people would see his giggles. I agree, they *do* have Tell-Hims, one overhears them. There is always a doddery, retired Colonel type of Father, and an old shaggy-haired Tray of a mother, and an irritating married daughter, and a son in a blazer. The trains coming back were full of them. June is really too late to go. It was fearfully hot, and Rome stifling. All one wanted to do was to lie down. And it's so silly to go all that way to lie panting in a hotel bedroom! Still I'm glad we went, and I think he enjoyed it all, but I feel America, and Latin America at that, is really his cup of tea! I would like a leisurely winter in Rome, and really get to feel 'in'.

I expect Branwell's galleys soon, and hope all that will be over by the time you come, so there will be no work.

All love, Tray.

※

Mena, Sunday 9 October, 1960.

Dearest Oriel,

I had a feeling you must have had 'flu. Isn't that just the thing one dreads? Ill, on one's own, and in another country, however much one loves it. Are you sure it *was* flu you had, and not some horrid virus you picked up in Elba?

Have you ever thought how frightened you would have been if, as a child, you had suddenly seen yourself in the future? I mean, supposing you, in Wales, aged eight and with your mother still alive, had suddenly been shown yourself *now*, alone in a houseboat on the Seine, with flu! I *can't* believe you would have been excited; you would have thought, 'How frightful. That white-faced thing in bed there *can't* be me!' Likewise myself, playing on the Heath with Jeanne, would be aghast to see an old grey-haired Track, doing her monthly bills at what used to be Mummy's desk, and knowing nothing at that age of Mena, would think it some shabby, old, Doomed house! So, if we would be frightened *then*, how much more frightened at thirty years hence? Track crippled, in some Old People's Home, and you – heaven knows – rather bad – moody, aged about sixty, and living heaven knows where. It's like the Brontës and their birthday notes – not seeing ahead, thank goodness! One clings to present security.

Your P. S. about the good news of a dramatic adaptation of *Sun Horses* suggests that you are going to write it yourself? What a glorious crumb! I see Nancy Mitford has written a book called *Don't Tell Alfred*, and I bet it gets rave notices. It comes out the same week as poor Branwell, who will be chucked. There is some hope re the Mena lease, by the way. It seems the heir will consent to a continuation of our lease, but no news yet for how long, or details.

Do write again when you are feeling a bit better. Take it easy now, and don't have a relapse. This Dooming, floodish weather is everywhere, and I bet '*la Seine monte!*'

Tons of love, Bing.

———

'La Seine monte!' was no joke but a dangerous reality when, with the spring and autumn floods, we rose almost to the level of the Boulevard. When we reached the tops of the trees, warning signals went out, and it soon became difficult not to become entangled in their branches. My Mississippi neighbour was forced to keep her kitchen porthole wide open, to avoid the glass being splintered by the invading branches. This made the boat extremely draughty, except in the kitchen, where the branches burgeoned and blossomed as if in spring, and she used them to hang her towels out to dry. One particularly rainy year, when the floods came early, she decorated the branches with coloured balls, and later forgot all about them. When we descended to the normal level of the river once again, it was almost impossible to believe that we had once been perched like giant birds, so high in the treetops. All through the summer, those Christmas baubles sparkled and tinkled in the breeze, and strollers along the Boulevard could be seen to stop, gazing upwards in amazement.

The floods left behind a layer of thick mud, like dark chocolate cream, which covered the gardens; everything planted seemed to thrive, and even the roses came to no harm from weeks of immersion under water. Never since have I seen such wonderful blooms as in the deep crimson, scented rose which twined itself round the trunk of an old tree at the water's edge; and ropes of orange and yellow nasturtiums cascaded down the banks into the water. To get rid of this mud was backbreaking work; my Mississippi neighbour made use of her students, and I invited the most stalwart friends to Sunday lunch, later inveigling them into doing some brisk work with a shovel. Most people were only too pleased to spend a

Sunday afternoon on the river; at weekends, our quiet backwater became animated, with oarsmen rowing up and down in their light skiffs, and an occasional motorboat, rocking *La Ronde* in its wash, and causing fury and perturbation among the anglers. A line of them sat in midstream, in flat-bottomed boats hired from 'Le Martin Pêcheur', a café-restaurant next door to my Mississippi neighbour, who carried on a brisk guerrilla war with the *patron* when he allowed his boats to move into her territorial waters. The 'Martin Pêcheur' catered mainly for fishermen, but often we gathered on its terrace on summer evenings for a glass of wine and a plate of *frites*, and chatted to the fishermen, who came from the other side of the river. They were a friendly bunch, and I liked to see them peacefully afloat in midstream, feeling that they would hasten to my rescue, if *La Ronde* should sink.

My first experience of 'La Seine monte!' had been traumatic. The previous owners had closed the boat each winter and moved to a less hazardous life ashore; in consequence, *La Ronde* was but ill-equipped with planks, ropes and all the necessary things to anchor it securely to the land. That first winter, I lay awake one night, aware of a sinister gurgling noise beneath me. This, I soon learned, was the sign of rapidly rising water, and it seemed likely that I would find myself floating out in midstream by morning. The ducks had elected to sleep on the mat outside the front door, and kept me company by quacking gently in their sleep. I hoped they might take off the minute anything fatal occurred, and prayed that I might be able to swim to shore as swiftly.

It was now that the community spirit of the houseboat-dwellers came to the fore; my neighbours did not only offer me wise advice, but solid planks, to bridge the widening gap between *La Ronde* and the shore. The boats were skewered to the banks by long thin tree trunks, with pointed ends like pencils, called *écoires*. These kept us stable, but they had to be moved up and down the bank as the level of the water rose with the spring floods, and this was a task far beyond my own strength.

My neighbours introduced me to Monsieur Bourguignon, who lived on a small craft further down the river and worked on the lock at Suresnes. Each morning, as he bicycled to work, he elected to keep an eye on *La Ronde*, and to deal with anything requiring prompt action.

On this particular occasion, the Seine rose so swiftly that within half an hour an ominous gap appeared between the gangway and the shore. This had to be speedily bridged, if one was not to be marooned for days, or even weeks. Monsieur Bourguignon pointed out that my gangplank would be totally inadequate in such an emergency, and he strongly advised me to get in touch with '*une maison sérieuse*' who would provide me with something more solid and trustworthy. He brought along his own Bible, the *Marine Directory*, and we perused this from cover to cover, but so many *maisons sérieuses* were listed that it was impossible to make a choice. Finally, I stuck a pin into a short list and hoped for the best.

Next day, a grave gentleman looking far more like a banker than a sailor, called upon me to discover what exactly was needed. He took extensive measurements of both the boat and the shore, then informed me that in his opinion, the best solution would be a telescopic gangway made of aluminium, which would be both light and solid. This could be extended to any length required, and would be hooked to a ladder climbing up the bank, thus providing me with an emergency exit, when the steps were under water.

It sounded perfect, and I realized that my future on the Seine depended on acquiring a telescopic gangway as quickly as possible. All the same, certain doubts assailed me and I hastened after him to enquire, as tactfully as possible, if he was really certain that all his diagrams and measurements would work out, when translated into solid fact. He smiled, and bowing with impeccable *politesse*, said gravely: 'Have no fears, Mademoiselle. Our firm helped equip both the *Normandie* and the *France*, and so far, everyone has pronounced our work to be satisfactory.'

Not only did my telescopic gangway work perfectly, but the bill was more reasonable than I had dared to hope. Once in place, I invited all my houseboat neighbours, and Monsieur and Madame Bourguignon, to inspect it. They were full of admiration and *La Ronde*, forgetting her humble origins with the *bâteaux mouches*, swelled with pride. Moper, too, became interested in my telescopic gangway. I showed him the diagrams, whereupon he pronounced the constructors to be 'first-class chaps', his highest accolade. Bing threatened to write to Pen Friend, so that he could boast of 'my friend's houseboat on the Seine at Neuilly, equipped by the same firm as the *France* and the *Normandie*'.

ༀ

Mena, 27 September, 1961.

Dearest Oriel,

I am so sorry I couldn't get a letter to you in time for your return.

The thing is – no need to tell you – I've had a frightful time with Moper again. Another bout, just before Doodie came. Then he got on his feet for the visit, which lasted from the Sunday to Thursday of last week, and which went off like a bomb. I expect he did not want to lose face in front of them, especially the daughter, who he took to immediately.

I must admit, she is a very sweet kid, and I loved her. Old Doodie rather dotty about her, and it is a wonder the child is not spoilt. But she is not. They had scarcely been gone before another frightful bout came on, so bad that I could hardly get him up to bed, and I was really frightened. The weekend was frightful, and he had to be got on his feet to go to a meeting in Truro today, and there are others all this week. I don't know how he will get through them. The doctor says he must have a drastic cure, but wants to do it here at home, with a nurse in the house. It will last about a week. Meanwhile, I had promised Kits I would go for a week to Aldeburgh with him, when he came out of hospital – this coming weekend. Obviously, Tod has now got to go instead, but if I can get away before the treatment is due, and if Moper is OK, I will go, because if I don't, I think I shall go dotty! I have had my galleys of *Castle Dor*, and that kept me going for a bit, correcting them.

Fond love, Tray.

⚜

Mena, 3 January, 1962.

Dearest Oriel,

I know it's about your birthday time, and it's so ignorant of me always to forget the real date. I can't think *why* I do, when you always remember mine. Anyway, I hope this letter arrives near the day, and many happy returns. I like the sound of 1962 much better than I did 1961 – I don't know why – the 2 looks better than 1, so perhaps I prefer even numbers! I do hope that it's a better year for myself, selfishly, and that it's a splendid year for you – it ought to be, with Main things piling up! First, I would like you to have a great success with the play, and then to bring off a triumphant Arcadia – and then to move into a bigger houseboat, or better still (imagining you have made a lot of money), into a cosy studio flat in Paris, and a heavenly little hideout somewhere in the country.

Do you ever have a silly sort of imagining thing that I do at times? I lie in bed, and imagine towns and villages, and what is happening at *just* that minute. For instance, I will think of a particular bit of Paris, a street corner – say the Rond Point or somewhere obvious, and try and 'see' exactly what stream of cars are passing at *that* moment, and the faces of the people walking by. Then I'll switch to Red Square, Moscow – it doesn't have to be a place one has been to (tho' it's better to do), and I'll think of silence, and snow falling, and suddenly a dark saloon car, and perhaps an old crossing-sweeper woman – anyway, it's such an absorbing game, and makes one feel like God looking down upon the world below, with a sweeping comprehensive gaze! It's a good game for sending one off to sleep.

Meanwhile, how goes the boat, and were the pipes frozen? It's been bitterly cold here, but no snow – rather disappointing, I do love it – but sunny and frosty, and tho' I still have a dreary sniffy cold, it's better than it was. Moper in good form, long may it last. I think he *liked* his quiet Christmas, he felt like Mr Darling in his kennel, with Mrs Darling concentrating on him, and Nana too, but I felt awfully like Mrs Darling with the empty beds, and I suddenly wondered if Barrie meant the flying away partly symbolic of how a mother feels when the children have grown up. I could have cried for twopence. It was not the grandchildren I missed, but somehow my own children young – Flave and Kits running about, with their stockings. I'm told Peter Pan is ruined now, with the pirates turned into silly comics, and the Lost Boys are put into prep-school clothes, can you imagine anything more silly? I adored those jerkins and berets they used to wear, which was how my Aunt Sylvia dressed all her boys, the originals, and I have lovely photographs of them dressed like it, in an old book. Oh well, it's so long ago – 1903 – I suppose they had to alter it in 60 years – it's amazing they keep it so long. But a tremendous jeer goes up now when Peter says, 'Do you believe in fairies?' so I am told – not in London, but in the provinces, which shows the dooming lack of imagination in children.

Old Phyllis Bottome has sent me the second half of her autobiography, I told you, and it's *so* good – the opposite of a Tell-Him, tho' so much about Austria, which actually has never interested me, but she makes the whole thing so interesting, just like a very good novel. You must read it when you come. And I bought myself a Henry James you would also like – *The Princess Casimassima* – which I loved. I have a thing about Henry James, and I love the peculiar way he writes, rather involved. This was an early one, and not too involved.

I'm plugging away at my Busson notes, but nothing has come yet from the research lady in Paris, and I've asked Hoffman *again* to put her in direct touch with me. I wonder if Monica Stirling has this same difficulty with research people, or was she able to do it all by herself at the Archives nationales, and just badger people? I am sure it is the only way. People simply take no notice if you just write letters.

What did you think of *Rebecca* on tv? I don't think it had dated too badly, but some things hit me – and it was silly, the way they made Rebecca hit her head on a block, instead of being shot by Maxim. And they muffed the fancy-dress ball, and the wreck: it was all too hurried, one did not know what was happening. In the book she had to go through the whole Ball without speaking to Maxim, who was on a hard chair beside her, and then it was in early dawn the wreck came. I suppose *you* thought to yourself, now Peg would have been *much* better than Olivier, and it would have worked out rather well, imagining Peg thinking of his first wife, and being plunged in deep thoughts . . .! Of course it was old-fashioned in 1938 when it was written – I remember critics saying it was a queer throwback to the 19th-century Gothic novel. But I shall never know quite *why* it seized upon everyone's imagination, not just teenagers and shop girls, like people try to say now, but *every* age, and *both* sexes. It certainly would not today, which shows how the world has gone ahead in the past twenty years, into a much more scientific, realistic sort of approach. I feel it myself. One terribly wants to get at the *truth*. Which is why I want to know so desperately *how* my Bussons lived, instead of being content to Gondal them. It must be something to do with the age we live in. Imagination, yes, but so that you use it to *perceive* the past, and relive it.

I have been looking into my grandfather's *Peter Ibbetson* again, and it's queer how he had these same feelings about forebears that I have – an almost agonized interest – and how part of his dream in the book was to *become* them in the past, and how they became *him* in the future. I can't think why he did not go out to Sarthe and find out about them *truly*, instead of Gondaling them, for they are there, in embryo, in *Peter Ibbetson*, but he has Gondalled them wrong – making them aristocrats instead of bourgeois – I s'pose a natural Victorian reluctance to be a bit honky!

I must stop, Piff is coming to lunch.

                                        Heaps of love, and happy birthday, Tray.

                                        ✠

Mena, 15 January, 1962.

Dearest Oriel,

It's a bore about there being no news yet of what is to be done re the play, but it's typical of theatre people. You may be kept hanging about for ages, so much better get on with your new brewing.

I am amazed at your *imagination*! In the same way that the ferryman, talking to Piff, was amazed at the film story of *Rebecca*. 'I don't know how Lady Browning thought it all out!' (Nor do I, looking back, but I remember going through torments of creation in the very hot weather in Alexandria, and scribbling the précis in a blue notebook, which Ellen of all people has now!) I am amazed how *you* can suddenly switch to that little girl and the dog kennel, and a host of adventures! You have got the most extraordinary vivid mind! The one snag is, how does the little girl talk to the village children, because she wouldn't speak French, would she? Be sure and have a fairly happy ending – I mean, *don't* send the child back to England. What on earth will you call it?

I've been busy every after-tea-time getting down all my Busson facts into Notes, and this takes me through until dinner-time. At last the Hoffman research lady has sent me some stuff – she sounds nice. What fun if you could meet her – she is a student of Balzac and is doing a thesis on him, but doesn't mind doing research for me *en même temps*.

Apart from these brewings, all has gone well, except I'm worried now about everyone's health *except* Moper's. He is fine, and had three teeth out last week without turning a hair; I should be prostrate. But poor Piff has got to have her gall bladder out next week, which is a nasty op, though lots of people have it these days. She will go into the Fowey Hospital. Tessa has caught chickenpox from her children, and had it *very* badly. Lastly, poor Kits is *still* feeling queer, tho' his appendix has been out for over a month. The doctor at Aldeburgh has finally hoisted in that Kits isn't just making a fuss, and he is to have tests, in case it's some sort of liver disease. I am really very worried – they ought to have checked on this before whipping out the appendix.

I do hate it when they get ill, and are all so far away! And Tod keeps grumbling about Aldeburgh and saying how cold it is. I have had my first US copy of *Castle Dor*, and it looks very nice. No more for now.

Fond love, Track.

※

Mena, 31 January, 1962.

Dearest Oriel,

Many thanks for your good Main letter of last week. First of all, everybody's health. Piff had her op last Thursday and is going along very well now. She felt awful the first 24 hours, and I could hardly bear to go in and see her, I could so imagine how she was feeling. She *is* so plucky about facing ops – as you know, I can't even face having a tooth out!

It was lovely having Tess and Kits. I think Kits' thing *must* have been hepatitis – he looks very pale, but was in good form, and eating well. I think he will be better if he gets a job, as just hanging about at Aldeburgh isn't very good for morale, especially with Tod as a constant moaning companion! Tessa also was OK, but I'm sure she gets fed up with the Grimsby life, and Peter *will* drink so much gin. She has chucked her Menace, so hasn't even a Peg to Gondal about. Moper still in tremendous form, and I go on wondering if it can possibly last.

Yes, it would be a very good idea if you could meet that Mlle Fargeaud. Your excuse could be that I am anxious to know if she got two letters I wrote to her? If she could have got down to St Christophe, and stayed at the little hotel-restaurant, Les Glycines, with that beaming woman, it would be wonderful. She could go to the Mairie, and see if old documents existed of how it was, when my Gt.gt.gt.-grandmother died there in the Revolution, and was called La Citoyenne Busson. The village's name was changed to Rabriat, God knows why – because they hated the 'St' in St Christophe, I suppose. I have got so much in notes now, that I think I shall try and start the book.* It began to brew *fast*, just before Tess and Kits came down, and I'm sure I could start it, and it would flow. I think it must be rather long and Main after all, and not just happening in a single time. I shall make it be told by my old Gt.gt.gt.-Aunt person, to her nephew (my great-grandfather), who had been born in London during the Revolution, and came back to France, wanting to know about his family, and his father etc (all this is true!). He gets a shock when he finds out that they were all for the new Régime, and not aristocrats at all! This will happened in a sort of *avant-propos*, and the first chapter will be the old aunt talking, as though to a nephew, as she tells the whole story of what they were, and so on.

As to your own brewing, I am rather concerned about it, because I thought you were so *on* to the new dog-kennel story? It's worrying that it should have faded so quickly. Yes, I do see that the houseboat is a chore, but it ought not to be such a fearful chore as all *that*, if you can heat yourself soup, or have cold sups at night. I think Peg may be a kind of unconscious stumbling block, and until you can make him a Main person, you won't get him out of your system. If you can, kill him off in the story, because then the Peggishness will go! I know, because when I had that (to me, rather silly, now!) 'thing' about Ellen, which was pure Gondal, it was only by making up *My Cousin Rachel*, and pegging the Rachel woman on to her, and making her die, that I was able to rid myself of it. For writers, the only way we can do it, is to *write* them out. I wouldn't worry about people guessing, who cares?

I don't think I need a Peg nowadays, because I feel so differently about menaces, after having C. of L. The sort of excited urge has left me. But I shall be happily interested in my group of glass-blowers, and if it's a

* *The Glass-Blowers.*

Tell-Him, *tant pis*. But *you* have years before C. of L., so you may as well make good use of all the Gondal urges towards a Peg. I remember doing *Frenchman's Creek* when the children were ill with measles, but so great was my Gondal-Peg urge towards the man in whose house we were staying, that *Frenchman's Creek* absolutely *tore* along! (Anything less like the Frenchman, really, than the poor man, there couldn't be, but I Gondalled him into it, and saw him that way!) Probably Peg isn't really like *your* idea of him at all, but is querulous, and grumbles about his slippers or something, and is mean with the household books! You see, *everything* is as one sees it, in one's prejudiced Gondal eye!

I'm a bit worried about the future of France. I feel it's on the edge of an abyss, and any moment poor old de G. might be bumped off. I don't trust the army. Hope to have brighter news of you next letter. Weather awful. Rain, rain ...

Love, Tray.

————

The adaptation of *Horses of the Sun* was providing me with an excuse not to get down to another novel. After a time, this exasperated Bing, who saw through my flimsy excuses with her usual perspicacity, but she would not believe me when I told her the truth – that I could no longer write the scenes and characters I saw so clearly in my head. The words would not flow, and did not make a satisfactory rhythm. I had read of writer's block, but had never believed it could happen to me. Now it had, and it was a painful and frightening experience. We had never been so close to being at cross-purposes. Bing's insistence that the Fresnays were holding me up was a mistake; with their day-to-day reality, their Peggishness had vanished. The whole point of Pegs is their remoteness, just as a place or a picture loses its grip on the imagination when we draw close to it. It does not seem to have occurred to either of us that I was simply suffering from physical fatigue. To keep *La Ronde* afloat, I had been forced to overtax my strength, ignoring all the warnings I had been given about a quieter life. Nor is it easy to conduct daily life in one language, while writing in another. I had gone in search of wider horizons, and deeper experiences, and with my usual impatience expected to reap a harvest overnight; unaware that the journey towards maturity is a long, slow haul and that those who believe themselves to have arrived, have not even started out.

It was during this period that I came close to death for the first time. One cold and misty evening in February, I returned from a concert in

Paris with friends who dropped me at the boat and drove off into the dusk. Crossing the gangway, I noticed that some dead branches had become tangled with the plastic pipes supplying us with water from the shore. The river was flowing swiftly at the time, and I knew they would be likely to break and cause trouble, so I hurried indoors and changed to more suitable clothes – oilskins and rubber boots. As I poked at the branches, leaning out over the river, my gaffe slipped, plunging me headfirst into the icy water. I surfaced close enough to the boat to cling to the side, but my boots filled with water and, heavy as lead, threatened to drag me under. I knew there was little hope of rescue. No one was strolling along the Boulevard on so wet a night, and all was dark and silent on my Mississippi neighbour's boat. She had gone to the cinema with her son, and would not be back until midnight. There was no one to hear me if I shouted, and it seemed wiser to gather all my strength to keep afloat. My fingers were slipping from the deck, and I realized with sudden cold clarity, that I could not hold on much longer. I felt no fear, nor did the past unroll like a banner before my eyes. I was only conscious of an immense fatigue, and a strong desire to let go and be done with it.

At that instant, I felt a hard blow in the small of my back. A sturdy plank had floated towards me out of the darkness and, by using it as a lever, I was able to haul myself up on to the deck, where I collapsed like a stranded whale. My first conscious thought was that I must have swallowed half the Seine. Knowing what was *in* that water, the mere idea made me violently sick, after which I dragged myself indoors and swallowed some brandy, in the vague hope that it might be a disinfectant. Then, still shivering and shaking, I rolled myself into my eiderdown and fell asleep. I did not boast of this incident, and took care to conceal it, even from Bing. I knew I had failed to observe the most elementary rules of safety on the river, and so far as it taught me anything, it was not to poke about, alone, in the dark, in rubber boots. To wonder how, or why, that plank had happened to be there at that precise moment was idle speculation. Nevertheless, I *have* wondered about it, on and off, ever since.

❦

Mena, 30 May, 1962.

Dearest Oriel,

Such ages since I have written, but I have been so fussed, with endless changes of plans! All due to Kits, who said he would be free to go to Ireland on 15 June, so I fixed accordingly, and then only a few days ago, he heard that Carol was going to start his film in Spain, mid-June. So to get the holiday in beforehand, we have to dash off to Ireland in the middle of next week. I have had to hurry through with the correcting of my *Souffleurs*.* I suppose I'm getting too set in my ways to chop and change at a moment's notice, and I'm all hot and bothered!

Another awful fussing thing is that we have suddenly been warned that the Queen wants to come here on 23 July – to Mena, to tea! She will be visiting Cornwall, and wants to come to Fowey in the Royal Yacht. It is the Doom of all time ... It means a commotion, and all her entourage, and policemen and chauffeurs – how *shall* we manage? It has ruined my summer! Piff says I ought to do up the house but really, one *can't*! It would mean workmen here forever.

Thank goodness *Souffleurs* is finished, but I still don't know whether to let it go to V. G. or not. I shall have it typed while I'm away, and then think about it. I think it's quite good – not wildly exciting or suspense-making, but rather nostalgic and mellow, if you know what I mean? I hate to think of it being put into a yellow cover, and boosted as a story of the Revolution, which only comes into it in the middle part. It's the story of a *family*, plain and simple, written with compassion, if you see what I mean?

                                        Tons of love, will send p.c. from Ireland, Tray.

                                        ❧

Mena, Friday 24 August, 1962.

Dearest Oriel,

Yes, of course, the 17th will do very well indeed (your letter [arrived] this morning, many thanks!). The only pity is that it gets to Equinox time, and the weather will be very doubtful for bathing or basking. It might be that time now, as it rains nearly every day! I haven't bathed or basked for ages, and the grass has got that long, glistening, early-autumn

* *The Glass-Blowers.*

look – Doom, Doom. Having had so little summer, it makes the stretch of winter loom endlessly, especially when one has no work in mind. I thought the other day, that it might be rather fun to have a book of musings, on various things and persons, and call it *A Day in Bed*. Because it's just what one does in bed – not reading a lot, but idly thinking about a number of things, either people in the Past, or Deep Thoughts. No one would buy it, but it would be rather amusing to do. I think it wouldn't be planned, it would be more or less written by mood. But I don't know if I shall get keen enough on the idea, for this winter.

Tod is down, with a lot of chitter-chatter, but not *too* bad, and busy making meringues that don't come off, and lemon creams etc, for the Spences. I don't know if she'll be here or not when you come, but if she thinks you are to be here, I'm sure she will want to see you.

Lots of love, Tray.

✿

Mena, 2 October, 1962.

Dearest Oriel,

So glad to get your letter, and to hear that you had settled in well (sounds like school!). I must say I envy you, just at this moment. I love autumn in Paris, and would love to be strolling about and looking up my old glass-blowing places etc. If by any chance you ever find yourself in the Palais Royale environs, do see if the little boutique in the arcades, No. 255, is still in existence, where my great-great-grandfather, Robert Mathurin Busson, once exposed his *objets d'art*, and where his poor little wife died – at least, she does in my book. I saw it so vividly when I wrote about it, and he definitely lived there, but perhaps the numbers are changed.

By the way, the enclosed was in that writing pad you left. Is it a copy of some prayer? Rather good. But it makes God awfully like a wise, fatherly Peg! God as a super-Peg is rather a thought. One wouldn't need anyone else. I wonder whether all religion is just a development of that feeling? God being a Father-figure Peg to all those who need a Father-figure Peg, and a great wise, comforting Mother to all those who need a great comforting Mother-Peg, and to some rather tender people, *l'enfant Jésus* is also a Baby-figure Peg! Perhaps to people like myself that old thing of Ancestor worship, which African natives sometimes have, and the old Chinese used to, is all part of an unconscious religious urge. My interest in glass-blowers is really like natives carrying the mummies of their ancient grandparents to some old mountain, and sticking them up on rocks, and then going to carry tributes to them once a year!

The instinct to be watched over, and taken care of, is basic to us all, and always has been through the ages. But it takes different forms, according to our upbringing and temperament etc, etc. Which would finally mean that no religion was really better than any other, that each was right according to his notions, and that was that! The only Doom is out-and-out materialism, which denies this spiritual side to our nature. Perhaps the development of that sixth sense you were talking about, would be the answer to many of these things, and we would all be put in touch with whatever this curious instinct is. The Thing is within us, and about us, and it's a question of making contact, like turning on a switch!

Fond love, Tray.

Mena, 19 October, 1962.

Dearest Oriel,

How maddening about *Marraine*. Publishers are all the same. They think of nothing but sales, and unless they've made a whack out of a book, it just gets wiped off and forgotten, no matter how good the reviews. I don't think I had any bad reviews for my Branwell, but right from the start I know old V. G. was bored by the thought of it, and he never made any effort to push it after it was published. It wasn't because of Gerin's, because hers didn't appear until months afterwards. Now, of course, he's all over me again, because he hopes *The Glass-Blowers* will do well. But I don't believe it will sell in great numbers, as it doesn't get exciting until halfway through, and readers are so impatient. But you know my thing these days about no books really selling enormously, except about animals – Elsa etc. Clara Vyvyan was told the same thing by her publisher, Peter Owen. She gets *excellent* reviews always, but her sales are small. She was complaining to Peter Owen, and he said bluntly: 'No one sells nowadays, not even Daphne du Maurier …'! Talking of which, I've just heard there is a great Main thing about my books, in the *Times Lit. Supp.* this week. It's not come yet, and I dread it!

Did you know that you left behind this old scribbling pad? It comes in useful, and there was a little, pale-blue, cheapish biro lying around, which also might be yours. I have found the Missal, in Blue Lady bedside drawer, as you said, and here it is.

The weather has been quite perfect here, too. Really what one calls golden days, and yet rather foolishly I have not bathed – I don't quite know why. I had put away my things, and somehow put summer behind me at the same time. I think if you had been here, and we had both been worked up to it, it would have been different! But I've basked outside the front of the house each day, and gloated. Tommy very well, and thinks he has now sold both boats, but if the new one isn't ready until next autumn, heaven help us all next summer – he will be lost – and so will Bib, for outings!

You could make a good short story, out of the Chevallier people, and their little routes bistro being ruined by publicity! *Do* do it, I can see how good it could be, and you could bring in a little group of subs! But I suppose you can't 'brew', until you hear about the play? The weather has been so heavenly, that *not* brewing hasn't mattered, but directly our horrid clock goes back, and it's dingy by teatime, I shall be lost, unless I can settle to something. In past days when I wasn't working, I used to do my Greek, but I'm off that. I would like to do some short stories, but can't think of one! I expect the thing is, I have got stale, and need a change of scene to ginger me up. Kits is due home in about a fortnight, and I long to see him, but if he is taken up with his Miss Ireland Beauty Queen, he may not want me at Aldeburgh, where it would have been fun, for a week.

Poor Tess is very unhappy. She is finding out more and more about Peter and his goings on – he now admits getting off and waxing with every girl they've had in the house to look after the children. Apparently gloats about it. Tessa thinks he's unhinged. She was in such a state last week she went up to London to see our lawyer, in case she could have a separation, but I do hope she lets her blood cool a bit, and sees if things settle down. The lawyer told her these things are very difficult – legal separations etc are often more difficult to fix than plain divorce. But you see, one must remember that Tessa herself was once what one can call 'indiscreet' a few years ago, and all that would have to be taken into account, if she really started 'proceedings'. I can't help thinking this behaviour of Peter's is a sort of unconscious revenge for that, if he did suspect it, which he probably did. Tessa, of course, *is* rather quick-tempered and impatient, and she says to me that she is *damned* if she is going to spend the rest of her life with someone who not only drinks, but is constantly and continually unfaithful, and completely hopeless about money. Well, one sees her point. If only he could make a fresh start – being a Catholic, one would think some very noble priest could have an influence on him. Those Jesuits at Farm Street can be brilliant, psychologically, I remember Alec telling me. Oh dear, oh dear, it *is* worrying when one's children's lives start to become unhappy. Short of boosting up a new Trust for Tessa, which I have done with the *Glass-Blower* serial, I can't *do* anything. If Peter won't go to a priest, I wish *she* would. I am sure they would give wise advice. I mean, surely they wouldn't just say, 'Dear child, this is a cross you must bear,' but would suggest a helpful course of action, don't you think? Not just any old Dodderer at Grimsby, but a really good Farm Street man. Tessa was so good at being a Catholic a few years ago – and gave me my rosary and Main Missal when I was unhappy about Moper in 1957, which helped me a lot, and now when she comes to her *own* crisis she is ready to chuck it up, and says it's been no use to her. I'm sure it's because she doesn't have any good priest to go to. She needs a kind of good, wise Peg. How good *he* would be! I'm afraid I'm being a bit like Ferdie and her Tell-Hims about this. But you are always so interested and sympathetic. I haven't said much to Moper, and nothing to Tod, because I don't want them to be put off Peter, in case it all settles down eventually.

Flave rings up from time to time, and seems OK. Her menace in Henley has had a riding mishap, so that keeps *him* at a distance for a time. Perhaps just as well! I always feel if Flave found a real menace, she might do something silly, and be off like a gun.

Tod goes back to London tomorrow. Rather a relief. She was beginning to get on Moper's nerves. She is so deaf, and says such silly things, and always seems to get hold of the wrong end of the stick. For instance:

TOD: My dear, I hear on the news that France is now bullying poor little Monaco.

SELF: (*patiently*) No question of bullying, Tod. There are a lot of firms in Monaco who are set up there to evade tax. Naturally the French government want to stop this.

TOD: Well, I don't know, the French government would be better employed clearing up the mess they've made in Algeria.

MOPER: (*beginning to grind his teeth*) Algeria has been independent for months now. What happens there is not the concern of the French government.

TOD: Well, a lot of French people *live* there. When I came back from Constantinople in 1923, the French had everything under control.

You see, one can't *begin* to explain!

No more for now. I hear the old gong go, and it means steaks are served. Let me know when you hear from Stevens. I'm so glad your old heart is better!

Fond love, Tray.

⚜

Mena, Friday 9 November, 1962.

Dearest Oriel,

Many thanks for your very Main letter that was written on 25 October, and for your PC today – such a pretty one, too! – with its gentle hint that I had not written. I don't know how it is that time goes so fast, for God knows I'm not doing anything! I seem to have been going into the town in the morning, for shopping – which I never do in summer – and odd jobs like planting out wallflowers (Tod!), and the Burts are on holiday, so I vaguely – *very* vaguely – cope with the evening meal. And I hate writing letters after it gets dark, I don't know why. It's just not routes. Unless I have the morning free they don't get written, except bills and things that have to be answered promptly.

I must tell you, I read Teilhard de Chardin in bed – another thing that made me late getting up! and liked it very much, but of course a whole lot of it I knew so well from Jung, and all his volumes, which you know I have been collecting for years. You ought to read *one* of them, at least, when you are next here, but that *Modern Man in Search of a Soul* ought to be in paperback by now. Did you know I once, a year or so ago, waded all through Thomas Aquinas, so I am up in him, too?

The Zulu front is a bit static at the moment, tho' Peter is apparently on the drink again, and what has actually happened to the German girl no one seems to know – she is supposed to have gone to France! I wanted Tessa to get in touch with the *very* nice level-headed Baroness person who runs the Grail, she might be better than a priest, but anyway she could advise on the best priest to go to. I think Peter is really in need of some help and advice right now, but he ought to be in some really good clinic run by monks (if such a thing exists!). He obviously needs thorough and proper medical treatment, combined with psychology. The children apparently are being very good, which is rather strange, but maybe they have sensed that something is amiss, and are reacting in a nice way. The idea is that they shall all come for Christmas, and I hope they do, as it would make Peter see we have nothing against him. If only Kits would come, he would make it all go! Re the Beauty Queen, he has got off with Miss Ireland of 1961 (last year's one), and they have been going it great guns over in Ireland. Now he is back, and she is in Manchester, or some place (she is a model), so they are not together, but heavens knows what they get up to at weekends! Kits is very frank, and says it's the first time he has been properly menaced. He says she is *not* a fool, but sits gazing into the fire, and reads Yeats! Anyway, I can't go and stay at Aldeburgh if she should be there, so must wait to hear their plans. (This also funny!)

The Carol film has finished, and Kits doesn't want a job before the New Year, but wants to do a short one of his own, with friends, like he did before. He asked me to think of a script, so I quickly thought one out this week, and sent it to him. A foreign girl (script called *Au Pair*) comes to London, and goes to a house where the husband tries to get off with her, and she has to go, and she can't get another job. She can't speak English, gets into a dreary nightclub and hates it, and then tries to be a companion to an old woman, who turns out to drink, and so on; and eventually has no money left, and we know the inevitable will happen.

The point is, the whole effect must be of wet streets, and loneliness, and the awful thing of trudging from address to address, with suitcases, and English people being horrid. I am longing to know if it appeals to Kits. I think it may. It's just a short film, about an hour. Can *you* think of an idea? As mine may be no good. But you must remember it will be acted by amateurs, so must not be too difficult. A lot of exteriors (interiors so difficult to do). Flave is apparently *brimful* of ideas, and good ones too. But I think she would crumb to get hers done by pros, whereas my 'au pair' thing was just to help Kits from passage wandering, until he gets a new job. (The au pair girl could be acted by the Beauty Queen!)

About your religious Main letter, I ought to discuss it when you next come. Or in another letter, when I've been having some Deep Thoughts. One must be in the vein! I sometimes get great veins of religious thinking, but have not had one lately. It generally comes with trouble. I agree, one does have to read a lot, and think, and study, to come to terms with trouble. That thing of loving God comes on in great waves, sometimes, with suffering, and I suppose it is very mixed up with emotional reaction. It's impossible to do, just with the intellect. And not everyone's emotions react in the same way. One might say, to someone blind with misery, 'Offer your misery to God,' and it could mean nothing. I think this is why the early Christians turned with such relief to Jesus. He seemed so much closer, and some of them had even known Him. It must be difficult today, for young people who have had the minimum of religious education, to feel the actual *personality* of Jesus – any more than you or I, admiring Socrates, could really be helped by the idea of *him* taking his hemlock nobly, centuries ago! Loving God is a queer, inner, 'aware' thing. I think it only strikes a person with a flash, at strange moments. And for a great many simple, ordinary folk – say like my old Aunt Billy, who has always been what is known as 'religious' – it is a thing like respecting the King or Queen, really second-nature to someone well brought up, and not to be separated from routes church on Sunday, and prayers.

To switch entirely – any news from that Stevens man? If he has written, be sure and tell me what he has said, and if he wants changes etc. I long for a short break. It's such autumn, with falling leaves, and the same routine, day after day. Moper fine though. No more for now.

Fondest love, Tray.

One day, a mysterious letter had appeared in my letter box. It was post-marked New York, but bore no address that I recognized. It informed me that the writer, who had been given a copy of my *Horses of the Sun* to take on holiday, had greatly enjoyed reading it and would like to get in touch with me, with a view to adapting it for the stage. The signature, Roger L. Stevens, meant nothing to me at the time, and I concluded that it was either a mistake or a joke. I meant to show the letter to Odette Arnaud, but my thoughts at this time all revolved around the roof of *La Ronde*, which had sprung a leak. So I put the letter away, until some time later, when lunching with Gordon and Lee, I mentioned it casually in conversation.

Their reaction was swift and violent. Lunch was interrupted, while they searched through a pile of old *New Yorker*s to find one which contained a profile of Roger L. Stevens. From this, I learned that he had recently been appointed Director of the Lincoln Center in New York. A frantic search for the letter reminded me that I had shut it into a book I had been reading at the time, and which had since been returned to the library. Once again, I was luckier than I deserved to be. On hastening to the library next morning, I found the book still on the shelf, and the letter inside it. I answered it, just in time to catch Mr Stevens before he and his wife set off on a trip to Europe. They came to see me on the boat; both were delightfully easy, simple and charming, and I greatly enjoyed our meetings, both in Paris and London.

Nothing came of the plan to adapt *Horses of the Sun* for the stage; apart from the production costs, which would have been enormous, there were casting problems to be overcome. One of the subs, for which Bing so often mocked me, was a donkey with a fairly large part to play in the plot; and no donkey with star quality appeared. Much as I would have loved to be working in the theatre, I was not too disappointed, for I had never really seen my story as a play, although had my godmother been there to play the principal character, a wayward, autocratic Contessa, it might possibly have worked – and *she* would certainly have enjoyed playing opposite a donkey.

Various adaptations were made, but all failed for more or less the same reasons. Each time, I found myself slightly better off, and this too seemed wrong, for *Horses of the Sun* had cost me nothing to write. I had tossed it off in a kind of golden Cotopaxi dream, and it had already enabled me to buy *La Ronde*, and brought me other, equally valuable things, such as friendship and goodwill. I had no cause for complaint.

🕉

Mena, Sunday 2 December, 1962.

Dearest Oriel,

I am so *dreadfully* sorry to have to say No, about your suggested pre-Christmas visit. It would have been a perfectly good moment, but for this unexpected setback of Moper's!

I went off on 20 November, leaving him in very good form, healthy and cheerful. I rang him every day, and he sounded absolutely OK. I had my week with Kits at Aldeburgh, and got back to London on 28th – had an amusing dinner with old Pen Friend, and up to Hampstead on Thursday to lunch with Irene. When I rang Moper on Wednesday night from the flat, he said he had a beastly chill. I thought little of it, as one does get chills at this time of year, so I was not prepared for what I found. I got the Riviera on Friday, and he was on the platform to meet me. I saw at once by his congested face, and rather incoherent talk, what was amiss, but ignored it, and intended to say nothing that evening. However, he did the routes thing of breaking down, saying he couldn't think what had made him do it etc, etc, but instead of stopping yesterday, of course he went on. We are right back to days in bed, and what Martin calls 'sweating it out', and I am praying he will be on his feet by the end of the week.

I *did* think it was OK to have my week with Kits, as Moper had been so completely well! We had an amusing time, working all day and each day, on our script – the Danish au pair girl in London – I typed, and he strode up and down, and it was such fun the way we *were* able to work together. Of course, if I had been doing a book, I couldn't have done it that way – but here, with just short scraps of dialogue and scenes, it was OK. Now he has to find his amateur cast to act in it! We saw Flave in London, and she is mad to be the Danish girl (!) so perhaps she and Kits *will* get going together after all. I can see she is aching to break out in some way! Kits has gone off to Dublin this weekend to see his girl. I hope he doesn't get *too* badly menaced, and ends up marrying her, but I don't think he will unless badly pushed. She looks *very* pretty, in a snap he showed me.

I love that little place, Aldeburgh. It gives me such a sense of freedom, even if I did have to work *and* cook *and* do the chores at the same time. I find myself singing, as I go off to buy meat in the little town, as one would in France. I suppose it *is* the freedom! I still long for a complete holiday, abroad. What a hope, though, now! I think Moper's thing must have been unconscious jealousy of Kits. I had told him on the telephone how we were working all day on a film script. He possibly resents our mutual interests, and that I don't take a similar interest in boat plans, and things to do with him. (But it's quite unconscious!)

No more for now, as piles of letters to answer.

Fond love, Tray.

When, in my mind's eye, I see Monsieur Barreyre it is always among his books; either in the shabby, cramped study of the Paris flat, where they made a rampart about his desk, and shared the sagging leather armchair with his beloved Siamese, Amok, or in the barn at the bottom of the garden in Normandy where, spectacles on nose, he scratched away with a steel-nibbed pen and black ink, writing down all that passed through his fertile mind. He was a poet, novelist and philosopher; a journalist, critic of theatre, music hall and circus, but also a *bon viveur*, one of the last of the old Parisian *boulevardiers*. He had known almost everyone worth knowing of his generation, barring politicians whose tortuous minds were alien to his kindly nature. Known affectionately as 'Toto' to his friends and colleagues, it could truly be said of him that he had not an enemy in the world, quite an achievement in the competitive world of journalism. Without speaking a word of English he was more knowledgeable about English literature than most people I had met, and he introduced me to Carlyle, Emerson and Thoreau (whose works did not fall within the scope of the Institut Catholique), while his enthusiasm for Dickens could not fail to strike a spark from the dullest listener.

But there were things he did not know, and would never learn. Finance remained a mystery he did not attempt to penetrate, leaving all practical matters to his wife, Madame B, nor did he know how to refuse a kindness, break a promise, or repulse importunate callers. I loved him from the moment we met in my new friend Madame Meg Catusse's salon, where his bulky, somewhat Johnsonian figure, and beaming countenance illuminated even that dark, ground-floor cage. His family came from Bordeaux and had once owned extensive vineyards; they had been close friends and neighbours of my godmother's family, which no doubt is why his door was instantly thrown wide open to me.

A benign Providence decreed that Monsieur B.'s newspaper *L'Intransigeant* should despatch him upon a summer cruise to Spitzbergen in 1939, two months before the outbreak of war; on the same boat was Madame B.. Without this kindly nudge on the part of Fate, it seems unlikely that they would ever have met, for they came from very different worlds. Madame B.'s childhood had been spent at the Palais du Luxembourg, where her father occupied the post of *Trésorier du Sénat*, one of those higher Civil Service posts that count for so much in France. Her father was a strictly honest, upright Frenchman of the old school. The family were comfortably off but never really affluent. Their only son had been smashed to bits in the trenches of the Somme in 1914; his mother made an heroic journey to the front lines, in order to bring him back to the *Hôpital de la Salpêtrière*, where she was acting as assistant to one of the big professors. They operated three times, but he died in her arms.

At the age of twelve Marie-Louise found herself an only child, greatly loved and cherished, but expected to make up to her parents for all they had lost. When she spoke of her brother, she always recalled that even as a child he had been: '*très sérieux, même triste, souvent ...*' – and his photographs bore this out. But nothing could have quenched Marie-Louise's natural gaiety and spontaneity, which she retained to the end of her life. She loved her parents deeply, and they were far from the stuffy bourgeois so characteristic of French bureaucracy. They both loved the theatre and music, and counted Sarah Bernhardt and Edmond Rostand among their friends. It was fun for a child to have the Jardin du Luxembourg to herself, once the gates had been closed to the public. In the company of the concierge's children, Marie-Louise instigated explorations of the subterranean tunnels under the Sénat, rumoured to link with the Palais de l'Elysée, but the tunnel was choked by fallen masonry, and she was hauled out, dusty and protesting, before she had got far enough.

After an unhappy first marriage which ended in divorce, following the death of their only child, she developed tuberculosis. A cure was successful, but to consolidate it further she was advised to take a cruise to an invigorating northern clime, such as Spitzbergen. Once embarked, she decided that the most amusing company on board was among the group of journalists, and attached herself to them for the rest of the cruise. By the time they disembarked at Le Havre, Monsieur B. was more in love than he realized, while Marie-Louise had decided that this was the man with whom she wanted to spend the rest of her life. But before any further steps could be taken, war broke out and all private hopes and plans were shattered.

Those newspapers which did not wish to work under the Nazis evacuated their staff to the Unoccupied Zone. Monsieur B. was sent to Clermont Ferrand and here, after a hair-raising journey across France, with bridges blown up before and behind her, Marie-Louise finally joined him. It was not possible to communicate with anyone en route, and as most of the towns through which she had to pass were heavily bombarded, for one nightmare week everyone imagined she was lost. During this time, Monsieur B. could neither work, eat nor sleep, but paced up and down, driving his colleagues almost to distraction. Finally, one of them, driven to the limit of endurance, exclaimed: '*Écoute, mon vieux*, if this is the way you feel about this girl, for God's sake marry her!'

Madame B. maintained that when eventually she walked into the hotel and saw his face, she knew she had been right to come, even at the price of abandoning her parents, her home, and her beloved dogs. Now she was safe, Monsieur B. continued to balk at anything so final as marriage, and photographs show him marching to the ceremony in the Mairie with bowed head and hands behind his back, like a condemned man walking to the gallows. Fortunately, the wedding-lunch photograph shows a more cheerful picture, of smiling faces, raised glasses, and a feeling of relief all round.

Soon, there was no longer an Unoccupied Zone, and Clermont Ferrand fell under the jurisdiction of the sinister Klaus Barbie, head of the Gestapo. Like many others, the Bs took part in underground resistance, hiding people from the Nazis and helping them escape, in daily danger of being denounced and arrested themselves. When I could persuade Madame B. to talk of those days, I listened spellbound. She was a natural *raconteuse*, and brought the smallest incident or odd character instantly to life – as Bing discovered when she came to stay, and egged her on. Looking at Madame B. with her calm, almost unlined face, grey hair coiled into a neat chignon and her *grande dame* air, it was almost impossible to imagine that she had once smuggled a friend on to a train wrapped in rugs (fortunately, he was small and thin) while the Nazis searched for him at the station.

When the war ended, Monsieur B. was in his fifties, newspapers were rapidly changing hands and it was not easy to find somewhere to live in Paris. On the death of Madame B.'s father, they were glad to accept her mother's suggestion that they should share the apartment in the rue Molitor at Auteuil, to which she had moved on his retirement. A genuine affection linked Monsieur B. to his mother-in-law, whom everyone called *Madame Mère*, and whose opinions he respected. It was this mutual respect for every member of the household which made it so pleasant a place to the many friends who came there. I sought refuge there when the Seine rose, or the pipes froze, always sure of a warm welcome and a hot bath. Bing grew very fond of the Bs, and always asked for news of them. She often begged me to ask for Monsieur B.'s advice on this or that perplexity, and she regularly sent them the French editions of her books. In time, these occupied a whole shelf in the overloaded bookcases, and were greatly treasured.

It was hardly surprising that an edifice as odd as the house in the rue Molitor should contain some equally bizarre individuals. On the ground floor, the concierge reigned supreme. Coming home late at night, it was prudent to call out one's name upon entering, or she would spring from her bed to glare out through her lace curtains – a terrifying figure with a Medusa's head of knobbly curlers. Two floors above, there lived a celebrated professor. I never discovered the exact nature of his celebrity, but it had something to do with zoology. From time to time, mysterious sacks reputed to contain rare reptiles were delivered at the *loge*. The concierge did not approve of this, and dumped the sacks out in the yard, among the *poubelles*, to await the Professor's return. On one such occasion, a large boa constrictor managed to escape, and to climb into the lift-shaft, where it twined itself around the central shaft and went to sleep. No one cared to wake it, although this caused considerable disruption to the normal usage of the lift, and those on the top floors soon formed a circle of protest about the *loge*, demanding that the police and *pompiers* should be speedily summoned.

Appealed to for his judgment, Monsieur B. mildly suggested that snakes had been known to respond to music. I could tell by the twinkle in his eye that he was enjoying the situation, but a radio was produced and tuned in to France-Musique; a lady warbled one of the Schubert *lieder*, and the snake climbed higher up the pole, presumably to get out of earshot! The Professor, arriving home early that afternoon, calmly unhooked the creature with a stick, remarking drily that it was a perfectly harmless and inoffensive specimen, and was in the process of digesting. 'Digesting *what*, mon dieu!' shrieked the concierge, with an eye on her cats. She would probably have said far more, had the Professor not been quite so celebrated, but no further sacks were delivered, and peace was restored.

The topmost floor of the building was inhabited by a family whose fits of Slavic gloom alternated with outbreaks of wild hilarity, in which they tumbled downstairs, scattering the contents of their *poubelles* on the way. It was constantly rumoured that they were under notice to quit, but they remained, long after the other inhabitants, including the concierge herself, had been swept away – the Professor to a higher post, and a grander apartment, and others to a still more elevated sphere. For change was on the way, imperceptibly at first, and then with gathering momentum. The friendly corner shops disappeared, to be replaced by the egregious banks, while the autoroute, the all-conquering *périphérique*, sliced away at the green and peaceful borders of the Bois, until only a few century-old trees were left in the Jardins d'Auteuil, as a sop to public opinion.

※

Mena, Monday 11 March, 1963.

Dearest Oriel,

I have thought for a long time that the boat chores, or indeed any chores, are too much for you, *plus* writing, in your K.M. state of health. You see, last year it was your heart, and now your throat, and it must mean that your basic anaemia won't let you do too much physically, and I still think a boat must mean a bit more sweat than a flat, because such queer things can go wrong. But if you can go to Normandy and work most of the summer, it should be the right answer.

I've just had the quarterly edition of *The Author* – and it's very Dooming about the difficulty all writers have these days in keeping themselves by their writing, compared with even fifteen years ago. The old established people are being chucked (Tray?!), and the younger ones don't become successful unless they strike a great lucky thing and become a sort of newspaper personality. It's all very Dooming indeed.

I *think* it will be all right about flying to Rome with Tess on 23 March but, so typical of Flave, she's backed out. I telephoned to make final plans, and she made so many difficulties that it was hopeless. Yet when I originally asked her she seemed very pleased. I was quite bad-moody and unhappy when she said No, as I had so counted on it, and it would have pleased Moper so much. As we get older, Moper and me, one's daughters will have to oblige now and again, or I shall never get a break. Anyway, I've now asked the Burts to come and sleep here, and be here in the evening.

What Tess and I want to do is to have about four days in Rome, and then go by car to Assisi, then my Urbino place, then back to Arezzo, then Siena, then down to Perugia, and back to Rome. It should make a lovely break for Track's culture! I wish it would inspire me for a new book to brew upon, and then do next winter. I do get so passage wandery when I'm not working, especially in winter. Summer doesn't matter because of basking. But as you know, there is really nothing else to do in one's life here, if one isn't working, except routes walk to Prid! Which is ideal as walking exercise when working, but awfully silly as the Main event of one's Day!

What DO you mean, you have written a song? It makes me think of a Jane Austen person, sitting down to the piano with her music, and singing in a 'clear treble', with gentlemen leaning over the back of the piano and the father saying: 'That will do, my dear. You have delighted us enough!'

All love, Tray.

It was in 1952 that Madame Mère decided to buy a small house in the country for summer holidays. She wished for one close to Paris, to save fares – not too big, nor too small, but with a garden; of necessity, it had to be cheap. Nothing seemed to fulfil these requirements, and she had almost given up the idea when she came upon a notice advertising the sale of a small farmhouse in Normandy. The Bs hurried off to visit it, and although only the roof could be seen above a tangle of unscythed grass, they knew at once that this was to be their home.

The house stood facing a village green planted with apple trees; there was a pond, with its *lavoir* still in use, and a village pump. The *notaire* seemed unwilling to disclose the name of this locality, but under pressure revealed that it was known as La Haute Folie. For many years no signposts existed to indicate this, the inhabitants being sensitive about their name. The Bs, however, were enchanted, and bought the house on sight, relieved to discover later that the walls were solid, and the roof sound.

Indoors, the dwelling was simple and rustic, with beamed ceilings and the floors laid out in a traditional diamond pattern of old red-and-black brick tiles. The garden was enclosed by walls of baked earth thatched with heather, upon which was planted a row of wild iris. Nowadays, when these walls crumble with age, they cannot be replaced; this art has now disappeared.

Even for those days, the house was absurdly cheap, and before moving in the Bs installed a kitchen, bathroom and electricity. The arrival of

'Parisians' was resented by the local community, and the Bs had scarcely moved in before a neighbour complained that he had intended to buy the house himself. As he had taken over three years to make up his mind, however, they saw no reason to feel guilty on his behalf. Soon, other houses were bought by city-dwellers in search of a weekend retreat, and the boom in *résidences secondaires* had begun. Prices rose accordingly; Madame Mère had been only just in time.

When, over ten years later, I came to La Haute Folie on visits from *La Ronde des Heures*, nothing much had changed. Although only 104 kilometres from the centre of Paris, as measured from the spires of Notre Dame, it was still a rural community. Those wishing to communicate with the outside world had to walk or bicycle to the main road, and use a telephone installed in the local *épicerie*, in the charge of two fierce harpies. To ask to use this machine was tantamount to proffering an insult, and entailed hours of patient waiting, while parrot-like shrieks were hurled down the line to the exchange who, becoming excited, shrieked back. When at last, the telephone arrived, it was a party line, and many were the feuds and disputes occasioned by this.

Milk was still fetched daily from the nearest farm. Standing about in the yard, waiting for the milking to finish, one soon got to know all one's neighbours, country born and bred and Parisian alike. The kitchen at the farm boasted neither washing machine nor television, and deep freezes were, of course, as yet unknown. Those without transport of their own were not despised, as they are today; all the local shops made weekly, sometimes daily, rounds. The greengrocer, an eccentric man, often came swaying over the fields at eleven o'clock at night, a lantern swinging from the roof of his ancient van.

Each autumn, a primitive kind of steam engine made its appearance on the green, and everyone brought sacks of apples, to be converted into Calvados, the traditional apple brandy of Normandy. For days, and even nights, the engine puffed and vibrated merrily, tended by an acolyte; to pass by, was to stagger homewards, overcome by the potent fumes. Soon, the distillation of small quantities of alcohol was forbidden by law, and the little engine vanished, never to be seen again outside a museum. Here, too, change was on the way. The *route nationale* to Paris, which had meandered through towns and villages on its way to the coast, became an autoroute to Brest, down which enormous lorries thundered day and night. Milk now came in cartons from the supermarket, and the chemicals sprayed over the fields killed the lovely wild flowers growing in profusion along the grass verges.

One of the last survivors of the past was old Madame Le Loer, who in her cottage on the green continued to live as she had always done, rising and going to bed with the sun. Winter or summer, her front door stood open to the four winds, as she clattered about the yard in rubber sabots, tending her few sheep, or fetching wood for her stove. She once confided to me, a little wistfully, that before the war everyone had gathered under the apple trees on the green in summer, to sew and gossip; or rou..d some hospitable hearth in winter, for what was then known as a *veillée*. Nowadays, she complained, all the doors were shut at dusk, as everyone gathered about their television. Her family installed a telephone, but she refused to master its use, and it stood mutely in a corner, covered with a knitted teacosy. This stubborn refusal to move with the times ended by causing grave problems to friends and family alike; growing old and deaf, she retreated into a private world of her own, refusing to open the door even to a familiar face. Peering out balefully from behind a screen of geraniums, see seems to me the last of an indomitable race, a dodo or a dinosaur; someone who valued her independence above progress.

Those happy years on the river came to an end in one of the coldest winters on record. Day after day, we anxiously watched the thermometer fall, until it reached seventeen below zero. The Seine froze, and to prevent our boats from being crushed like walnuts in its iron grip, it was necessary to break up the ice every two hours or so, day and night alike. It was hard to turn out of a warm bed at 2 a.m and to stump around the deck, cracking the ice with a garden fork, and pushing it away from the side. Yet it was splendid too, to be out in the steely air, in a frozen world, with a ceiling of stars overhead, bright and sharp. We fed the starved birds that perched on our railings, and for a time I harboured a little cat, which sought shelter in my garden.

Then I fell ill. For days I had been suffering from a sore throat to which I paid little attention, expecting it would turn into a common cold; I could not abandon my nightly round of ice-breaking. Instead, it grew steadily worse, until one night I woke up convinced that I was being slowly strangled. My throat was closing up, I could hardly breathe, and when I attempted to suck hot water through a straw, I could not swallow. In a panic, I remembered that Madame Garonne, a new friend and houseboat neighbour, had insisted on giving me her own doctor's address, in case of need. By this time I was light-headed, and could barely see the numbers on the telephone dial. When I got through, all I could do was to whisper my address, and beg the doctor to come at once. He did not know my name, and I doubt if I had summoned sufficient strength to mention Madame Garonne's, but he knew the houseboats, and to my eternal gratitude, came at once.

The physician wanted to despatch me straight into hospital, but I refused to abandon ship, and managed to persuade him that to do so would be tantamount to scuttling *La Ronde*. The days that followed are hazy now. A white-coated nurse came daily to give me injections, and treated me with disdain; people who lived on boats were no better than gypsies in her opinion, and deserved all they got. I feigned sleep, and was glad when her brisk footsteps clattered away over my telescopic gangway. Once again, the community spirit of the houseboat-dwellers came to the fore; my neighbours rallied round, and I was never alone. Madame Garonne called daily, bringing thermos flasks of home-made soup and delicious *crème brulée*, while my Mississippi neighbour banged and crashed about the decks, breaking up the ice around *La Ronde*. A young couple further down the river brought their little girl to feed the ducks. The cat, to my distress, had disappeared, and I always suspected the white-coated nurse, who considered all animals to be insanitary. Even Tod wrote me an anxious letter, offering her services. '*My dear, you had better let me take charge* ...' I could not imagine her on *La Ronde*, of which she had always been highly suspicious, but was grateful all the same.

In due course, the ice melted, and when I looked out of the window, there were daffodils in the garden and primroses on the banks. I had taken longer to recover than if I had gone into hospital, the white-coated nurse declared, but all I needed now was a good convalescence. As soon as all danger from the floods had passed, the kind Bs came and removed me on shore, to their comfortable flat. There, cocooned in loving care, I gradually became resigned to my fate. When everyone, including Bing, seemed determined that I should get rid of *La Ronde*, Monsieur B's was the only dissident voice raised, apart from my own. He declared it was important for me – for *any* writer – to have a place of my own in which to lead a personal life.

I agreed wholeheartedly; it proved as hard for me to leave *La Ronde* as it had been to tear myself away from the Villa Racine, for where I am happy, I quickly put down roots. At first I went back often, to visit my neighbours and to listen to their tales of floods and disasters, but gradually the pressures around me became more and more insistent; the cheque was brandished once too often, and before the end of the winter, *La Ronde des Heures* had passed into other hands.

That icy winter of the early 1960s brought disaster to many, besides the houseboat-dwellers on the Seine. As usual, the homeless suffered most, although the métro stations stayed open all night to provide them with warmth and shelter. On one frozen morning, Madame Mère, opening her window to distribute largesse to the starved birds huddled on the balcony, caught a chill which swiftly turned to pneumonia. I was in England, and hurried back, in time to say goodbye to her. There had always been a special understanding between us. Madame Mère was precisely the grandmother I would have chosen for myself, had my advice been asked. She was wise, intelligent, humorous, with just that touch of irony that adds zest to life; and she could laugh at herself, as well as at others. Her going left a tremendous void in that closely-knit household of the Bs, and she was mourned by many who had turned to her in troubled times for help and advice.

⌘

Mena, Friday 3 May, 1963.

Dearest Oriel,

I was so glad to get your letter of 25 April, and to know that you are better. But your health is so K.M.-ish that I feel you will be whisked away to Switzerland before long – perhaps to live at Crans or Montana, up above Pen Friend! Two abscesses recurring in the throat is bad. There is nothing so out-of-sorts and lowering as throat trouble. That stupid tonsil of mine is only now gone quiet, and it still looks lumpy. So I began to think you and I both had some sort of budding cancer, and would die within the year, and how sad it would be – two writers, friends, cut off in their prime! It made me feel so depressed, too, and you know how it takes a lot to make me Doomed.

Autre chose – I am *thrilled* about the play being on again, and I can foresee everything working out OK. But don't commit yourself to some awful plan of working on it in England, which will Doom your summer. All you need is to come over, meet him and talk it over. It would be a good plan to come here for a week, so you could have Tray's wise advice, and then go happily back to France. I *did* so enjoy the days when I did plays, and it was exciting going to rehearsals, and rather frightening too. One never went the first two weeks, but let them get it roughly into shape, and then went along for the last two weeks, and of course for the first week of the tour. But of course everything may be changed since 'my day'. It's fourteen years since I did *September Tide*. And if I wrote a play now I wouldn't even be able to get up to London to discuss it, much less watch rehearsals! Just as well I have not brewed on one.

Oh, I know a thing that *did* add to my sadness. My cousin Nico Davies sent me a lot of family letters to read, all about his father and mother dying, you know his mother was my Aunt Sylvia – Daddy's beautiful sister – and when she died, Barrie adopted all the boys. Well, anyway, these letters were about the gradual death etc, and they were so brave and noble, I can't tell you – it made one ashamed of one's own stupid grumbles. You know, I *do* think people were more noble then – 1910 sort of period – and they had such courage, and good ways. I shall have to send them back to Nico, otherwise I would love you to read them. I'm not surprised my poor Cousin Peter threw himself under a train after collecting them together (which he did). He probably compared *our* day with theirs! Uncle Arthur (the husband) died first of slow cancer of the jaw, and then about three years later she died of a sort of lung cancer – but it was their devotion to each other, and their courage in front of the little boys, that was so wonderful. I suppose two great World Wars have made people very different; more kind of grumbling, and unable to cope with vicissitudes.

Fondest love, Tray.

༄

Mena, 5 August, 1963.

Dearest Oriel,

So glad to get your letter. It was lovely having you to stay, and looking so well in spite of that throat all the winter, but I do think you would be wise to consider parting with the houseboat, if you can do it at not too big a loss. I would have thought it ideal for some young (healthy!) artist or writer, possibly a man, but so often these sort of people can't raise the necessary cash. The spring would be a likely time, or if we get a *really* hot summer, when people get whipped thinking how pleasant to live on the water, but I doubt if there would be any bites in the autumn!

I was thinking about your life, after you had gone, and it seems to me that you could be between the patterns, as it were, and sort of Waiting for Godot, if you know what I mean! One does strike these slightly passage wandery patches in one's life, but I think one should accept them, as a marking time for meditation, but not for planning. At one time, when I was younger, I used to think that planning ahead was good, but now I don't. I think one has to accept what comes, but not in a dreary way, in a sort of welcoming way! Of course there is sadness at the end of an era in one's life that doesn't come back. And if one passes the place, there is a sort of resentment that it doesn't belong to one any more! If I pass a place I once lived (like at Hampstead), I often do a Gondal, whereby I go into it just as if it was still mine, and take my coat off, and somehow settle down, and then try to imagine the amazed surprise of the *new* owner coming in, and how one would behave in the Gondal just as if they were not there, and one was still in possession. I always think the house – or in your case the boat – would be on *one's* side, but of course the other person's furniture would be hostile, and perhaps rear up crossly from the walls, and yet the atmosphere would be for *one*. It would be rather queer and hateful, and I think in the end the new person would send for the police, thinking one was mad!

Another thing I Gondal about, is supposing one suddenly went and rang at a person's house, who was a Fan – I often have long Tell-Hims from people who have read a book of mine, full of gush – and one said, 'Look, here I am. You wrote me such a long letter, I thought perhaps you would like it if I came to stay!' And their *amazed* look, trying afterwards to welcome one, but really, of course, there would be no sort of rapport at all, and they would never have bargained for one in their Day, which would be all messed up for plans. Or again, when you don't know people well, and have stayed a night (for some reason or another), and just as you are going, and the suitcase is in the car, you say, 'I would rather like to stay on. Is that all right?' and get out again. What would the immediate reaction of the people be? Would they say, 'Oh … oh well, how nice!' and settle to the Day again, or quickly make out it wasn't convenient? Such a silly thing to think about!

We have just had an old American Witherspoony woman to stay, only two days and she was harmless, but I wondered what would happen if she suddenly turned to me and said, 'May I stay on for the rest of the summer?' or alternatively, if I said to her: 'May I come back with you to the States?' Whose reaction would be the quickest? (You don't know this old person, but she was the widow of an old American boatbuilding pen-friend of Moper's.) She was over seventy, and a harmless old thing really, and it was not much trouble, still … Moper felt he couldn't watch telly, and so there was Tell-Him talking after sups, but about *nothing*, just that conversation the English and Americans have about their children and their grandchildren. Now, in France it would be great Questions of the Day, or books, or some Aspect of Life, if you know what I mean? (Tho' I must admit I didn't get that from old Ferdie last year, it was all that friend-of-friends stuff!)

I keep vaguely brewing my Urbino story, but it takes on so many aspects, and doesn't brew to one Main deciding point, which means it isn't ready. You know there is a small University in Urbino, as well as the Ducal Palace which is the main tourist sight, and somehow I keep seeing someone there who perhaps teaches, and is a remote odd sort of figure, who has always Gondalled all his life about the past in Urbino (he is half-English, half-Italian). He has a much younger half-brother, who goes there as a student, and the young one knows about the older one's Gondals, and is a bit worried in case they get out of hand.

It is the summer term, and there is to be a great *son et lumière* thing that the elder brother is to arrange, and which will enact a great scene from the past at the Ducal Palace, when there was an insurrection from the people of Urbino against the Duke of those days, who got hurled from the tower of the Palace. In some rather nanny, hypnotic way this elder Gondally brother works up the students and the people from the town who are doing the pageant, into *really* doing this. Suddenly 'turning' on the people watching, and there is a *real* tragedy, with perhaps the head of the University or some Main person hurled from the tower. That's as far as I've got, but do you think it would work? Would it be very difficult to do? It would have to be a novel of atmosphere almost entirely, and if only I could get a title for it, I believe it ought to have one that would be somehow like *Son et Lumière*, but of course it wouldn't make sense in English – or else a very long title like *The Night the Eagle Fell*,* except that the Eagle would be the emblem of these old royal Dukes of the past.

You ask about the film script. I did do some alterations, and also brought the girl in a bit earlier on, and now it is supposed to be with some crumby great Columbia man, but needless to say neither Kits nor I have heard one word from him, and I doubt if we ever will! I wonder how writers would exist if they just waited hopefully for an answer from managers and film tycoons!

No more for now. Tons of love, Tray.

※

Mena, 20 August, 1963.

Dearest Oriel,
  Very many thanks for your goodly Main letter, commenting on Gondals and Urbino. I've had a worrying time since then because Moper, who had a sniffling cold, suddenly began to run a temperature, a high one –

---

* It was finally called *The Flight of the Falcon*, published by Gollancz in 1964.

102 – and Luther came and gave antibiotics, but they have only just started to work, and it must have been near-pneumonia, he says. This means he will be ages picking up again, and it's a bad outlook for the winter. To add to this the dentist said I must have two teeth out soon. They are infected, and of course I can't start on myself until Moper is OK. Added to which, Tess is here with the children, and two dogs, and although the children do seem better behaved, it is an added cope when Moper is in bed, and one has to minister to him.

This sounds like a moan from Tod! Oh, and I had a worse thing too, in that some wretched man began making a fuss – did I tell you? – that he had written a book called *The Birds*, and it sounded just like mine. He was getting all worked up and cross, saying Hitchcock had taken the film from his, and not mine. Then he apparently took Counsel's Opinion, who said it was no good him doing anything, so luckily he is not to go on with his claim, so-called. But at least three fools in America have made 'claims', saying they have written books or stories about savage birds, and my heart began to sink, in case some awful great Main case started up in the US (like that *Rebecca* thing) and I had to fly out, and give evidence. These brutes just do it for publicity and money, and film people like Hitchcock don't care; it makes *more* publicity, and any claim always comes back on the author. There seems to be no protection for well-known authors when this happens, because after all it's only one's word against somebody else's, that one has never read their stupid stories! And as these people are always insolvent, there is no hope of making a counter-claim against them, or getting them to pay costs if they bring a case. Actually, I don't think anything will come from it all, but I can't help remembering that awful *Rebecca* lawsuit. That person's story was rotten, and not a bit like *Rebecca* at all, but they were still able to file a lawsuit, and one had to go to America, and do all that witness business. Imagine the hiatus if I had to go, leaving Moper here, it would be too awful for words! So you can imagine how all this has been fussing me.

I had a letter from Frank the other day. Not tiresome, but nice, and he had been seeing Ellen, who was doing her usual summer thing of having people out to Long Island to swim, and Puck was having some play put on, and everyone sounded in good form. No, I've thought no more of Urbino since I wrote, what with one thing and another, but I don't see how I can ever get down to writing it, unless I have another glimpse of the place. One has to get the 'feel'. One quite nice thing last week was the brief visit of a charming little student from Tours, bringing me a gift from an old professeur person, who had helped me with some *Glass-Blower* research. I was struck at once by her intelligent conversation, and nice polite ways; not a bit made-up or anything, like silly English girls of nineteen would be! The poor thing had sweated all the way from Bristol by train to visit me, and had to swallow her lunch, and dash back to Bristol again. She was staying for a few weeks with an English family, and she said she was rather disappointed because they knew *nothing* of books, or pictures, or music, and she had understood Bristol was a good centre for that. Well, of course it *is*, but imagine English Witherspoons caring two hoots what went on. It's only in termtime she would have found other students who would be interested. I felt so sorry for her. She will think England the shilling of all time!

No more for the present. Moper does seem better today.

All love, Tray.

Mena, 2 September, 1963.

Dearest Oriel,

I was delighted to get your letter, and the very interesting and, I think, psychological politics dream. I have discussed it on a separate piece of paper enclosed, and shall be interested to know if you think it far-fetched or not. Thanks also for the photos, which are good, although Tray does look such an old Track these days, with her grey hair, and lines. It's only when one sees oneself in a photo that it strikes home. It's like that Queen in *Snow White*:

> *Mirror, mirror on the wall,*
> *Who is the fairest of them all?*

For years one crumbs and is quite content, and then one day, near C. of L., one looks – and it has all gone. For fair people worse than dark, because they fade so, and lose depth and colour.

Oh, I must tell you, so interesting. You know that *Birds* man, who said he had written a *Birds* book too, and was cross, and I was afraid there would be another Main case? Well, this man, Mr Frank Baker, wrote me a nice letter and sent me his *Birds* to read, saying he had read mine in Penguin's, and thought it very good. So I began his, rather smiling derisively, thinking it would be nonsense, and it's *frightfully good*! Much more psychological politics than mine, and going into great Deep Thoughts, I was quite absorbed! *His* birds were not ordinary birds like mine, but great strange things from outer space (and this was written in 1936), and they turned out to be the *souls* of all the people in the world, who had somehow pushed them out of their inner selves; and so the wretched souls, turned into birds, were furious and sought revenge.

He gives marvellous descriptions of awful old people being pecked to death, who really deserved it, and there is a woman having an abortion in a hospital, and suddenly a great squawking thing flies into the hospital and plucks at her innards; and then there is a great service in a Cathedral, full of pompous Witherspoons, and suddenly it's invaded by these birds, and all the choir and congregation go quaking with terror as these birds swoop on to them.

The author seems to be Welsh (he gives a wonderful description of noble thoughts on a Welsh mountain near Cader Idris) and I do think it's a shame his novel never seemed to sell back in '36. Hitchcock would have been well advised to have bought his, and not mine, as I hear from Kits that the story he has made is not like mine, *or* poor Mr Baker's, but is all about irritating people in San Francisco. Isn't it interesting? I wrote off at once to the poor Mr Baker, saying how much I had liked his Birds, and how terribly sorry I was that his book had not caught on in the way my short story did, but perhaps in 1936 people were not ready for such psychological politics, and perhaps the war made them wake up. Anyway, I now long to know this man, his Deep Thoughts are so good, and he has a wild sense of humour, too, making his birds do such funny things, like palling filthy smelly pal on the top of very Witherspoony women's feathered hats!

That old Clementine American woman wrote me all gushing from California about her records, and I thought I had kept the letter to show you, but can't find it. Another maddening American woman turned up suddenly yesterday, just before lunch – so awkward, with old Jim Orr having just arrived, and having drinks – and I went to the front door, and she flung her arms round me, saying: 'I must touch you, I must touch you!' as if I had magic powers, and then said she read everything I wrote, and *she* had started a book now herself, and was bursting with words, and she was sure her style was like mine, and she was writing about Cornwall, and that's why she had to touch me for luck! Thank God she then went away. Actually she was quite royal, and rather handsome but what a gushing *fool*! So different from the quiet little French student I told you about.

Fond love, Tray.

Mena, 23 September 1963.

Dearest Oriel,

Many thanks for your long Main letter on getting back to the boat. Rather a pity you had to make the *rentrée* so suddenly, as Normandy sounds nice.

Yes, I think you do sound rather unsettled. *No*, I don't think it's a retrogressive step to live on land. It's sensible, *truly*, especially as you are not robust. The months are few when one really wants to be on a boat. I am sure if you can get down to a routine and work you will feel much better. I think I shall have a try at my Urbino book during the winter, even if I have not been back there (which looks hopeless), and just make it all up. I shan't call the place Urbino, but make-up names, and then I can Gondal the place a bit too, and it won't matter if it's not correct.

Kingsley Amis has asked me to contribute a science fiction story to the series he is to edit, deadline March, and although I don't know a thing about science fiction, I thought I would have a go – it's rather a challenge – and do a sort of telepathy thing about a person dying, and yet scientific at the same time. I'm brewing it now,* and will have a shot in the autumn.

Our excitement of the past weeks has been Kits announcing his engagement in the *Times* etc, to make it official! He has given Olive a ring (pearls, for setting, provided by Moper!) and she is thrilled, and all seems to be well. They are to be married in Dublin in January, and to go to Mexico for their honeymoon. (I'm supposed to pay for that!) I can't help feeling, like Flave, it's all rather 'let's pretend' to him, and he can't get over the fun and novelty of dashing about in his Jag with a pretty lovable girl, and having happy waxing. It's the aftermath one wonders about, and bills, and babies, and arguments etc, etc.

Must stop, shilling people coming for a night,

All love, Tray.

A series of events had been set in motion by my illness; they had obviously been lying in wait for me, biding their time. My wretched quinsy sank *La Ronde* more surely than any iceberg; for once on shore I had to face a storm of protest against life on the Seine: it was far too hazardous, the winters too harsh. Even those who had once been encouraging turned

* 'The Breakthrough'.

against me. Odette Arnaud pointed out that I had done no real work since living on *La Ronde* and this she considered to be *pas sérieux*; a writer's business was to write, not to mess about with boats! Winifred agreed, and when even Bing voiced her doubts, my confidence was shaken.

To open the door of the Bs' flat, where I was enjoying my convalescence, was to be greeted by its own special smell, compounded of goodly cooking, and the rich leathery scent of old books. It looked a muddle, but ask Monsieur B. about Plato or Montaigne, Diderot or Voltaire, and he would be able to lay his hand upon a copy at once. Like Dr Johnson, he was not gentle with his favourite books, but treated them robustly, cracking open their spines at a favourite page, or turning down the corners. The pockets of his favourite wine-coloured bathrobe sagged with the books he thrust into them, for he always read three or four at a time. He worked late at night, and whenever I came home from the Abbaye nightclub, I would see the light on his study desk shining from afar as I emerged from the métro. Only much later did I comprehend that he always waited up until I came safely home; nothing was ever said, so careful were the Bs to preserve my sacrosanct independence.

※

Mena, 4 November, 1963.

Dearest Oriel,

No word from you since you got back, and I expect you are busy shifting from the boat to the Bs' apartment for the winter? I do hope you are feeling less depressed. You must not let yourself get into an '*à quoi bon*' thing about writing, because that really would be the end. Without our writing, where would Gondal people like you and me be? It's not as if you were some poor brute who has never been published – *Horses* got very well reviewed. I *do* feel sorry for poor Piffy, whose book has been out a month, and she has had no reviews *at all*.

It can be an awful 'autumn' thing, that '*à quoi bon*' feeling. When I was younger, I always had to be looking forward to something, some holiday, some event, some encounter, dividing one's year into interests; and there would be a Gondal Peg hovering somewhere around, from which one could create something. (No matter if one knew, *au fond*, that one *was* Gondalling!) If you look back into my life, since you knew me – and before that, when you didn't – it has always been fundamentally rather monotonous and uneventful, from a worldly point of view. Just being a person down here, Moper coming at weekends, and the children at school; the Main events, my books being written, and leading a queer Gondal imaginary life. If I had *not* written, and *not* Gondalled, I should probably have gone raving mad, or taken to looking out for some sort of menace, to make an interest! All people, male *or* female, in their youth and prime, *do* have the urge towards menaces of some sort, and even if a lot of it is imaginary, it's all a part of life!

All love, Tray.

———

Like my own grandfather, whom he so closely resembled, Monsieur B. suffered from diabetes. Later in life his sight began to fail; he begged us to find him stronger magnifying glasses, but when these proved unavailing, accepted the infirmities of old age with his usual philosophy. One evening in early March 1979, I went into his study to say goodbye as usual, before going out to the theatre; coming home at midnight, I looked for the guiding light, but this time all was dark. He had not admitted feeling ill to me, for fear of spoiling my evening's pleasure – a gesture typical of his courtesy and consideration. They had taken him to the Hôtel Dieu, the hospital which faces the cathedral of Notre Dame. From the window of his room, he could see the great towers and hear the bells; he asked for it to be left open, so that he could listen to them. He died there, on 30 March, as he would have wished to do – at the heart of the Paris he loved so much.

With Monsieur B.'s death, a part of Madame B. died too, and the world they had loved and shared – that Parisian world of theatres, first-nights and galas – lost its savour, and presently ceased to exist. Madame B. had given up her part-time job as curator at the Musée du Tabac to care for him, and now it was time to think of the future. In 1984, at the age of eighty, she gladly retired to the country, to La Haute Folie – the little house she had created and loved, and where for nine more years she managed to outwit old age by the force of her personality. She never lost her quick wit and sense of humour, nor her passionate interest in the world about her and in other people. Many of them came to visit her, seeking comfort and advice, or simply the delicious meals she conjured up in the kitchen, where she reigned supreme to the end.

❦

Mena, 24 November, 1963.

Dearest Oriel,

Many thanks for your letter on Saturday. I had to read it over today more calmly, because yesterday morning I was in such a state of numbed shock at Kennedy's assassination, that I really could think of nothing else. He was one of the few leaders for whom I had an enormous respect, although he may not always have been right about things in Europe – but he was so far-seeing in so many ways, and so progressive in America itself – anyway, I can't tell you how it has moved me, and Moper too. We both felt so shaken we could hardly finish our sups.

About your writing, I think you must try and forget about the 'could-have-been' of *Horses*. Everyone who read it loved it, it had splendid reviews, and I would think that was the greatest pleasure you could have. You don't know how hurtful it is to have rotten, sneering reviews, time and time again throughout my life. The fact that I sold well in the past, never really made up for them. Of course making money has been very useful, because of being able to afford Mena, and bring up the children, but I somehow don't connect money-making with the writing, not in my mind. Now, if I were a person like Ian Fleming and the James Bond stories, I see the point in being a success. He has an interesting life, always travelling, and a house in Jamaica etc, and another in London, and another in the country – that's the *sort* of best-selling life that ordinary best-selling people do. But if by chance *Horses* had had a wild success, I can't see *you* doing that! You would still have been on the boat, and perhaps had it done up, but that's about all!

No more for now. Write again re plans.

Fond love, Tray.

✠

Mena, 19 January, 1964.

Dearest Oriel,

Many thanks for your good Main letter, which came many days ago, and I ought to have answered it before.

Poor Tod, I am really very worried about her, as she has had several X-rays on her innards. She really *has* got some growth there, and has got to face having an operation. She will go to a place called St Mark's, Bethnal Green, where they specialize in these sort of things, and a very good surgeon will perform but, after all, a growth is no joke for anyone, especially when they are over seventy. I would be dreading it, if it were me! She is fundamentally so healthy that I feel it can't be cancer, but *any* op is bound to pull her down, and make her feel like death afterwards for weeks. I am sure she will need nursing, and am hoping she will hear of a good Convalescent Home where she can go after leaving hospital.

Meanwhile, we face the wedding this coming week, and Moper says he would rather go back into the trenches on the Somme in the 1914 war! But he is going to go. I wish I could look forward to it, but I can't. It all seems such an effort, and I can't even feel that I shall see the funny side, as one would do if it were nothing to do with oneself! I feel rather frustrated, and wanting to get down to my Urbino book, but I am still not clear on the story, and it is so difficult to brew it without another glimpse of the place. Perhaps just the effort of the wedding will make me *changer les idées*, and the Urbino story will start to click. What worries me at the moment, is not really knowing enough about a University in Italy, and how it all works. It's silly to try and make it up, when I might be so wrong, like some silly Italian person writing a book about Fowey Grammar School, having stayed one night in Fowey! And it's got to take place all in, and around, that University, because that will somehow be the point. Still, perhaps with completely disguised names, it will work out.

Meanwhile, lots of love, and many, many happy returns, and a very successful Main brewing. I'll write when the wedding is over, and we're safely back.

Fondest love, Bing.

༄

Mena, Friday 31 January, 1964.

Dearest Oriel,

We arrived home safe and sound from Dublin last Sunday. Well, it was a tremendous success, and I enjoyed every moment of it, and wouldn't have missed it for the world. It was much more fun than the girls' weddings at the Savoy; I suppose because it was more original. I thought I might feel *triste*, because of being so silly about Kits, and that irritating thing people always say about, 'A son is a son till he gets him a wife'; but I didn't a *scrap*, and felt thoroughly gay the whole time! Moper put up a very brave front when he got there but on the way he might have been en route for the salt mines of Siberia! We had a wonderful suite at the Gresham, high up and bright, and I would willingly have spent a week there, taking my ease.

We had to take out the Whites to dinner. They were a *very* nice couple, and the dinner went well, tho' Kits insisted on taking us to a rather silly place in the basement; not a bit Irish, pseudo-Chelsea. Afterwards we went to see the presents in their little house, which was full of sisters and relatives, and the parish priest, who was to marry them – a blissful, madly menacing chap, about seven foot tall, and quite young. The presents were laid out on the bedroom floor (where Olive shared a bed with her sister), and the bridesmaids' dresses and the bridal gown all hanging up on a curtain. It was simple, and touching, and just like something out of an Irish tale, but the odd thing was that it truly *was* awfully like the house in my script, and the parents very like Tim and Maggie too! (How waine if it is ever done, they would think I was mocking them!)

Before we left, the priest started up a song, with all the family clapping and joining in the chorus! Just imagine an English C. of E. parson doing that, or even bothering to go and sit with the bride's family before a wedding! The wedding itself, tho' in the presbytery (becos of Kits not being Catholic) and Mass afterwards in the chapel, was very simple and nice. Outside, the crowds were incredible – like waiting for the Beatles! – Olive being an ex-Miss Ireland, and on Irish TV, was of course well-known. Shouts and cheers, and the priest had to jump on the wall to ask the crowd to give way.

As she got into the car, one old Trackish woman called out, 'Ah, she'll niver want for nothing no more!' which I thought was a lovely phrase to remember (hope it proves true!).

The lunch – a great sit-down affair at the Gresham, but the cream of the reception was the priest's address to them afterwards, so moving and sincere, and when he had finished he said, 'Now, how would it be if I led you all in a song?!' and broke into a rollicking chorus, something about 'The girl I do adore', which was so spontaneous and natural. Then they soon went off to change, and so to the airport, in a cloud of confetti!

We followed in a later plane, conducted to the airport by Mr and Mrs White, who embraced me and said, 'Please God we meet again,' which was so touching and sweet. I feel either it will be a *very* happy marriage and an example to others, and both of them being sweet to their children – which Kits easily might be, as he is so like my daddy, who was always so fond of us and so jolly – *or* they will be fighting within two years, she with an Irish temper and he selfish – you just can't tell!

Moper in very good form now he is back, but says he would not go through it again for a million pounds – though truly there was not much to go through! Now the excitement is behind us I want to concentrate on Urbino. Weather mild with snowdrops everywhere, and buds on the rhodies.

No more then now. Write soon with all your news.

All love, Tray.

❀

Mena, 23 February, 1964.

Dearest Oriel,

So many thanks for your lovely Main letter, including synopsis, which I return. Forgive me for being laggard in my answer, but I have been brewing too, and thinking, and slowly putting the outline into chapter headings, in my notebook. I don't do it in the same good precise outline that you do, but notes that only I can understand. I am being so slow about it, chiefly because it's rather like a soldier, an attacker, before a battle – I have to study the plans and postcards of Urbino, and the books about the University there, day after day, so that I could, in a way, find my way blindfold about the place! Then, if I close my eyes, I am there. All this has been rather taking precedence of the actual notes, and then when I come to outline the story I find the first suspense idea, and the *son et lumière*, all become involved with deeper levels – I mean, there has to be an explanation of *why* the person directing the acting in the *son et lumière* (a professor at the University), begins to make it all come real to himself, and to the students etc, etc, what is his deep unconscious motive in wanting to re-enact history, and the wicked Duke. So ... it's much more difficult than I thought, hence the slowness of the notes.

Now, to return to your 'Arcadia'. I am *delighted* with it. It really does sound good, with a very good story, all working up to its climax of the old lady dying, and then still exciting afterwards, so there is the constant wanting to know what will become of the children. *All* the characters sound good, children *and* adults. It sounds a thick book too, plenty of reading, and I like that deeper thing underneath them all somehow about to embark upon Life (symbolized by the boat). No, I can find nothing to criticize here, only to praise. I return the synopsis, as you may want to refer to it. I can find *no* subs to steal the thunder! Only person to watch might be Emma, to see she doesn't become another Laura. I'm sure I shall love Comus. He must have a certain *quick* malice, like French children occasionally have.

Now, as to your proposed flat – perhaps it is now decided upon, or discarded? It's most attractive by the sound of it, and full of character. Only snag – and I *do* think a snag, as you found the boat so small – is just having one room. You *do* like to have a sitting-room *plus* a bedroom, which you had on the boat, and one of its snags was that you wanted an extra room to put a friend up occasionally. In this flat, you would hardly have room to turn round! I don't think it's practical to say you could build a room on to the balcony. How!? However, I don't want to put you off, but this was the snag that seemed to stand out a mile when I read your letter. You didn't mention a bathroom? Anyway, I shall be most interested to hear what comes of it all. Don't LEAP!

Poor Tod is still waiting for an op, which might be the end of the coming week, but they still don't let her know. I will send you a wire when she has had it, and you can write to her at the hospital. I do hope she'll be OK. I'll tell her about the beaming nurse of Madame B.'s Madame Mère. I must say, I should be dreading it. Another thing, poor Winifred is not well – she has something wrong with her throat. She can only talk with difficulty – I heard this via Tod, who was to lunch with Winifred and the Milton Runyons tomorrow. I don't like the sound of it. Could she have some growth in her throat? She is always rather hoarse, isn't she?

Two more things I meant to tell you, ages ago. I have put on Marraine's record, and I simply *love* it. Gosh, how beautifully she plays! Really inspiring. It immediately made me 'brew', and have a person in the Urbino book who plays beautifully! The thing she does so well is that Debussy piece I remember learning years ago, but Oh, such wonderful touch! And I am mad about the thing called *Fileuse*, by Ruff? I've never heard of it. It would make a wonderful *pas de deux* in a ballet. The other thing, Tommy says to tell you, is that the little plant you gave him for his birthday is going great guns, and is still in profuse flower! We have moved it to the dining room, because the telly-room was too warm, and it graces the whole room, the dear little thing. Perhaps it's magic! Tommy has had a horrid head cold, but otherwise OK and in good form. I am well, only bored with not getting on fast enough with my Notes. Because if I don't start actually writing until March, it means I will be working through the summer, April, May, June – possibly July – and I do so hate to be indoors in the summer! It's not routes, it's routes to write in the winter months. Still, *tant pis*. I don't like to go to the Hut these days, either, with Tommy at home.

I have been reading a Main book I loved, called *Twilight and Sunset*, and it's the journal of that old art critic man who lived in Florence and died not so long ago, very old. It's his journal between the ages of eighty-two and ninety-four. He was a wonderful old man, full of Deep Thoughts, and I just could not put the book down. If you have any book tokens left, do get it. It's expensive, 42/-. I got it on the Harrods Libe list, so after Moper reads it (he is enjoying it) I'll have to send it back. I'm in the middle now of *The Little Girls*, Elizabeth Bowen's first book for nine years, but so far I'm disappointed. It's muddling, and written in such an involved way. It sounded so good, too – three middle-aged women who used to be friends as children, and meet after years, and then you go back and see them as children. But they're all such shillings when you *do* go back, at any rate as far as I've got – not a bit K.M.-ish, as I'd hoped.

Will you still call the book 'Don't Bother About Arcadia', and will some person say it in the book? I'm thinking of changing *The Night the Falcon Fell* to *The Flight of the Falcon*, because the falling part might give away what is to happen, and the flight could be a two-fold thing, with a deeper meaning.

Piffy is going to be sixty next weekend! Doesn't it sound awful, like old aunts one had as a child, and yet I always think of Piffy as someone who still says, on a Saturday afternoon when I'm trying to get her to play Catholics and Huguenots, 'Oh, I don't think I will play,' and stumping off, with two plaits, to read, or do something else. Jeanne was much better at playing, with her little friend Nan, who did lessons with us, and I always got them to play *my* games, in which I was the leader, so I suppose it gave me Power! One's dress tucked into one's knickers for a doublet, and a woollie over one's shoulders for a cape. I still think that when one writes a book, it's the same thing. It's all pretending, and like dressing up!

Weather has been east windy, and bleak, no sun, but today much milder, and one begins to see the daffodils struggling to get to bud, and already it's light after tea, which gives one hope.

No more now. Write again soon, and tell me about the flat plans.

Heaps of love, Track-Tray.

※

Mena, Sunday 15 March, 1964.

Dearest Oriel,

I did love getting your long Main letter, and do forgive a scrap now, but we have a Tell-Him cousin of Moper's and his wife here, self-invited for the weekend, and one has to cope, and all last week I was actually down to the writing of the book. I decided I was delaying too much over the jotting down of the notes, and the précis – rather like what you said about yourself, and putting off the moment of getting down to the writing! So I decided I *must* make a start, and I did last week, and I am so glad I did because I have now begun to get into the swing, and although I have not quite done fifty pages yet, it *is* properly launched. You start too, and we'll keep in line together. Rather fun. The Book, I mean! Oh, it makes such a difference to one's day. Instead of feeling constipated and restless, I can now sit down in the morning at the end of the Long Room, after taking Bib for his trit, and I do the same after lunch, and then – after routes walk – again after tea. I now feel settled, and grudge interruption.

Oh, poor old Tod is installed in St Mark's Hospital, City Road, and she was so pleased to get your flowers, and the horrid op is tomorrow. But, poor dear, already she is grumbling, and going for everyone there, and puts up the backs of the doctor and surgeon. I do feel so dreadfully sorry for her, and I know she will be in agony next week, but if only she would not purge at everyone, it would be easier for her in the hospital.

How very sad about your Boat neighbour, I am so sorry. It will have made everyone sad. Interesting about the KM. book. You know I went to Fontainebleau, and found her grave in the cemetery, and saw the stone that Richard Murry put up to her; not old Murry, the husband. The *guardien* told me how she had been in the *fausse commune*, and then Richard, the brother, had her moved. He was always nice in the letters, do you remember?

Forgive me now if I stop.

Fondest love, Tray.

The 'Boat neighbour' to whom Bing referred lived further down the river, on one of the grander houseboats. Some fifteen or twenty assorted craft lay between us, and I might never have met the owners of *La Garonne* but for an accident of the kind which all too often befell me. Returning from my summer holiday, I was unpacking my suitcase out on deck, when it slipped from my grasp and was borne away on the swiftly flowing current. It was a light cardboard suitcase from the goodly firm of Marks & Spencer (where quality is assured) so it did not sink, but floated along with a bobbing motion. My Mississippi neighbour's student was standing in a dinghy, painting the side of her boat. Alarmed by my cries, he seized the oars and set off in hot pursuit. I knew he had little chance of catching up with the suitcase, which was now whirling along at an ever faster pace, so I hurried up the steps, and raced along the Boulevard, trying desperately to keep it in sight, over the garden hedges. All I achieved was a stitch in my side, while the suitcase bobbed merrily along, presumably on its way to the sea. It soon developed a slight list to starboard, however, which made it slacken speed, and veer gently towards the bank.

When I judged it was close enough I raced down the garden of the nearest houseboat and pealed frantically at the bell. This was opened by an august person in a striped waistcoat, who took one look at my bare feet and cotton slacks and seemed inclined to close it again forthwith. I pushed him aside and dashed headlong down a passage, and into a room where, to my horror, a lunch party of the most formal kind was drawing to its close, with coffee and liqueurs. It was a charming room, its walls hung with red and white striped silk, like a tent, while a crystal chandelier sparkled on the silver and glass, and on the jewels of the elegant guests, whose light summer dresses and straw hats might have stepped straight from a painting by Marie Laurencin. There was nothing nautical about the scene, except the wide expanse of river outside the windows.

Everyone naturally stared at me in stunned surprise, and I felt that only some dramatic explanation could excuse this intrusion, so as if inspired by my surroundings, I cried, 'Ma valise! Mes bijoux! Au secours!'

At once everyone leapt to their feet with cries of alarm and dismay. 'Mon dieu, quel désastre!' the elegant ladies cried, wringing their hands, while their husbands hurried down to the landing stage, where my suitcase could be seen, bobbing gently shorewards. Their host summoned the person in the striped waistcoat and bade him fetch a long gaffe, with a hook at the end, to secure it when it came within reach. He did so, giving me a look of intense dislike, with which I could only sympathize as in so doing he went into the water up to his ankles.

My own feelings were no less distressed, for my suitcase, far from containing any priceless jewellery, merely held books (including Bing's latest, *Castle Dor*, which I should have been sorry to lose) and an old, battered toy rabbit, the companion of my early days, which I sometimes took on a visit to Mena to hobnob with Bing's and Moper's bears. This could hardly be explained in public, and I received the dripping suitcase into my arms with mixed feelings. It was somewhat unsavoury by now and everyone prudently backed away. Madame Garonne, rivalling Ellen as the perfect hostess, begged me to open it at once and to check that my jewellery was safe.

At this point the student appeared on the scene, flushed and panting, having nobly pursued his quarry to the end, so, with profound expressions of gratitude I hopped in and bade him cast away. The dinghy sank low down into the water, and as we were rowing against the current, progress was slow. Every time I looked back I could see the whole company, still assembled on the landing stage, staring after us in amazement.

'Why are you in such a hurry?' my companion panted, peevishly. 'They might have offered us a drink.' I sympathized, but could only urge him onwards as I feared we might not reach *La Ronde des Heures* before sinking. It was a long hard pull upstream, and after rewarding my companion with an enormous tea and all my spare cash, I sat down to write a note of apology to my hostess, to send with some flowers.

The next day, while I was swabbing down the deck, I heard the garden gate click and saw Madame Garonne, elegant as ever, coming down the steps. She came, she said, to thank me for the flowers and to see if she and her husband could do anything to help. This neighbourly gesture touched me, and over tea in the garden we made friends. Her family came from Lyon, and for centuries had owned a silk and lace manufactory. It was she who created the designs for the delicate lace wedding veils they sold, and the tablecloths which graced some of the most elegant Paris restaurants. When I saw these I was filled with admiration for the beautiful and complex designs she conjured up out of her imagination, in which flowers, feathers and snowflakes were finely spun. During our friendship, I learned all about lace from Madame Garonne, and treasure the pieces she gave me, almost too fine to be taken from their tissue paper.

On that first morning, I learned that the lunch party into which I had so rudely intruded was a business lunch, and the personage in the striped waistcoat had merely been an 'extra'. Later, I was often to be a guest in that enchanting dining room, with its French windows opening onto the deck, where the same striped hangings formed a canopy to protect one from the sun. When life grew too turbulent in the proximity of my Mississippi neighbour (whose life was never without its drama), I would often seek the calmer waters of *La Garonne*, and the gentle company of my new friend. Like the others who gathered round her, I found a sense of peace and rest in her presence, where it would have been unthinkable to raise one's voice or lose one's temper; and I never heard her say an unkind word about anyone. She was all too often mysteriously unwell, but it was a shock to learn that she had cancer, for which at that time there was no other treatment than the cobalt rays, which were often as hard to stand as the disease itself. Every time she returned from the Clinic after one of those treatments, she seemed weaker. When her husband was forced to be away on business, she would sometimes ask me to come and sleep on board to keep her company, but she would never call me in the night, and I never heard her complain. Her end was as quiet and gentle as herself; she left a gap in our river community which could not easily be filled.

꙼

Mena, 5 April (Low Sunday. Why?).

Dearest Oriel,

So many thanks for your Easter card, which went at once on to the mantelpiece in the Long Room, routes, besides one for Mother's Day from Kits. (I'm sure he doesn't know about it, and Olive made him!) Forgive me not writing before, but they were here over Easter and went on Tuesday. Then I was working all the week, but suffered interruptions from various Witherspoons who were in Cornwall, and would ring up, and one had to have them for tea, in relays. Such a bore!

It was lovely seeing Kits and Olive, and Flave the weekend before. The young marrieds were very happy and nice, and it was very easy. Kits unchanged, but a bit more responsible, I thought, and more adult in a way. It's psychological politics, because he is with Olive awfully like the way he was with Flave, when they were young. She had to go and play Badminton in the Old Libe (such a sweat for her!), and he talks of himself in the third person, like he does with me, so it's as though he has been able to continue the old family routes with a wife, which is *just* what I hoped would happen. You know I have this thing, that it is really what people (unconsciously) want to do, to find the old security in their adult life, that they had as children. On the other hand, he is not babyish, or clinging. I suddenly saw that all that French family thing will come out in him, when they have children. He will be an *excellent* father. She is a dear, and I like her, and have great hopes they will make a stable thing.

As to myself, the book is going like a bomb. I hope it doesn't mean I shall get badly stuck, later on. I've done a hundred and forty typescript pages now, which perhaps is some forty-two thousand words, but I never can calculate. It's always more than I thought! I'm keeping more or less to the Notebook, but as you said, as one goes on things somehow branch out, and although I don't go in for subs as much as you do, I think there *will* be more subs than usual. It's tricky, because everyone is Italian, and while I never thought twice about having everyone French, I can't say I really know about Italians, so I have to think myself under their skins – perhaps wrongly. Who can tell, until it gets translated into Italian? If I go to Urbino, I will be stoned. Not that I make them beastly, but after all – if an Italian wrote about Fowey, with awful things happening, how tut-tutting all the Fowey people would be!

Tod is on the mend. I ring her up every evening, and there is usually a moan about the food, and so on. But I honestly think she is feeling better. She hopes to be away in another week, and going to stay with a friend in Winchester, who has a good cook! Poor Winifred has had to have some op on her throat. You know how hoarse Winifred always is? Well, it was some sort of cyst – not very nice, is it? But it seems that it is OK.

There's to be a great invasion of Doubledays to Claridges this month, and a big party, but I shan't go to it. I really *can't*. If I work hard and don't get a hold-up, I might be finished by the end of May, and then could be free for a boatified, basking summer. The boat is to be launched in May, and Moper will be hard-chairish if I don't take an interest, and go out in it.

Fondest love, Bing.

After his retirement, Moper had involved himself in various local activities, including Civil Defence for Cornwall. Bing worried when he was out late at meetings, fearful that in male company he might be tempted to exceed the very few drinks which were all he could safely absorb. On one occasion, he had been unable to resist, and in consequence had become involved in a minor car accident, as a result of which his licence was suspended for six months. The damage had been negligible, but to Moper the incident was a tragedy which sent him into a spiral of guilt and remorse. On my next visit to Mena, he seemed resigned, although rather quiet and withdrawn. I remember standing with him one day at the edge of the lawn, looking out to sea. We had been for a short walk, and it was the end of a fine, sunny winter's day; wood-pigeons flapped in the trees, and all around us was calm, and peaceful. I turned to speak to Moper, but on his face was such an expression of inner sadness that my words were silenced.

Mena, Sunday 24 May, 1964.

Dearest Oriel,

You will be feeling terribly sad about poor Winifred. Barbara* rang me up, at your suggestion, and I sent flowers, but there was nothing else one could do. It was all so sudden. I have been writing to Barbara today, and saying how wrong I think it is that doctors do not tell patients and relatives when they have a malignant growth. All they need say is: 'Look, this is malignant, but there is a fifty-fifty chance that deep X-rays *might* do it good, so?' And the person says if they want to have X-rays or not. Winifred would not have minded. She went into hospital anyway, and died there, and whether she died of cancer or of a queer thyroid thing hardly mattered by then. But at least her friends and relatives would not have been so shocked. They would have said, 'Well, of course we *knew* it was cancer, and so did she.' But Barbara, only a week before, had said there was no question of cancer, it was just to do with thyroid. So naturally one didn't do anything, and you didn't go down to see her at Bexhill, imagining it was a temporary thing to do with her throat.

Moper's new boat is to be launched on Tuesday, and there is *such* a to-do about it. People have been asked to watch, and Mrs Treffry from Place is to launch her with champagne, and it's almost as big in Moper's life as when we had the Queen to tea! He is all worked up and can't sleep, and I only hope he will be OK on the day. Anyway, he hasn't drunk a thing since that day in December with the awful car business.

Kits has got the Second-Assistant job on the film *A High Wind in Jamaica*, and it means going to Jamaica end of June. I *wish* I could see them before they go. I would terribly like to fly for about five days to my Urbino, when I've been through my book; and if Tessa could come to be with Moper, I will. He couldn't mind for five days, and I do so long to see the place I've been living in since February!

All love, Tray.

❦

POSTCARD

Friday.

Urbino even more beautiful than I had remembered it. Keep this postcard, so that you can look at it when you read Track's book! I am

---

* Barbara Noble, Winifred Nerney's successor at Doubleday's London office.

now looking at all the places, and seeing if I have got them right. Kits and Olive very good and helpful. The weather is glorious, and we had some good swimming at Rimini. I would love to live here for about three months!

Love, Tray.

※

Mena, 30 June, 1964.

Dearest Oriel,

My trip to Italy with Kits and Olive was bliss, and they were so sweet to be with. Urbino was lovely, more lovely than I had remembered, and it was such fun seeing all the places I had written about from memory – not all quite the same, but it doesn't matter. Victor is pleased with the book, but as always, silly old thing, wants my – as I thought – funny bits about tourists in Italy cut out. I know it has some 'Deeper' Thought layers, but I'm sure Victor has not spotted them, and just thinks it's a suspense story, the ignorant old man.

Rupert and Norwegian nanny arrived yesterday. Rupert has a backlash cough from whooping cough, and foolishly we let him go in the water yesterday, and he is not very well today; looks white and is staying in bed. How awful if we have made him worse! Also, we have a new dog, to be a companion to Bib! Also came yesterday. His name is *Murgatroyd*!! Morray for short. We saw him at the vet's, his owner did not want him (he's a West Highland, like Bib), and the vet said they were trying to find a home for him, so we have him for a week on trial. They are quite good together, so far.

Why is it that children you make up in books are always nicer than real children? Think of Lord Fauntleroy, seven, and Humphrey in *Misunderstood*! I think Rupert might be a bit like them, but he seems to me very young for nearly six.

All love, Track.

※

Mena, Tuesday after Bank Holiday, 4 August, 1964.

Dearest Oriel,

Victor is going to publish *Falcon* in January now, not December – just as well, I think. It has not gone yet for a serial in the States, and I haven't heard of it being chosen as a Book Club choice, which makes me think it won't go all that well over there. I'm afraid people are not going to understand it at all, but I am glad you liked it. Tell Madame B. I shall be most interested to read the Urbino book. Yes, horrid old Cesare Borgia went and took the city from poor Guidobaldo, the good Duke's son, but he got it back again later, if I remember rightly.

Why does Monsieur B. write about marionettes?! I have a theory that people who use marionettes, but more especially one big doll, like ventriloquists, can't have true relationships with people, and by jerking their puppets about they get the power they don't otherwise have! I also was thinking the other day, how awful it would be if, instead of getting older, after middle age, we regressed, and the person of sixty suddenly jumped to twenty (though still feeling sixty), and then at seventy (Tod, say) looked like ten, all short and with socks and things, and had to buy child's clothes to dress in (can't you *imagine* Tod's rage?!) and then at eighty, although perhaps quite lucid still, had all the indignity of having to be carried, and napkins. But the point would be, the looking forward would be so fearful. I mean, *now*, I can look forward say to a reasonable old age, and death around eighty; but what if I had to plan for my schooling once more at ten, and for someone to look after me at seven – would Tessa or Flave? The idea has frightful possibilities. Do ask Monsieur B. how it would fit in with his philosophy? It would so throw everything out!

Tons of love, Tray.

X

Mena, Sunday 23 August, 1964.

Dearest Oriel,

It was so sweet of Madame B. to send me the book on Urbino and I have written to thank her in atrocious French. I hope she will understand it. Tell her I speak better than I write, but am what Tod would call very 'rusty'!

Now, I am rather disturbed by your own restless mood. Do you remember how it was the same last year, about leaving the boat? You felt at the end of a great epoch, and now it's the same again, brought on by your father being ill. I wonder if, in a way, you are trying to blame yourself for his illness in that if you had not gone to live abroad but stayed at home, he would not have remarried, and would be rushing around, beaming, with two sound legs and no stroke? It's partly because you are Pegless, and it makes a great gap. You remember how I told you that when I was younger I always had to have some sort of Peg to hang things on, whether it was a character in a book developing from a real person, or a real person being pegged from a character (*very* muddling!) – and this, quite apart from my ordinary married life with Moper and the children?

The Peg made an interest, and one's dream life (which you and I, as imaginative writers, have) centred round this Peg, although one's reason told one it was non-adult and absurd. It must be a lot mixed up with sex because now I don't feel I need Peg any more, but before C. of L. my Peg images were very strong. Looking back now, although they served beautifully as characters in books, it was awfully silly, *au fond*, pegging them as *people*. I learnt my lesson, and I have told you this before, when having pegged Gertrude (bits of Maria in *Parasites*, bit of *Rachel* etc) and then she died – I was quite *bouleversée* by the death; *not* because how sad, a friend had died, but how bottomless – a Peg had vanished! A fabric that one had built disintegrated! Though your Peg has not died, it could be that the myth having disintegrated (for you see it now as a myth), has left you bereft. Vanity, vanity, all is vanity, as you say. *Why* write? *Why* think out silly stories that aren't true, about Gondals that don't exist? I've been through all this. But where it is harder for you is that you do not have your husband and children in the background. Try and work out your present trouble (of course Winifred's death, before your Papa's illness, didn't help), but I think, basically, you may be making these deaths and illnesses a cover for your Pegless life. It does take time to break out of this mood, I know full well, and in the long run, a book is the only hope – *writing* one, I mean.

Fondest love, Tray.

Bing at Kilmarth

La Ronde des Heures

Yvonne Printemps and Pierre Fresnay in *Les Trois Valses*, 1938

Yvonne Printemps and Pierre Fresnay at home in Paris, 1960

Marraine (Yvonne Arnaud)

The Bs on board *La Ronde des Heures*, 1961

Mr B

Kilmarth

The view from Bing's bedroom at Kilmarth

The chapel at
Kilmarth

Bing looking out to sea from the garden, Kilmarth

Tray with Freddie, at Mena

With Freddie, at Kilmarth, 1969

Bing, about 1970

At Kilmarth, with Mac and
Kenzie

Coming up Thrombosis Hill (with Tod's much-painted tree in the background!)

Mena, Saturday 5 September, 1964.

Dearest Oriel,

Your long Main, very interesting letter finds us in trouble here. I'll answer the letter when I've given you the news. The thing is, poor Moper's foot has boiled up badly. He has been in bed for a fortnight with a clot on it, and that is a horrid thing that has to be rested completely. Anyway, it seemed a bit better, when at the start of this week, a corn between his toes on the bad foot got some sort of infection – nothing to do with the clot – and he is now in torture with *that*, and off the clot pills and on to penicillin for the new thing. It's awful how painful it must be, and each time I go into the room he seems to be writhing with it, then now and again it will ease.

What clashed with all this was a cable from the *Good Housekeeping* people, saying would I hurry with their silly alterations, and write a last chapter to round everything off, and then Ken,* over from New York, added his voice to this, saying *he* might like to print the same version as *Good Housekeeping*. This threw me into a tizzy, because one has to take more trouble for a book than for a mag, and the rather silly sentences I had written for *Good Housekeeping* didn't seem right for Doubleday! So, you can just imagine, what with rushing up and down and ministering to Moper, and minding wretched Morray, and dashing stuff on Bibby's eczema, and then this rewriting or adding bits to *Falcon*, I hardly knew where I was!

And oh, a last thing. You know that Rashleigh house that I was interested in – Kilmarth, above Polkerris, where they want to make a horrid holiday village? Well, it turns out that the Rashleighs have not *yet* got the lease back, and the daughter of the tenant who died wants to sell the nineteen-years lease, and just for interest's sake, Tess and I went all over it. No doubt, the site is superb, the most glorious view of the bay, and the house itself, though not large and gracious and lovely like Mena, has a definite charm and *could* be made very nice, if money were spent on it. I wish you could have come too, to see the Kilmarth place. It was certainly much nicer than I had expected, and as a second string to Mena, very good indeed. Actually, the crowds everywhere have been so awful this summer, that I'm afraid Cornwall is ruined anyway in the summer, and one must make up one's mind to that. A swimming pool is one's only hope, wherever one is, and staying in one's garden.

Do write soon, and say how things are down South. Yes, I'm sure

* Ken McCormick, Daphne's American editor.

Moper would love a big bright postcard of Monte Carlo harbour with its boats, and news of all the boats you can see.

Fondest love, Track.

※

Great Western Hotel, Paddington, Sunday.

Dearest Oriel,

The operation on the leg *does* seem to have been successful, the blood circulating again OK, but I am not happy about Moper's condition. He is very low and weak (I s'pose like people get after a major op, which he has never had before), and he is running quite a high temperature which won't come down; he is being plugged with antibiotics every six hours. He looks awful, so drawn and grey, and the day before yesterday he was quite light-headed and thought he was on the boat, and he kept saying I was keeping George waiting; it was agony. Yesterday lucid, thank goodness, but dreadfully tired. Today more irritable, and still a temp.

I am just praying they will get the answer to his temperature, and that he will begin to pick up. We have been here over a week now – it seems like eternity.

Managed to see Tod's flat yesterday – it is super, she is so *bien installée*! Hope Papa is OK?

Fond love, Tray.

※

Greenwich Hospital, Plymouth, 16 September, 1964.

Dearest Oriel,

I have left you *sans nouvelles* since my last Main letter, because a crisis developed very rapidly. Moper's foot got worse, he had to go quickly by ambulance last Wednesday (a week ago) to this hospital, to have an operation to try and restore the circulation to his foot. The operation is the one the King had (George VI) when the circulation went in his foot; it worked with him, and works with most people. Unfortunately (the op was Friday), it has *not* worked with Moper – the arteries to the foot were too far gone. He has been in great pain, as owing to the nerve pills he takes they could not give him morphia to allay the pain after the op. It has been a nightmare to see him suffer, and for him to know that the op has not worked after all. The thing is now to try and control the pain in the foot, and to get him home, restore his morale, and see how he gets on. The only alternative, for a younger, stronger man, would be to amputate the leg. This I have firmly said No to, and the surgeon entirely agrees. Tommy would never stand the shock. Already his morale is terribly low, not only from weakness but from the feeling that the op has not worked, and he is so pathetic and humped in his bed.

There is no more the doctors can do for his foot, except try and kill the pain, and if they can do that they will send him home, perhaps Monday. Then, it will mean rather hobbling about, perhaps on one floor. I don't know, I must cross that bridge when I come to it. Nothing matters, as long as we can keep him free from pain, and reasonably fit.

Send another cheerful postcard to Moper at home – if still here, I can bring it.

All love, Tray.

While I was ministering to my father in the South of France, Bing was having an even more worrying time at Mena, and once again there was little I could do to help her. I could only send Moper a series of cheerful postcards. He faced his disability with courage, and soon was able to get out in his new electric chair.

☸

Mena, Wednesday 23 September, 1964.

Dearest Oriel,

It was lovely to get your letter, and comforting, in a curious way, to know that we were going through much the same sort of distress, though I think yours was more acute around the time you were here, and Papa was in hospital. It's a case of living day to day with Moper and seeing how it goes. He is very plucky with his two sticks, and gets up and down stairs, but only once in the day. I help him dress and undress. He is not wandery or dopey, though awfully fatigued after bouts of pain.

Don't expect a lot of news as I have little time for letters, but you know I will keep you in touch more than anyone. I do get tired, but it's not the angry fatigue of the days when poor Moper drank – I have so much more sympathy now, and somehow it's less tiring. It's draining, yes, and I suffer every time I watch *him* suffer, but I remain calm. I don't seethe underneath, which the drinking made me do. I suppose it's all part of the lesson of Life.

No more for now. Do write again soon.

All love, Tray.

————

For some time my father's health had been causing us concern. A highly nervous man, he had made a second marriage late in life and had settled at Cap d'Ail in the South of France without, of course, speaking a word of the language. They had hoped to lead a busy life among the British colony, but the reality proved to be something of a disappointment. My father, already a sick man when he married, was soon forced to lead the life of an invalid. Under these conditions my stepmother grew bored and increasingly impatient with my father's slowness. Her visits to England became more frequent, and she would send me an urgent telegram to warn me that my father's health was deteriorating. I would hastily pack and set off, only to find my father his usual self and slightly surprised to see me. But I came to welcome these interludes, for at such quiet times my father and I drew closer to each other than we had ever done before. His illness had made him gentler, less nervous, and more at peace with himself. He liked me to sit beside him on the terrace, or to accompany him on a daily drive into the surrounding countryside.

A favourite place for these outings was Notre Dame de Laghet, a place of pilgrimage high up in the hills. For centuries the chapel walls had been decorated with pictures, representing the miseries and disasters from which so many grateful souls had been rescued by the intervention of Notre Dame de Laghet. These seemed mostly to be shipwrecks, but there were carriages plunging over precipices, burning buildings and fallen tree trunks, while crutches of all sizes were festooned about the altar. These disasters did not appear to depress my father's spirits; they amused him and we often came here, always out of season, for I never remember seeing any other visitors.

Sometimes my sister would come out from England to join us, and then we would do our best to remedy my stepmother's somewhat spartan ideas of housekeeping ... I well remember her horrified surprise when I suggested that a visitor might enjoy two croissants for his breakfast. '*Two* croissants?' she exclaimed, in the outraged tones of Lady Bracknell. 'Who could possibly eat *two* croissants for breakfast?' Most occupants of the

Villa found no difficulty in doing so, and in her absence we freely encouraged them to indulge in this, and other such excesses.

🜚

Letter from Tommy
Mena, 27 November, 1964.

Dearest Oriel,

Thank you so much for the cards and news, and was glad to hear you are having lovely weather. Here, thank goodness, it has been the mildest November ever, I should think, so I have been able to get out quite a lot in my electric chair, which gets me round the Cedar and Palm Walks, and the drives etc, though not good across country!! The old foot still gives me a lot of pain, especially at night, but the doctors continue to say this is a good sign!! They also say it is all a very slow process, but I could have told them that! *Yggy III* was put to bed early of course, as I missed the last two months of our good summer, and she is now back in the shed where she was built. No alterations required, as she proved so satisfactory, except for that boarding ladder, which we are having put right, so one steps straight into the cockpit, which will be much more satisfactory. Apart from the old foot, Bing and I are flourishing, though the former has had a pretty trying time, with a semi-invalid on her hands for three months. She has certainly been wonderful, and very patient, as when one is in pain, even an angel can be fractious!

We have got the whole outfit coming down for Christmas, which with my disabilities, will be rather a major operation, but still all very good fun. I hope your father is well and not overdoing things? Have you found a permanent home yet, as I know you have been looking for one?

Bing sends her fond love, and let us have your news when you have a moment to spare.

With much love from Tommy.

🜚

Mena, Saturday 21 November, 1964.

Dearest Oriel,

Your Main letter came today, and I thought I would answer it while it was fresh in my thoughts. Also, to say *don't* send the comfits, if you mean those glazed fruits that look so lovely, as we neither of us touch them. We used to get them from someone, I forget who, and it was such a waste, as we didn't like them. But if there were fresh mandarins ready to send in boxes, they would be lovely, but maybe a bit early for them?

Monte Carlo weather sounds lovely, and it would be nice to have that sort of break. Yes, I agree, I can imagine Doodie at 'the tables'! I hope *you* won't take to it, like your grandmother. It's *very* eighteenth century, isn't it? Old Pen Friend is going to Genoa in January, for the climate!

Tons of love, Bing.

※

Mena, 4 March, 1965.

Dearest Oriel,

Oh Doom ... Oh Doom ... Thank you for your last letter, but things are still so bad with us. My dreadful jaundice thing is better, but I am still yellow and confined to my room, and have lost a stone in weight. And poor Moper caught some awful bronchial flu out of the air, somehow, last week, and has been terribly ill – right back to before he left hospital. He has been in bed nearly a week. He looks ghastly. I can't believe he can get right after this, and his leg was going on quite all right. Why is it that a sudden Doom descends on people in a flash? I don't know when I shall be strong enough to cope. Tessa came for a few days, but had to go back again yesterday. Thank goodness for the two excellent little nurses.

No more for now, but I wanted you to know about us. Perhaps you will telephone some time, about seven in the evening, and I will speak from my room? It is bitterly cold weather. How I long for the spring.

Fond love, Tray.

———

Death is always unbelievable, until it happens. By this time Bing had accustomed herself to Moper's invalid life and tried to live from day to day, with no thought of what must ultimately take place. The shock was all the greater when, going in to see him at breakfast-time, in the routes way, she was called back again a few minutes later to find that he had slipped away. In spite of all misunderstandings, there was that bond of love and trust between them which, stretched to the limit at times, cannot be broken; and she mourned him deeply.

🪷

Mena, 19 April, 1965.

Dearest Oriel,

This is just to say I am so looking forward to seeing you next Tuesday. I would have written before, but I had our lawyer down for three days, and we were very busy over something called Probate. I have to put in claims, which seems so waine as I don't need them, for Widow's Grants and Pensions. I said to the lawyer, 'Honestly, it's not necessary,' and he had to explain that I wasn't taking bread from some poor person's mouth, that all this is legal, and is more or less automatic.

My letters are more or less finished, although they still trickle in from people who had been abroad when Moper died, and are now home and horrified, so one has to start all over again. Still, the letters did give me something to do. It's pretty ghastly from mid-afternoon onwards, not so much because I am on my own, but because Moper isn't here, and wanting his routes coffee, and then tea, and later our sups together etc, etc. I miss doing things for him – which, if I look at it dispassionately, is self-pity. No doubt if I was working on a book, and had my mind filled it wouldn't be so bad. It's funny how many rather silly people have said, 'Anyway, you have your writing!' as if – Bang! – I was going to sit down and reel off a thriller! I seem to remember, after Marraine died, you were blocked and numb, in the writing sense, for a long time.

Yes, there is all this long-term planning of a house to consider. Kilmarth is the house I told you about, that was to be Moper's and my second string, when Philip Rashleigh wanted to come here. Now Philip is being horrid about *both* houses, and everything is in a muddle. I think I shall ask him over here, and find out if it is he who is being horrid, or just his lawyers.

Tons of love, Tray.

———

One of the greatest trials the bereaved must face is the kind advice bestowed upon them by their friends and relatives, who all too often urge them to move at the earliest opportunity. This is often a fatal mistake, for nothing is so wearying as grief, and no one should be forced to take any major decision in those first restless months, or even years. All that Bing wanted was to be left in peace at Mena, to enjoy her own peaceful routes and the summer ahead and consider the future at leisure; above all, to hope that inspiration would come and set her mind brewing again. These hopes were to prove disappointing; the summer was unusually wet and cold, and her landlord, Philip Rashleigh, seemed unable to decide whether or not he intended to renew her lease for another fifteen years.

I had been shocked to learn that, for years, Bing and Moper had no legal lease for Mena other than a gentleman's agreement with old Dr Rashleigh, who lived 'up country' in some modern villa and had no intention of ever inhabiting Mena. I well remember Moper saying: 'Well, ducks, we had better get something more binding. We are none of us getting any younger ...' A new lease had been drawn up and was ready to be signed when old Dr Rashleigh suddenly died, and the future was thrown into the melting pot once more. No one knew if his heir would ratify this agreement or not, and meanwhile various alternatives came up for discussion, none of them wholly satisfactory.

At one time, Bing and Moper were keen to build a new house in the grounds of Menabilly, protected by the trees and the ever-present rhododendrons, and with a splendid view out to sea. We had often visited this site, but I always secretly felt this was a Gondal, and indeed the scheme quickly fell through. The other alternative was to move down the road to Kilmarth, the Dower House to Menabilly, but here too there were objections. The house stood high upon the cliffs, exposed to all winds, and had not been lived in for many years. From a quick, trespassing visit with Bing inside the grounds, I felt that to restore it would be almost as great an undertaking as to build a new house.

Bing, naturally, hoped to be allowed to stay on at Mena and when, at the end of July 1965, Philip Rashleigh agreed to renew her lease she was greatly relieved. Almost at once, she began to feel the first faint growth of a new story pricking her mind.

※

Mena, Saturday 22 May, 1965.

Dearest Oriel,

I have thought of you so much since you telephoned, and I am afraid you will be having a very anxious, unhappy time. I think a great deal about your father and hope that whatever he is going through is not too hard for him. Being like Moper in many ways, he may have that apprehensive thing which is so distressing, and one would want him to be spared it. It is no use my speculating, because it could be better, or worse, than you expected, and I had better wait to hear from you before I say any more. I will go on at once to tell you ordinary things.

Flavia and I went to fetch my little DAF car, which is a dear little thing, and I am driving it about the paths and in the park, to give myself confidence.

Ellen's visit passed off very happily. She was just as she always was: not Tell-Himish, and only drinking White Dubonnet, and wine at sups. She was not keen on TV, so it did mean settling to talking after dins, which was a bit tiring, but oddly enough I did not find it too exhausting. She seems to be resigned to living in Honolulu and likes the people she knows out there, and says it is a much 'wider' circle than Oyster Bay, with intellectual people (!) and University people, and a lot of music etc. (She never used to like music!) So I think her friends there are a new lot she is *in* with, rather like you now have friends in Paris that you didn't once.

As for myself, I am ploughing along, and it does seem to get better – it started to do so when you came, so perhaps there is a lot of beaming down going on? Marraine may have organized it a bit, but I feel less wanting to cry, and more routes and cheerful. No fresh news either about Mena or Kilmarth; the lawyer is waiting to have a meeting.

Fondest love, Tray.

꽃

Mena, May 1965.

Dearest Oriel,

O, I have not thanked you for your French bread-basket, which is so goodly, and now Esther can get loaves of so-called French bread from the baker when he calls, which Mrs Burt heats up for sups. Isn't it providential? Foy sent me the original of *Alice in Wonderland* for my birthday – it's been redone in Lewis Carroll's handwriting, and suddenly I thought, Alice is exactly like *you*! Honestly, the things that happen to her, and the way she expresses herself, is *so* like! I laughed more than I had ever done before, because of this. She is so polite to that old turtle thing on the toadstool, although she says to herself: 'I wish these creatures wouldn't get so easily offended!' and I could see *you* falling down that rabbit-hole, and having Deep Thoughts as you fell! You *must* read it again when you come, I've put it in Blue Lady for you.

As to my woes of Menabilly and Kilmarth, no, I can't say I'm being noble and brave; it's one of those things that happen in life, to which one has just *got* to adapt, and where I should be thankful is that so far, unless it all disappears, I have resources behind me (that old Veteran Trust) which, if money has to be spent on either place, will be forthcoming. But if it *must* be Kilmarth, and it looks unhappily like it, it *is* a sweat, certainly, to think of all that would have to be done there. And rather silly at my time of life, to embark all over again at reconstructing a property! But, there again, that old house is there, and if it was *not* it would have been worse, for I would have had to have moved God knows where. Also, I have three years ahead of me in which to do it. Who knows, who knows, what will come about? It's no use getting Doomed and fussed, I must get on with this book, and work through *that*, and as the agent of Philip's is away on holiday, and all these lawyers and people take such ages to settle anything at all, I am going to put it aside from my mind. Ellen, by the way, said that Kilmarth had immense possibilities, and the site was wonderful. It was nonsense to say it could not be done, or must be pulled down! She came all over it with me, and was so helpful, and as you know, she has now built *two* houses. Of course, I don't go all the way with her – dishwashers and laundries in every corner! – but she did give sensible advice, and said how really charming it could be made, providing imagination was used. So, just as she cheered me last year, so she did cheer me up about this year's problems.

It was funny, your dream about Moper – one never knows how much these dreams are psychically true, or how much they are one's own unconscious fears. I had a very vivid one about Kits, just after he and Olive left for their holiday in Portugal last week – that he was desperately trying to find his nursery again, and had suddenly gone back to being four years old! It was dreadful, I was so worried. Then I wondered if I was mixing him with Freddie, who had gone to stay with Flave, and might be missing *his* nursery at Tithe Barn. Anyway, I rang Flave, and Freddie was as cheerful as a cricket, and I had a letter from Kits, happily basking in the Estoril sun, so *que voulez-vous*?

Oh, now, could you do something for me? Tessa has heard from a friend of Ferdie's in Paris that she, Ferdie, is very ill in the American Hospital in Neuilly, having had endless goes of *pleurisie* and *bronchite*. She is now in there having tests, and *prises de sang*, and explorations, and the Lot! I have sent her a telegram, and have written to her just now, but I do not know if she is *so* ill she is on some danger list, or is having these tests before some nasty op, or what? The friend did not give any details. I am wondering if you could possibly telephone, or even call at the Hospital? I dare say that her Mayor person at Le Mesnil St Denis, and being Deputy-Mayor herself, has ensured that she is getting every attention, but it's dreadful if she may be facing some fearful op, one just does not know. So I would be so grateful if you could find out for me. There must be a Matron or a Floor Sister who would surely know?

I was saddened, talking of illness, by that book of Simone de Beauvoir's, *Une Mort très facile** which I read in English, about her mother dying. It was beautifully written, and so moving, and reminded me so much of poor Gran.

Well, now no more. The reason I did not write last weekend was that I had to do all the letters that came for my birthday from people I don't know so well, and *they* have to have priority or they would never be done at all!

Tons of love, Tray.

🜊

Menabilly, 15 June, 1965.

Dearest Oriel,

Many thanks for your letter, which came yesterday. I seize the chance to write now, before Pen Friend arrives this afternoon. You can imagine how my time will be fully filled, attending to his wretched gourmet needs! Tessa is here, came yesterday, to help me out with him, but of course the weather has now changed from basking bliss overnight, to solid drenching rain! That will be a great bore if it continues tho' I feel sure he won't mind nodding off before the Long Room fire.

I am so dreadfully sorry about your poor father and his ups and downs. It does sound so like Moper in lots of ways. I shall always be glad that Moper died here at home, and not in hospital. In fact, I have an awful feeling that when the nurse told him that morning, just before he died, that he might be going into Fowey Hospital the next day for a blood transfusion, the shock of hearing that did the trick, and brought that clot dashing into his heart. He said, 'It wouldn't be for long, would it?' very anxiously, and she said: 'Oh no, twenty-four hours,' and then in a few minutes she had called me, and it happened.

I have had a meeting with Philip's estate men, and they said that Philip

---

* *A Very Easy Death.*

is very difficult to budge in any direction; what would I suggest myself? So I said *if* they gave me fifteen years from now (1965) until 1980 at Mena, I would agree to pay for the pulling down of the back.

I think it was Ellen who said rather a true thing about moving to new houses, in that it was very different when there was someone with whom you were going to share the house; but cold-bloodedly to plan a move into a house just for oneself, was hard going. This she meant for the widowed, who had shared a home for years with their married person. Quite different for you, who might be planning an apartment on your own. It's the thing of having been married once, and had a home, that the planning loses its point. That's why I do cling to the Mena routes I know.

Fond love, Track.

❦

Mena, 1 July, 1965.

Dearest Oriel,

I was shocked to get your letter this morning, and I fear when you read this it will mean that all is over for your father. I'm so frightfully sorry that twice now you have had to sit by the hospital bed of someone you love, and be without hope. Well, you will tell me in your own time how it happened, and I won't harp on it any more now, because you will have to face up to the performance of the funeral, and the great strain of all that. I don't know why people have to have those awful great Memorial Services, but I think it gives a self-righteous feeling to those left behind – I don't mean family, but friends – like a 'send-off', when a person catches a boat-train. Moper *loathed* them, would never attend them, and that is why I would not allow one for him, and put in the *Times*: 'No memorial service at his own request.'

What I didn't realize at the moment of Moper's death is that for many years I had been living under a strain of angst about his health (whether physical or mental), and although when he was OK I was perfectly happy, there was an underlying worry. Now, suddenly, that has been lifted. I still feel the happy feeling that I felt when he was here, but the apprehension is no longer with me. Hence, I have a sort of contentment.

I have the faintest, faintest 'brew' – a subject I used to think about some years ago – of a civil war, or an invasion of this country, and how it would affect a place like Fowey. Who would collaborate, and who would be Resistance? The title is possibly *The Take-over Bid*. It's only a faint seed, but I do see the possibilities of an exciting story in this. It could be satirical as well – showing up the sort of people who are 'in' with the invaders, and the ones who are not.

Fondest love, Tray.

When, two months after Moper, my father died in June 1965, it was something which had been expected, and could only be considered a relief. But his death was followed by an unforeseen blow. During the years when I had been happily living on the Seine, prices had risen steeply on land, and time was needed to bridge this gap before I could move into even a small flat on land. Meanwhile I had entrusted the money from the sale of *La Ronde* to a friend, who was also a competent international lawyer; perhaps he was not competent enough, for he became entangled in risky business deals and absconded with his clients' money. In France, all would have been repaid by the Chambre des Notaires. Although he was a member of this august body the Law Society disclaimed responsibility, however, and I could not afford a lawyer to press my claim.

I had been a slow learner for most of my life, but was now brought face to face with the fact that life is not a pleasant Gondal, but a battle. Since I had always secretly been on the side of the losers and underdogs, I did not find it hard to identify myself with them, and was even proud to join their ranks. Life becomes simplified when one's choices are reduced to a minimum; then one learns with a startling clarity who one's real friends are – and they are rarely those one had expected.

For some time I felt like a piece exposed on a chessboard, checkmated at every turn. Upon leaving *La Ronde des Heures*, I had rented the attics of the Bs' Normandy cottage, in which to store my furniture, and also Madame Mère's old room in the rue Molitor. Overnight, it seemed, I could not afford even this modest rent, and felt I must tell the Bs so at once. I had no fixed job, and no prospects; work permits were necessary then, and they were not easy to obtain. The Bs waved such scruples aside, declaring that having lived precariously themselves, they had never looked upon money as a sacred cow, but as a commodity to be shared with anyone in need; where there was enough for two, there would always be enough for three. I was deeply touched by their generosity, and accepted; and the years ahead linked us together, with those ties of the heart which are often so much stronger than the ties of blood.

Bing was the first to learn of this disaster, through the papers. She rang me at once, and was a constant tower of strength through the difficult years ahead as, indeed, were my friends the Gilberts and the Runyons. Both Stuart and Milton helped me find translations, which I hoped would tide me over, and enable me to keep on writing. Instead, these slowly snowballed, putting paid to any further books, for I did not have the stamina to do both. I concealed this from Bing as long as possible, cherishing my independence as fiercely as ever, and determined never to accept any help that I could not hope to pay back in due course, with interest.

I wish I could believe that I was grateful enough to the Bs in those early days. I was selfish, having inherited *this* quality at least from my Latin forebears. To sell *La Ronde des Heures* may have been the right decision, but I timed it badly, and by my impatience lost not only all my money but my independence, too. At first I felt cramped in the Bs' flat, and deafened by the noise of the traffic on the Boulevard Exelmans. I was openly critical of life on land, and did not hesitate to make my feelings plain, yet never once did the Bs reproach me for this cavalier attitude. Slowly, but surely, that shabby old flat began to weave its spell; the mutual love, and respect for all opinions, rubbed off even upon me, and gradually taught me to be more tolerant.

I also learned the art of managing on a small budget, and admired the sleight of hand which enabled Madame B. to produce such delicious meals out of very little; and yet there was always enough for unexpected guests. It was a lesson in itself, to accompany Madame B. to the market, which twice a week spread its richness almost upon our doorstep. She never let me venture there alone, maintaining that I bought whatever came to hand indiscriminately, instead of just making a careful round of the stalls, checking prices, and haggling over bargains. Like most thrifty French housewives, she had her favourite stalls, knew their owners by name, and listened sympathetically to their family histories. We always stopped to chat to a little old man with two wooden legs, who played his flute at the entrance, and like some benevolent Pied Piper, kept his eye upon dogs and babies, while their owners shopped.

※

Mena, 30 July, 1965.

Dearest Oriel,

Thank you for your goodly Main letter.

If my books had not been financially rewarding, and if I had not married I feel sure I would have led very much your sort of life. Probably managed to find myself a small cottage in Cornwall, and just made enough to pay a 'daily', and perhaps go for trips to France now and then. I could never have held down a job, although my physical health is stronger than yours. Yes, we both like our comforts, but not as madly as all that. You've never yet had a car, or entertained in lavish style, or wanted very crumby clothes, and furs and things. As to my own affair, daylight is glimpsed. Philip *has* consented to my having another fifteen years here, until 1980, with the proviso that I could build my Dower House in 1980 if he wanted to come in then. For this agreement, I will consent to pull down the back, providing the sum of demolition does not exceed five thousand pounds. I am happy about the decision, because I did not want to leave Mena. It's my home, and my routes, and the thought of starting up all over again with a Kilmarth, and perhaps not liking it when I got there, was a bit of a dread. So I do feel secure. And really, fifteen years – who knows? Grilled herring and St Cuthbert's Home for Old People still seems a long way off.

No more for now, and keep well, Tray.

🜨

Mena, 11 August, 1965.

Dearest Oriel,

I was so glad to get your Express letter this morning, as I was afraid the news about X would have been a terrible blow to you. Did you get the long letter I wrote to you, about a week ago? You did not mention it, but I expect you did. Meantime, don't despair, you are still some way from St Cuthbert's – we hope!

If Philip does not come here in 1980, I could begin to turn Mena into a St Cuthbert's, and house my poor ageing humble-circumstanced friends! You had better book Blue Lady and its bathroom in advance, but of course you'd have to have a cooking facility in one corner – unless you paid extra, and used Moper's room for a kitchen! I often think if there was another war, and Mena was taken over by Civil Defence,

I might ask to stay, and I'd put myself in Tod's flat. It really is very nice.

Don't despair, and let me have more news when you have time.

Fondest love, Track.

※

Mena, 11 September, 1965.

Dearest Oriel,

I have a Doom, but a conceited Doom. Kits, when he was here, took some photographs of me, and also a proper photographer came from St Ives to do me too, and I crumbed they would look well for future books. But they make poor Tray look just like an old peasant woman of ninety – *far* older and more wrinkled than Lady Vyvyan, and I nearly cried when I saw them. I know I am lined, but I had not realized how badly! And the awful expression on my face, like a murderess. Talk about being ready for St Cuthbert's – *well*! The thing is, everybody these days takes photos with tiny cameras and no lighting, so I suppose one's bad points come out worse. What a blow to one's Silly Values! Oh, me ... And there I was, swishing about thinking I looked quite nice.

Kits said bluntly: 'Well, Tray, you must realize that you do look a lot older than fifty-eight in real life!' and I was very shaken. The only way to treat it, is to think I'm a throwback to old glass-blowing provincial *aïeux* – you know how peasants etc get very old and wrinkled by forty and bent, and in shawls, carrying pails of water to cows! Maybe I'd better go the whole hog, and start to dress like that, it would be in keeping! You and I had better take adjoining rooms in St Cuthbert's – me for my great age, and you for your great poverty, and we'll cook our humble herrings together. I was *most* amused at Madame Peg's reaction to your lack of means, and the lovely 'sans importance' about a husband for you. Anyone with a bit of money would do! Perhaps she would marry *me* off too, as it is perhaps not right to be a '*veuve*!'

No more for now. Write again soon.

Tons of love, Track.

※

Mena, 27 September, 1965.

Dearest Oriel,

I thought I would send you a short letter, before setting forth tomorrow. I go up by train to Slough where Kits meets me, and I stay with them at Tithe Barn until Thursday morning, when Jeanne and I take off for Venice. We shall be in Venice for a week, so it's worth your sending me a line there to the Hôtel Monaco. It's always nice to get letters. After that, we shall motor about for a second week, and back to England on the weekend of the sixteenth, which I shall spend with Flave, then down home on Monday the eighteenth. Tod comes to stay for a week or ten days about then. If you like to book your time in November now, do so. I suggest mid-November, or later if you like, so that you won't overlap with Tod – you know how I like to space my visitors out.

I think it's a *fearfully* good idea your writing about Ste Thérèse. I have read a lot about her, and the best book is, I think (but won't swear to it) in French, and with all the direct sources, statements about her life at home, and the sisters, and the mother who died, and how she had tantrums as a child, and all that. Avoid in your reading, the *sugary* lives. I am sure such a lot of her was psychological politics, in the nicest way. In fact, if you feel at all stuck with a novel, I would almost switch to her life during the winter. Biographies are all the thing – I read a piece in the Sunday papers about it. I am sure novels are not selling so well, unless one is very Main and in Fashion, like Graham Greene always will be, and big names like that. There is a new person who has rather taken over from me called Mary Stewart, who sells a lot. I don't, now. My *Falcon*, which everyone said was a Best-Seller, only sold about twenty thousand copies in England, and you remember, in the old days, Track sold about eighty to a hundred thousand. (It's my Great Age!) So, whatever I do next, I shall not expect to sell.

I was much amused at Madame Peg being so *in* with you, and of course when I come to Paris I shall love to have dinner with them. But we would not dare look at each other! I think the thing is that a Frenchwoman like Madame Peg always seems to have more personality than a man, because they make more to-do about it! A man with a similar personality would be rather more tiresome.

Tons of love, Tray.

It was at this time that Thérèse Martin – Sainte Thérèse de Lisieux – known in England, alas, as 'The Little Flower', re-entered my life. She had been there ever since I received a copy of her autobiography, *The Story of a Soul*. A brief glance at the frontispiece, depicting a soulful young nun clasping an armful of roses, led me to consign this to the back of my bookshelves. Years later I came upon a biography of Thérèse called *The Hidden Face* (1959) by Ida Gorres, from which I learned that the picture I had disliked was not an authentic one, but merely an idealized portrait drawn by her sister Céline. In the same spirit, Thérèse's autobiography and her personal correspondence had been 'corrected', if not entirely rewritten, by her elder sister Pauline (Mere Agnès de Jésus). I could imagine no more heinous crime than to tamper with someone else's private papers. What induced them to do so? In 1955 the Carmel Convent of Lisieux produced a facsimile edition of the cheap school notebooks in which Thérèse had inscribed her spiritual testament, but it was to take another ten years for a team of thirty-five Carmelites, archivists and historians, using the most modern techniques, to restore the original texts beneath Mere Agnès's heavy erasures.

After a childhood marked by psychological suffering, Thérèse Martin entered the Carmel of Lisieux in April 1888, when she was just fifteen, a critical time in adolescence. She did so with her eyes open; years of visiting her sisters there had taught her what to expect; and yet the pettiness and stupidity, even the spitefulness of many of the Community, could not daunt her. She was entering Carmel to seek God. Once within, she did not rebel or criticize the laxity she found there, but fell back upon obedience to the prescribed Rule, and to the promises she had made on entering. This did not make her popular; even her sisters were disappointed, having expected her to join them in forming a family circle within the convent. Instead, Thérèse deliberately sought the company of the tiresome or eccentric nuns whom everyone shunned at Recreation. No doubt the spirituality, and the general level of intelligence in the Lisieux Carmel was neither better nor worse than in most nineteenth-century convents, but it was certainly pretty low. At a time when few choices were open to women, it was often the neurotic, the physically delicate, and those without a dowry who entered religious houses, and once within, struggled as best they could to develop a vocation.

As I pondered on the stifling, hot-house atmosphere of that provincial convent, my admiration grew for a young girl, spoiled and adulated at home, who could free herself from the various conflicts going on around her and strike out a new path for herself, one of pure abandonment to God's will, and love. This became known as the 'Little Way', and it was not really new: in the seventeenth century, writers such as St François de Caussade had proclaimed the way of loving abandonment to Divine Providence, calling it 'the sacrament of the present moment'. Almost from her entry into Carmel, Thérèse was plunged into what mystical writers label 'the dark night of the soul'; God seemed further away than ever. She died on 30 September, 1897, after months of a suffering so intense that it did indeed amount to martyrdom. 'I want to spend my heaven in doing good upon earth', Thérèse boldly declared, and promised that she would not only *beam* down, but would *come down*. It was these promises that caught the imagination of a world soon to be plunged into the darkness of World War One and which forced the Church to canonize her, in record time. For Thérèse did keep her promises, as hundreds of well-attested miracles prove; these include an unusual number of personal 'appearances', in the years following her death.

As usual, I longed to share my enthusiasm with Bing, and at this time must have despatched pages of Tell-Hims about the Martin family. Fortunately she *did* become interested, particularly in the untouched photographs by Céline, whose main objective was to photograph her sister Thérèse, but who also made some charming studies of the Community, going about their daily tasks in the laundry or the hayfield, and gathered together for Recreation in the chestnut avenue. In 1973, a centenary edition of Thérèse's collected works, including her family's own correspondence, had begun to appear, volume by slow volume. These did not wholly satisfy me; there were too many deliberate omissions. After a frustrating visit to the Carmel at Lisieux, I decided to abandon my project of writing about Thérèse. I had adopted her maxim for my own: '*Je n'ai jamais cherché que la vérité ...*' but I had not been allowed to find my own truth, and I would not settle for less.

Bing was annoyed by this decision and tried to persuade me to go on reading between the lines, but I knew this would merely be guesswork, and could not agree. Finally, she made one last and, for her, supremely generous gesture. When we visited Lisieux together, she suddenly announced at lunch that she intended to knock at the Carmel door herself, and seek admittance on her own account. I did not believe she meant it, until we found ourselves outside that forbidding portal. Without the slightest glimmer of a beam, the nun at the Turn (both were heavily shrouded), slammed it shut with a curt refusal. (I had provided little support, having collapsed with laughter into a nearby laurel bush.)

When Bing joined me, she was laughing too. 'Well, at any rate,' she said cheerfully, 'that's one place where Rebecca will never penetrate!'

I felt that somehow, somewhere, Therese was laughing, too.

✤

Mena, Monday 20 December, 1965.

Dearest Oriel,

I went down on Sunday, pouring rain, to see Miss Wilcox. You would think she would be cutting her throat, but not a bit. She was pottering about in the cottage, hardly seeing a thing, little radio going, her cats licking their paws, and she was full of cheerfulness. I finally got a humble list of Christmas cheer things she wanted, and which I said I would get for her. She said, quite proudly, that she had ordered a chicken, and would be quite happy having her Christmas alone; there would be the radio (remember she is nearly blind, so can't read), and I suppose she will follow services etc. I suddenly felt that she was doing a tremendous Little Way on her own, because she is by nature a bit grumpy and fault-finding – but there she was, prepared to cope, and being quite beaming about it. Not a word from Philip Rashleigh about her rent. He *might* have acknowledged her letter at least.

Fondest love, Tray.

☙

Mena, Friday 7 January, 1966.

Dearest Oriel,

I got an idea during Christmas for a money-making scheme. You know those rather irritating books that are in fashion nowadays – they are called 'coffee table books', and they cost about three guineas, and people have them displayed as a status symbol? No one ever reads them! Well, I suddenly thought I might jump on the bandwagon and do one called *Romantic Cornwall*, and get Kits to do heaps of coloured photographs, and black-and-white ones too. The writing would not be heavy, but somehow describing the bits of Cornwall I like best. What do you think? Anyway, I know at one time Doubleday were doing these sort of books in conjunction with some English firm, and they bought the copyright outright, and that was that – for a lump sum down. I don't believe it would take long to do; it would start me off on something that did not mean brewing too hard, as I really don't feel like fiction yet.

Tons of love, Tray.

☙

Mena, 23 January, 1966.

Dearest Oriel,

I've had such a shock – Philip Rashleigh's agent wrote to say that after all these months, when I thought it settled, Philip was *not* going to sign my lease after all. For a moment it was like you with X. I thought, 'This can't be!' My own lawyer was away, and there was no one to consult. I just had to wait until Wednesday the nineteenth, when he said he would call and discuss the matter with me. Talk about Doom, Doom ... Well, he came, and was very nice, and I think all is not lost. He had dined with Philip the night before, and with great discretion had somehow worked him round to say grudgingly that he would let me have the lease, but as Gibbins points out, the lease *must* be ready to sign as soon as possible before Philip changes his mind again.

To go on with Thérèse, I am not sure that I absolutely agree with her bit of the Little Way, that makes her take such trouble with the tiresome, grumbling nuns. What I mean is, that it sometimes almost borders on insincerity. She literally *forces* herself, needlessly, to take pains and smile and beam on the people who irritate her, and then those old nuns used to crumb, and preen their feathers, and probably be more tiresome than ever! It's a bit like Doodie, who would say to girls at school who bored her: 'Oh, what a pretty dress, *how* it suits you!' and I would know that she really thought the dress ghastly. Or people in theatrical dressing rooms who gush to the star, '*What* a wonderful performance!' when they have not liked it a bit. I know Thérèse did not mean this in *her* Little Way, but it could have come rather near, and if after her death, any of the surviving grumpy nuns had read her *Story of a Soul*, they would have felt rather upset, and perhaps would wish that Thérèse had told them to their faces that she was irritated by them!

No more for now. All love, Tray.

🕉

Mena, Thursday 10 February, 1966.

Dearest Oriel,

I am still *Doomed*. That beastly Philip has gone back on his word again. When my lawyers, and his, and his agent, all met up in London two weeks ago, to finalize the terms of the lease, a letter had arrived for the agent, saying Philip did not want me to have the lease after all, nor did he want me to build a Dower House, or *anything*. He said he wanted to move in here in three years, when this lease is up. Everyone is in a fearful state, his agent and the lawyers, *all* on my side. I think he must be going really potty, but what can any of them do? I am resigned to whatever Fate may bring. If it is possible to get Kilmarth, despite its disadvantages, it would be better to try for it rather than be left stranded with nothing. I have had no news now since then, two weeks ago, and I wait to know what is to happen. Talk about the Little Way – however, it's no use going over it all until there is more to go over.

I remain calm, and am working hard on research for the Cornish book, in case Kits and I can get on with that. Tho' it's a bit Dooming too, because although Doubleday think it is a good idea, they have to find out if they could get the world rights, though not for English-speaking people. Meanwhile, Kits is not so Doomed, as CBS in America are enquiring about buying his Yeats film, so he felt rather jubilant. Even if they pay a small price, it would at least be a feather in his cap, and he could say, in a voice like Pen Friend, 'I have sold my Yeats to America ... I don't know the terms ... my agent arranges these things ...' (Quite untrue, Kits will have to write to them, pretending he's the agent himself.)

All love, Track.

🜊

Mena, 27 June 1966.

Dearest Oriel,

I have a moment to write, because I have had to stop for a whole week – that Hetty person (the mother of my godchild, Mary) came to stay – I think I told you? But unlike you, she is not a person one can cliff, and get on with one's writing when she is here; she is a *visitor*. She has brought her dog, a poodle, well-behaved but it means keeping Morray on a lead, which is a bore!

But I want to tell you of one lovely expedition, in her car to the Carmelite convent on the north coast, which I had been writing about in my book. So we went over, and as Hetty is Catholic, she asked the housekeeper at the presbytery if we could see the Prioress. And after a bit, we were ushered up to a room with a double grille, so like prison, and then the curtains were whisked aside, and behind the further grille was the Prioress. She had a great black veil over all her face, like a sack, so one couldn't see her at all. She said at once, 'Praise the Lord!' or something, in a very Irish voice, and I could see (or not *see*, but hear) that she must have been *beaming*, behind the sack. Anyway, she talked away, so pleased to see us and welcome us, and Hetty told her some Tell-Hims about her Catholic relatives, and I told her Tell-Hims about mine, and the beaming went on. Then a bell clanged, and she said she had to go to Vespers, so we asked if we could go too, and more beaming of Yes, and we went. To the main part of their chapel, but they were all behind their grille. And their pathetic voices caterwauling, but so nice. There are only twelve of them. (A hundred years ago, in my old research book, there were twenty-five or more.)

Then we went up to the visiting room again, and she once more emerged in her sack behind the grille, and more beaming and goodbyes, and downstairs I bought some goodly jam they sell. When I got back, I daringly sent her some books (*Loving Spirit* as being harmless, not sexy, and *Hungry Hill* because of Ireland), and this morning a letter full of thanks from the Prioress, so beaming, and I will always be welcome. I thought it might be a thing we could do when you come, except that I am a bit doubtful of driving there, the roads are twisty. But knowing how you are to do with Carmel, you could crumb to the Prioress about your book on Ste Thérèse.

Tons of love, Tray.

🪦

Mena, Monday 15 August, 1966.

Dearest Oriel,

First, I have finished the book* as I told you, and it seemed all right when I went through it, not too heavy, or what Kits calls 'golf balls'. This comes from when he and I went years ago to a film, and before the Main one came on, there was an interminable documentary film all about how golf balls are made, and forever afterwards this sort of dull film or book, Kits has called golf balls! Well, I don't really think mine *is* golf balls, but there had to be bits of history which some people might think a bit slow (not you), but on the whole it moves well, and is even amusing, in bits. The only thing is, I am so rude about tourists, I shall be stoned by the people who encourage them.

Now, poor Ferdie. I have heard nothing from Le Mesnil, and I can't help thinking if there had been a Will leaving things to me, I should have heard from some lawyer by now. Kits says it will be like a Maigret-

---

* *Vanishing Cornwall.*

Simenon film, and furious relatives will gather at Le Mesnil, to search the house and rumple through poor Ferdie's drawers and letters. Well, I can't do anything until there *is* some word. When the Zulu children go to stay in France at the end of the month (*with* this French child who is staying here with them, and is a friend of Ferdie's – the parents, I mean) it would be a good idea if Tess went too, and went over to Le Mesnil.

I suppose Moper's death has hardened me to other people's deaths, but though I was very sorry to know poor Ferdie had died, and had had a wretched last few months, I did not cry, or feel that awful sad feeling I thought I should. I feel nowadays that if there *is* a 'beaming down' and an afterlife, then really it is almost better to get there as soon as possible! It must be so much nicer for ill people, or old people, to get there as soon as they can, rather than hang about suffering in the world. Do you see my point? So, though it was sad for Ferdie to leave her dear little house, and her cat and dog and routes, how lovely to see her Maman again, and old Papa, who has been dead for years, and a cousin she loved as a girl in Normandy, and all sorts of things and people. Or, if there *is* nothing – well, one goes to sleep, and that is pleasant, too!

I went over to Kilmarth yesterday. It was looking so peaceful and nice. The farmer who has the meadows (and is my tenant!) met me, and he is going to cut all the grass and weeds etc, when his harvest is over. He was the real old-fashioned Cornish type, I did like him. I'm beginning to be rather torn between *both* places! It would be fun to have both, and to move between the two houses, as my whims increased with my old age!

※

Mena, 4 November, 1966.

Dearest Oriel,

You know the article on widows I wrote? Well, I let them do it in the American *Good Housekeeping*, because they sent two thousand dollars to the Airborne Security Fund. Incidentally, there is a barracks built in Aldershot called the Browning Barracks – such a nice crumb for Moper. Do you think he beams down about it? And now that *Woman's Own* magazine wants to do it here I did not know *what* to say, but thinking how the Airborne would like more money, I showed Grace* the article

---

* Tommy's sister.

(my carbon copy), to ask her opinion. She said definitely NO. It was much too revealing – like being naked in Piccadilly – and although she liked the article personally she said she was afraid that Moper's friends who might read it would be waine, and think I was being self-centred. So I shan't let it go, and am relieved, as I would have been waine, actually, had people read it over here. That is the difficulty about being personal, and one of the reasons I think it is almost impossible for a person to write an autobiography. If they *don't* reveal, it's a Tell-Him, and if they *do*, it's waine! I have much enjoyed Harold Nicolson's *Diaries*, published recently, which keep a good balance.

Oh, such a dreadful Little Way is threatened for me and Piff. Have I ever told you about an old cousin of Daddy's aged ninety who is an old Tell-Him person? Well, she is getting rid of her cottage in Kent, and has found a one-roomed, ground-floor flat in Tywardreath of all places, and is coming down there to live. It means we must cope with her a bit; and she is not content on her own, but loves to be taken out and about. Piff says we must each have her to lunch once a week. Oh dear, it sounds so cruel to mind. But I can foresee binds ahead, can't you? And aged ninety! She is sure to be ill, or break a leg, and ask to be nursed here! And she *never* stops talking, all about how the Prince of Liechtenstein used to be in love with her in her young days. It's funny once, but not every week.

Heaps of love, Tray.

––––––

The arrival of Cousin Dora was a stone flung into the quiet pool of Mena days, and caused almost as many ripples. While Piff and Bing were bound to their equally aged Aunt Billy by the strong ties of love and childhood memories, Dora was almost a stranger, and I admired the way in which they both rose to the occasion and made her welcome. With time, Piff's patience became somewhat frayed, and she withdrew slightly, leaving Bing to cope with Dora's constant claims for attention and her pre-occupation with the aristocratic dancing partners of her youth. These, we suspected, were mostly Gondals, but at least they helped to while away the long, rainsodden winter days in her dark, ground-floor flat at Tywardreath, where she had chosen to lay her old bones. It was a bold move, and a courageous one, to pull up her roots so late in life and transplant herself to this alien Cornish soil, but Cousin Dora was both canny and strong-minded. Having presumably worn out all her immediate entourage with her ducal Tell-Hims, she had decided to move closer to her remaining relatives, who might prove hospitable and sympathetic.

She had chosen well. Dora was quickly added to the list of frail and elderly neighbours whom Bing visited regularly, and helped. Amused by her graphic description of Dora's arrival, I could not wait to meet her, and on my next visit was driven up to Tywardreath where all was (and remained) in a state of wild confusion. The one room was of a comfortable size, but was perpetually blocked by some large black trunks, from which a strong smell of mothballs wafted every time the lids were raised, which was two or three times a day, since the trunks contained all that remained to Dora of the past, and she constantly rootled about among them, stirring the past, and muddling everything up. She was delighted to have a fresh audience, especially one who lived abroad, and might therefore be receptive to her tales of the Vienna balls of her youth. We made friends and Bing, only too glad to share part of her Little Way, would wander off with the dogs, leaving me to the Tell-Hims and the trunks. Piecing Cousin Dora's past together was no easy task; it shifted about like the pieces of coloured glass in a kaleidoscope, but what she did decide to recall was told with a certain panache, and a wicked humour, which amused me. Old grudges quickly rose to the surface, but her rages against a world in which she no longer had a place were nothing more than the basic human need to be loved and wanted.

Dora had been to a convent school in Paris, and she liked to air her French, which was still good. On her shelves were many French classics, and she sometimes asked me to read to her from these or she would recite long-forgotten verses she had learned at school; La Fontaine's Fables, or that depressing epic poem by Victor Hugo, *Waterloo, Waterloo, Waterloo, morne plaine* ... But mostly she preferred to talk about herself, for now her world had narrowed to this room and this old body, with which she grew increasingly hampered and bitter. In such a mood, no one found favour with her except Bing, when she could be persuaded to listen. Conversations always seemed to come full circle, ending as they had begun with Austrian Dukes, and Prince Metternich, for whom she professed unbounded admiration and who was, I suppose, a Peg upon which to hang her *folie de grandeur*. She once confided to me that she wished most fervently that she could claim to be descended from him. This seemed to be stretching things a little far, even for a Gondal, and I gently hinted that it might after all be good enough to be, however remotely, a du Maurier.

Dora brushed this suggestion aside, and sent me delving into the black trunks in search of proof that she had once danced with some ducal figure, who could claim some distant link with the Prince. The trunks contained a mass of old newspaper cuttings and dance programmes, dresses that clinked with silver tassels and jet, and a moth-eaten fur with glass eyes that I could not bear to touch.

I never knew whether to be glad or sorry when Bing put her head round the door, and announcing firmly, 'Lunch-time!' swept me off in the red DAF before Dora had time to start on a fresh Tell-Him. Rocketing homewards down the hill from Tywardreath, Bing refused to be cajoled into sympathy with Dora's dreams of grandeur. 'Now *don't* get Dora in your mind, or you'll be turning her into a sub!' she warned me crossly.

❦

Mena, Tuesday 27 December, 1966.

Dearest Oriel,

My time in London was OK but so exhausting. Christmas shopping, and always pouring rain, and taxis so expensive, and I had to see Pen Friend, and old Aunt Billy etc, and a good dinner with the Menace, Sir John Wolfenden and his wife, which was fun. I stayed in Tessa's flat, which was nice, but not half so nice as Tod's. (Tod very pleased at that!) Then back home, and all the preparing for Christmas. Everything was made doubly exhausting because of the awful Little Way I had with that old Cousin Dora, who had to be settled into her flat at Tywardreath the week *before* I went to London, and coped with after, too. The thing is, she *never, never, never* stops talking for a single moment, so that one is absolutely worn OUT, before one has spent half an hour with her! Her flat is the shambles of all time, and I had to get Henry and Esther to help get it straight, and all she did was to stand about smoking endless cigarettes (at ninety and a half!) talking about the dukes of her youth, and asking them to find her a map of Austria, so she could show them where she used to stay! I thought of Thérèse helping that old nun who bored her so – honestly, it was the Littlest of all Little Ways!

Anyway, she was settled into her flat, and then the whole crew came for Christmas – great fun, Towers, Zulus, Brownings and Piff and old Cousin Dora! All well but for poor Olive, who thinks she may be starting a miscarriage. We all coped with Freddie, who is quite a handful, but such bliss. Kits is heavenly with him; gets him up and feeds him, and together we gave him his bath last night – in the bath where I had bathed Kits – and the two of us now bathing *his* son, it does make a continuity, doesn't it? And I'm sure the love I gave Kits he now gives to his son, so it is a thing of: 'As ye sow, so shall ye reap', and love does bring forth goodly things, don't you agree? If I had beaten him, *he* would now be beating Freddie. Everyone else OK and Marie-Thérèse *much* improved, and helping, and very sweet with Freddie, and she is getting nice to look at, too. Rupert going through rather a plain stage, with missing teeth, but very nice, and Paul a bit silent, but OK. Flave in a very gay mood, gay for gaiety's sake, and Alastair full of good solemn advice about Kilmarth, which everyone has been beeding at. He says it is too nice for holiday flatlets, it would be better as a house. It looks much better than it did, with a lot of the undergrowth cleared away, and windows open, with sun streaming in.

Well, now I am getting exhausted with typing, and everyone still here, so will close, as they say. In all this I have not thanked you for your goodly Vent Vert, *many* thanks.

Happy New Year, and tons of love, Tray.

———

Esther and Henry Rowe lived in one of the cottages scattered about the grounds and woods of Menabilly; a stone's throw from the house, but screened from it by a belt of tall trees. Esther was Cornish, born and bred (her photograph, by Kits, appears in *Vanishing Cornwall*). In 1958, she was looking out for a part-time secretarial job when one day, much to her surprise, Tod came knocking on the door with a different proposition: would she consider helping out at Mena while the cook was having her baby? This idea did not greatly appeal to Esther; she was not a professional cook, and felt that she had enough housework in her own home. Two days later, Tod returned to the charge, insisting that it would only be a temporary job so, somewhat doubtfully, Esther accepted. Thirty-one years later, she was still faithfully at her post (the cook's baby having turned out to be twins).

Esther did not find it easy at first to adapt to the strange ways of the household. Moper was always kind and thoughtful, and immediately put her at ease, but he was away in London all week, and Bing at this time was an elusive figure, who disappeared to her Hut every morning and rarely gave orders. The person most to be reckoned with was Tod; it was she who ruled the household, gave orders, and expected everyone to conform to her own strict, somewhat old-fashioned ideas.

Later, when she departed to London, to 'see folk' and lead her own life, Esther gradually became the mainstay of the household. Bing was pleased to have someone young and cheerful about her, and since Esther also valued her independence, they got on well together. Later, when she had moved to Kilmarth, Bing came to depend more and more upon

Esther as her secretary, as well as housekeeper, answering letters, paying bills, dealing tactfully with the nurses and always with a warm welcome for visitors.

🜓

Mena, Thursday 6 April, 1967.

Dearest Oriel,

I was most impressed by your Little Way on the plane coming back, and what a help it must have been to the poor woman, and the old aunt. I feel sure it will have done vast good, and their lives will be blessed by your Saintlike ways!! It would be rather good, if the woman in the Cornish train that last time, met the new woman going to France, and they told each other their experiences of the 'sweet young lady' they had met, and then a great myth would spread, that it really was Ste Thérèse in disguise coming to earth, and one of them would say, 'Did you notice the scent of roses about her?' and that is how these things begin!! I read the Ste Thérèse book you left, and I think it was very good, because it did say so much about her being headstrong, which we know she was, and determined to have her way in things, which actually *isn't* very saint-like. But I think her saint-like time really began that last year, when she suffered so, and had such doubts, and she became very brave and noble in consequence.

That Mr Pascoe man at Kilmarth turns out to be rather nice, and has Understanding of Nature! He had to do mending to the roof here, where the bees are, and has taken such trouble that the bees should not be disturbed, and brought in a special bee-man, in a great helmet like a spacesuit, to cope with them. There were two huge nests, and the bee-man has left me one in a corner, with holes in the new boards for them to get in and out, and I let him take the other nest, to start up a great hive at his own place. He got me some honey, and it's so good, dark brown and very tasty, and I have it for brek, rejoicing in my own bees and their labour!

To go back to the children (who are out of the room at the moment), I get on with them fine, but I wish they were more like Kits and Flave were, and played imaginary games. They do passage wander when *not* being taken for outings, and soon get bored with telly after tea, and then they play cards for about five minutes, and get bored with that. It's rather an aimless existence – what goes on in their minds, I mean. As I said, neither wants to read. Paul doesn't kick a ball about like Kits did, or even tear about armed to the teeth with imaginary sword or gun. Their only 'letting off steam' is to fight on the floor, and shout at each other! But perhaps they will develop, and grow up. Poo likes to put on nylons and find some lipstick, which is rather silly at twelve. She will have so many years ahead in which to do that! But she is very amiable – like a flighty au pair! They are both very pleasant to me, and sweet, but that is perhaps because I don't nag, or go for them, or tell them to wash or anything! I still build my hopes on Freddie, but it's a long time to wait! *His* thing at the moment, Kits says, is to follow the gardener around trying to help, and always frightfully busy at something, which I hope continues. I know Kits will play football with him, which he already enjoys, at barely two!

Tons of love, Tray.

※

Mena, 27 May, 1967.

Dearest Oriel,

I must tell you about my Little Way in the Woods, which is such a saga! You see, I had not gone down to see Miss Wilcox directly I got back, because of my sinus thing, and I went early last week, and was very disturbed to see she looked rather queer, flushed as if with a fever, and staring eyes, and could hardly walk. She said it was nothing, and her legs were stiff with rheumatism, but I was worried, and when I got back I rang up the vicar. He said she had been 'failing' since I went away, and he would go and see her, and ask the doctor to call. Well, he reported her to the doctor, who said he would go in a few days (lazy brute!). Then I went again, and she looked a bit better, but last Sunday that man who cuts bamboos in the woods came tearing up to the house here, to say he had seen Miss Wilcox and she looked 'bad', and what should he do? So I quickly telephoned the doctor on duty, a young man, and he said he would go and see her at once.

Almost at once he came rushing back, saying he had seen Miss Wilcox and he thought she had a thing called erisypilus (can't spell) and he must send for an ambulance at once. He could not go back to her, as he had other calls, so as I could not bear to think of her waiting in the woods alone, I put on my mac and boots and tore down to her. I found the poor old thing crouched in her chair, trying to air a pathetic flannelette nightgown by her meagre fire. Luckily, I had brought my Swan's Hellenic overnight bag, so put that in it, and some soap, but the chaos of her poor little house ... I could hardly see for the mess, though doubtless she knows where everything is, although she is blind.

I found her best coat hanging behind the bedroom door (not worn for years) and the bed not slept in – she had been sleeping below in two chairs, with cats all mewing around her. I helped her put on her coat over her very dirty clothes, and found her bag and purse with all her papers and then *ages* afterwards there were voices at the door. It was the ambulance men from Bodmin, who had lost their way and gone to the Farm instead. She had to get on to a stretcher and be bundled into the ambulance, and I sat holding her hand as we bumped through the drive to the park, but she was so brave, and I kissed her, and said I would telephone the Truro Hospital, and explain all to the Sister in charge. Anyway, Miss Wilcox got to the hospital, and the vicar has been to see her, and she is not dying or anything, but on the mend and cheerful, though she is in the Isolation Ward. What if Tray comes out with erisypelus? [*sic*] It would be a fitting end to my Little Way! I think *she* is a saint, she was so brave.

No more now. With fondest love, Tray.

༈

Mena, Tuesday, 27 June, 1967.

Dearest Oriel,

Your letter came at tea-time, and I felt I must answer it at once, because I can so understand the sense of Doom! First of all, you must get it into your head, as I said before, that the disappointment of the play is, I am really sure, just temporary. This is the game of the theatre, its ups and downs, you know it so well. It's a great temporary setback, but there is no need for it to put you off 'Arcadia', which is a novel, and you were eager and fully brewed to continue with it. But I know so well how one gets these blocks.

But I repeat, I do so understand. One wakes up, one passage wanders; if it's a wet day one does bills – you probably go out and have your hair done, or make the time pass somehow, and all the while there is that nagging feeling: 'Oh, if only I could be writing, the time would whizz by!' I've been doing this all the past week. Glancing at *Country Life*, picking flowers, taking the dogs down to Prid and thinking, 'Really, what an aimless existence!' But I know it is only temporary, and I refuse to be Doomed! So easy to say, I'm sixty, I've had my life, I'm just an old has-been who is stuck down in Cornwall, and wait for my grandchildren to visit me. That is no way to look at life! Yes, the only thing to do is to carry on, and the storm *will* blow over. I think you will feel better when you get into the country, and have the feeling of Life and Nature going on around you. A city, even Paris, is not the place for depressions, unless one is a whirring-about-the-gay-life-Silly-Values sort of person, and you are not. Have some good Deep Thoughts discussions with Monsieur B. or Peg, who sounds so sensible always, and very understanding.

I went to see Miss Wilcox, in Truro Hospital. She was quite bright and OK but oh dear, I thought, looking at the ward next to hers, where there were lots of senile old ladies, supposing she, or I, were facing *that*. It was raining, too, and so easy to get depressed. But no, no, NO. Life goes on. Life is everywhere. One must *never* be defeated!

Now I must stop, and put my tatties on to boil for sups.

Much love, Bing.

꙰

Mena, Saturday 14 October, 1967.

Dearest Oriel,

Yet another blow!

My lawyer rang to say that Philip Rashleigh's agent had telephoned him in an awful state of depression, to say that Philip *had* at last made up his mind, and he *does* want to come here, and not to renew my lease. He said Philip was going to call on me to tell me so himself, so at least I was prepared. He came yesterday, and the poor man was in such a state of waine, mopping his brow and obviously afraid I was going to attack him with fury, that I had to Little Way like mad, and say of course I understood, I hoped he would be very happy here, and it was better he should come while he was still young enough to enjoy it, and better I should move and get routes at Kilmarth before I got too old etc, etc. The poor brute looked so grateful that I almost agreed I would go and live in a dog kennel if it helped him! *But* I was firm, and said it would take at least a year for me to get Kilmarth ready, especially the stable block to be converted into a cottage for 'my staff' (!), so I hope that sunk in, and he didn't think I was going next week.

I have prepared Esther, and she and Henry are thrilled at the thought of a new home designed for their comfort, so that is one great relief. So ghastly, if they had said, 'We are so sorry, but we really feel we had rather stay here, and look after the Rashleighs.' At least I am spared the expense of pulling down the back, and what would have gone there can go on Esther's new cottage. I will look on it all as a challenge, and get more *in* with Kilmarth, week by week all through next year, so that I don't mind too much. Actually, in time I might even brew a book about it, as an old person in Tywardreath is looking up records, and it *does* date back to 1329 (centuries older than Mena), and he is going to find out who lived there.

All love, Tray.

⚜

Mena, 10 November, 1967.

Dearest Oriel,

I am sorry I did not write before, but you know how it can be. Tod was on the go nonstop, with carting plants and things backwards and forwards to Kilmarth, and she really *is* amazing at eighty – her *energy*! Old Dora was out here to lunch today, and I had to hear all about the Duke of Liechtenstein for the umpteenth time, but it had to be part of my Little Way. She is really quite OK at her flat, with her Daily going in morning and evening, so she is quite well looked after. But she said how nice it was to get out, and to have some good talk (??!) so I get rather coals of fire. It was lovely having Flave and Alastair – Flave in very good form, and dear grave Alastair is so helpful about my finances – what a pity you never had *him*, when you knew X! He is sure the lawyers and people can get me some money from that old Trust thing, and is going to put up all sorts of ideas to them. If they won't agree, I don't know how I shall manage, because turning Kilmarth stables into a cottage for Esther is going to cost an awful lot. But I must do it, and I never could live there without them.

I took Flave over to Lanherne Convent, to give a copy of my book to the Rev. Mother, and she received us behind that grille thing, with another old nun, both draped in black sacking like the witches in *Macbeth* – Flave did not dare look at me – but they were so sweet. I crumbed about you, and said a dear friend was going to write a Life of Ste Thérèse, and concentrate on Léonie, and the Rev. Mother was thrilled and could hardly wait. She said she thought a book *had* been done about Léonie, but it hasn't, has it? She also said that she thought the Papa and Maman ought to be canonized too, but I wouldn't have thought so, would you? I mean, the old Papa went potty! I must take you there when you next come. I asked permission to see the whizzing cupboard where they keep the vestments, in the sacristy, and I was terrified we would get giggles there, because the cupboard whizzes round to the enclosed bit, and one can hear the Vestment Nun breathing behind it. They asked if we wanted to see the Relic they have, which was the skull of Father Mayne, the martyr. So of course we said Yes, and the cupboard whizzed again (rather like a Demon in the pantomime!) and there was a white skull with a bleeding wound in it, where the poor martyr had been impaled! I did wish you could have been with us.

The Zulu children have begged to come to me here for Christmas, which is awfully touching, and I'm *so* pleased. It *is* good that they obviously feel secure here. And Flave says *they* will come too, so I will have a Mena Christmas after all. Kits will be cross, he wanted me to go to them, but it would be such chaos with Olive in the middle of having her new baby. I really think it would be better to get *her* mother over to cope. She is so good in the kitchen etc, and Track is really pretty useless. Anyway, it's nice that *anyone* wants one, if you come to think of it! Awful if they were saying, 'Oh God, who is going to cope with Bing?' Perhaps they will, when I am eighty, at Kilmarth.

Oh, I forgot to tell you – I have been made a Member of the Nationalist Party of Cornwall, called *Mebyon Kernow* (Sons of Cornwall) and given a badge to wear, and a thing to stick in my car, and I can hardly wait to go and blow up a bridge, like your Welsh Nationalists! There should be a similar thing in France, for Madame Peg – 'à la poubelle', as she throws her bomb! I told you about Ferdie's house, and I have got to be the Maigret person who signs the papers; it's all rather worrying. I hope it can be sold to the Clinic next door.

Fondest love, Tray.

⚜

Mena, 30 November, 1967.

Dearest Oriel,

I really am getting rather brewified about Kilmarth in olden days. I've sent for some research books to do with Tywardreath and the fourteenth century, and I have found a sort of Tell-Him old Research man who suggested other books which have now come from the London Library. They are all about Tywardreath Priory in 1329, and some awful old monks, and one monk called John de Meral, who was 'the sick sheep infecting the flock', and had to be sent back to Angers. The monks were all French, as it was a sister-house of the Abbaye of Angers, you see. And this was the time that Roger Kylmerth was living, so you see I began to brew madly that this Roger Kylmerth was *in* with the monks, and knew the sick sheep! And then Mr Pascoe the builder found a great well that no one knew about, in the patio bit at Kilmarth, and I began to get so excited, and to brew some more.

Then I thought, what if that old Professor Singer and his wife, with their embryos in bottles, got up to queer discoveries? I looked them up in *Who's Who* and they used to know about Alchemy, so I thought – what if they found some secret way of going back to the past? And suddenly I began to see the whole countryside in a fourteenth-century way, and the sea roaring up past Par, and touching Tywardreath and the Priory above, and my Roger Kylmerth man may be being rather wicked ... Oh yes, the brewing does sort of begin to come!

That awful thing called the Black Death came to Cornwall a few years later. What if germs from the Black Death should be in the well? I suggested this to Mr Pascoe and he looked so shocked and said, 'Oh, Lady Browning, surely not,' and I said he must get a ladder and go down the well to investigate. Instead, he went and got some plants in pots, to put in the entrance porch, to distract my attention. But I shan't be put off! Perhaps there is hidden treasure in the well, or some old Alchemist treasure of the Singers! Anyway, you can see from this, I am not passage wandering but deep in past days, which is all to the good.

I read *A Swan in the Evening** and was not so mad about it as you, tho' I liked it, because I did not think the spiritualist part convincing. The thing is, it read to me much more like the experience of someone on the verge of a nervous breakdown, and suffering from shock – *great* shock. It reminded me rather of my strange C. of L. feelings, and she may well have had C. of L. at the time when the daughter died. This is not to say that I don't believe in beaming down, and an afterlife, because you know I *do*, and I am sure her nice daughter *is* beaming down – but that queer out-of-the-body feeling that Rosamund Lehmann got is much more like frightful shock, and the unconscious mind's attempt to get out of the shock, than what I would call definite contact with the dead. Also, she tells the reader almost nothing of what the daughter said to her in their talks from 'beyond', but was vague, like all spiritualists are vague, and just went on about the good new friends that she, R.L., had made since she had taken it up.

I am so glad for her sake that it has all made such a difference to her sorrow. She, R.L., was always a person who had such a strange life, always suffering from thwarted love affairs, and is almost *over*-sensitive, I think. Even as a child things seemed to have the most devastating effect

* by Rosamund Lehmann.

on her. I have always been interested in her, and her family. They are contemporaries of ours, and we lived near them in the First War, and went to a dancing class at their house. R.L. is about Piffy's age, I think; she used to be rather handsome, but now looks very distraught and haggard, poor thing – it's her suffering that has done it. Still, shock does have an awful effect.

Tons of love, Track.

⚜

Mena, 5 February, 1968.

Dearest Oriel,

I was horrified to hear the news of poor Peg, and do hope he is better, and rested. I am so terribly sorry, and can well imagine how it must have shocked you. But it also made me think of Charlotte and Monsieur Héger, and how she would have felt if he had fainted at a lecture in Brussels! She would have written pages to Emily about it, who would have smiled scornfully, but written back nonetheless, telling Charlotte it was no business of hers, and not to be fussed. (If *only* we had her letters!)

I plod away at my research for my fourteenth-century story, but get rather sidetracked from Kilmarth itself to the whole Manor – as it was in those days – of Tywardreath. (I don't mean a Manor *house* – I mean the thing they called a Manor, which is like a Parish, and the head of it was the Lord of the Manor.) I have found out that he was Sir Henry Champernoun, and so obviously he was the most important person in the district, and my Kylmerth man would have known him. The Main thing I can't find is – where was the original Manor House? There is no record of the site, which is most unusual, as most old manor houses are still farms. So I go out in the car to explore – rather fun – and go round all the old farms in the district with field glasses, and I am sure people think that I am a spy, hovering about in hedges! It's so childish, really, and so like the games I used to play on Hampstead Heath, when I was a child. *On revient toujours à ses premiers amours!* But it's not passage wandering.

If only I can find the site, I shall see the Champernouns more clearly. Roger Kylmerth being a go-between, and the old monks in it, too – I have quite a lot of information about *them*. My great ploy is studying the old Tithe Map, and filling in the names of all the fields. It's just like being a detective, when some old field one always thought was just a Tell-Him, turns out to be called 'Bishop's Down' or 'Prior's Meadow', and you think, 'Aha, *this* was part of their land!' Useless information perhaps, but not to me, seeing an old Bishop in his litter travelling down across-country from Exeter to Tywardreath, to admonish the Prior! So this is really what I've been doing these past weeks – going for little trips in the car in the morning, then routes walks with the dogs in the afternoon, and my maps, and perusal of documents between tea and sups. The time flies.

All love, Tray.

Mena, 4 March, 1968.

Dearest Oriel,

I'm working hard at the Notebook stage* and only wish I had got the story all clear in it, so that I could get down to the actual writing. I'm about halfway through the Notebook, and because of my great age, it all takes longer to do than it once did. My *stories* get so involved, and I want this one to switch between the past and present. I want my 'I' person to discover a drug that keeps sending him back to the past, and he becomes a sort of addict to the switchback. He just can't stop, and his wife can't think what is the matter with him, and imagines he is drinking, or has some woman on the side. And all the time he is obsessed with this past which he keeps getting into, and the family of that time, who are having fearful problems of their own. He is much more interested in *their* problems, than his wife's rather tiresome ones. I think I shall make her rather maddening and social, wanting people for weekends, just when he wants to give himself a 'fix', to get back to 1327!

Tons of love, and forgive this sudden rush! Tray.

Mena, 24 March, 1968.

Dearest Oriel,

No, no, truly and really NO! It is *sweet* of you to want to buy the drawings by Grandpapa, but I simply could not let you do this. You see, the thing is, had we looked at them down here *ages* ago, when they were

* of *The House on the Strand.*

lying around, I would have said, 'Oh, do take what you like,' only too pleased that you showed appreciation. There have always been heaps of these drawings lying around. Look how pleased I was when Ken [McCormick] showed appreciation, and I gave him *carte blanche* to take what he wanted. Now, it was only lately, one time when Tod was down, she did her 'My dear' thing of saying they must be worth quite a bit, and then how she sold some for my old Aunt Billy. So I told her, 'Well, why don't you do the same for me?' and we got quite excited at the thought. She hoped my fortune would be made (!) but I didn't think it would. They *may* go up in value after Mrs Ormond brings out her book, but Kicky will never be in the fortune-making class. Anyway, I could not bear to sell drawings to *you* of all people – so interested in Kicky, and all family stuff, and my friend and all. So please don't be offended at my sending this back. I am only too pleased for you to have the drawings. If by chance you suddenly make your fortune and whizz down here in a Rolls Royce, with a chauffeur, and I am standing with a begging bowl outside Kilmarth to attract the tourists, *then* I can say, 'Oriel, about those drawings. Do you think perhaps *now* ...' But let us wait until that noble moment! Anyway, many thanks for wanting to do this, and I do appreciate it.

No more for now, and tons of love as always, Track.

卐

Palm Sunday, 7 April, 1968.

Dearest Oriel,

I'm reading such an interesting book, called *The Astonishing Christians*, all about the early years of Christianity (after Jesus was dead) and the various schisms that went on – Paul having *his* idea of what the future should be, and Peter and James having their more Jewish idea, which they felt represented what Jesus *meant*. I've never been madly for Paul, and this book puts me off him even more, and rather on to old James, who of course is more on the Messiah line; and Paul more on the Hellenic thing, of making Jesus more Apollo-ish, to appeal to his Greek audiences. It's very fascinating. I've always been puzzled by the contradictory sayings in the Gospels – one moment Jesus is being so noble, and saying everyone must love each other, and then in the next He calls everyone vipers, and 'let the dead bury their dead', and all that. So either He was a *very* contradictory character, or else there is great confusion about what He actually *did* say. I suppose the arguments will go on for ever!

Tons of love, Track.

———

I was in England when 'les événements' – the stirring events of May 1968 – took place in France. These began with a legitimate revolt on the part of university students, in Paris and elsewhere, against the over-crowding and the impossible conditions under which they were expected to study and to live. The government of the day (which was almost entirely General de Gaulle) took action, fearing a full-scale revolution, and soon, all legitimate grievances had become a struggle for power, of which the only result to ordinary people was a decline in the quality of life and a rise in the cost of living.

When I read that tanks were rolling down the Champs Elysées, and had been stationed in the Place de la Concorde, I knew it was time to make tracks for France and home. Voices were raised to dissuade me from taking what they imagined to be a fatal step, but Bing was firmly on my side. Later, she told me that she had thought of a plan to rescue me, if things became too dangerous in France. I was to get myself to Brittany (how?) and she would persuade the kind occupant of Pridmouth cottage to fly over in his plane and pick me up. I do not know if she divulged this plan to the person most concerned as fortunately it never became necessary to put it into practice. Tod was also on my side, much to my surprise. On my last day, I went to tea with her in her cosy flat close to Battersea Park. She had made scones, and her famous lemon cake, and all was reassuringly familiar. I was excited and elated at the thought of the journey ahead.

It was not possible to fly directly to Paris, as the airports were closed, nor was it easy to get a seat on a plane, but I had done so through the kindness of a journalist friend who intended to travel on the same flight. I thought this would reassure Tod. Instead, she became agitated. 'My dear, never trust a journalist!' she exclaimed, in shocked tones. 'I should take a good book with you, if I were you!'

It proved one of the easiest journeys I had ever made, with no hanging about in detestable airport lounges, and a smooth swift flight to Brussels where, to my relief, the bus was waiting. It waited some time, until another plane from Dublin flew in, bringing home a reputed French expert on trout fishing. He finally arrived, loaded down with rods and nets, and wearing a squashy green hat covered with fishing flies.

It was a clear, bright evening, of the kind that often comes at the end of a hot day, and the bus threw long black shadows across the road as we ambled through the peaceful countryside. We might have been a party of tourists returning from a day's outing, but everyone concealed secret anxieties. En route, the driver turned round and asked us if we had ever visited one of the Flanders war cemeteries; there was one quite close, and he thought it would be worth our while to do so. I, for one, had not, and those long, straight lines of white crosses against the setting sun have remained with me – proof, if proof were needed, of man's stupidity.

It was two o'clock in the morning when we reached Paris, to find an eerie, empty city, with no light in the streets but that cast by the moon; not a soul abroad, and every shop and café barred and barricaded. The bus deposited us and our baggage in the deserted rue Royale, and rattled off homewards. There were no taxis, and the métro gates were locked; most people picked up their bags and made for the nearest hotel. I knew the Bs would be waiting for me to call, and when I did so a kind neighbour insisted on using precious petrol to come and collect me. When he saw our plight, he extended his services to others as well.

Shortly after this, life slowly began to return to normal. While de Gaulle scurried to and fro between Colombey-les-Deux-Églises and Paris, politicians of both Left and Right blamed each other for the sinister deeds done under cover of the 'revolution'. Little was achieved by either side, but nothing would ever be quite the same again, for like an evil genie violence had been let loose, and could not be thrust back into its bottle. The Paris I had been just in time to know, and to love, would gradually disappear, to be replaced by a greedy and mercenary society in which more and more people would find it harder and harder to survive; and it was certainly not the politicians who would come to their rescue.

※

Mena, Friday 10 May, 1968.

Dearest Oriel,

I have had to break off work today, because of Tod arriving so I thought I would at least start to answer your letter, even if I have to break off and finish later.

I'm getting on not too badly, but I found it quite hard to start working away on this one, after the non-creative book of *Vanishing Cornwall*. But by sitting down firmly every day, morning and afternoon, the discipline of sitting and concentrating helped my mind work. It is imperative, I think, to feel yourself involved with your characters, and this is why I find I have to be an 'I' so often. I can think much better as an 'I', and it begins to flow! But I assure you, it doesn't flow so fast as it did when I was younger, and I get tired much more quickly. If I work from eleven to one, on again after lunch from two to three-thirty, then take my walk with the dogs, have tea, get their sups, and go on again from five-thirty to seven-thirty, I am quite exhausted, and glad to have my sups with 'telly', at which I sometimes fall asleep!

If I were you, I would try to stay out in Normandy on my own; you would find being alone quite perfect for forging ahead. I don't believe I *could* write any more these days, if I had to live in a house full of people! Solid getting on with a working routine is much easier alone (but of course, I would be done without Esther doing the lunch!).

Tons of love, Tray.

✠

Mena, 29 August, 1968.

Dearest Oriel,

I was so pleased to get your good Main letter this morning. I am so very pleased the tour was a success, but I wish you could have been longer in St Christophe – as you say, even writing there, and with a motorbike, because then you could have gone to Chenu and found the Maurier farm, and got to know the district well. I must say, I would love to go again, but it might possibly be that waine thing of, if one went, they would want to show one off a bit, and clients would drop in for a drink, and be introduced. It's so much nicer if no one knows who one is, because once known, one has to avoid the place forever more.

It was a relief to have my work finished before my invasion. For over a week we were twelve or fourteen in the house, it really was a bit much. Though it's fun for a Christmas weekend, it becomes rather exhausting for longer, because the families split up into rival gangs, and everyone gets heated in conversation! Kits is getting *so* like Moper in some ways; he likes to sit at the end of the table and thump his fist, and lay down the law, and brook no argument, and then the girls start arguing back – Tessa pitching, and Flave rather scornful, and although it amused me, it was a bit tiring. Kits and Olive were OK and the babies adorable. Freddie is such an angel. I don't know what it is, there is some sort of psycho-bond between us. We went off for our little trits, and he used to run about the house shouting for Track at the top of his voice. It's odd why some children are so endearing, for no reason. It's not just that he's Kits' son. He's much more *endearing* as a character than Kits at that age.

I have not yet sent my book to Sheila, as she has been away on holiday. I hope she likes it. I think it is exciting, but also funny. Let me read your synopsis about the Nannies. I will send it back.

Tons of love, Track.

🜗

Mena, 7 October, 1968.

Dearest Oriel,

Tod comes down next week for a spell. I still think early December would be the best for you. Now autumn is upon one, although the weather is still mild.

It's a bit passage wandery without my book, but I got the seed of an idea for a short story when in Ireland, and may brew upon it.* I wanted to look up an old friend of Moper's I had not seen for years, who was very kind to us when we got engaged. He was a Brigadier, Irish and quite mad; and then some sort of coolness developed between him and Moper, I never quite knew why. He left the Army, and went to live in Ireland, and Moper used to say he was sure he was behind the IRA! Well, we spent two days at Kinsale Harbour, and I felt sure that this was where 'Chink', as he was called, had gone to live. I could not find his name in the telephone book, and I remembered Moper had said that he had changed his name.

Anyway, we never did find him, but when we went to Killarney, there was a rather sinister lake, with an island in the middle of it, and I suddenly thought, one could do a good story about a widow who went to trace her husband's best friend, with some dying message from her husband, and finally tracked him to this mysterious island. She is warned by the locals *not* to call, as the Brigadier does not like visitors, and lives as a recluse – no telephone, no means of communication! Anyway, rather daring, she gets a boat and lands, and comes to the house, surrounded by trees. There seems to be no one there. She looks through the window of the living room – quite snug, but very bachelorish – and there on the desk (she steps into the room), much to her surprise is a large photograph of a wedding group – *hers*, taken years and years ago. She steps nearer,

* 'A Borderline Case'.

and sees that instead of her own husband standing next to her as bridegroom, the figure of the Brigadier is there instead, and she has an awful feeling of discomfort and fear. Has the Brigadier been living under some unpleasant fantasy all these years? She feels she can't face him, and runs away from the house, down to the boat, but it has gone. She is marooned on the island, and it is getting dark! I've got to get the IRA into this, and various nanny sort of happenings! And last night, on telly, there was an account of protest marches in Northern Ireland, and a great to-do, and they say the IRA are behind it; so I got quite excited, and wondered whether the *real* ex-Brigadier, the Chink man, was behind it! Though he must be about seventy now. Even so, a frightening old man of seventy might get up to all sorts of things! But I could make him younger in the story.

Anyway, it will give me something to brew about. And there is still a Jerusalem story* to do, and that story about a husband and wife in Venice† that I told you I wanted to do, where the husband suddenly sees his wife passing in one of those vaporettos on the Grand Canal, and yet he knew he had seen her off to fly home to England that morning! I might get about six longish short stories, that would fit into a book, and be sold separately to *Journal* or *Good Housekeeping*, in America.

Tuesday 8th
So fussing for poor Esther! Henry has not been at all well, and has jaundice, and now the doctor says he must be taken off to Truro Hospital, there might be some obstruction (bowel?). The ambulance is coming at any moment.

All love, Tray.

———

Poor Henry Rowe died in Truro Hospital a few days later; his jaundice had been a sudden revival of the hepatitis from which he had suffered so badly during the war. Once again, the world seemed to split apart and Esther was left, a young widow with a son to bring up on her own, and totally unprepared for such a shock, which no one could have foreseen. It was impossible to imagine Mena without Henry, a lovable man, always so kind and capable, and one of those quiet personalities who never put

* 'The Way of the Cross'.
† 'Don't Look Now'.

forward their claims, and who would be the first to be surprised at how greatly they are missed.

I remember Henry coming to meet me a few months previously at Newquay Airport where, owing to a rail strike, I had flown across England by helicopter – a glorious experience on a clear summer's day. We drove back to Mena through the narrow Cornish lanes, talking of this and that; of the war and the waste of human life, and of the world which could, and should be a good place to live in. How could we have guessed, then, how little time was left to him?

🜚

Mena, 14 November 1968.

Dearest Oriel,

I think this must be calamity autumn! Another awful shock. Those darling little boys, Freddie and Robbie, have been in an awful motor crash, and are both in hospital. Their new nurse (very nice) was driving them in the car the day before yesterday, and suddenly some man, overtaking, crashed into them. The car was wrecked, and they were all three removed to hospital near Slough. The first Kits and Olive heard of it was a ring at their front door, in the morning, and a policeman to break the news. They tore off to the place at once, a great impersonal Hospital, Children's Ward, and there was Robbie, who had had stitches put in his baby forehead, and Freddie with a fractured leg! The nurse with several stitches on her face.

They say Robbie will be able to go home soon, but Freddie will have to be there, with both legs tied together under some sort of cage, until the New Year. I am so shaken and upset I can hardly write. What it must be for Kits and Olive, God alone knows, the empty house without their children! They seemed fairly calm, but they said the Hospital was terribly understaffed, and it's not one of those places where the mother is allowed to stay and see to the children. Freddie was so brave after it happened, and told Kits, 'Nasty car ran into us, ambulance came ringing its bell, and took us away, and Daddy's poor car all broke, Daddy will have to take Freddie to buy a new car.' So brave and full of initiative, but later, when they had to leave him in the strange hospital, and in pain, he was crying bitterly ... Oh Oriel, *what* wretched Doom, and after Henry's awful experience in Truro Hospital! One wonders if the leg has been properly set, and if everything will be OK, or if there will be worse Dooms to come?

I felt I had to write and tell you. It's awful here, just sitting and passage wandering, and thinking about it. Meanwhile, poor Esther is being so brave, and trying to get over *her* awful shock. She came back from staying with her mother last week, and started working again. She said it was better for her with something to do, and her routes. I put off all those people who were coming to stay, thank goodness, but it will be all right for you to come on the twenty-seventh, and perhaps the children will be on the way to recovery by then.

Tons of love to you, Tray.

※

Mena, Christmas Eve, 1968.

Dearest Oriel,

It's so queer having no one down here for Christmas. I have not done my routes decorating, but have put all my cards around, and have lovely flowers everywhere, and an arrangement of holly on the centre table in the Long Room, and so it all looks very cheerful. If I thought about it too deeply, I might be rather sad, but I don't. Anyway, I am so excited about those men in orbit round the moon I keep dashing to the telly, to see what has happened! To me, it's the most exciting thing that has happened, historically, for generations. At last Man is out of his own hemisphere, and the thought of that capsule thing streaking away into the unknown, just *gets* me. It's like Columbus discovering America, and Stout Cortez on his Peak in Darien, and Hillary on Everest, and more besides, and it makes me think of those lines I love, by Humbert Wolfe:

> *To plunge upwards is the way of the spark,*
> *By burning up and out, even as we die,*
> *We shatter and dominate the nameless dark,*
> *With our gold death – and that is my reply!*

All well with the family. The little boys are at Tithe Barn, and brave little Freddie dragging himself around on one leg, and so much better. His new thing is to open a book, and pretend to read aloud to Robbie, making things up, and Robbie beams, and says, 'Ah, ya, ya,' nodding his head and pretending to understand. I do think they are bliss.

I pottered round Kilmarth yesterday, and tried to think of being there next Christmas. It was a queer feeling. I *know* I can make the house cheerful and welcoming. I think the thing is always to look ahead in life, and never look back, except in gratitude for happy times past. After all, one might be in one room, like old Dora. She comes to lunch tomorrow, with Piffy, and will talk about the good old days with Austrian Princes! As for Miss Wilcox, I've sent her down a pheasant, and some goodies for eating, and she will be so busy listening to carols on her radio, she will be as happy as a bee. What a contrast in character!

Lots and lots of love, Tray.

※

Mena, 16 January, 1969.

Dearest Oriel,

I am so glad the brewing is going fast and furious. I'd love to see a synopsis, but don't lose your head and get *too* many subs, or you will get sidetracked. My method is to keep a Notebook, as you know, and put the chapters in it, just like a Main book, but of course only the briefest of précis. *Par exemple*, in my last notebook Chap. 1 would just have: '*The walk across the cliffs, back in time, the discovery of the Priory conversation between Prior and Roger, self watching, the trek home and sudden waking, basement of old Kitchen, Kilmarth,*' and that would be my basis to follow, when I came to write the real Chapter One.

I do the whole Notebook like this, some of it very shorthand and nobody but myself would be able to follow it, but it makes a good guide for myself, although to write the chapters properly, I often don't keep strictly to what I have said in the Notebook. Of course, your great synopsis may have the same effect for you, but doing it in chapters does help when one gets down to the start of the proper book.

All well here, but awful weather. Esther is very up and down. Some days her old self, with her hair done, looking smart, and the next crying, and saying it is so lonely. All I can say is that it is just time that slowly heals, and it's only three months.

Oh, Ruth Gollancz, Livia's mother, came to lunch, and she is *not* a great dark Matriarch at all, but rather a sort of humped Track, with fair hair gone grey, and in slacks all jam-along, although she is seventy-eight. We had interesting discussions on Life, and she was very interesting about her widowed status. She said she *did* understand that thing of feeling out of things, after a husband of great personality has died. She does find Victor's friends rather cliff her. But she is nobly turning to new interests, and goes to lectures and classes, and things she never did before, which is wise.

I am reading about the Black Death at the moment, just out, which interests me in particular, because it does come into my book. It sounds so like the way I describe it! Perhaps I am psychic too.

Fondest love, Bing.

✄

Mena, Monday 3 February, 1969.

Dearest Oriel,

I'm having rather fun with the Cornish Nationalists, *Mebyon Kernow*. I wrote the article for their paper, and am all in with the editor, and now it seems that M.K. are vaguely in league with the Welsh Nationalists, and the Breton ones too, and the Bretons have a black and white flag, like ours. Do you think I shall be joining some great march – *'à la poubelle'* to de Gaulle, and all 'imperialists'?! I had a letter from some anti-M.K. man, saying: 'Do you realize that you are playing with fire by joining M.K.' and going on to say that it would mean all of Cornwall turning Roman Catholic! I must say, that is the *last* thing I should imagine Cornwall would do, as they are nearly all chapel! Anyway, it all rather amuses me.

Kilmarth progresses slowly. The paper is up in the bedrooms on the first floor, and they all look nice, also the washbasins and bathrooms are fixed.

Esther seems brighter again. I think her last depression was due to a sort of Doomed feeling that she was getting on, and what was her life to be – you know the sort of thing. Last week, I made her go to a dance at Newquay, and she wore my best fur coat and stayed the night at Newquay, and I think it cheered her up. Today she has gone off to look at a kitchen unit for her new cottage. But it *must* be sad for her, having to plan without Henry. I often feel it's sad too, planning for one's foolish self, but that is Life! Only, I'm so much older than Esther, it really doesn't matter.

My Perrette* novel goes from turn–down to turn–down – no mags seem to want it, which is certainly a blow. They all say they found the story compulsive reading, but not really right for their *women* readers. What a Doom if it is a fearful flop! I crumbed after Sheila was so keen on it, and Livia too, but one can be so wrong about one's own work.

All love, Tray.

✄

* *The House on the Strand.*

Mena, 20 February, 1969.

Dearest Oriel,

Have awoken to thick snow all around, and I get such a childish feeling of excitement when I see it, and want to prance out and kick it about, and the dogs love it, too!

But oh, such a Saga of dramas to tell you, and Little Ways, and Old Age! The first casualty, ten days ago, was Dora, who on top of a touch of pleurisy, suddenly started black diarrhoea (like the Black Death), and the doctor couldn't get her into Fowey Hospital, and she wouldn't go anywhere else, so relays of people had to sit with her! I kept ringing the Matron of Fowey Hospital, and thank heavens, a person in bed there went, and so the ambulance came for Dora last week. She must have the constitution of ten oxen, because she is still there, getting better, had a few blood transfusions (like Dracula, she is nourished by blood!) and is now asking to be allowed home, and cursing the nurses because they don't make the tea as she likes it!

Hardly was this drama over, when Miss Wilcox's Home Help came rushing up one Sunday morning, to say that Miss Wilcox didn't know where she was, said her sight had quite gone, and was sitting humped in her cold kitchen. (Below freezing, ice and snow everywhere.) I tore down to Southcott, where the doctor met me, and the poor old dear kept saying, 'I don't know where I am!' and clutching on to me. Oh dear, oh dear! Martin took one look, and murmured, 'Hospital,' in my ear. So the ambulance came and whisked *her* away, and I thought how hopelessly in the hands of Fate we are – from one day to the next, Doom falls upon us! But poor Miss Wilcox, with her mind confused, and unable to see, must have wondered what the hell was going on, suddenly being taken off by ambulance (like Jews to Belsen!). Luckily, the nice vicar went down next day, after I telephoned him the news, and found her not too bad, and making sense again. I am glad she is in hospital, because really, in this weather she could never have survived at Southcott.

All the wild birds are coming in, and the east wind has been piercing. I still think it is fun (apart from the Doom of the Aged!) like a siege! Every day I clear out more drawers and more cupboards. Mr Pascoe takes things each time he comes, which is so much better than a Main move in June. Little Arthur has gone (the furniture, I mean), and is all installed in the Pink Room, with its pink bathroom, at Kilmarth (your room), and so it goes on, bit by bit. Which really does help, because by getting myself denuded here, it's like a baby being weaned.

The Postmaster has just telephoned to say he can get through with the mail, and will take any letters going, so I will stop, to let this go. Write soon and let me have all news.

Fondest love, Tray.

⚜

Mena, Saturday 1 March, 1969.

Dearest Oriel,

I have to take time off to visit old Dora, who is *thriving* after her blood transfusions. From looking as if she were going to die any minute, she is now practically back to normal, sitting up in a chair in her room at the hospital – lipstick on her lips, and puffing at endless cigarettes! She *is* like Dracula, who survived the centuries by drinking blood! They still don't say what is wrong, but suspect an ulcer, for which she is on a strict milk diet and declares they are starving her. So, really, one does not worry too much, except that she will soon want to get back to her flat, and will have to have her Daily more often, and she won't like forking out for *that*!

Miss Wilcox still 'down Truro', and they think she had a tiny stroke, which has made her definitely blind, poor old thing. I'm afraid this means she can't go back to Southcott, but will have to go into a Home. Everyone is trying to find a good one, if possible at or near St Austell, where we can all go and see her, and where (most important) she can have a room to herself. Not easy! I feel much more sorry for her, than for Dora.

Oh, what *do* you think? Peter wanted to come here for Easter, with his new wife. I *do* think he is insensitive. He said it would be a good way for his children to get to know his new wife. But really, Tess might be dead! And Mena is all connected in the children's minds with Tess and Peter filling stockings, and routes Christmas, and hols etc. If he wants them to meet her, they *must* meet on neutral ground. So of course I wrote back and said I was sorry, but it was not on. How awkward too for his wife!

All love, Tray.

———

The farewell to Menabilly hung like an ominous cloud over my last spring visit there. Bing, as usual, was feeling more than she would show;

wisely, she resolutely turned her thoughts towards Kilmarth, where preparations for the move were going on apace. We went up there almost every day, and this left little time for brooding over the past. Those high, wide rooms at Mena had begun to echo strangely; they looked bare and sparse, as more and more furniture vanished daily up the road in Mr Pascoe's van. Bing refused to name a day for the move, leaving herself free to turn the key in the door and walk away, whistling. Meanwhile, everything we did felt horribly final; the last walk down to Prid, through the woods, a last climb up to the Gribben; and this was foolish, since all these walks could later be taken equally well from Kilmarth. Twice Bing quoted, 'Never glad confident morning again!' I had come to hate Browning's *Memorabilia*, for it had a dirge-like sound.

Next morning, as the taxi bore me away, I leaned out of the window for one last look at Mena, as I remembered it. Bing had always stood out in the driveway, waving to the last, but this time she had not waited. She had gone back into the house, closing the door behind her – and this seemed to make it more final still.

When I was back in Paris, she sent me a poem she had found by C. S. Lewis, with a cryptic note saying: 'This says it all ...'

> *You, beneath scraping branches, to the gate,*
> *At evening, outward bound, have driven the last*
> *Time of all times; the old, disconsolate,*
> *Familiar pang you have felt as in the past.*
>
> *Drive on and look not out. Though from each tree*
> *Grey memories drop and dreams thick-dusted lie*
> *Beneath; though every other place must be*
> *Raw, new, colonial country till we die;*
>
> *Yet look not out. Think rather, 'When from France*
> *And those old German wars we came back here,*
> *Already it was the mind's swift, haunting glance*
> *Towards the further past made that time dear.'*
>
> *Then to that further past, still up the stream*
> *Ascend, and think of some divine first day*
> *In holidays from school. Even there the gleam*
> *Of earlier memory like enchantment lay.*
>
> *Always from further back breathes the thin scent,*
> *As of cold Eden wakenings on wet lawns*
> *And eldest hours had elder to lament*
> *And dreamed of irrecoverable dawns.*

> No more's lost now than that whose loss made bright
> Old things with older things' long-lingering breath.
> The past you mourn for, when it was in flight,
> Lived, like the present, in continual death.

༄

Mena, 9 April, 1969.

Dearest Oriel,

I've owed you a letter for weeks, ever since your last of 26 March, when you got back. But I've been so frantically busy that I simply have not had one moment in which to write, and even now it won't be very Main, but a sort of précis of events. My cold has gone, and all well in body and mind. Miss Wilcox home again, and when I saw her last, before Easter, in cracking spirits, walking well, and her legs gone as slim as a débutante! Her sight, even, not hopelessly wrecked, and she looked to me ready to go on for some time to come.

My rush has been due to Kilmarth. Up the road every day, giving decisions, doing things about carpets and curtains, ordering things, getting furniture moved – rush, rush, rush, and then the preparations for Easter, with Tessa and the Wolfendens descending on Maundy Thursday. Thank heaven the weather was bliss and it all went like a bomb. Sir John menacing – went all through the books, and wants my manuscripts for the B.M. Lady W. nice as ever. Tess well, Zulu children arrive Friday, and I gather have got on well with Peter's new wife, who turns out to be nice, and Tess likes her! So that is a huge relief for everyone. Well, the Wolfenden visit was a success, as I said, and they loved Kilmarth, and we beeded round it, and they walked to Prid and did the routes things.

I forgot to say that before they came I had Philip Rashleigh and his mother to lunch, and showed them all round Mena. Poor Philip waine, and shaking with nerves, but the little mother rather sweet and frail, and very grateful; and then the week after I let them come all on their own (I had to be out) and bring pasties to sit by the Long Room fire, so they could beed on their own. Very nice letter from them both afterwards. So it shows it is right to turn the other cheek. Meanwhile life goes on, and I don't pretend that as it (the move) gets nearer, it's not unlike Operation Overlord in the war, with landings in Europe ahead, and who knows what outcome? Still, it must be faced, and I'm so busy there is no time to think. Esther seems better, I have a feeling she has a menace somewhere hovering, as she is always rushing off looking smart with earrings, but I could be wrong!

I've got to face up to an awful crumby invitation, which it was my first instinct to refuse, as always. Then I thought both Daddy and Moper would tell me to accept it. I've been asked to that Royal Academy Dinner, that comes annually – a kind of banquet thing, that women have only been invited to since last year, when the Queen went, and women like Violet Bonham-Carter (Baroness Oxford, she died lately, you remember?). It's a great honour, I know, and I felt it would be wrong not to go – 29 April. Piffy has an evening frock she will lend me, and I shall go up by train, have my hair done, stay with Tess, go to it, and come whizzing back again. After all, I don't have to *do* anything. What finally clinched it was that Sir John Wolfenden has been asked, and he said he would escort me, so there will not be that waine thing of being announced on my own, and looking a fool (I shall do that, anyway!).

No time for more, but lots and lots of love, Tray.

🎋

Mena, Whit Sunday, 1969.

Dearest Oriel,

I can't begin to tell you what life is like here. D-day and the Expeditionary Force landing in France doesn't match it!

Tod and Kits and Olive came for my actual birthday, and were helpful with packing up things etc. Kits took a lot of things for the Tithe Barn, and for Flave at Yiewden Lodge as well, and I had to wait for a Pickford's van to remove them. Which came, of course *after* they had gone, and just at lunch-time, when some man from the *Manchester Guardian* had arrived to interview me! Tod packed a lot of china and glass, and also planted things up at Kilmarth – but as you know, she never stops talking, and I nearly fainted with fatigue at the end of the day. I am writing this in Mena Long Room, with awful echoes all round me, and only my routes chair left, and a table. So hence the reason for my silence. I am just at it, nonstop.

Every time I go for my morning trit in the Palm Walk I nearly cry, knowing there are only a few weeks left here, and I think part of my fatigue is nervous exhaustion, because it's just like facing an awful op. But it's no use thinking like that. I mean, this is Life, and it has got to be faced. After all, I might be going to live in some back street, instead of a welcoming house like Kilmarth.

Well, no more news at the moment, except to say your Kilmarth dates are perfectly OK. I know you will be helpful. I think we shall be comfy in the house, but dreadfully non-routes for our walks, with the fields below Kilmarth all wheat or barley, and that non-routes beach below. We shall have to pretend we are on a holiday somewhere. If there is a heatwave we can bask, but what if it rains? Walk up the drive and back?? What a ghastly shilling! Or drive the car to Barry at the Gardens, and walk down to Prid by the fields, with all the tourists? It's a lesson in Little Way, and humiliation. Re which, the most blissful book I've just read is *Against All Reason*, about the monastic life.

Now I must stop, and do my routes telephoning. Flave comes down to help on 5 June, and she will be very useful.

Tons of love, Tray.

𝔛

Kilmarth, 6 August 1969.

Dearest Oriel,

The little boys went home on Monday. They are both very sweet indeed, but I was rather relieved to see the back of them, chiefly because I was not fully in a routine to cope with them, and had guilt because I was not seeing enough of them every day.

Freddie is very intelligent, and will make a good little companion, when one has the time to spare. He came to lunch most days, and says most interesting things. Quite out of the blue, he pointed to a chair and said, 'That's Oriel's chair,' and it was true, it was, but you would think Oriel had gone from his mind. Then, for no reason, he said, 'And that's Moper's chair, and Moper watches us when we eat our lunch. Though actually Moper is a spirit now, and lives with God.' (Beaming down in his mind, I suppose.)

Anyway, as I said, I felt a bit guilty, being pleased when they had gone, and suddenly I had the house to myself, and it gave me such a feeling of freedom! I took the old rug and went to the grass just above the wall and lay down, staring at those trees overhead – the mysterious ones like a Rackham picture from a fairy tale – and then sideways to the sea, with about ten ships anchored off. It was very sunny, about six o'clock, the warm aftermath of a summer's day. Then suddenly a plane, like a Comet, went high, high overhead, a tiny white arrow, no noise even, and a trail behind, and there was only sky, and the plane, and the mysterious trees, and I had a sudden feeling of absolute *bliss* – it was quite spiritual! It seemed to me that what I was seeing was Life. The Comet streak, the sky, the trees, the sea below, it all added up to a great

Main Goodness. And if this was Life, so was Death, and everything was in harmony, and one ought to be grateful, all the time for every moment, instead of getting irritated and put out by the stupid things of day by day. Well, of course I tried to repeat the experiment next day, but it was not the same; there was more of a wind, and Bibby kept scratching, and anyway I was tired because of a boring man who had come to interview me for *The Lady*. So you see, spiritual experiences are too rare to be repeated! At least, for a bit.

I do hope all goes well, and love to you all, Tray.

———

It felt distinctly odd, arriving for the first time at Kilmarth. Turning into an unfamiliar drive, stopping at a small white iron gate ... and there was the house, with its slated front and the glassed-in porch, bright with potted plants ('my dear, I *must* take some cuttings'). The first familiar sight was of Bing, hurrying down the garden with the dogs at her heels; yet even she looked a bit odd, both strange and familiar at once, as in dreams. The inner hall was still lined with Moper's bows and arrows, with the iron toad family in its place beside the front door; the old Mena furniture looked as if it was feeling rather strange too, among the bright new carpets and chintzes chosen by Tessa and Flavia. Bing admitted that she felt the same, and she had insisted on keeping her own bedroom and dressing room upstairs as shabby and familiar as possible, with the same carpet and wallpaper. It was like the prow of a ship, with windows looking out to sea running along two sides of it, and out to the mysterious, Rackham-like trees, which successive winter gales had twisted into strange shapes. At night, when the lighted ships lay offshore, waiting to come into harbour, it was beautiful.

At first Kilmarth felt extraordinarily like being on holiday in a strange seaside hotel; perhaps because everyone who came to stay was in holiday mood. Yet no matter how strong first impressions may be, they never last for long. Slowly, surely, every place imposes its own personality and, in becoming familiar, can never be seen in quite the same way again; and so it was with Kilmarth.

Kilmarth, 19 August, 1969.

Dearest Oriel,

I'm afraid I get more and more selfish about liking the house to myself, and feel guilty in consequence. The Zulus arrived a week ago today, and the nonstop arguments go on every day. The trouble is, their absolute inability to amuse themselves. They have their bikes here, there are plenty of buses at the top of the hill, going to both Fowey and St Austell, if they wanted to go off. But all they ever do is lie on their beds and listen to pop music! A book is never opened. Sailing bores them, walking bores them, and so one is really rather defeated. Luckily, they like their quarters in the flat, and they listen to TV there in the evening, and Ralph* goes up to join them (for whom Poonie makes big eyes, and sort of jigs around, hoping he will be menaced!).

Pascoe and Co. seem to have finished at last, and one of the final things they did was my Chapel, which is really bliss, does look holy, one feels one ought to kneel whenever one passes it! I shall get the vicar out, to bless it.

I went to see Miss Wilcox yesterday, for the first time. She was in good form, and glad to hear all the news. It was queer going through Mena gates, and leaving the car halfway down the Park. Rather oppressive and gloomy, like passing a grave. Odd. And in a strange way, I was relieved to get back into the car, and return to welcoming Kilmarth. The Rashleighs are in, it seems, and Philip is digging up the side lawn for a vegetable garden! And they are doing the inside painting themselves. It *is* like someone dead, but much more final! For a dead person beams down, and poor Mena can't!

Tons of love, Tray.

———

Bing had arranged her chapel at Kilmarth in one of the mysterious stone basement rooms, where one rarely penetrated. The way down to it was by a twisting stair, opening out of the front hall. On the altar she had placed a crucifix, and all her holy relics, and each week she arranged a little vase of fresh flowers for it. She loved this little chapel, and was proud of it; she often went down there to say a private prayer. In our last conversation on the day before she died, she surprised me by saying

* Esther's son.

that she had gone down there, and said a prayer for me; this might have warned me of what was to happen, but it did not. Perhaps I did not even want to know.

⚜

Kilmarth, Bank Holiday, 1 September, 1969.

Dearest Oriel,

I *am* getting settled and it's not so much like staying in a house lent by friends, and it is a very happy, relaxed place, especially with so much sun always. I do like the little beach, which even at holiday times is never full of people. I am sure [the] people here before were happy, and made a glow about the house. Foy came for tea one day, and told me about the people before the Singers – a family called Lubbock, who loved it and kept peacocks, and lots of collies. And I know the Singers loved it too, so I crumb that they beam down, all the people here before! I remember in '43 creating my own atmosphere at Mena, because it had been empty and lonely so long. I bet now it has reverted to a sort of Rashleigh gloom, with all those frowning portraits on the walls! Though perhaps Philip thinks they are beaming down at *him*.

To switch to your writing plans. I'm all for your getting on with the book, but don't make it too full of subs! Not a nibble yet for *Strand*, despite the fact it is heading all best-seller lists. Ten years ago, some film person would have snapped it up, just because it had sold so well. Kits says everything is sex or violence or spies, and it has to be perverted sex at that – homos, lesbians, incest etc. Honestly, what is left!

Yes, you must read my old Diaries when you come. They are so naive. Even at fifteen, the endless games of cricket, lots of riding and bikes on the Heath (again, we would be enemies chasing each other, which made it more exciting), and the endless lists of books I read. We also seemed to go to the theatre every week, which I had forgotten. It seems to have been a very broadly-filled childhood. Yet in the middle of it I had this awful thing about my Cousin Geoffrey, aged thirty-six, but not knowing a thing about waxing, and I would have been dreadfully waine if he had kissed me! I suppose he was some sort of Peg. But again, a completely different world to Poonie's. I do think it's such a relief to be sixty-two, and have no thought of menaces, past or present, and to be so frankly bored by the idea that I can't even think of them. I must be fortunate, because some women of my age still crumb and hope for something. I suppose it is basic loneliness, or dissatisfaction for them. And perhaps I am being complacent, which sounds rather dull!

> Heaps of love for the moment. Tray.

————

There was not a single silent watcher at Kilmarth, in spite of its long line of past inhabitants. Foy Quiller-Couch sent Bing some photographs of the Lubbocks, posing before the front door. There was a little girl with long hair and a serious expression, and two boys in Norfolk jackets, looking like E. Nesbit's Bastables, clasping one of the collies. Nothing had changed much, since 1913; there was the front porch, and the stone steps down to the garden, where the children were seated. Bing dubbed the little girl 'Little Miss Mary', and insisted that I should write a story around her. She said she would write to Foy Quiller-Couch for further information. Foy, who always knew everyone, had visited the family at Kilmarth, in their day. Gradually, as we Gondalled, Little Miss Mary and the peacocks became quite real to us. At night, lying in the four-poster bed, I wondered if this really *had* been Miss Mary's own bedroom, and if she had climbed out at night, when the cross grandmother was snoring, and gone off on secret expeditions to the beach, with the boys and the collies. Bing said the grandmother would have been on the lookout, and the peacocks would have screeched, raising the alarm …

�֎

Kilmarth, 26 September, 1969.

Dearest Oriel,

Many thanks for your Main letter of the 12th. I have not been able to answer it before as it has been nonstop, with family here.

First, the Towers – very nice, and so easy and helpful in the house. Flave good with her helping with chores, and Alastair's choppings and clearings in the garden. Rupert, a happy little boy doing whatever anybody else did, and very well brought up. Flave is now the most excellent mother, and copes with him continually, either taking him for walks to the beach twice a day (I really can't cope more than once!) or watching TV with him in the children's wing. Then when they had gone, it was time to prepare for Tess, and her weekend here with David Montgomery. It was successful, and I like him very much, but he is rather exhausting, a nonstop flow of conversation – perhaps he was trying to make an impression. He and Tess were out a lot sailing, and I should think he would wear her out with his ceaseless activity (rather like Prince Philip must wear out the Queen!). In the midst of all this, I have been, and am, so worried about my poor Bib. He is ageing fast, almost completely blind, and deaf, and the vet thinks his kidneys are packing up. If it must be, it must be, but you can imagine how distressed I feel.

Tons of love, Track-Tray.

⚶

Kilmarth, 14 November, 1969.

Dearest Oriel,

Nothing much happening here, except gales of rain, and wind, and although my bedroom ceiling is now intact, after the first ominous drip … drip … the new place it finds to enter is under the French window in the Long Room. French windows can be hazards, but the night storage heating is very successful, and does keep the house nice and snug.

I have been asked by *McCall's* magazine in New York to write a 2500-word article on 'Women's Intuition'. It sounds Silly Values, but they pay well, and it will all help. The line I shall take is that of course women are *as a rule* more intuitive than men, because of having been made to play the lesser role through the ages, rather like natives in Africa, and having to sense the mood of the male etc, etc, but that with equal education these days, they may lose their old arts, if they are not careful. On the other hand, there are of course exceptions. Peg, for instance – more intuitive than Madame Peg? This might set you off on a discussion, the next time you all dine (but *not* saying anything about the Pegs themselves, *bien entendu*). Then no doubt Madame Peg will launch forth on her great noble intuition! I think it goes with psychic awareness, and again, as a rule there are more women mediums than men. Quite an amusing discussion for you and I on a walk!

Tons of love, Track.

⚶

Kilmarth, 7 January, 1970.

Dearest Oriel,

So many thanks for your good Main letter, and do forgive me for not having written before, but it was quite hopeless when the family was here, one had no time for ordinary letter-writing routes.

I went down to Miss Wilcox this afternoon. She was feeling the cold and was running out of coal, so I was able to come back and telephone for some to be delivered; it was a good thing I went down. Dora OK, but grumbling continually(!). Piffy and I are much more worried about poor old Aunt Billy in Golders Green, who although not flu-bound, is rapidly losing her memory, and rings up Tod to say she has no food in the house, and then Tod dashes up in a taxi and finds she has plenty of food! We want to arrange for Gran's nurse, who was so good, to go and stay with her, but Billy will not hear of it, she is so stubborn. How it makes one dread old age!

I heard again from Foy, who said Mary Sadler was so pleased to hear from me, and told her that the Belgian refugee did not stay long at Kilmarth, to the best of her recollections, because she and the cross grandmother fell out about planting potatoes! I thought so much about the little girl Mary on Christmas Eve, and how she had hung up her stocking in your room, with hopes, and found it empty in the morning! And of there being no sign of Christmas at all. I wonder why the grandmother was so hard and cross? And who were the spirits she communed with? Yes, I am certainly keeping her letters, and the one from the refugee, with the snaps. Perhaps Foy can get her down to stay, next time you are here. I love the thought of the donkey with the hat tied on with ribbons. And how queer it was, that Mary thought *she* heard peacocks screaming, when she was reading my book!

Well, this does not sound too cheerful a letter for the start of 1970, and I always thought 1970 would be good, because I like the sound of it; the 7 next to the 0 *sounds* a bright, pleasant type of year! Anyway, we must all hope for the best, and face the future with a brave heart. To keep healthy is the first thing. It is *such* a Doom to be ill in any way, and brings the spirits down headlong. I *can't* believe caviare from Madame Peg was so full of vitamins, but she might have some deep wisdom! I *do* so see her being good with herbs, and things.

Lots and lots of love, and to the Bs too, Tray.

No matter how many spirits Miss Mary's grandmother may have communed with at Kilmarth, they had all been blown away by the sea-gales which, in winter, rocked the house, hurling themselves against the windows. Indoors, it was a safe house without a silent watcher in any of the rooms. I was all agog to hear more about Miss Mary, and had begged Bing to get in touch with her; curiosity winning out over prudence, for Gondals, like Pegs, so easily disintegrate when confronted with sober facts. Fortunately, Bing was as intrigued as I was, and we wondered endlessly about the cross, spirit-communing grandmother, the peacocks and the collies. I decided that the grandmother must have disliked poor Miss Mary, to have been so mean and grudging to her on Christmas Eve, when she hung up her stocking, only to find nothing in it in the morning – surely an unforgivable trick to play on a child! Bing said she had probably been too wrapped up in her spirits to remember that it was Christmas Eve; but I thought this a poor excuse.

⚜

Kilmarth, Friday 20 January, 1970.

Dearest Oriel,

I had a visit from a dear old monk from Buckfast Abbey (who knows Jeanne), and he brought me some automatic writings from some medium, who had said they were all directed from long-dead monks from Buckfast! Well, honestly, they *were* rather silly. And I had to write and tell him so. To me, they were the sort of thing that someone who, in her youth, had read Walter Scott and other historical novels and had forgotten them, would scribble down, quite genuinely thinking they were being spiritually guided. And this led me to think how imaginative writers, like you and me etc, really must have the same sort of feeling when we do our Gondally novels. If a chapter is going well, you know how it flows, and the story seems to pour out in an automatic fashion. Well, doubtless some old medium would think, 'Oh, how wonderful, it's the spirits guiding me!' While really, it's their imagination, which they did not know they had! And I've always felt that everything one read as a child *does* go into the unconscious, and comes flooding out in niggling ways when one *does* write. So in a sense, it's the same thing! Look how all the early Gondals and Angria influenced Charlotte and the others, and they might have been quite cross if someone had said it was a mass of digested thoughts etc, that came out in later years. But they certainly would not have thought it was spiritual guidance! I wonder what the old monk will say?

I hope he won't be offended. I *am* rather sceptic about such things. I know there *is* a sixth sense; we all have it, and *do* get forewarnings about things quite often, or premonitions, but I don't see why it should be one's dead mother, or someone, hovering all the time to pump the idea into one's mind. *Do* ask the Bs and Pegs what they think. Being French, they will have logical minds.

I went for my hair this morning to Mrs Hamilton, and before she came in to start on me, I tried on one of the many wigs that she now has displayed on little stands. I tried on a curling, rather menacing one and God, I looked such a fool! You see, it didn't go with one's age, and it gave me quite a shock! And then one of the girls came whisking through and saw me, and I felt *such* an ass, and quickly took it off, and I bet she said to the others afterwards, 'I saw Lady Browning trying on one of the wigs. I wonder if she wants to make herself look younger.' In point of fact, it made me look older than Dora! So it's no use, one can't get away from the person one is. I suppose the real thing to do with a wig would be to have one made the spit of one's real hair, like false teeth, but then the Gondal change of one's appearance would have lost its point! In a way, it's rather like my liking to write sometimes as a male narrator, and sometimes as a female narrator. It gets one away from the rather dull old Lady B. person one really is! But of course, fundamentally, one can't fool oneself, and one knows *who* one is, *what* one's name is, and how old one is! So it's all a gigantic Gondal, to fob off reality!

Tons of love, Tray.

☙

Kilmarth, Saturday 24 January, 1970.

Dearest Oriel,

Family all well, and I have a feeling Tess is boiling up to make a match of it with David. This is a Gondal in a way, I suppose – the start of a new life. But how queer to be Mrs Montgomery, after being Mrs de Zulueta; the *person* is the same! I am expecting an official announcement at any moment. I suppose tiresome newspapers will telephone me.

Re Great Age, you know one could do a very good story about a person who got in a muddle about his or her age, and said they were only ten, or something, when another person died, and then it was discovered to be wrong; and so the poor person in the muddle gets arrested for murder, because the police think the muddle was a deliberate lie, to act as an alibi! Then, as this age question gets discovered, more and more waine incriminating things come to light, which the poor arrested person (who was *not* guilty, of course) had simply glossed over in their past, and so in the end the Doom is appalling! You must admit, one could do quite a frightening story on these lines. Or, better still, do the age the other way round. Dora, let's say, is really only sixty, and *not* ninety-three, and *is* a criminal; and when it's dark, goes rushing around Tywardreath doing awful murders. Of course, no one would suspect a dear old lady of ninety-three! The whole aspect of age is full of possibilities!

Meanwhile, tons of love, and I do hope you will feel better soon.

Tray.

卐

Kilmarth, 2 February, 1970.

Dearest Oriel,

This long wet winter is really too much. I don't think I have seen the sun for days, and I've never known it do this, in old passage wandering winters at Mena. It's quite impossible to face the routes Far From the Madding Crowd walk, and a hurried shuffle up the shrubbery, taking only seven minutes, with Moll looking equally bedraggled and depressed, is one's only hope! As for passage wandering, the trouble is, there are really no passages at Kilmarth in which to wander!

Well, I knew reaction, and missing Mena was bound to come about some time, but if I am really sensible, I don't suppose it would be any better if I were *there*, except for the walks which I could do in the rain. So I must just get on with it! And I should be thankful not to have had flu, like you, not even a cold, just sinus and catarrh, which is probably due to smoking too much! Everybody seems to be feeling down and despondent, even Kits, and Flave too. As for Tess, of course she is riding high. You may have seen that she married David last week. Rang up in a glow of excitement and delight, and I am so happy for her. I feel sure it will be a success, because it's not as if they were youngsters, and it gives her a *raison d'être*.

As to your driving lessons, I am overwhelmed with admiration. I can't imagine the nannyness of driving around the Place de la Concorde and the Étoile. I know I could never do it. Those *agents* blowing whistles, and the giddy whirl of it! I think what I shall do is ask the local garage man to order my new DAF for about May, and say I have a buyer for the old one, and would it be possible to make the exchange through him, so that I can get him to overhaul it first, and see if it was in good order for you. *He* might say it was not worth £250, or whatever the official price is, second-hand. Anyway, he could always keep it until you were ready for it to be borne off by someone. But I still think you ought to have a left-hand drive.

Now, back to Kilmarth and Days. Passage wandering has been slightly kept at bay by my being suddenly asked to write something for a great Gift Book that is to be given to Prince Philip on his fiftieth Birthday. All sorts of sporting people have been asked to contribute, like Peter Scott and Uffa Fox, and mountain climbers, and cricketers, and heaven knows what-all, and I couldn't think *what* to do, but it would have been rude to refuse. You know those Gift Books – I remember there was a Queen Mary one years ago, and the money is given to charity. Anyway, I suddenly thought I could do a piece and call it 'A Winter's Afternoon, Kilmarth' and describe a typical day here, with descriptions of ghastly weather, and the Far From the Madding Crowd walk, sheep, and the ships at anchor riding in the Bay, and then coming back to find the chimney smoking etc, and making it *funny*, which I did! I thought it would be quite different from the other people, and would make Prince Philip laugh, if no one else! So I did it, and it really occupied a number of evenings, brewing it, and then typing it out.

Re *proper* brewing. No, I never intended to start thinking about that novel, it's too soon. It's not nearly ready in my mind. Part of the trouble is that I can't settle to a real place to write in. If I try the library, it's rather dull, because I like to move in there for evening telly; it's no change. I love the Long Room, and it's OK for the Prince Philip piece, but for proper story or brew it's more difficult, as there isn't room for a proper desk. I really almost need a Hut! But to fight my way out to one in the weather we've been having would be out of the question! Anyway, I realize that a change might do me good, after the effect of last year's move, which has now rather caught up with me. (I'm not depressed or anything, just rather unsettled.) So, Kits and Olive and I have decided to take a little 'trip' for a fortnight, on 18 May. Kits has been looking up brochures, and we are going to fly to Athens for a couple of nights, then have six days in Crete, and six in Rhodes. I have suggested writing some sort of travel article about it, and Kits could do the photographs, and then we would flog it to some magazines, and it could help pay their fares. Kits is such fun to be with, and I really think it would be a lovely change, and help whip up some ideas, which I could settle to when I got back. Anyway, that's the plan for the moment.

My plot for Lent has been seeing Dora more than ever, and Oh! it is a Little Way. She is getting more grumbly than ever, and with her talk of the 'Lower Orders'. Her new thing is to keep changing her will every week, telling me what she wants to leave to everyone, and I must see it's done. *You* are to have some of her books! The Council people might let her have a bungalow for Old People, and if they do, the thought of the Move will kill me stone dead, because as soon as it's done, she will say it's too small!

Miss Wilcox is temporarily in a terribly nice St Cuthbert's at St Austell. Even I would not mind it. Like a very nice hotel, and she seems perfectly happy, and I can't help thinking it would be a good thing if she stayed, and did not go back to Southcott. Being blind, she can't *see* her neighbours, who are a bit doddery, but her bedroom is so comfy, and the lounge place too, and there is a very nice dining room, with tables set for four. Of course, Dora would take one sniff and say it was for the 'Lower Orders', but I don't think they are too bad, and I would far rather be *there* than some stupid, badly-run place for grumpy royals! I told the Matron I would book in for my eightieth birthday and she was pleased, and beamed.

Poor Billy is not too good, but thank goodness Mummy's ex-nurse *has* gone to stay with her, to look after her for a month, but after that Piffy and I will have to think again. She *cannot* be left alone, as her memory is going; also she nims in bed, and doesn't know it. Oh dear, that final decay of Old Age. If only they could just be snuffed out at the right moment! Piffy wants to put her in a Home but I would rather pay a nurse, or a kind person, a lot of money to look after her in her own home, where she has lived for so many years. She could not take her little dog into a Home, and would be miserable. The Miss Wilcox place wouldn't do for her, because it is for local people and they don't nurse anyone there.

Now I must go and draw all the curtains against the howling wind and rain. I can imagine Mary's cross old step-grandmother, Mrs Lubbock, communing with the spirits tonight. I wonder what she said? And the peacocks, where on earth did they roost in this sort of weather? Perhaps they had a kind of peacockhouse, like a henhouse, and perched on a great plank and screeched when the dawn came! It must have been rather eerie.

All for now. Tons of love, Tray.

Kilmarth, Palm Sunday, 22 March, 1970.

Dearest Oriel,

I suddenly became inspired to begin one of the short stories I had been brewing upon. The rather nanny one about Venice – it's been on my mind for years! I think what gave the final impetus was that Colin Wilson came to lunch last Saturday. He came at one, and stayed till six, and he talked and talked, very brilliant and interesting talk about Great Intellectual Thoughts! Anyway, he said the Will was supreme, and every difficulty could be countered by an effort of Will – depression, passage wandering, everything. So when I knew you weren't coming I decided I would make an effort of Will and start the story, and it's worked! I am steaming ahead. It's rather a nanny story, very psychic.

The problem at the moment, for Piffy and me, is what to do about Billy. She *can't* be left to live alone any more. The discussions on the telephone are endless. I have said I will pay for a furnished bungalow, or even an unfurnished one, down here where she could live near us, but it still means finding a nurse or a person to live with her. She might not want to leave her own little home in Golders Green. It's Dora over again, only worse, because Dora is still capable of being on her own. The reason I could pay for a bungalow is that my Life Insurance has been realized, and I could advance money from that. My maxim is that, 'You can't take it with you' and if money like that can be used to help others, as my own wants are few, then *tant mieux*! Well, we shall have to see, but Billy is far from an easy problem to solve, and neither Piffy nor I could face the thing of having her to live, *plus* a nurse, in the house. Piffy had it for years with Gran, and she was younger than I. I had it latterly with Tommy, and it was a strain, admittedly. In the days of big staffs, these things were not so hard. People sat about in different rooms, waited on by servants. Well, there it is.

Tons of love, and I wish you could get down to the country again soon,

Track.

'Don't Look Now' appeared in a collection of short stories called *Not After Midnight* which Gollancz published in 1971. It was later made into a magnificent film with only (for once) a minor aberration on the part of the director, who insisted on showing, in gruesome detail, a child drowning in a pond – which had no part in the story. It was one of Bing's most gripping tales, the result of the eerie and sinister atmosphere of Venice that she evoked. 'Don't Look Now' must surely take its place with 'The Birds' and 'The Blue Lenses' as the most frightening of Bing's short stories. I never knew where this macabre streak sprang from; possibly from that nightmare zone of the unconscious which some writers tap at will, and others prefer to leave unstirred. It is in Walter de la Mare, and M. R. James (in Henry James, too) and often contains a touch of sadism, which Poe and Dickens exploited to the full. On the surface Bing was blithe, always ready to turn events and people into mockery, but under the laughter, as in an empty room when everyone has left it, there was this twilight zone of secret fears and anxieties into which it was impossible to probe too far.

⚜

Kilmarth, Tuesday 30 March, 1970.

Dearest Oriel,

I will *start* this letter, but when I finish it is another matter! It sounds so silly to say I have been busy, but truly, the backlash of irritating mail has been going on, and then there have been such to-dos with irritating Dora, who of course after less than a week in the nursing home at Tavistock was writing to me purging about it, and wanting to be taken back. So typical!

Had my godson Toby for his routes lunch, and walk. I rather enjoy his visits; he is an original little boy, and had had a bad report from school, but I think it is just sheer pranks, and having fun in the dorm, and high spirits. He is so amusing, and so at his ease with me, which I enjoy. I *do* love boys!

Tuesday, after tea.

Back from St Austell. Nothing wrong with my eyes – didn't even need my glasses changing. What a relief! Oculist said his eyes also got flashes in them for no reason – it's to do with tear ducts getting less free in one's increasing years, or words to that effect! It's so waine, going to oculists, because they peer so closely into one's eyes, one dreads having bad breath, so that they might stagger back! I then bought myself a three-quarter-length camel coat to travel to Crete in – I really think I can wear trousers, everyone does these days in planes, and a new shoulder-length bag! Such a pity there is no Marks and Spencer's in St Austell, because they are so much better with their wares. Came back, and did the flowers. Camellias out, and that good yellow forsythia, so Long Room looking very pretty. I'm sure I shan't want to go away on the fifteenth, but it will be goodly once embarked, and no turning back, and lovely to see the Tithe Barn lot, and that silly fat Ned for the first time, who is always grinning, it seems, with his first tooth protruding!

I have been reading *Lytton Strachey by Himself* – his *Letters and Diaries* – so like Pen Friend I laughed aloud and read the book to myself in Pen Friend's voice.

Tons of love, and to Bs and Pegs, Tray.

———

One hot August afternoon in 1969, I had driven over to Chartres across the flat golden plains of the Beauce, and came home in the cool of the evening to find a telegram announcing the birth of Kits' third son, Ned – my godson. I was thrilled, having mainly goddaughters (despised by Bing). I could not be as good a godmother as I should have wished to be, owing to the distance between us, but I always tried to remember birthdays and Christmas and in an incredibly short time, so it seemed, was confronted by a tall young man, endowed, like all the family, with good looks, intelligence and – one can only hope and pray – the du Maurier luck.

❦

Kilmarth, 13 April, 1970.

Dearest Oriel,

Weather just starting to improve, but it's been pretty cold right up to today, and today is the first time I've been able to have French windows open in the Long Room. The boys are quite fun to have, and not too much sweat, because they enjoy the afternoon scramble down Thrombosis Hill to Bewly Beach or Par, and of course go leaping out on rocks for the tide to sweep round them, and get wet feet in consequence. I think 'Boys will be boys' and T.N.N., but imagine the shouts from respective mothers, if they were here! 'Unconscious of their doom, the little victims play,' I murmur to myself, wondering what their fate will ultimately be?

Rupert improves on knowing. He has a great sense of humour. We watched the Miss England contest, and he sat with critical eyes, and when someone's vital statistics were called out as 35 – 25 – 36, he turned his eye on me and said, 'Those are my mother's statistics. She should have entered the contest!' (He is 10!) Such a mixture of giggling Flave, and grave Alastair!

They are all useful for my long-term novel project, the one about the old lady surrounded by a mob of boys, when England is either invaded by a foreign power, or totalitarianism, and these boys form the nucleus of a local Maquis underground. I must have the two younger ones also, types like Freddie and Robbie. And pompous old Generals and local Leaders of the invading or Totalitarian party, never suspect that this little handful of crafty lads are up to anything. I was going to call it *Take-Over Bid*, if you remember, but some other tiresome person has bagged the title – some book about Tycoons, out very soon. So I thought of another title, *Rule Britannia*, which rather pleases me – it's very subtle!

Billy is down at Piff's, and came to tea yesterday, and was so much sweeter than grumpy old Dora, but of course not so intelligent. I whipped her up about a bungalow, and I hope we can get her one. You know the chemist's at Par – he wants to sell his very nice one at Tywardreath, so there is hope, and if Billy could sell her Golders Green house, it would cancel out. Dora will be very jealous, because if Billy has a bungalow in Tywardreath, she will be keener than ever to move, and there will be Rivalry between the Aged. It's all going to take time, though. I sent Kits my Venice story, which he thought was very good, and frightening. Its title is 'Don't Look Now'.

Lots of love, Tray.

––––––

Rule Britannia was one of Bing's less popular novels, and one can see why. It required an immense feat of imagination on the part of the reader, to believe in the occupation of Britain by an American army, and of the guerrilla warfare between the occupying forces and the main characters – an eccentric elderly actress and the six orphan boys she has adopted. When Bing discussed her latest brewing I had contested this point, wanting her to make the invading army some unknown Eastern or South American state, or perhaps even some Gondal country of the mind. Bing disagreed; she said that whether in books or plays, the public have always found it difficult to believe in a Ruritania, and it is the mixture of reality with fiction that gets them. I pointed out that it would almost certainly upset American readers, too, but Bing waved all arguments aside. I could see that she had really got the Gondal bit between her teeth, and would gallop wherever her fertile imagination led her. Once you accept the American invasion as a possibility, it is an amusing and original book.

The character of the heroine, Mad, was based upon Gladys Cooper, whom Bing had known and loved all her life and who she hoped might be tempted to play the part in a film. I secretly thought that Mad resembled Bing herself – and that she had put more of her own character into Mad than she realized. It was the first time she had drawn her characters so openly from life. Pa was partly her new son-in-law, David; the old Welsh beachcomber, a fellow bather whom we met on the beach with his dog; and the boys were Freddie and Robbie, with her godson Toby thrown in for good measure. It was the last time that Bing allowed her imagination free rein. After this, she embarked upon the lives of Francis and Anthony Bacon, which kept her grounded in historical facts, to be followed by *Growing Pains* – an unwilling plunge into autobiography, and then, silence ...

⚜

Kilmarth, 21 May, 1970.

Dearest Oriel,

Do forgive delay in writing, and even now it may not be very Main. Hordes of letters to answer, and Tod in the house, with her usual little patter – 'My dear, I have put in some cos lettuce, but really, the weeds are beyond everything, I must get some Slug Death ...' and so on, *you* know, so that I couldn't settle to things. But she is a wonderful old dear, and her energy far exceeds mine!

Then there was Dora to get out, grumble, grumble, and poor old Billy and her new bungalow to see – which she forgot we had shown her the very next day, and wanted to go back to Golders Green! Her memory is very bad, since her fall at Ferryside. She is now, temporarily, in a tiny furnished cot in Fowey, with the nurse Piff got.

The nicest thing that happened this week – on Monday – was the arrival of Foy for lunch, bringing with her 'Little Miss Mary'. I wish you had been here! I rushed to meet them up the drive and my heart sank, because instead of a shy little girl with long brown hair, I observed a stout, white-haired, rather beaky-nosed elderly woman of seventy or so, and I thought 'Oh no, it *can't* be!' then pulled myself together. My heart warmed as she said, 'Oh, I can see the tree where I used to climb up and sit with a book, to get away from Grandmother –' and suddenly I saw that she too, in her mind, was looking for the little girl. Oh dear, oh dear, the thing of Time ... Anyway, she turned out to be very nice, and so interested in *everything* and kept remembering things, and I had to show her all over everywhere. (Foy, so discreet, wandered off with Tod to look at her Tell-Him plants!) Mrs Sadler – Miss Mary – came here at eleven, and left at seventeen, and *was* in that half of your room, as I thought. The bathroom then was the room where I have the telephone downstairs, and her darling collie Crib died there at her feet. The Grandmama said she used to hear him go up and downstairs after he died, but then she was a spirit-communer anyway.

One day, Miss Mary had a bad appendix, and she remembers the doctor coming and operating on her in the playroom, where Freddie and Robbie go – which used to be a bedroom for staff, I suppose. She sat there, gazing around her, saying, 'Oh dear, I do so remember lying here, and the nursemaid would keep on crinkling her newspaper which made my head ache dreadfully, as I had a high temperature.'

I just saw it all with her, and I said to her, 'If only you had known *then*, what all your life would be, and that you would come back and sit here like you are now,' and she agreed, gazing around her with her plump face, and the beaky nose.

Then we searched for Crib's grave in the woods, but no good, it was so covered with undergrowth and she did not know the exact spot. There were sixteen dogs buried there, she said. I *must* get Mr Burt to find them! The peacocks were called Ruby, Emerald and Jade, I think, and slept in the trees. The parrot in the kitchen screamed 'Bugger!' whenever the Grandmother came into the kitchen!

The afternoon went all too fast, and then they had to catch a train back to Trelowarren. I said she must come again. I don't know what her life is, I didn't like to ask, but she seems to be a widow and has five grandchildren, and she has a flat on the river at Putney. I wondered what her Day was? She said as a child she lived entirely in a world of her own here, mooning away in the grounds, and on the cliffs, with dear Crib. She was born in San Francisco, but to me she looks Peruvian, and she has travelled all over the world. The Grandmother was kind, but very strict and disapproving. The old Grandpapa a dear. The boy in the photograph was some friend, not a cousin. There was a horrid aunt, but I must ask Foy about this – I couldn't very well ask *her*.

If you met Mrs Sadler in a hotel you would say, 'Oh, just another rather deadly Witherspoon,' but this is the awful thing – that imaginative little girls become Witherspoons! Anyway, I think if one got to know her, one would find she was *not* a Witherspoon at all, but had quiet reflective thoughts, and I am sure a sense of humour, otherwise she would not have told me about the parrot saying 'Bugger!' The mother was pretty, and liked smart hats – she had twenty hats in her cupboard but she died tragically, of TB I think, at Newquay, when Miss Mary was away at school. I think her young days must have been rather sad.

Forgive no comment on your letter, but I was so full of Miss Mary, and I knew you would be able to 'see' it as I did!

Lots and lots of love, Tray.

🦂

Kilmarth, 6 June, 1970.

Dearest Oriel,

Many thanks for your letter of last week, which I would have answered before, but my Little Way is going full blast! Your questions first – re radio programme. This was a discussion about my Great Works by a group of people – Monica Dickens (very nice), some other woman critic (also nice), Colin Wilson (very nice), and sneering Ronald Bryden of the *Observer*, who obviously hates me! It was most amusing. *My* voice interposing was a rehash from that programme the BBC did at Christmas, from a tape recorder. I sounded quite nice, I thought! It brought a flood of mail, unfortunately, which I try to answer – all but the silly Jehovah Witnesses, who always think I need to be Saved! So much for me.

My Main preoccupation has been poor Billy, who has had a setback – not a fall this time, but dizziness and tummy-trouble – and has been in bed over a week now, in the little furnished cot in Fowey. I go down each day to sit with her, to give nice Chris, the nurse, a break. (Piff away on hol in Scotland.) Chris says she is going to need a full-time nurse from now on, and is prepared to stay, and to go with her to the bungalow I have found for her in Par.

I have only been able to do my article on Crete so far, no time for one on Rhodes, or to start on the short stories. I'm so glad I got the Venice one off my chest, before I went on holiday.

Lots of love, Tray.

———

With the arrival of Aunt Billy in 1970, Dora lost her claim to be the only pebble on the beach and, as Bing had foreseen, this led to a certain amount of Rivalry among the Aged. The jealousy was all on Dora's side, for no two characters could have been more unalike, Dora so bitter, with a life which had not fulfilled her ambitions, and Billy, gentle and sweet, with years of unselfish service to others behind her, and a firm faith to uphold her. At times her memory tricked her into a belief that she was still in her own home, but at other, better times she was perfectly content to enjoy the present – visits to Ferryside, or Christmas lunches at Kilmarth. Dora, who considered herself superior in both mind and body to Billy, held forth more than ever at these reunions, but she was secretly envious of Billy's contented life. Nothing would satisfy her but to move into a bungalow too, and soon this became one of her main preoccupations. It seemed a pity that some of Billy's serenity should not have been granted to Dora, but she would have scorned it; her Gondals and her grumbles kept her going. Physically, too, they were miles apart – Dora with cigarette dangling and red lipstick slashed on recklessly, and Billy, cocooned in soft shawls pinned in place by a cameo brooch, her grey hair framing a gentle face, unlined by ambition or by greed.

❦

Kilmarth, Saturday 18 September, 1970.

Dearest Oriel,

   Yes, you are very right about 'draining' visitors. And why is it that Gondal people *don't* drain one, only real ones!? It's rather an indictment of oneself, and of course people like Maugham *did* take his characters from real people, and so probably could not have enough of them for his brewing. But if one is the other type of writer, who has to 'make up' (tho' we may take snippets from real people, too!), the ordinary day-by-day of people coming to stay is a fearful waste of time.

   I *was* tired when the Zulus/Montgomerys left, and then Kits arrived for his three days, and that was different – though tiring in a way, because we had to go dashing out, up and down to Bewly Beach two or three times a day for photographing, to catch the weather! He was his usual cheerful self, and happy to eat cold ham and watch his telly in the evening. It's funny, I don't think he has changed his routes in the slightest over the years, and Olive has somehow just happily adapted to them! *How* lucky it is. He went off a week ago, and since then I have made a few alterations or adjustments to the Crete story, as Sheila said the end wasn't quite clear – certain references to mythology. It's silly; people surely know that Dionysus is the God of Intoxication, or do they only know the Roman equivalent, Bacchus? There have to be rather magical, sinister implications in the Crete story, and I don't think Sheila saw the point. She is rather factual, you know, and is inclined to want everything explained!

So now I've got *that* clear, I must brew on the Irish story, but have been thinking I must change it from the woman going over there, to the house on the island (and seeing her *own* photograph as a bride in the ex-best man's library, with him substituted for the bridegroom instead of her real husband) to her *daughter*. I tell you why. If it was the woman about thirty years later, it would make her over fifty, and readers don't want to have a story about a fifty-ish woman! Also, surely the best man would recognize her, even if he had not seen her since the wedding. Whereas, if the woman's *daughter* came, he would not know her, and it would be equally creepy for her to see her mother's wedding group with this man as the husband, instead of her father, and she knows she must find out more. And then, because the man thinks she is a journalist, come to get his life history (he is ex-IRA, perhaps still in it), he won't let her leave the island. *She* doesn't know this, but is all whipped up by seeing the photograph, but decides to stay quiet about it, and not reveal herself as her mother's daughter. I think she must get menaced by this man, and he by her – but from there I've got to brew! The only thing is, I wish I were in Ireland to get the 'feel', like I was in Crete, earlier on.

The 'feel' of Ireland has a bit faded, since 1968. Strangely enough, a first cousin of mine, of my own age (the daughter of Mummy's brother, my Uncle Willy), who was a great friend of mine when we were young, suddenly turned up with her husband on holiday in Cornwall, came to lunch, and guess what! – they live in Ireland, on a lake, and have a cottage on an island on the lake! She begged me to go and stay, and of course had I known earlier about her house and the island, I might well have arranged to have gone. But just now it's too muddling and I think I must just brew it without too much description, and perhaps go and stay at some later date. It will obviously be a year before the stories come out, so there is plenty of time.

All love, Tray.

⚜

Kilmarth, 2 November 1970.

Dearest Oriel,

Many thanks for your last Main letter, written from Normandy. Now you will be back in Paris, and the translations will keep you going. But you will be thinking of little Madame Daf laid up for the winter in the Normandy garage.

Tod has been here ten days – no, twelve! – and goes tomorrow. Busy all the time with gardening and sketching. But she *will* talk all through TV, so I just have to switch off, and thereby miss a series of Garbo films! She does get hold of the wrong ends of sticks, too. You know that awful fire in the dance hall at Grenoble. I was saying how dreadful it was and she said, 'I suppose they were just a lot of hippies.' *Really!* Why should those poor young people out for the evening, be hippies? Oh dear, I do hope I don't get so generation-blind when I am eighty-three!

Billy is in good form, nurtured by Chris; really she is in clover. Dora is full of grumbles. She got a wrong number the other day, and when an unknown woman answered, she told this woman she was ninety-three and blind, and all alone with no one to do anything for her, and the woman was so horrified she walked all the way from St Blazey in the rain, to see if there was anything she could do to help! Of course Dora opened the door, and was perfectly OK and asked the woman in for a cup of tea and a gossip. I should have been *livid*, had I been the woman! Miss Wilcox, on the other hand, has got *folie de grandeur*. Someone has given her a black velvet overcoat, and she wants me to find a wine-coloured frock to wear under it, and a hat to match, so she can cut a dash at church on Christmas Day! I have searched Fowey, can't find anything suitable.

Also, I am worried about Piffy, who keeps getting giddy turns. The thing is, Piffy does too much, and will tear about making speeches for Tories, and clergy. She has promised to ease up. But there again, dashing around makes her Day! Without it she would passage wander. She can't just sit humped at Ferryside.

I have finished my 'Borderline Case'. (Sheila thinks the title very good.) She is pleased with the story, too, tho' I agreed with one or two modifications. It's rather an awful story, really. The end, I mean. My next story, 'The Way of the Cross', will be the most difficult. The Jerusalem one, a bunch of people who all find *their* Cross when they get there – some awful fall of pride, or sense of loss, has to strike them. I have not brewed it yet, and am waiting for Tod to go.

I've got a new thing for you to discuss with the Bs and Pegs. You've got to imagine waking up one morning, and finding everyone in the world dead except you. T.N.N. thinking about bodies, the point is you are *quite alone*. Where you live is the same – me here, you in Paris. How long do you think you could exist? Because at first, of course, it would be easy to break shop windows and get in food. But no one would man the electricity or Mains or anything. So light would go, but you could get candles and matches from a shop. I suppose in time the water would stop coming from a tap, so where would you get water? Well, you could get bottled Evian etc and wine, to keep you going for some time. But, if you think it out carefully, I bet there would be something necessary that you could not find, and death would come very soon. Madame Peg couldn't *poubelle* anyone, so I think from sheer frustration and rage, *she* would die first! In a way, it would be worse in a city, like Paris. All those empty streets, and houses too. I might survive for longer here. But I would have to walk down to Brewer's at Par each time, as I should not know how to get petrol from the pumps for the car!

Those idiotic Tories have helped all the tycoons with their mini-budget, and the poor people are poorer than ever. I shall turn Communist!

All love, Tray.

———

Dora's stories of her past might amuse for a short time, on a visit, but her constant bids for attention wearied those who had to listen to them daily. She quarrelled with her neighbours, including her kind and patient daily help, and usually ended by ringing Kilmarth and begging Esther to come and restore the peace she had so rudely shattered. Her Day bored her, as anyone could have foreseen, but there was little to be done about this, and the greatest excitements were the little jaunts to St Austell or Truro, on which kind-hearted Esther took her as often as she could manage it. The acting talent of the du Mauriers was not lost on Dora.

One afternoon, when Bing drove her home after Sunday lunch, at which she had held forth at length about the Prince, Dora seemed to become smaller and sadder with every mile, hunched up in a corner of the car like a child who knows its bedtime is near. When we left her she bemoaned the fact that she could expect no other visitors until the following Sunday. On our return home, I discovered I had left behind my handbag and we went back to retrieve it, only to find Dora, hand on hip and cigarette alight, in full spate to a captive audience of kindly neighbours, who assured us that they always looked in on a Sunday evening. They received little thanks from Dora. She dubbed them all 'yokels', and members of what she always described as 'the lower orders'.

This infuriated Bing and raised her Republican blood to boiling point. 'A la lanterne!' she muttered as we left.

Kilmarth, 16 December, 1970.

Dearest Oriel,

I hope this will reach you for Christmas, but life has been chaotic anyway, with all these electricity cuts.

It was such a good thing you went back when you did. One was never told when a cut would come, and if in the evening, the whole house went black in one flick, and one stumbled about looking for candles, which all Par and Fowey had run out of! If in the day, then the cooker went off in the middle of doing lunch! People all over the country were livid, and started throwing manure at electricians' houses; or milkmen refused to deliver milk at their house etc. Psychologically, this fascinated me, because it bore out the great Trackstein theory that in this country, perhaps in others too, chaos would rapidly break out if there was really a national breakdown in essential services. Everyone, instead of being noble as in wartime, would gang up against each other! If Fowey was lighted up when Par was black, people said, 'It's because the electricians are giving a party there,' or something quite silly. So imagine what it would be if there was a breakdown in food! The people of Polkerris would say, 'I hear Lady Browning has got her basement full of potatoes!' and they would rush up the hill, to break in! It all paves the way for my novel about crisis in England, if it ever gets written!

I should think there will be a funny meeting here on Christmas Day, between Billy and Dora. They probably won't speak, and it will be so Little Wayish trying to get them to agree! Dora, who came for her birthday last week, literally *cannot* engage in any conversation unless it is about herself. Billy just sits and beams, and can't hear, or else gets muddled and thinks she is somewhere else. Chris, the jolly nurse whom you met, likes to talk about her wartime days in India – Dora will be bored stiff at *that*. Jeanne and Noël will talk about horses, and Dora will then say how in *her* young days she used to ride the Archduke's thoroughbreds in the Austrian Royal Stables! You could make a play out of it all!

Tons of love to all, and I do hope you have a happy Christmas. Yes, of course a post-Christening visit will be lovely.

All love, Tray.

Kilmarth, New Year's Day, 1971.

Dearest Oriel,

A Happy New Year! But I always think it's rather mean the way one cliffs the poor Old Year which, after all, did its best! If it's gone wrong, it's only the fault of the people who did foolish things in it, or great natural catastrophes occurred, which wasn't the fault of the year. Actually, 1970 was a very happy year for me, with a nice healthy holiday in April, a lovely hot basking summer, work on the stories and no nasty things happening. I hope you and the Bs are not freezing, and Madame Peg doing a *poubelle*. *Dear* Madame Peg, and her 'Non ... non ... NON!'

Well, Christmas went very well. The house radiant, with cards and flowers and plants in pots everywhere, and your little crib all set in the chapel, with candles. Billy was in beaming mood, and after lunch and the Queen, I turned on the telly for her to watch *Cinderella* (the ballet), which she loved. I really did not mind it being an 'aged' Christmas at all, and was pleased the rest of the family had all gone to the Tithe Barn, where Kits had a terrific do, just like I used to have at Mena; which shows the childish things *do* remain, and when one is older one remembers, and carries on the tradition.

I had a wicked extravagance! You know Bull, that you gave me last year? Well, going to St Austell for the dentist recently, in a shop window I saw the most blissful china Shire Horse, a bit bigger than Bull, and all togged up in a leather trappings and blinkers, and I was *mad* about him. But it was dreadfully expensive so I knew I mustn't buy ... Then I remembered a story I used to read to the children about a horse called Hannibal who ploughed the fields, and I rang up Flave who reminded me how Hannibal did a Gondal and dreamt he was a racehorse and won the Grand National and was called *Prince*, and ridden by an Indian Rajah. Anyway, I couldn't bear it any longer and I tore into St Austell and brought him back, paying by cheque!

All love, and to the Bs and Pegs. Tray.

———

I was glad that Bing had quelled her conscience, and bought Hannibal Horse. She had so few personal wants, and was the least acquisitive person I had ever known. I was perpetually guilty over buying books, being unable to pass a second-hand bookshop without emerging with two or three books weighing down my conscience. Bing preferred to order books from the London Library, and she was constantly being sent proofs, in the hope that she would write enthusiastically about them; these overflowed into the corridors and bedrooms upstairs. I was tired of giving her Vent Vert toilet water for Christmas, and when one day in Fowey, Bull caught her eye, I was delighted. He was beautifully red and prancey; we had him carefully wrapped in tissue paper so that she could open him on her birthday, but she unwrapped him as soon as we got home, and placed him on the table beside the sofa. Hannibal Horse was bigger, and more dignified; he could not have won a race in all his leather trappings, but he was dearly loved, and Flavia has him now.

It was in 1971 that Bing was made a DBE in the Queen's Birthday Honours list. She accepted this with her usual diffidence, pleased and honoured, but it could not make her take herself, or it, any more seriously. I was staying at Kilmarth when she was preparing to go up to London to receive this honour, and as usual she worried herself into a panic over what clothes she should take with her, planning to keep the whole journey as short as possible. Once in the train she relaxed, and to pass the time we tried to summon up all the Dames we could remember from nursery days, from the Dame who got up to bake her pies, or to sweep cobwebs from the sky, to the Dame who found that her cupboard was bare. I remember that we counted twenty before reaching Plymouth. When all was over, she rang to say it had all gone off well; mocking herself as usual, and obviously relieved to put all such grandeur behind her and get back to her own simple routes.

৵

Kilmarth, 24 July, 1971.

Dearest Oriel,

Weather broke about three days ago, with heavy skies then pouring rain, so the lovely after-tea routes of bathing had to go, and basking, too. Actually, it worked out OK because I have had a heavy week, with people coming, ever since last Saturday. On Monday, a man I had booked since March (or rather, Gollancz booked for me) came with a tape recorder, for me to spout into about my stories. My heart sank as he arrived at the gate with a wife, and two gigantic dogs! However, they turned out to be rather nice, and to my surprise had read the stories and had understood them. He loved the Jerusalem one, ['The Way of the Cross'] and said death was preferable to any of the things the members of the tour went through!

Then Piff came to lunch on Wednesday, with Bet Hicks* that was,

---

* Seymour Hicks' daughter, an old childhood friend.

and that was all right. Bet is a dear. Then, inevitable Dora yesterday – purge, purge, purge, all the time. Kept on about her relations being fools. I have a new thing, that when she *does* die, she will realize how tiresome and boring she has been, and be annoyed with herself. She will meet those relatives she says are fools, and they will be rather cross! Today was sunny, and sea wildly rough, so I tore to the beach, but really too nanny and high to swim, so I went in to where the waves were just breaking, and rolled over in the splashing bits, just to get the goodly glow! The old buffer was not there, but while it was fine he came every day, and was inclined to hover with his Tell-Hims. He meant no harm, but one *can't* have a Little Way on the beach, as well as with Dora!

Such a relief, that old deaf male cousin of Tommy's put me off, so my weekend is quiet, with time for my own movements, after all. I don't know what I would have done with him. I'm sure he would have wanted a cooked breakfast at eight! I'm enjoying the Thomas Merton paperback, by the way, which I dip into in bed, after the *Times*. Oh, and I must tell you Tod's reaction to my stories.

'My dear, I didn't like the first one at all, *most* unpleasant. I like the one about the schoolmaster, with his painting!! But as for that Irish one, I think that tiresome girl was the Borderline Case, not the nice Commander, at all!'!! She obviously missed the whole incest point. Thought the girl was trying to get off with a friend of her father's. O, heavens, she *is* bliss; and it's so L.M.-ish,* really!

Now am at the bottom of the page, and it's time for my Campari.

Love to the Bs, and tons to yourself, Track.

⚜

Kilmarth, 12 March, 1972.

Dearest Oriel,

The Montgomerys, Tess and David, and the two Zulus came for Easter, a week. I had two outings with them – one to Lanhydrock, all open now and lovely, the National Trust have done it well. (Foy was away, but her quarters at the back looked a bit cramped.) The second outing to Carhays, where the gardens were open to the public. I felt like Tod, being taken out! David and Tessa in good form, but I got giggles,

---

*L.M. was Katherine Mansfield's faithful, but too-fussy, friend (rather like Tod!).

because I have made a person in my book *just* like him, and he kept behaving just like the man does in the story. He is bound to guess. I am now much more in with David, and *entre nous*, I think it's because making a caricature of him in my book, I feel I know him better, and can tease him and mock him, and he seems to like it!

Now for Flave. I'm afraid it is a bad lookout. She now says her marriage was an error from the start, and wants to have a divorce. She and Alastair will have to pull themselves together for Rupert in the holidays, but I confess myself appalled. Well, I won't harp on, but it is all very distressing. It's quite different when French husbands and wives have *amants* and mistresses, and are still fond of each other, and keep the home happy. Stupid English people never see it that way, hence the endless divorces! I don't know what Tod will say! And the person I dread ever knowing is Mr Burt, who always thought the world of both Alastair and Flave!

Rule Britannia goes to Gollancz this weekend. What will they think of it? It's controversial.

All love, Tray.

ℋ

Kilmarth, 23 June, 1972.

Dearest Oriel,

Many thanks for yours, and you will have heard from Madame B. that I sent a wire to Paris, saying that 13 July is OK. Actually, I think it's a much better date, because surely with each week the weather *must* get better? It's still colder than it was at Easter – in fact, Jeanne and Noël, who were over from Dartmoor last week, said that it was colder than when they came to stay for Christmas! I've still got the heating on, which is unheard of. I know last summer I was bathing and basking in June.

Moll gets stronger every day, but still can't do Main walks, and so I have rather a shilling routes of taking him down Par Beach every morning for his Main walk, instead of the shrubbery, which he thinks a shilling. Then having palled, I don't have to walk him properly again. So I slip out myself in the afternoon for a Mainer walk, but I am getting a bit bored with routes down–fields–to–cliffs, because it's the same as winter. Different if I was going to swim. This afternoon, I hardened my heart, left him shut in the Long Room, and did the Grib, which stretched my legs, as I was able to walk fast. But very chilly all the same, and even wearing my car gloves!

It's very important for you to have your Thérèse family letters, also to settle the Bs happily at La Haute Folie. I have checked the train from Exeter – you will have a bit of a wait, I'm afraid, as there is not a train until just after six. It doesn't stop at Par, but at St Austell. I shall probably get the Goose* to meet you, not knowing whether the train will be late, or what Esther will be doing. You can't do that change at Bodmin Road thing, because there isn't a connection at that time. I do so hope it will be goodly weather by then!

I've just been listening to the news, and they say we have a 'floating pound'! Doesn't it sound like a floating kidney, in some poor patient? I don't follow it one bit. I'm sure Heath has gone too far, or got muddled. But I was rather horrified and shocked when my accountants told me the other day that if I died my actual copyrights would be worth a tremendous lot, and when I asked couldn't I give them away *now* to all the family, they said the Inland Revenue don't allow one to do this, which seems so mean. I just don't understand finances one bit, but it shocks me that a stupid old person like me should possess assets that can't be put to some goodly use. I think I *shall* turn into a Granny Tray, and say that I will leave copyrights to grandchildren if they will do some noble deed first! Like Poo doing a training as a hospital nurse (but not having to *become* a nurse if she doesn't want to, just to get the training), and for the boys to do their training in a Parachute regiment. It would do Paul a power of good, and Poonie too.

Doodie was over the other day, and rang me up, and talk of Silly Values, she said her Zef and Jean† had given the most enormous party at their château, the biggest there had been since before the war – with all the Parc lit up, and various bands, and lights on all the trees! It sounded like Versailles before the Revolution, and *this* shocked me! Such a frightful waste of money, and Stupid Values. *Do* ask the Bs what they think, and the Pegs. I'm sure Madame Peg would poubelle them. I *do* poubelle at wanton extravagance; it must come from those thrifty, hard-working French glass-blowing forebears, who tried to make their own small community prosper, don't you think? But then of course the son Robert was a dreadful spendthrift person, so it shows blood can be very mixed!

No more for now. Moll is doing his routes bark outside the porch, and I must see to my sups (a kidney – that thing you hate!). I'll send this to Paris, for safety.

Fond love, Tray.

* A local taxi-driver.
† Doodie's son and daughter.

Kilmarth, 26 October, 1972.

Dearest Oriel,

It must be over a month, maybe more, since we were properly 'in touch', and I feel awful about it. But this is the thing about going off on a holiday, because everything gets disorganized, and then coming home again is equally a fussation of picking up the routes, and sorting things out.

Well, the hol! Great fun, and so different from anything we had done before, but on balance, I prefer staying in one place, like Crete, instead of going from place to place, which is more tiring. I don't really enjoy sitting humped in a car. Both Kits and Hakka [Olive] lovely fun to be with, so never a problem there. The places we saw were goodly, and that Dordogne-Midi-Provence country all so beautiful, and guess what – madness perhaps! – David and Tessa, who also motored around the Dordogne, have bought a tumbledown farm with fifty acres! They say they are going to take two years doing it up, and go out and live in a caravan while they do it, and can talk of nothing else, they are so excited. I was damping when they told me, because I at once thought of the problem of what happens to a property in one country, when one lives in another. I mean, unless they are there a great deal, it will just get damp, and old French Mr Burts will just sweep leaves now and again, but not really cope – and what about the fifty acres? David gets so excited, and sees us all going out to stay, and me writing a novel about it! Well, Cannes was nice (noisy), though the actual flat in an old building comfortable, and it was fun going to the market to get one's food etc, and Track's old rusty French came tripping from her tongue, but I can't imagine what I would have done there on my own without the others, because to be in any town is not one's routes. Tho' thank heavens no one is smart now. Everyone English, French, royal or not, is in trousers.

The thing you would be amused by was our trek over to Cap d'Ail to see Doodie! I knew she would be on a hard chair if we didn't. Well, it sounds a bit unkind, but really her villa is a bit creepy, like something by Agatha Christie, or more Algernon Blackwood. It's kind of oppressive – very ornate décor and *objets d'art* everywhere, and rather dark, though it was admittedly a poor day, with rain – and a kind of stifling atmosphere. Doodie has become what I would call a typical Anglo-French exile (you have been warned!), dressed in a nice pastel-pink Chanel suit (I doubt if she has ever worn trousers in her life!) and rather old-fashioned shoes with heels – but of course, chic with it all, though somehow like the Thirties – I wonder if you know what I mean? A smart lunch of grilled trout and Vouvray, then *framboises* served by a maid. Oh, I *do* sound mean! I had a long afternoon with her, while K and H went off to meet some friends at Menton, and Doodie was very sweet, of course, and glad I had come. But she embarked on a long, involved story about neighbours who had done her a bad turn, some Americans – I don't know, but I would think the milieu of Cap d'Ail, with rather middle-aged French riffraff, and old ex-patriate Maughamish English, is a bad one. I should hate it; but I *did* think how very different it was from Kilmarth, and how bored she would be with *my* life! Kits and Hakka behaved well, but told me afterwards they thought the setup was sinister, and Doodie probably has orgies in her music room!

Flew back on Sunday fifteenth, and the little boys springing to their parents' arms when we arrived at the Tithe Barn, like the Darling children when they came back from Never-Land, which was good to see. Silly Ned scarlet with excitement. They are dears. Oh dear, I do hope nothing goes wrong with *that* marriage.

I don't know how the book goes in its first week – no, this must be the second, because I don't get press cuttings, and the ones I have seen were mixed. The ones written by men, always better than those by women! Yes, they do say I'm anti-American, and I was prepared for this, though it's obvious, in a Them and Us story, that someone has to be Them; and to have made Them Russian, or Chinese or Asians, would have been to turn it into any old war story, or even science fiction. The whole point was, to make them speak our language, and be our allies. Tod is very shocked, being pro-American, and is afraid the Runyons will be offended!! 'My dear, I don't like that character called Madam. She orders everyone about too much.'! Isn't it funny, how you can never predict how people will read books? Auntie Grace, who might have been shocked, simply loved it!

Tons of love, Tray.

※

Kilmarth, Saturday 5 November, 1972.

Dearest Oriel,

I guessed you must be working hard, otherwise I knew I would have heard before now, and I am so glad all goes well. I can so see how much nicer it is to be in the country in a routes, and your own time for your own movements, and things like planting bulbs thrown in, it truly is such a good life. And you don't seem to be lonely at all, which is such a splendid thing.

As to my news, I had an invitation to that Silver Wedding thing last Monday, in Westminster Abbey and, my heart sinking, I knew I must go, for Moper's sake. So trundled up last Sunday, spent the night with Tess and David, tore off to the Abbey – had a great front seat on the aisle, was terrified I might faint, very hot, two buffers on either side of me I didn't know, but a wonderful view! The whole Procession passing in front of me. So, actually, a good thing done, historical-like, and I'm sure Moper beamed down!

I am now happily settled in, I hope, for winter, surrounded by heavy-going books about Bacon, and trying to make notes. Whether or not I *really* get down to doing him, I don't know. So much of interest about him seems to be hidden away in the British Museum or Lambeth Palace, like Thérèse's stuff is in Lisieux! However, it makes a ploy for winter evenings, reading what I have got on hand, and sorting it out. Tod came, did her planting, and was in good form, and then went after ten days, which is routes ('My dear, I don't know where Esther puts all the knives ...').

All love, Track.

🕉

Kilmarth, 22 January, 1973.

Dearest Oriel,

Do forgive me, I have quite forgotten your birthday which is, I think the 20th, and although I always get muddled by it, I always remember to write during the birthday week! No excuse, except that I seem to have been so busy, with things happening, and my evenings are filled with research on the Bacon brothers. Surrounded with books from the London Library, and am getting more interested in Anthony than in Francis even, he was so *in* with Essex, and with secret spies in France, and apparently spoke perfect French, which is always menacing. Stayed with Henry of Navarre before he became King, and as *Love's Labour's Lost* is all about the Court of Navarre, I get more interested than ever! Supposing brother Anthony was really the hidden Shakespeare person, and *not* Francis? I have got old Tudor maps of London, and am poring over them, to see what it was like in those days. Anthony lived in Bishopsgate, next to a theatre! His mother, very disapproving, writes that he liked low company!

All love, Tray.

✠

Kilmarth, 14 July, 1973.

Dearest Oriel,

Documents are coming in rather slowly from my Research woman, but still I peg away, trying to sort the Tell-Hims from more important ones. She did go to Gorhambury, and had a very interesting visit. Nice secretary woman devoted to the place and mementoes, and has a *thing* about Anthony, like me, and thinks a portrait there – said to be Essex – *may* be him, but no proof. I *must* get myself there sometime.

The thing that *maddened* me this week, on TV, was that writer called Margaret Drabble, who went to Haworth and had a programme on the Brontës. It was obvious that she had only read *Jane Eyre* and *Wuthering Heights*, and Mrs Gaskell, and she flounced about in one of those long Maxi coats, with flowing blowsy hair, even on the moors, and talked about the three unhappy sisters, sex-starved etc, and longing to break away. I could have HIT her! Not a word about Gondal – quoted one of Emily's Gondal poems as if it were Emily's own life; the poem about being Doomed, you know it well. Said all Branwell ever did was to drink at the Black Bull, and that Charlotte hated the Parsonage. It was a travesty! Why on earth didn't the BBC get Margaret Lane or Winifred Gérin to do the programme? It's just as though some *fool* suddenly did Thérèse, without any modern research, and calling her the Little Flower, and nothing else, but that she died young in a convent, of consumption. Oh, one's rage!

Billy and Dora about the same, and I do Little Way every other day but Oh, it must be awful, just sitting all day. Not so bad for Billy, because of her pretty garden, and being so well looked after, and she Gondals and sleeps a lot – but poor old Dora, yearning for dukes in Düsseldorf, it *must* be her Purgatory! I sometimes wonder if God thinks it was a dreadful error to have made *people*, and wishes he had stuck to animals, even old things like scaly dragons with wings! My dear swallows have left their nest in the garage, and are flying about so happily. Their *Day* must be so much better value! I'm sure Madame Peg would agree with me; do give them my love.

Tons of love, and to the Bs. Track.

When the Bs' Siamese, Amok, died at the age of seventeen and a half, he was mourned as deeply as any member of the family, and the Bs swore that no other cat should be allowed to take his place. He was a proud cat, as befitted his noble lineage, and disdainful of all humans, other than his own family; but a loving complicity had grown up between us, and he would even answer to the name of *Nonni-chat*, which I had bestowed upon him, and would lie on my back as I lay outstretched on the grass, reading. He was buried in the garden in Normandy, and the house seemed suddenly empty. After his death I noticed that no other cat seemed prepared to trespass there or, should it jump over the thatched walls enclosing the garden, it trod warily, glancing over its shoulder as if at some unseen presence. I have always believed that animals survive death as surely as we do, for Christ taught His disciples that even the sparrows are of importance in God's eyes; how much more so, the loyal animal friends that we bind to us by ties of love in this life? There is no doubt that all the churches, and the Catholic church in particular, are responsible for much of the cruelty and suffering endured by our brothers the animals, in spite of the shining example of the saints.

Presently, I suggested to the Bs that to give a loving home to a dog, not a cat, would not be a betrayal but a blessing; and shortly after this came upon an advertisement in an English paper for a litter of Yorkshire terriers, available at once, in a London suburb. Acting as usual upon impulse, I rang the number given, and reserved one of the puppies by telephone. I cannot conceive how I could have been so foolish; it is essential to choose a four-footed companion personally, as carefully as any other friend.

By the time I was free to cross the Channel and claim my pup I was confronted by the rejects of the litter – two of the most miserable little specimens I had ever seen, both obviously shunned by wiser purchasers. The sensible decision would have been to reject them at once but this I could not bring myself to do, and when the more hideous of the two crawled towards me, shivering, and rolled over waving its thin paws in the air, I knew my fate was sealed. I brought it home in a basket, and even the customs officers at the airport looked upon it with distaste and waved me hastily on.

I knew the Bs had prepared a loving welcome, with a cushioned basket, bowl and baby harness, but even their kind hearts quailed when they saw the miserable little object that emerged, and crawled away into the darkest corner of the room, as if ashamed of itself. I saw their faces fall, and felt guiltier than ever. I feared that Madame Peg would instantly consign it to the nearest *poubelle*, for she had been against the idea from the start. 'C'est cela, un Yorkshire?' Madame B. exclaimed, disappointment tinged with disbelief. I had to agree that it looked more like a bat, for its ears were large, and without a single hair; nor were there many on the rest of its body.

'Enfin!' sighed Madame B., with the expressive shrug that covers so many of life's disappointments in France. Not a word of reproach was uttered as with her usual energy she set to work to make the best of a bad bargain. Daily the bat-like ears were rubbed with baby-oil, and in time became covered with soft, silky hair. The thin body filled out, and became plump and silky too. Before long, people were stopping us in the street, with shrill cries of, 'Ah, le joli petit chien!' and demanding to know where we had obtained so charming a creature.

It had seemed so unlikely that she could ever live up to the name prepared for her, Bellina, that I shortened this to Boozlebee, in derision. Soon, no one knew how, this had turned into Beezle, and Beezle she remained during the eleven years of her happy life. A loving, cheerful, fearless little companion, she was a great solace for Monsieur B. in his declining years. Once she was certain of our love and admiration, she took over the entire household. Even Yvonne Printemps melted before her. There was no talk of *poubelles*, and she allowed her more licence than her own well-disciplined dog; Pierre, however, was always a little wary of her, because she was so small. Bing followed the entire saga of Beezle from the beginning, and was enchanted by the first photographs, taken in all her glory. She insisted, though, on calling her *Poozle*, which she said had sprung to her mind from the instant she saw her picture – and so Poozle she always remained, at Kilmarth.

※

Kilmarth, Wednesday 10 October, 1973.

Dearest Oriel,

I arrived home here on Sunday evening, the seventh, having left on 18 September – the day *you* arrived in London! We flew across to Bordeaux the next day, the nineteenth, and you will have had my card from Montauban now, I hope.

But your news first. I was *horrified* to hear of your disaster – it must have been terrible for you and poor, poor Madame Daf. Oh dear, the sort of thing one so often imagines happening, and then it did! But really, your escape was a miracle. Talk of Ste Thérèse beaming down! I feel sure you must have been, and still are, suffering from shock, and can so imagine one's trembling hands and weak knees. But at least, thank God, you are safe and unhurt, but how worried everyone must be, and of course Madame Peg wanted to *poubelle* everyone! And how bereft without the car ... Oh, dear ...

Well, awful anticlimax to proceed with my own Tell-Hims. Our tour was as follows. From Bordeaux to Agen, and went from there to Montauban, which I told you about on my card. I wished in retrospect that we had stayed longer in that part, because we could have done 'Navarre', and all that Gascon part that Henry IV came from, and I bet it was at Pau that Anthony Bacon went, when he stayed with him. But *tant pis*. We went north instead, to the Loire, near Luynes, staying at a very crumby hotel, and 'did' various châteaux from there – the routes Chenonceaux, Le Plesses les Tours and Chinon, and I took a day to do my Le Maurier farm again, for Kits to take more photographs. Then we took a day off in the Dordogne (this was before the Loire place), to find Tessa and David's farm, but I'm afraid I thought it an awful shilling! Huddled, ramshackle place in fearful state of disrepair, which will need thousands spent on it! It was so awkward and Tell-Them that I couldn't rave, but I had to be frank. The thing is, one sees enchanting old farms all over France, and especially around the Dordogne, with mellow walls and roofs – indeed, Le Maurier is a case in point – but theirs made me think of Miss Wilcox's Southcott, only not so snug! Nice views, yes, but it could have been Dorset! I am afraid I have offended them for life by not enthusing when I got back!

The day after we got back to Tithe Barn, Kits drove me to Gorhambury, the Bacon place near St Albans, which was good. Lovely pictures etc, and the owner, Lady Verulam, gave us tea. I felt I was at Longleat, so crumby! Friday, up to Tess and the dentist, and to a private showing of the film *Don't Look Now*, which comes on this week. Very well done, the photography glorious, and though they have not really kept truthfully to the original story, it wasn't badly altered. The funny thing was, there is a terrific bedscene in it (not in the story), and I was shown the version in which it is cut!! But the version that will be shown in London this week has it in, and Kits says one sees *everything*!

Oh Lord, it's pouring again. I shall have to sit humped in the Long Room after lunch, and read. It's funny, I don't mind how long I lie *out*-of-doors doing nothing, but it's all wrong *in*doors!

No more for now. Write news soon.

All love, Track.

Bing's DAF had served me well until that fatal day in September 1973 when she came to an untimely end on the Route Nationale 12. A juggernaut lorry, travelling towards us at immense speed, lost a wheel and this, hurtling towards us like a thunderbolt, hit Madame DAF amidships, and sent us flying across the road, almost under the wheels of a second lorry. Only after we had taken to the air, and dived headfirst into a ploughed field, did I have time to realize that one side of the car was missing, and a jagged piece of metal was pointing dangerously at my ribs. By a miracle, I emerged unscathed, to find a shocked crowd gathered round the wreckage. The lorry driver, head in hands, was moaning: 'Mon dieu, mon dieu!' When I tapped him on the shoulder, he turned green, obviously under the impression that he had seen a ghost. Oddly enough, this incident gave me renewed confidence. It was the second time I had narrowly escaped death and I was, I felt (however unjustifiably), *a survivor*.

My *baptême du feu* at the wheel of a car occurred on the day Pierre Fresnay asked me to drive Yvonne Printemps to a certain restaurant, while he led the way with the Bs. I had not long passed my test, and had so far avoided taking the car into the centre of Paris. It was the hour when everyone seemed to be converging upon the Étoile, and my heart sank as, joining the giddy throng, we whirled round and round the Arc de Triomphe more times than was strictly necessary. I soon realized I had lost not only Pierre and the Bs, but also my way. When we finally reached our destination, half an hour late, Yvonne said accusingly: 'Vous aviez peur, n'est-ce-pas?' I could not deny it. 'Très bien,' she added, approvingly. 'You did not show it. One must never show it, when one is afraid. When *I* am afraid, *j'attaque*!'

✠

Kilmarth, Thursday 8 November, 1973.

Dearest Oriel,

Your letter came this morning, so I will answer it right away. The reason my letters are few is that my mornings are so tied with visiting the old ladies, or trying to take them out, in turn, and then early-afternoon walk with Moll, and as soon as tea is over, I try and get on with my Bacon stuff. This only leaves me about two and a half hours for work a day, because my eyes are too tired after 7.30, and I never work after sups.

This is apt to leave letters until Sunday, and now I don't have Mrs Burt, I have to do my own lunch, so letters get unanswered! I will have to alter my days now that winter is upon us, and not visit the old ladies so much, so that I can work in the mornings too. When I actually get down to writing after Christmas (I hope!) I must be really firm. It's only that poor old Billy was so bad after her fall, and Dora now so incontinent, that I get guilt if I don't see them. I just feel it's heartless.

Now to you, poor thing. I'm not surprised, as I said on the telephone, that you have a shaky heart, and feel upset and Doomed! This is delayed shock, and it's just as bad as if you had been properly hurt, with broken limbs. *Then*, of course, you would have been obliged to go into hospital, and be nursed. But not having broken limbs you have tried to carry on as if nothing had happened, and this of course was very bad. You mustn't panic about getting finished. I know the feeling, I get it with Bacon, not even started! But to push on when one is exhausted is madness.

As for driving – well, you see what those bloody Arabs are doing with their oil. Petrol rationing may be upon us any minute, and then we shall have had it. I am so ashamed of the English and French govts. for giving way to blackmail. The only country that has tried to be firm is Holland, and they are going about on bicycles. Good for them! I am really appalled over the way England, and Europe, has behaved over this Israel-Arab war. It makes me think of Munich all over again, although, I must admit, at the time of Munich I was relieved when Chamberlain appeased Hitler, because I was so afraid the army would be on standby, and Moper ordered to war! Now, as a stout-hearted old widow, with nothing to lose, I'd go out myself with bows and arrows, to help Israel! Or better still, if I could make an atomic warhead, I'd drop it on the oilfields, and the whole world would then have to go about on bikes! *À la poubelle!*

I can't remember, when I spoke to you on the telephone, if I told you that poor old Tod never turned up for her birthday after all. She fell in London, when going out to dinner with the Runyons, and broke a bone in her arm, and had to have it in plaster, so she was really handicapped and the whole outing was put off! It's too late now for gardening, which she couldn't do anyway with a bad arm, and no flowers to paint, or little views, as one can't sit out, and it's not as though she can come for routes walks, like you. So I am rather hoping she will give the visit a miss. Flave has been to see her twice, which of course delighted her. 'Flave quite her old self!' said Tod, on the telephone. Rupert has been back for half term, and all went well, but poor Alastair still hovering. What a pity you could not have taken him on, as a reliable man to advise about insurance etc! I agree, one does need a man for that. Kits is good these days. It's difficult for a mother not to think of him as a prancing little boy demanding a new Dinky car, but I must say that he is mature these days, and I would always ask his advice about things.

The film *Don't Look Now* is doing wonderfully in London. It's getting the sort of audiences that James Bond films get, tho' quite different, and the reviews were all very good. You must see it when you come in December. A pity about the sexy bit though – so unnecessary.

Fondest love, Track.

———

On my way back from Kilmarth, I had always tried to find time to visit Tod, knowing how it pleased her to have first-hand accounts of Bing. Her flat was in one of those redbrick Victorian mansions running along the side of Battersea Park. A long corridor, stretching away from the front door, was hung with Tod's beautiful flower paintings. To have tea in her cosy sitting room, surrounded by photographs of Bing at all ages, and regaled with home-made scones and jam and Tod's special lemon-cake, was like going back into past days at Mena; soothing, and sad at the same time. Sometimes Flave came with me, but more often I went alone.

For many years, Tod seemed exactly the same, brimming with energy and full of projects. On coming to London she had joined a water-colour society, and made a circle of new and interesting friends – 'seeing folk' at last. Then, all at once, she seemed to grow smaller, and to nod her head more often; she fell once or twice, and in the winter suffered from pains in her arm, which stopped her painting. In time she could no longer be left alone, and nurses came and went. Later, it was felt necessary to send her away to a Home. She had expressed a desire to return to Cornwall, to be near her beloved Bing, but the Home chosen was on the cold northern coast where Bing, by this time ill herself, could not easily visit her.

Tod died alone there in 1983, yet she is not forgotten, for it is surprising how often her favourite phrases spring to mind. 'My dear, we must keep on hoping ...' or, 'My dear, what next! I never heard such nonsense ...' And she is there, in her blue tweed skirt and sensible shoes, raising an admonishing finger.

🙏

Kilmarth, Saturday 2 February, 1974.

Dearest Oriel,

All has been such Doom. I can't tell you what the weather has been like, absolutely throat-cutting! Fearful gales and storms and teeming rain, day after day nonstop, and I have never known anything like it in all my years in Cornwall. One feels it terribly up at Kilmarth, which is so exposed. I have barely been able to go out, far less on Thrombosis Hill, and even on flat Par Beach one can barely stand up, with all the sand blowing in one's eyes. This sort of thing played up my residue of cold and cough, so I saw Martin, and had to have more antibiotics. Only when I had finished them did he say that I had had bronchitis. Well, if he had told me, I would have asked Esther to have taken out Moll for his routes walks! No wonder I was gasping for breath and feeling wretched. You know I never get low-spirited or depressed but truly, I could hardly drag around. Thank goodness I now feel better, and have even made an effort of will to begin Chapter One – Lady Bacon as a young woman getting married to Nicholas Bacon, as a background introduction.

Mrs H. is still clearing up Dora's pathetic things, and I have to go and check from time to time. I agree with all you say about her now – if not actually beaming down, having met all her family, and being a bit reconciled to a new environment – but probably saying awful things about what life is like down here, in the world of today! I made a great to-do with her ashes, had them in the chapel here one night, and lit some candles, and read some prayers from my French missal! As to 'down here', Billy thank goodness is much better.

Don't worry about me, because I'm really better, only longing for the gales to stop, and the house to cease from shaking!

Tons of love, Track.

༅

Kilmarth, Monday 13 January, 1975.

Dearest Oriel,

It couldn't be a more Dooming day – teeming rain and a gale, impossible to go out, and I thought of you facing the same weather in Paris, and going to dear Peg's funeral.*

I think the thing of 'beaming down' does take a bit of time to filter

---

* Pierre Fresnay died on 9 January, 1975.

through, and though you may suddenly get a wonderful feeling of Peg being close, which would be a great comfort, you still have to get on with, and plough through, the usual day-by-day. I'm all for crying, and even going to bed for a day or two; but one *has* to get up again, and where you will be hit more than most people who lose family, is that it's not only the close friend, but the PEG that has gone! Few people but writers will grasp this. I feel sure that, as you worked, no matter on what, something of the person who was writing latched on to Peg, wrote for Peg. Unconsciously, or even consciously, you thought, 'Peg would see the point of this' or, 'Through knowing Peg, I feel this'. Therefore, work will suddenly seem pointless. BUT – when one considers beaming down, it could be that in this world, Peg would never have been able to give you the real comfort and inspiration you would have wanted from him (and he realized this), with all that *poubelling* etc going on but *now*, once the beaming down begins, the link may suddenly, or very gradually, become very strong indeed. I don't mean silly table-rapping, but the real *feel* of a link, and a source of strength. Then, as you shake yourself out of natural grief, you will feel I *will* go on. Peg isn't lost, he is stronger than ever without any awkward ties, and because of it I will make my life fuller, without the dependence of him coming to dinner, or anything else that may have held me back unconsciously.

It may take time, but by severing that *earthly* tie, a mental and spiritual tie should become stronger. And in a way, you should become more *free*. I wonder if this makes any sense to you? Mentally free, if you see what I mean. I don't mean you 'cliff' dear Peg in your thoughts, quite the reverse. But you are not hampered by the earthly bonds. Now, naturally, this type of thought would not apply to heaps of people, but it's because you are a writer that I feel it's important. Non-writers would go over happy days spent together, for consolation. Very religious people, by being endlessly on their knees. Others by putting flowers on graves. All these being *memories*. But a writer should ask *more* than this, should want an advance on the past. And if a complete sceptic said, 'You mean, use your imagination?' – well, yes! That's what imaginations are *for*! For exploration, if you will.

Now, this is not some noble philosophy I have worked out for myself. I've written this straight to you now, off the cuff as it were, never having thought any of it out before – so, if *my* imagination is now of use to you, hurrah!

I'll leave off now, and you can mull it all over, and meantime, I can only hope the next week is not too terribly hard to endure.

Tons of love, Track.

Pierre Fresnay's funeral, like most funerals, was totally unreal, and I have mercifully forgotten almost everything about it, except the pain. It was raining; people swarmed over tombstones and blocked the cemetery paths, like an army of avid black ants. From the houses opposite, someone flung out an armful of red roses; spiralling downwards, they were crushed underfoot in the muddy street.

I remember my return to Paris and the interminable drive through the dark, rain-washed winter streets, while Madame B. broke the news that Pierre had collapsed on stage during rehearsal, and was not expected to live. This was not wholly a surprise; for months, years even, he had been pushing himself to the limit of his strength in spite of two serious heart attacks and constant warnings from his doctors. Although Yvonne proudly wore the title of *Directrice*, it was Pierre who carried the entire responsibility for the theatre; in later and more difficult years, this had proved an increasingly heavy burden. Yvonne alone seemed unaware of how exhausted he was becoming; for her, all must be as it had always been, and Pierre the solid rock upon which their lives were built. Like most actors, he had always hoped to die on stage and I remember that this, at least, was as he had wished, and tried to feel grateful for that.

We drove straight to the hospital where Yvonne met us, wearing a strange white coat. Holding out her hands, she said sadly: 'Venez lui dire adieu ...' The Bs sensibly refused, and she led me into an alien place where there was no life, only noisy machines pumping air into an empty shell. We stood side by side, in silence, looking down at a form beneath a white sheet, struggling painfully to breathe, and there was no more to be said. Nothing now was left of that person who had always been so kind and thoughtful a friend to us all. I looked at Yvonne's stricken face, and knew that all we could do was protect her, as he had always done – a forlorn hope, it seemed then, and so it later proved to be.

※

Kilmarth, Sunday 9 February, 1975.

Dearest Oriel,

I do hope things are a bit better with you, but the aftermath must still be awful, and the realization that Peg is not there any more. I was so glad to have your long Main after-it-all letter. Poor Madame Peg! I think it would be wonderful if you could write about him, perhaps something like you did for Marraine, and could it be in French, or is that too much of a crumb?

Back here, all I have done these past weeks is to read through various translations from the Latin – unfinished works of Francis Bacon! Difficult to concentrate when one's mind is not at top peak, but golly, talk about Deep Thoughts! Montaigne is easy and chatty in comparison. But apparently, F's Latin stuff was thought very highly of in Europe, France, Italy etc, and that's why he wrote so much in Latin, so that his Deep Thoughts could be widely read. It's no good my trying to write about him, unless I can somehow explain his Thoughts! Scholars, of course, know – but not my sort of reader!

They have been doing a very good TV film of *Jane Eyre*, which I think I must have missed the first time round. Jane excellent, reminds me of you, and a very good menacing Rochester – in fact, everyone good. Last night they did when Blanche Ingram comes to stay with that house party, and Rochester pretends to be a gypsy. Oh dear, poor Charlotte, with memories of Héger and her old Angrian tales all mixed up!

Lots of love, and I hope you are not too sad, Track.

🛠

Kilmarth, Easter Day, 1975.

Dearest Oriel,

Your goodly Main letter came, the day after we had spoken on the telephone. Typical! Never mind, because we did catch up on the news, and was so glad to know all was well. I guessed you were doing translations, as well as Thérèse, but feared you might still be sad, because of the Pegs.

Beaming down is all very well, but I often think that I would be so interested in what there was to see, quite apart from meeting dead people, like one's own family, or more distant ones – Mary Anne, or my Bacon brothers, for instance. (Though rather waine if they suddenly appeared, waving beaver hats and bowing!) What *would* one say? And you meeting Thérèse, and apologizing: 'I'm not sure if I got that bit right, where you ...' and her saying kindly: 'Je vous en prie, Mademoiselle,' – because she *would* be very polite! So it would be a bind, suddenly having to beam down to see what everybody was up to, down here – sad, too, with people crying, so that one would be torn!

Now that I take Moll for his morning walk down Par, I do a rather sketchy one later in the day, out on the routes fields, and am very 'in' with all the sheep and their lambs, and baa at them! (*Poor* old Lady Browning!!) And I got very fond of one poor, mentally retarded sheep that had been a lamb last year, but never sold, and the rest of the flock shunned him. I called him Matey, and honestly, he knew me! Then, a fortnight ago, I couldn't see him. Went on a bit further and to my *horror*, there he was lying on his side, with his face bleeding. I patted him, and wiped away the blood, and helped him to his feet, but he collapsed again. He was far too big to lift and be carried, so I tore back home to ring the farm. Then much later, I learned that Paul had gone and shot him with his gun, because it was the kindest thing to do. I was so upset, as I know you would have been – I thought of you. Oh dear, Nature is hard, but then that is Life, and think of all those children in Vietnam, and places. It doesn't make one an atheist, I think rather the opposite.

Meanwhile, I peg away at Francis, and have done a hundred pages, which isn't bad. It's strange, isn't it, how hooked we get on our people – you with Thérèse and family, and me with the Bacons! Re your coming here, I promise I'll let you know as soon as I can. Meanwhile, heaps of love, and don't let Poozle hear of Dog's Liberation! Moll is *awful*!

Track.

𝔰𝔨

Kilmarth, Friday 10 October, 1975.

Dearest Oriel,

Your mainstay must be to crack on with Thérèse, and be fully occupied – I really think it is *very* interesting, you know. I only wish I could decide what to work on myself. I sometimes wonder whether to check through my old diaries, and do a sort of Looking Back thing, on how I started writing. But I do find, when I read people's autobiographies, that unless the person has led a really full and interesting life they are Tell-Hims, and I hate the revealing sort of intimate kind that some people do, and equally the trivial, social chitchat about their friends! However, it's no good going into it Mainly with you now, because there's heaps of time to ponder on it during the days ahead.

Re the broadcast, my voice came over well, and I've had some nice letters from kind fans – generally of one's own age-group, who remembered the Peter Pan music I started off with. But I don't think it's such a good programme as *Desert Island Discs*, because the interviewing person doesn't have a conversation to lead one on, but just says, pressing his tape-recorder button, 'Start now, your first choice,' and one has to improvise, talking by oneself. And time was so pressing, only half an hour, that they had to cut the good *Warsaw Concerto*, and the Ravel *Pavane for a Dead Infanta*, because they couldn't be fitted in.

You know that person who had a thrombosis, and I went to do a Little Way, and talk to him? It's now become quite a routes. Well, I had not realized that he and his wife are very religious (her father was a vicar), and they have a tremendous thing about a woman called Dorothy Kerin, who was a Healer, and wrote a book about it. Have you heard of her? I had not, but Piff says she is terribly well-known, and has founded a great Healing Centre, and people have been cured just by thinking about her! The Varcoes lent me this book, and it *is* very interesting, and she reminded me so much of Thérèse. She had a great shock when her father died, when she was about ten, and from then on she got iller and iller, had diabetes, was paralysed, had TB – the lot – and then, about seventeen or eighteen, was so helpless that the doctors said she had only a few hours to live.

Then, suddenly, lying on her apparent deathbed, an amazing light came over her face and she said that she saw Jesus holding out His arms to her, and she got up from her bed, walked across the room, and told the nurses that she was going down to the kitchen to get some food. (Nothing had passed her lips for days.) Doctors were sent for, were amazed, said the cure was a miracle – and from then on, she never looked back. Went about doing good, healing people, had endless visions etc, etc. Finally died in the 1960s, but the book did not say of what. Only, how *does* one explain this sort of thing?

Silly old Pen Friend wrote telling me that Francis Bacon is a Jew. He's *not*, poor old thing! He came of honest farming stock from Suffolk. Pen Friend has Jews on the brain!

Lots of love to you, and to the dear Bs and that plucky little Poozle. Old Moll well, and sends her a wag.

Track.

I had never heard of Dorothy Kerin and was mystified by Bing's references to her. Years later, in the mysterious manner that I call 'the Providence of books', I was browsing through a second-hand bookshop when I came across a slim paperback by Dorothy Kerin called *Fulfilment*, which traced the rest of her life after her miraculous healing. This has been so well attested by the doctors and hospitals who had treated her over the years, and by bishops of all denominations, that only a militant humanist would have dared to challenge it.

Once again, Bing and I looked at such matters from a different point of view. She, as always, seeking for a purely psychological answer to the healing, while I felt that although the shock of her father's death had triggered off the original illness, it was the family's firm faith and Dorothy's own religious upbringing that had brought about the cure – as at Lourdes, where one rarely hears of a complete sceptic being cured. Christ told those He healed that 'their faith had made them whole'. I am certain that we all possess psychic gifts which mostly remain undeveloped in this materialistic age or, if cultivated, are put to wrong uses, and commercialized. Many of the saints have been mediums; the Curé d'Ars and Teresa of Avila were greatly bothered by the psychic powers they generated, and which they did not seem able to control. Wise young Thérèse of Lisieux was wary of such manifestations, since the two visions she had experienced – of her father's infirm old age and her own miraculous healing in childhood – had brought her only trouble and perplexity. However, she had extremely intuitive dreams and can be described as a 'Sensitive', in the true meaning of the term.

Dorothy Kerin's later life was extraordinary enough; she founded a Centre for healing the souls, as well as the bodies, of those who sought her help. Most of those who sought it, appeared to be people who were wealthy and influential, to judge by the glowing testimonies at the back of the book. A princess, a duchess and bishops galore wrote with enthusiasm of their lifelong friendship with Dorothy Kerin. She adopted nine children, who were brought up by a succession of nannies and governesses – who left with suspicious haste (for she does not seem to have believed in discipline) – nor did she have a special call to poverty or asceticism. It is easy to despise the rich, especially if one is in straitened circumstances oneself, but they need spiritual and bodily help as much as others. Perhaps more than most, as Mother Teresa has pointed out.

🕉

Kilmarth, 9 January, 1976.

Dearest Oriel,

I have kept meaning to write since Christmas, but you can imagine how busy it has been. Even when it was all over and everyone had gone home, there was the aftermath, and then all the clearing up. I hate having to take down the decorations, and strip the tree, and pack up all the Xmas cards (which go on to that Mother Teresa person in India. I can't think what she does with them!) and put away the crib in the chapel. And one gets a bit of a Doomed feeling, that heaven knows what may be happening by next year – don't you, too? Perhaps it's one's age! I'm sure I never used to, but eagerly looked forward to the spring, or to whatever was going to happen next. One nice forward-looking thing is that Kits and Hakka may pay me a flying visit at the end of this month. Little boys are all fine, and your Ned always answers the phone, and is so chatty. He is a dear little man. Report was good from his day school, and it said that he 'read very fluently, and with expression'! Flave was in great form when she was here. I loved having her, completely her old self, and very jam-along.

I am still passage wandering re work, because if I do try attempting early days and 'the making of a writer', I feel I must base it on something – like houses, and the influence they have on one's development. I remember very vividly Cumberland Terrace, where I was born, and of course Cannon Hall, but there were other houses in the country which Daddy and Mummy used to take for us that also had their influence, and especially that great house Milton, belonging to the Fitzwilliams, where I stayed aged eleven, and never forgot, and which was really the *Rebecca* house, more than Mena. I would like Kits to get photos of all of them, and then send them to me, and they might inspire me. Oddly enough, the houses in France are very vague in my memory, though Paris itself vivid! Well, we must see. There's lots of time because I bet Gollancz won't publish *The Winding Stair* before late summer, or autumn.

A. L. Rowse came to lunch on Wednesday, and never stopped talking! Very complimentary over *Golden Lads*,* but says he will poison me if I suggest in *Winding Stair* that Bacon had anything to do with the Shakespeare plays. And kept saying I ought to write a *novel* about Shakespeare's life. (I didn't dare tell him what I *have* said about the Shakespeare plays in *Winding Stair*!) Also I said I couldn't write a novel any more, about a person who had really lived, because nothing could be proved about that person. Which he dismissed as 'middle-class'. I don't see that it is! I mean, it's not middle-class if you refuse to make up things about Thérèse, which you might have done once. It's just not honest! One can make up anything about a person who is imaginary, that's quite different. Don't you agree?

---

* *Golden Lads: A Study of Anthony Bacon, Francis and their Friends.*

Have you had your Brontë *Transactions*? They are rather good this year, and not *too* scraping of the barrel.

Must stop. All love, Track.

✠

Kilmarth, Sunday 15 February, 1976.

Dearest Oriel,

No excuse for not writing, having spent the most monotonous Tell-Him series of weeks since I last *did* write, after Christmas! The thing is, I just can't work up enthusiasm for going over childhood memories, and what made me write etc, etc, and keep putting it off, day after day. I did turn out a lot of articles and things in my desk, which I think are quite good, also some poems and very early stories, thinking they would make a thing called 'Scrapbook'. I sent them to Sheila, but she said though interesting, they would have to have a basic theme to hang them on, and I see her point. So I suggested doing chapters on the various houses that made an impact on me, like 24 Cumberland Terrace, and Cannon Hall, and a place called Slyfield Manor, and that Milton where the Fitzwilliams live, and of course Mena was already in 'The House of Secrets', an article I sent her. So she said, 'Oh yes, a good idea! Do get on and see how it goes.' But I keep saying to myself, 'Who cares, if I don't really care myself?' They are going to do *Winding Stair* in July, and a volume of what they think are my best short stories next Christmas – already published once, so Tell-Him plus to me ... and that leaves plenty of time for any old *Scrapbook*.

Meanwhile, I do realize that I ought to take a break from my day-to-day, and Tess and David have persuaded me to go on an Hellenic cruise with them in April, and I have agreed. I don't look forward much to the cruise – a sweat with clothes – but I do see it would be a real break, and might give me new ideas for stories. It *is* bad to sink into quite such a rut as I have done.

As for family, talk of being in a state of nerves about *them*. Kits goes off tomorrow to do some nanny film for an Oil Company in Libya, and will be gone two weeks, and I keep thinking that awful Gadaffy will imprison him and his unit. And Tess and David are off next week to San Salvador, that place next to Guatemala, where they have had the earth-quake. It's *too* much! Don't you see my point in feeling that Doom and better Doom, is all around? And then the IRA are up to their bombs again in London, and a virulent flu, it seems, is sweeping the country – headlines about an epidemic in all the Sunday papers. So now it's your turn to answer me with all the Doom that surrounds *you*!

Heard at last from Ellen, who is OK, and also a long letter, rather incoherent, from Puck in New York, who has written a novel. Tod all right, and no flu troubles so, 'We go on hoping!'

Fond love, Track.

穀

Kilmarth, 7 April 1976.

Dearest Oriel,

I do feel awful about not having written, and have now found your last letter, written 15 Feb, such a long while ago!

The thing is, I'll be quite frank. Instead of passage wandering, I have done nearly a hundred pages of my childhood thing, and though perhaps a colossal Tell-Him, it has kept me interested and busy all through March, and as you know, once I am down to writing everything else goes by the board. Then poor old Monty* dying, meant telephones and things to David and Tess – I dreaded they might want me to go up to the funeral, but luckily not. I watched it on TV, and it was very moving – better really than Churchill! David had to be interviewed in the evening on TV, and was very good. Then poor Tod has been awfully ill with a shocking flu, and had nurses etc but now is a lot better, but rather pathetic, and she absolutely depends on me to ring her every evening at 7.30, so it's my Little Way! I'm always in the middle of writing, and look at the clock, and think, 'Oh, lord, I must ring Tod!' I wish Flave would make a more routes thing of going to see her. She has been twice, and taken goodies, but I suppose it's not having a car that makes it difficult. I was relieved when the cruise had to be cancelled. We had decided against it before old Monty actually died, when he got ill. I was not really looking forward to the sudden uprooting, and getting clothes, and being plunged into communal life on board ship.

Various things have kept cropping up. Richard Attenborough sent me the script of the Arnhem film they are to do, called *A Bridge Too Far*. I didn't like the scenes with Moper in them (to be acted by Dirk Bogarde), because

---

* Field Marshal Viscount Montgomery, David's father.

they made him out to be a typical Guards officer, who only thought about polished boots, sort of thing. I made a fuss, rang up Attenborough, and he was polite and said they would make changes. But I bet they won't! Bogarde may be a good actor. I saw him in *The Servant*, and he was a homo in that. Whatever Moper was, he certainly *wasn't* a homo!!

I don't know how much more of my Tell-Him to do, but I think I shall end it just where I am about to start on my first book, *Loving Spirit*, because it is the *making* of a writer. I thought a good title would be *Growing Pains* – the *shaping* of a writer, and as it would not be very long, only a quarter of one's life, they could include some of my early stories, and the poems that were my apprenticeship, if you see what I mean?

Now I simply must stop and get a breath of air.

Tons of love, Track.

꿎

Kilmarth, 12 May, 1976.

Dearest Oriel,

I had such a sad news thing a few weeks ago, and rather psychological. I came back late for lunch, after being to the hairdresser, turned on the news and heard: '*Sir Carol Reed has died at his London home, very suddenly.*' As you know, he was my 'steady' before I met Moper, and the psychological thing about it is that only the day before I had been writing about him in my book, and how we used to go out together, and were menaced, and I had said to myself, 'I wonder if Carol will mind, but somehow I think he will be rather pleased!' and then, the news! Then his wife, very bravely, rang me up out of the blue, and said, 'Daphne, I wanted to tell you that Carol died on Sunday, very suddenly. He was reading in bed, and I had just filled my hot water bottle in the bathroom, and went back into the bedroom, and he was lying on the pillow, but he was dead.' Poor woman! She went on to say: 'I wanted you to know. He loved you so much. He often talked about you.'

Now don't you think it was queerly psychological? Kits went to the funeral, and was very moved. He said they played the tune from *The Third Man* very slowly, as the coffin was borne down the aisle, at Chelsea Old Church. I knew you would understand how sad I felt. Yet nice for *him* – now beaming down, one hopes – and not having to have a long drawn-out heart illness.

All love, Track.

꿎

Kilmarth, 22 July, 1976.

Dearest Oriel,

Just a quick word, after our phone talk. It's too awful, the emptiness without Moll! His heart had got steadily worse during the heatwave – pant-pant-pant – and he could hardly move. I had to carry him out to nim, and up to bed, and he didn't seem able to relax at all. He had an injection at the vet's which didn't really help, and on Saturday I took him down again. He shook his head and looked at me, and I understood. Said, 'Do what you must,' and rushed from the surgery. I *know* you will understand, everyone with dogs does. I could not bear to know his distress might go on, and that he was suffering, and at twelve and a half would never improve. Everyone says, 'You must get another!' OK, in time, but it's like saying, 'You must quickly find another husband,' after poor Moper died. Honestly!

Don't answer this. Heaps of love, Track.

卐

Kilmarth, Saturday 14 August, 1976.

Dearest Oriel,

Your sweet letter was awaiting me here, when I got back last weekend. Jeanne brought me, and stayed for a couple of days, which was lovely, and it had been a good break at Manaton. Frightfully hot there too, of course, much too hot for long walks, and I did feel very tired, but she and Noël are sweet to be with – and while Jeanne is routes, being sister, Noël is intellectual, which I enjoy for Deep Thought talks, about every sort of subject from politics to religion. Their Day, being different from mine here, was good for one. Their very nice doctor came with his family for tea, and I got him on his own for a while, and asked if it was silly to feel so completely shocked after losing a dog. No, he said. Absolutely natural, like when a person dies, and *don't* try to thrust it aside, or pull oneself together. His partner and wife had lately been through the same loss, and the wife had really felt quite ill with shock. I was relieved to hear this, as I thought I must be going gaga!

Very good review of *Winding Stair* in the *Sunday Times*, and in papers one doesn't see, like the *Yorkshire Post* and others, but that old *Observer* man is always bad. As you know, I never expected wide reading for this, especially as people are all on holiday. Forget if I told you that Sheila was delighted with *Growing Pains*, which they hope to do next May. I must plan something for the winter, but am pretty fallow of ideas. Would like to find out more about Kilmarth, and who lived here in earlier centuries, after old Roger Kylmerth died in *House on the Strand*. There were some crumby people, I know. Plaque to a woman in the church, in 1626, which interests me.

Meanwhile, in the heat, my evening swim down Bewly keeps me in trim, and is something to look forward to. I always feel better afterwards, despite the climb up.

Fond love, Track.

⚘

Kilmarth, Tuesday 5 October, 1976.

Dearest Oriel,

The reason I am writing now, is that I am really off for my break on Thursday the seventh. I go up by Riviera and am to be met by Kits. Then down to Tithe Barn for the night. The next day we fly off to Inverness and stay the first two nights at a place called Culloden House Hotel. I shall beed at the Battlefield. Then Kits hires a car, and we are to tour round the Ross and Cromarty country, because I want to see where the clan Mackenzie fought, Mary Anne's mother having been a Mackenzie. Well, you never know, I might get inspired by old Scotch ancestors! Back to the Tithe Barn on Sunday – a couple of days in London with Tess and David, and will see Tod, and then back home on twenty-second. So that's the schedule. I only hope the weather in Scotland will not be too cold and wet, but at least it will be a change of scenery, and goodly mountains.

Look out for your *Sunday Times* colour supplement of 17 October, because that woman who is potty on the Brontës has an article in it, and photographs she has found, which she says are of the family. She keeps ringing me up about it, over the moon with excitement. She sent me a copy of the photos, but they weren't very clear, and I would not like to swear to identity in a court of law.

I do hope all is well. It was lovely having our discussions about everything.

Tons of love, Track.

⚘

Kilmarth, 4 November, 1976.

Dearest Oriel,

What I meant to say in my postcard from Scotland, about travelling, is that flying to a new place *is* like our thing of dying and alighting at a new station. Not to be met by one's family or friends, but strangers, as at an airport. Driving from Inverness to our first hotel, Culloden House – rather a grand bedroom, with bath, and everything strange, smart dining room below – I thought one has got to get accustomed to this, and strangers around, just as one would to an afterlife. It was all new, and different, and one hadn't time to think of one's life back home, and Kilmarth empty, etc. Of course, I had Kits and Hakka, which made it OK, but it would have been awfully queer had I been alone, as one might be at death! Actually, one of the first things I saw out of the window, as we approached the hotel, was a little West Highland dog running along with a wagging tail, and I thought oh, what a good omen, it means old Moll is beaming down.

Anyway, our nine days up in Scotland were very interesting – glorious scenery in the Highlands, mountains, lochs etc. Rather mixed weather, and pretty cold, and of course driving every day *is* tiring, sitting as a passenger and looking out. But there was so much territory I wanted to cover, in search of my old Mackenzies. One lovely castle, a place called Eilean Donan on Loch Duich, which had been their stronghold in Jacobite days; and one could Gondal a bit, but not clearly. And then further north to Ullapool, then back across Ross and Cromarty to the Easter Ross, as it's called, and ending once more at Culloden House. Kits took masses of photographs. And one day we were crumbingly asked to lunch by the Earl and Countess of Cromarty at their house, Leoud Castle. We dreaded it, but they were so nice, a jam-along, middle-aged couple doing for themselves, and she had obviously cooked the lunch.

He is head of the clan Mackenzie, and showed me Family Trees, but obviously Mary Anne's mother, Elizabeth Mackenzie, must have been of humble stock – probably a crofter's daughter – so I couldn't find her. But maybe in older days her forebears had been more crumby, and might have come from the old stronghold in the Western Highlands. I wish I could think of a story about it, but one really ought to have beeded longer, to let everything sink in, and not rushed from place to place.

Do try and get the November number of the *Harper's & Queen*, because it's got this article by Antonia Fraser in it called 'Rebecca's Story' – she has written an account of what she thinks Rebecca might have been like. Charming and sweet, and Maxim the villain all the time, perverted and cruel! Very ingenious and amusing, and they – *Harper's* – asked me what

I thought, so I wrote an epilogue to her article, very tongue-in-cheek, agreeing and saying how misled I must have been when I wrote *Rebecca*. The *Harper's* editor told me the staff at the office were in hoots of laughter at my wit! So do try and get it.

Write when you have a moment, and fond love to the Bs, and that Poozle.

Fond love, Track.

🔆

Kilmarth, 21 January, 1977.

Dearest Oriel,

My bronchial cold is over, but I *feel* the cold so, and it must be through losing weight with the silly non-fat diet; also the cold, too, that pulled me down. Weather ghastly – force ten gales and rain nearly every day, so one can't go for routes walks. I have to shuffle up the shrubbery, out of the wind, such a shilling. One nice thing was Tess came this week, but only for two days. She cooked sups at night, and I thoroughly enjoyed it. I know one of the reasons I don't eat is that it's so uninteresting, on one's own. And it inspired me, when Moll was here, to drop bits. You know, when one is entirely alone, eating is rather a Tell-Him, and I've never been a greedy person. Tod has always said I live on the smell of an oil-rag! I envy you your translations, because it does keep you busy, even if it means keeping Thérèse back. If I *do* start, I want to get interested in the people who were here in 1620–30 – the woman Jane Baker, who has a plaque in Tywardreath Church. I think I *could* Gondal about her and do a novel, but I've got to get more keen first.

So glad your old aunt is better. I do see her point about being confused in time. I always think *I* shall get like that. Imagine we are all back at Mena, and be cross because the rooms look different, or even think I am back at Hampstead. I sometimes think that doing *Growing Pains* about childhood was rather bad for one, because I *did* go back in time, writing it, and it somehow became more vivid than my life now. Do you see my point? I can see myself in the day nursery in Regent's Park, and going for walks, far more vividly than anything in my adult life. In fact, my adult life is more or less a blank. Oh, dear ...

Awful waine, but John* and Sheila, and all Gollancz wanted to make

* John Bush, Sheila's husband and Gollancz executive.

a great thing of my seventieth birthday, and publish *Growing Pains* just before, and have a great party for me up in London. I said, 'No ... no ...' I hate that kind of thing, so reluctantly, I gather, they have abandoned the idea. I don't mind Kits doing some sort of film about the book, perhaps with my voice chiming in, but he could do it *here*, and no great party, with newspapermen and publishers. Quite unnecessary!

I don't really think I have anaemia, and truly I feel on the mend now, if only the weather would pick up. I am as jolly as anything, going in my car to do routes shopping in the morning, and saying hullo to old routes people, who all have colds too! Then after lunch I take my ease, but feel a bit flat, and really it's much better at this time of the year when it's evening, and I draw the curtains, and at seven have my good whisky and ginger ale, and look forward to my telly. I know a hell of a lot of the emptiness is still missing Moll, but I do hope to get pups, or a pup, later on. If only for the example of Piff, who has thrown off ten years since she had her two pekes. She dotes on them, and they on her.

Tons of love, Track.

꽃

Kilmarth, 16 February, 1977.

Dearest Oriel,

Dear, dear Madame Peg, what a truly sublime finish,* and I do so absolutely agree with all you felt about it. Her moment had come, and it wiped out any of her little tiresome ways that had gone on before. It was a sort of Divine Healing. It was consoling to know that her end was so truly good and peaceful. And in a strange way, it was like a curtain call at the end of a play, do you see what I mean, so right for *her*. And as to yourself, that is the worst of it. The shock of the loss, with *both* of them gone, and the end of an era! Yes, I do agree, the Catholic way of Sacraments for the Dying, is *so* good. I am sure it helps people. Although I am not a church person myself, I do think religion is very important, and I think half the trouble in this country today is the fact that religion has been dropped so terribly – fewer and fewer people go to church, mostly of Piffy's age group, and it's hardly taught at all in schools. This is very wrong.

---

* Yvonne Printemps died on 18 January, 1977.

I often wonder, if Piffy got ill, or helpless in some way, whether she would come to live here? I would get Chris or someone, and could afford it, but she would not want to leave Ferryside. Or if Jeanne got ill, she would not want to leave Manaton. And if I got ill – I am talking of helpless illness, like strokes – I would rather be here, under my own roof, with a nurse. But supposing the family said I had to go into a home, or Tessa said she had fitted up a nice little suite of rooms for me? Oh dear, it *would* bore me! Years ago, it would not have seemed a problem, but as one gets older these things *are* problems. But you are a long way off from old age, and it is a more practical living that you have to plan for, in the years ahead.

You asked about when I mean to get a dog. I've been in touch with the breeder of West Highlands and she has two brother pups, born before Christmas, and I said I would have them both. She will semi-train them, and wants to bring them down around 23 April. I have called them Mac and Kenzie. So if you come in April, you had better come before they arrive. No one has yet booked in for Easter. Would you like to stake a claim?

Fondest love, Track.

—————

I had not forgotten Madame Peg's recipe for courage, '*J'attaque ...*' but savoured this as a typical remark to pass on to Bing. It explained a great deal about her character, for Yvonne *was* afraid – like everyone – of old age and death, perhaps even of life itself. This fear had begun in childhood, when she and her mother had been abandoned by a fairly well-to-do father, at a time when no law existed to oblige him to maintain them. By the age of twelve, she was already hard at work, and not all her later celebrity could wholly obliterate those early years, the scars of which she carried into adult life. She never forgave the father she had never known, and this I think coloured her attitude to men, even those she loved best. She accepted them for pleasure, but she never really trusted them – not even Pierre Fresnay, who loved her the most loyally and the least selfishly, and who understood her best.

At heart, Yvonne Printemps was a simple, down-to-earth person, who loved her house and garden, her dogs and cats, and had no real ambition, other than to love and be loved in return; and I do not think she ever knew, or even cared, how much she earned. If Pierre could only have been satisfied to lead a quiet domestic life, and grow old contentedly beside her, she asked for nothing more, but of course he could not do so, and she could not forgive him for not doing so. No one who knew them well could fail to be aware how deep their devotion to each other was; perhaps they did not always love each other wisely, but they never broke the bond that linked them.

After Pierre Fresnay died, Yvonne Printemps lost all desire to live without him; she tried for a little, but died two years later almost to the day. She had always suffered from insomnia, and had acquired the foolish habit of smoking in bed. A lighted cigarette dropped upon a newspaper and set fire to her bed, and although she woke in time to press her pillows down upon the flames, she received third-degree burns. The horror of her recent experiences in a hospital made her refuse to go back there; and since no one, not even an eminent doctor, could make her change her mind, she was treated at home, where she lingered, in great pain, for many weeks.

I saw her often at this time, and crossed the Bois several times a week to take the dogs for a walk. She liked me to stay and talk, but on occasions would dismiss me abruptly, saying: 'Partez, partez ...' Later I learned that this was when she expected the nurse, to dress her burns, and did not wish me to hear the cries she could not always suppress. I was filled with admiration for her fortitude and courage; there was no word of self-pity, or complaint. She was, however, tormented by the feeling that God, as well as Pierre, had deserted her. Ordering God about, as she did everyone, she had trusted Him to arrange that she should be the first to go, but He had ignored her prayer, and she was outraged.

The day before she died, I found her radiant. All was now well, she assured me; at last, she had felt Pierre's presence, and knew that he was coming to fetch her. I could only pray that she would not be kept waiting long. That afternoon, a Dominican friend, Père Carré, (whom she had hitherto refused to see each time he called, out of her pique with God) was inspired to visit her once more, between two trains. This time, she received him with open arms. She made her peace with God, and died the following morning. Madame B and I called shortly afterwards, and were surprised by what I can only describe as a blazing look of joy and triumph, from beneath her half-closed lids.

I stood at the foot of the bed, and laughed aloud, remembering '*J'attaque!*' I felt certain she had won, as in the end she always did.

THE SAD YEARS
1979 – April 1989
❧

> *Like a child who has wandered into a forest*
> *Playing with an imaginary playmate,*
> *And suddenly discovers he is only a child,*
> *Lost in a forest, wanting to go home ...*

T. S. Eliot, *The Cocktail Party*

After *Growing Pains: the Shaping of a Writer* was published in 1977, Bing was left with nothing in mind to follow it for the first time in her life. Always before, she had threaded one idea upon another, like beads upon a string, and this blank space must have frightened her. Every artist knows moments when the mind lies fallow, waiting for a seed, planted even years before, to germinate and sprout into a book, play, or picture. Such moments may even be welcome, and are not at all the same as the dark and empty limbo which shrivels the mind and heart.

Writers seem to fall into two main groups: those who like to write openly about their lives and experiences, and those who prefer to wear the mask of fiction, and to escape from themselves. We know that Papa Brontë made his children don a mask, in order to answer his questions truthfully; although, knowing little of the subconscious, he could not really interpret their answers – which were surprisingly practical and down-to-earth for such sensitive little creatures.

Bing was a mixture of both kinds: intrigued by her family past, she wrote about them many times, in *Gerald*, *The du Mauriers* and *Mary Anne*, but in her novels she preferred to disguise herself and to wrap another, different personality about her like a cloak. So completely did she become these characters that, had she not been so private a person, she might well have followed Gerald on to the stage. She loved her family dearly and was a loyal and generous friend, but I always felt that no one (except Kits) was as necessary to her as this secret world of her imagination. Something very early in her life had made her wary and cynical; as a small child, she would take nothing on trust, resenting adult authority –

including God's. This resistance was an inner one. A shy, well brought-up little girl, she did not openly rebel against her beloved family, but needed more and more often to escape from them, to Cornwall or to France.

I often begged her to write her memories of these early years, if only for the sake of her grandchildren, but she refused, maintaining that to write openly about herself, or others, was against her nature. Who would want to read it, she demanded. I was surprised, but pleased, when she told me that after rereading her early diaries, she had begun to 'brew' upon her childhood and adolescence, but only as a stopgap while waiting for her second Bacon book *The Winding Stair* to be published.

Growing Pains came out in time for her seventieth birthday, and was later published in America as *Myself When Young*. It had a good reception in both countries but the miracle did not take place, and nothing further sprang from it. For a while, she played with the idea of writing a family saga around the Baker family, who had once lived at Kilmarth, but so little was known about them that she gave up this idea. Not so long before this would in itself have been a challenge. More promising seemed an idea that she might once again dig back into the family past, this time on the Scottish side; Mary Anne's mother had been a Mackenzie. To encourage this, Kits and Olive took her on a tour of the Western Highlands (*see* letter of 4 November, 1976). Here, as she admitted to me, '*One could Gondal a bit, but not clearly ...*' Once, a Gondal would have sprung to life unbidden and she would have longed to stay somewhere close at hand, on her own, to walk and brew at leisure.

For the first time, I felt that the days had begun to weigh more heavily upon her, even at Kilmarth. When not working, the old familiar 'routes' no longer filled them as satisfactorily as before. There were hints of this in her letters, but she was so anxious to conceal her fears that I failed at first to read between the lines. She had always disliked the idea of anyone living under the same roof with her; Esther's cottage was only a stone's throw from the house, but she had her own family commitments, and although she was often in and out, from the early afternoon until breakfast-time next day and from midday on Saturday until Monday morning, Bing was alone in the house.

To fill in the long winter evenings, she relied more and more upon the television for company, especially plays, debates or documentaries. She read all the daily papers, and *The Western Morning News* from cover to cover; the stool before the fire in the Long Room was strewn with every kind of magazine, from *The Illustrated London News* and *The Geographical Magazine* to the humbler *Lady*. Letter-writing had always occupied her time on Sundays, but presently she abandoned this in favour of the telephone. These calls became another kind of 'routes'; they were precisely timed, and even now I sometimes find myself glancing at the clock at 7.15 on a Sunday evening expecting the telephone to ring.

At first, the calls were long and chatty, and a good substitute for her letters, which one had missed. Later, they grew shorter and shorter, until in the last years one felt that she merely needed the reassurance that one was there, at the end of the line. After a brief exchange of news, she would ring off, with the same excuse each week: 'I expect Kits will ring directly ...' but long or short, the calls were always cheerful and loving, without the slightest hint of self-pity.

When I felt that this lack of inspiration was becoming a problem I begged her to come out to France, a country she had always loved and which had never failed to inspire her in the past. In the autumn of 1979 she did so, but the outward journey was nearly a disaster. Nervous of travelling alone, Bing had begged me to come to Roissy to meet her, and I had left in plenty of time to do so, but by one of those mismanagements to which airports and stations are so prone, I was directed to the wrong exit door, and took some minutes to find the right one.

When I did so, I found poor Bing in a state of complete panic. Shaking with nerves and breathless, she could only clutch me, whispering: 'I thought I'd lost you!' A kind couple had stayed to comfort her until my arrival, and then melted discreetly away. On our drive out to the country she grew calmer, and of the remainder of her visit I have only happy memories – of quiet walks in the autumn woods and of gathering sloes, as large and frosted as small plums, which she afterwards made into her special brew, carefully pricking each one with a silver fork.

We visited Chartres, and followed Ste Thérèse to Alençon and Lisieux. This interested her, and she became her old self once again, amused and amusing, but now and then still faintly mocking herself as 'an old bygone Trackish being'. Her French came back to her, as it always did, with surprising rapidity, and she chatted happily to Madame B., with whom she instantly felt at ease, and with neighbours who chanced to drop in. Knowing her love of privacy, I had told no one of her visit in advance, but with these chance callers she appeared perfectly at ease, and is still remembered with affection.

Yet underneath it all I could sense the hidden tension, of which her panic at the airport had been a first sign, and tried to get her to put this into words; but she would not, or perhaps could not, do so. When she got back she wrote one of her rare letters.

❦

Kilmarth, Friday 26 October, 1979.

Dearest Oriel,

I keep thinking of you both, and I also keep thinking of the little house, and all its rooms, and the routes, and how you were both so wonderful and understanding to me – the silly, rather bewildered Track, looking about her!

I think I told Tototte* about the flight, and the nightmare of Heathrow – honestly, airports are hell – and then Tessa turned up, and I went to have tea with Tod, before Hacker fetched me to go back to Tithe Barn for the night. Poor Tod has been very ill again. So her birthday was, I gathered on the telephone from here, a shilling, despite flowers, cards etc, because she felt ghastly. The good neighbours above looked after her, and now the nurse is back, and she sounded much more cheerful when I rang yesterday. But all the family are warning me she can't last long, and it's so fussing, poor old dear.

Loads of love to you both, Track.

———

Before Bing left France, we settled the date of my next visit to Kilmarth, carefully chosen for that time of year when the hounds of spring are definitely sleeping, and the days are at their coldest, dullest and wettest. In January 1981 she sent a letter in time for my birthday – the last I was to receive from her.

🜕

Kilmarth, 15 January, 1981.

Dearest Oriel,

I hope that a Westminster cheque will be OK? – and forgive this scribble. I can talk OK, but my writing is awful, and my typing worse. What *is* happening, I ask myself? Otherwise feel OK, and sleeping well, with Mogadon tablets. Happy birthday, and I will be telephoning.

Fondest love, Track.

* Madame B.

It was a *cri du coeur*; once again, I did not understand. Over the telephone she sounded perfectly herself. But not long afterwards Bing, driven to desperation by solitude and in fear of losing her mind, swallowed a quantity of her sleeping pills, and then phoned Esther. It was a second call for help. She was rushed into hospital at Truro; no one now seems certain what really happened there. She came out a permanent invalid, and from then on a series of nurse-companions were engaged to keep her company, and to regulate the drugs which, as usual, was all the doctors could suggest. These made her memory worse; she knew it, and it frightened her.

When in the past Bing had talked mockingly of her old age, she had always declared that, above all else, she wished to remain at home. Now, at Kilmarth, her daily routes went on as usual, outwardly at least, but all who loved her knew that the heart of it, the mainspring of her life had broken, and no one seemed able to mend it again. At this time, I did not always see eye to eye with Kits and Flavia about this. For some reason, I never spoke of these fears to Tessa. As the eldest, it was she who took charge, grappled with the various problems of doctors and nurses, and was generally efficient. We had never been in close touch, as I had with the others, and she was often away with David, visiting some far corner of the world. It seemed to me that they accepted too easily the changing of this wise and brilliant person into a sad and puzzled stranger. 'Old age ...' they murmured, sad but resigned, for to the young their parents must inevitably seem old. But I had known Monsieur B., and others in their eighties and nineties, whose minds had remained undimmed by the passing years, and I felt that seventy-four was too soon to suffer such an eclipse.

Bing fought back bravely against her failing memory. She would question one endlessly upon every subject under the sun, and in particular books and their authors. She kept a pile of reference books to hand on the stool in the Long Room, and constantly begged one to look up facts and check references for her. And once she asked me, still with that haunted, bewildered air: 'Do tell me, did I write *Gone with the Wind*, or was it someone else?'

On my first visit I had been struck by her look of panic, almost of fear, as she came to the door to greet me. Clutching my arm, she whispered, 'Oh, Oriel ...'. It was the airport all over again. Now, more than ever, her daily routes spelt security; everything had to be timed exactly to the minute, and nothing could ever be changed. For each day, she planned a definite objective. There were weekly visits to her sister Angela at Ferryside, and to close friends and neighbours in turn. Once a week she drove up to Mena, when kind Veronica Rashleigh would accompany her round the Palm Walk. The family came to visit her as often as they could, but no one could stay long enough to make any permanent impression. The nurses were all kindly and efficient girls, but to them Bing was simply another case. They had not been trained in psychology, and had little interest in uncovering the person she had once been; few had read any of her books, although all had seen the film of *Rebecca*. There was little actual nursing to be done and so, understandably, they quickly grew bored. Knitting and boyfriends occupied their minds, and their bright chat soon came to be as much of a Tell-Him to Bing as Tod's talk of slugs had once been.

Nurses came and went, but the mainstay of the house remained the kind and faithful Esther. Over the years she had become a trusted friend, running the household, answering letters and smoothing out the manifold small problems which inevitably arise in a household of women. She was always there to give one a warm and reassuring welcome at the end of what had now become a long, sad journey.

As time went on Bing seemed to withdraw more and more into herself, and at each visit it took a little longer to establish contact again. After one such visit, I wrote: '*Nothing now will make Track budge one iota from her "routes", and she shuts herself off from the world behind a wall of newspapers, or turns on the radio to prevent anyone from talking to her, although I don't believe she is really reading, listening or taking anything in. She has simply given up.*'

The best time for getting through to her, I found, was after tea, which was followed by the dogs' playtime: an established ritual, in which Mac played with an old tennis ball, tirelessly catching it in his mouth, and tossing it back to Bing. For some reason, Kenzie was excluded from this game. After this Bing was permitted a nightly tot of whisky, which warmed her, for she was painfully thin. This nightcap was one of the few pleasures she still enjoyed, and it was the best moment for talking. I would remind her of the past, of places and people she had loved, and she responded to this, even though they had grown somewhat shadowy figures now.

After each visit, I would go in to say goodbye to her in bed, before catching the morning train, and she would ask anxiously, 'When are you coming back?' And always, insistently: 'Are you writing?'

This question troubled me and once, impulsively, I asked her in my turn: 'Track, do *you* miss not writing any more?' but she merely shrugged and said sadly, 'I don't think I miss *anything* much, any more!'

In January 1988 I was surprised to get a birthday card from her, on precisely the right day. Her inability to get this date right had been a joke between us for so long that it was almost 'routes' for her to forget it. I guessed that Esther must have jogged her memory, but when I opened the card I found that she had written inside, in her rather shaky writing: '*I went to newsagent, walked to where they had rows and rows of birthday cards, and the first one I saw was this. Isn't it strange?*'

It was a reproduction of Dürer's *Praying Hands*, and the usual trite verses within proclaimed our need to be guided by God's own plan in our lives, no matter how little we may understand it, or how dark the path we have to follow may be; for all paths will ultimately converge, and all our questions will find their answer.

On her last day, she rang me and said: 'I went down to the chapel today, and I said a prayer for you!' Then I felt sure that her card had not been just a banal birthday greeting, but that in some mysterious way her questing mind had been satisfied, and deep inside, in what French spiritual writers call '*la fine pointe de l'esprit*', she had found her own peace.

In time, even her beloved dogs came to mean less to Bing. Mac died, but this was not the sharp grief it would once have been. She ate even less, and grew thinner; her walks on Par Beach grew shorter, but she continued to keep in close touch by telephone. A trusted nursing friend, who had always promised to come back to her when she was needed, returned to give her comfort and support in the last weeks. In her care Bing seemed better, and there came a week in which she wanted to visit all her close friends and neighbours, returning the books she had borrowed. She asked to be driven to the places she loved best: to Angela at Ferryside, to Mena, and down to the beach at Pridmouth.

Her telephone call to me that Sunday evening was longer than usual, and she sounded more like her old self. She asked when I was coming over. In ten days, I promised. Next day, the telephone rang in mid-afternoon and I was surprised to hear Bing again at the other end of the phone. 'Is anything wrong?' I asked anxiously.

'No, no,' she said. 'I just wanted to speak to you.'

'I'll be coming very soon now,' I assured her.

'Yes, I know,' she answered. 'Are you writing?' and as I hesitated, she insisted: 'You *must*, it's the only way!'

For the rest of the day I was faintly troubled, wondering what had made her ring me again so soon, and at such an unusual time. When Flavia called me early next morning, to tell me that Bing had died in her sleep an hour before, I was not entirely surprised. Apparently she had rung her bell at the usual time, and had then lain quietly back on her pillows, closing her eyes. When Esther came upstairs with her breakfast, she did not open them again.

Those who loved Bing were torn between gratitude that her release had been so peaceful and serene, and sorrow that one who was so much a part of all our lives had vanished; and with her going, a world had vanished too. But all who read and love Daphne du Maurier's books in the future will build their own inner world out of the Cornwall she loved and the characters she created; and that is how she would have wished it to be.

⚘

After the service in the crematorium, the little chapel beside Mena was filled with Bing's family and friends, just as she had requested. When Kits' young daughter Grace got up to read the poem she had chosen, looking so like the young Daphne of the photographs, suddenly I felt the continuity of our existence – a circle completed. There will be other circles, other times, but in the end, 'all shall be well, and all shall be well, and all manner of things shall be well,' as Blessed Juliana saw. Not sorrow for the past, but gratitude and love, and hope for the future. Somehow, somewhere, Track would always be with us.

⚘

Late that night, as I was leaning out of the window of an unfamiliar hotel and looking across to Kilmarth on the other side of the bay, a poem of Kicky's flew into my mind, which Track had loved and quoted, and I whispered this into the darkness.

> *'A little hope, that when we die,*
> *We reap our sowing, and so goodbye ...'*

Index

❋

Daphne du Maurier is referred to throughout the index as Bing. A figure 2 in brackets immediately after a page reference means that there are two separate references on that page.